RESEARCH IN ORGANIZATIONAL BEHAVIOR

RESEARCH IN ORGANIZATIONAL BEHAVIOR

Series Editors: Barry M. Staw and L. L. Cummings

Recent Volumes:

Volumes 1–20:   Research in Organizational Behavior – An Annual
Series of Analytical Essays and Critical Reviews

Series Editors: Barry M. Staw and Robert I. Sutton

Volumes 21–23:   Research in Organizational Behavior – An Annual
Series of Analytical Essays and Critical Reviews

Series Editors: Barry M. Staw and Roderick M. Kramer

Volume 24:   Research in Organizational Behavior – An Annual
Series of Analytical Essays and Critical Reviews

RESEARCH IN ORGANIZATIONAL BEHAVIOR

VOLUME 25

RESEARCH IN ORGANIZATIONAL BEHAVIOR

AN ANNUAL SERIES OF ANALYTICAL ESSAYS AND CRITICAL REVIEWS

EDITED BY

RODERICK M. KRAMER

Graduate School of Business, Stanford University, USA

BARRY M. STAW

Haas School of Business, University of California, USA

2003

ELSEVIER
JAI

Amsterdam – Boston – Heidelberg – London – New York – Oxford – Paris
San Diego – San Francisco – Singapore – Sydney – Tokyo

ELSEVIER Ltd
The Boulevard, Langford Lane
Kidlington, Oxford OX5 1GB, UK

First edition 2003

A catalogue record from the British Library has been applied for.

ISBN: 0-7623-1054-5
ISSN: 0191-3085 (Series)

Transferred to digital printing 2006

CONTENTS

LIST OF CONTRIBUTORS

Vikas Anand	Sam M. Walton College of Business, University of Arkansas, Fayetteville, USA
Blake E. Ashforth	W.P. Carey School of Business, Arizona State University, Tempe, USA
Corinne Bendersky	The Anderson School, University California, Los Angeles, USA
Sally Blount	Leonard N. Stern School of Business, New York University, New York, USA
Joel Brockner	Columbia University, USA
Gelaye Debebe	Simmons Graduate School of Management, George Washington University, USA
Jane E. Dutton	William Russell Kelly Professor of Business Administration, University of Michigan, USA
Kimberly D. Elsbach	Graduate School of Management, University of California, Davis, USA
Michael A. Hogg	University of Queensland, Australia
György Hunyady	Eötvös Lorand University, Budapest, Hungary
Karen A. Jehn	The Wharton School, University of Pennsylvania, Philadelphia, USA
John T. Jost	Graduate School of Business, Stanford University, USA and Radcliffe Institute for Advanced Study, Harvard University, USA
Daan van Knippenberg	Erasmus University, Rotterdam, The Netherlands
Tanya Menon	Graduate School of Business, University of Chicago, USA

Jeffrey Pfeffer Graduate School of Business, Stanford University, USA

Amy Wrzesniewski Department of Management and Organizational Behavior, New York University, USA

PREFACE

Volume 25 heralds/celebrates the first quarter century of publishing *Research in Organizational Behavior*. From its inception, *Research in Organizational Behavior* has striven to provide important theoretical integrations of major literatures in the organizational sciences, as well as timely examination and provocative analyses of pressing organizational issues and problems.

In keeping with this tradition, the current volume offers an eclectic mix of scholarly articles that address a variety of important questions in organizational theory and do so from a diverse range of disciplinary perspectives and theoretical orientations. A number of the chapters also directly engage contemporary events and dilemmas of considerable importance.

In the lead chapter, Ashforth and Anand present a major new framework for conceptualizing how corruption not only can gain a toehold within organizations, but can manage to even flourish and endure. The authors argue that corruption within organizations often becomes normalized so that it acquires a taken-for-granted quality over time and thus is more easily perpetuated. Ashforth and Anand identify three mutually reinforcing mechanisms that underlie the process of corruption normalization. The first is institutionalization, whereby an initial act of corruption becomes entrenched in ongoing organizational processes and structures. The second is rationalization, whereby decision makers promulgate self-serving ideologies to justify and even valorize corruption. The third mechanism they identify is socialization, whereby organizational newcomers are exposed to the corruption and inured to its existence, leading over time to its acceptance. Ashforth and Anand's analysis is not only theoretically rich and sound – drawing on an impressive variety of insights from extant organizational research – but also especially cogent given the recent exposure of widespread corruption at not only major private organizations such as Worldcom, Tyco, and Enron, but also once venerated institutions such as Arthur Andersen. Their paper thus provides a remarkably timely and important analysis, exemplifying both rigor and relevance.

If Ashforth and Anand help us understand how corruption can become normalized within organizations, Jost, Blount, Pfeffer and Hunyady clarify why individuals become more accepting of organizational processes and outcomes than we might otherwise expect. In particular, their provocative paper addresses a seeming paradox in people's beliefs regarding the acceptability and legitimacy of the social and organizational systems on which their very well-being depends. Opinion research demonstrates that people routinely espouse egalitarian ideals and acknowledge the fact that substantial inequalities exist in society. Yet, at the same time, these same individuals perceive the economic system to be fair and legitimate. To explain this rather peculiar pattern of perception, Jost et al. argue their exists a fair market ideology, which contributes to system justifying tendencies among individuals embedded in the social system. In defense of their claim, they explicate a variety of cognitive and motivational underpinnings of this fair market ideology, including self-deception, economic system justification, and belief in a just world. Their analysis has important implications for understanding not only why individuals might endorse extant social and organizational regimes, but also why they might resist attempts to change them.

The next chapter also takes us inside the heads of organizational members as they attempt to make sense of the phenomena they encounter. In recent years, there has been increasing recognition of the importance that subjective construal processes play in how social perceivers interpret the worlds they inhabit and also how they act in response to those interpretations. In this tradition, Wrzesnieski, Dutton, and Debebe develop a model of interpersonal sensemaking to understand how organizational members construct the meaning of their work. In contrast with previous models of the meaning of work, which often highlighted individual social information processing tendencies, the original framework advanced by Wrzesnieski and her coauthors highlights the central role that social interactional processes play in the construction of meaning at work. According to their framework, sensemaking is often triggered by interpreting cues in the workplace, including prompts that make salient affirmational or disaffirmational processes. Their analysis affords particular prominence to the role various kinds of stories play in this sensemaking process.

The next chapter also highlights the role social processes play in organizational interpretations. More particularly, Menon and Blount's chapter addresses the important question of how decision makers value knowledge in organizations. In contrast with rational actor and garbage can models, the authors posit a social relational model, according to which relationships between knowledge messengers and knowledge recipients directly influence knowledge valuation. In particular, Menon and Blount identify two key dimensions of relational perception, which they characterize as social identification and threat appraisal. Social identification reflects the extent to which the parties to the knowledge transmission and valuation relationship share a common social identity or not (i.e. enjoy ingroup versus outgroup status). Threat appraisal refers to the evaluator's perception of the other's relational status (e.g. enemy or friend). Using these two dimensions, the authors generate a useful taxonomy of relational schema types and then show how the types affect knowledge valuation within organizations.

From normalization, acceptance, and constructive sensemaking, the next contribution, by Jehn and Bendersky, turns us toward consideration of the subject of disharmony and conflict within organizations. Intragroup conflict in organizations has been the focus of a very large number of empirical studies over the past several decades, reflecting contributions from a variety of social science disciplines. Yet, as the authors note, there have been surprisingly few attempts to bring conceptual order or coherence to this vast, sprawling literature. Jehn and Bendersky admirably tackle this daunting task, providing a much-needed review of this sprawling literature and then advancing a comprehensive and original model of intragroup conflict. Their framework identifies several types of conflict moderators, including amplifiers (variables that amplify conflict-outcome relationships), suppressors (variables that weaken conflict-outcome relationships), ameliorators (variables that decrease negative effects and increase positive effects), and exacerbators (variables that increase negative effects but decrease positive effects). Jehn and Bendersky use this framework to develop some normative principles for the constructive management of intragroup conflicts.

Few topics in the organizational literature continue to attract as much attention as leadership. The result is a voluminous literature that sometimes has the feel of much old wine in not-so-new bottles. Happily, in their provocative and insightful paper, van Knippenberg and Hogg advance a fresh perspective on leader effectiveness drawn from social identity theory and research. According to their framework, a leader's effectiveness derives in no small measure from the fact that the leader is a group member and can motivate followers on the basis of salient, shared group identity. Particularly important in their analysis is the extent to which the leader is prototypical of the group. Drawing on an impressive number of recent empirical findings, van Knippenberg and Hogg demonstrate the power of a social identity perspective by comparing and contrasting it with a number of major contemporary approaches to leadership effectiveness, including charismatic leadership theories, leader-member exchange theory, and leadership categorization theories.

Elsbach's chapter also provides a rich conceptual lens from which to view a vast, extant literature in the organizational sciences on impression management and related topics. Her analysis presents a fresh, integrative perspective on a set of inter-related topics of enduring interest in the organizational literature, viz., how organizational spokespersons protect and manage positive images, identities, and the reputations of their organizations. Heretofore, these literatures have remained somewhat distinct and isolated from each other. Using the new construct *organizational perception management*, Elsbach illustrates how spokespersons engage in effective perception management in response to a variety of what she characterizes as triggering events. Her model details, for instance, the strategic use of verbal accounts, categorizations, symbolic behaviors, and displays of physical markers to effectively influence and shape audience perceptions of the organization, especially during periods of organizational crisis or change.

The final contribution by Brockner urges organizational scholars to more thoughtfully ponder and systematically explicate the psychological determinants of cross-cultural differences. Brockner begins by noting there has been a long standing interest in how national cultures influence organizational members' workplace attitudes and behaviors. Yet, less attention has been afforded to carefully and systematically explicating the psychological determinants of those differences. To illustrate his thesis, Brockner reviews prior work on a variety of topics, including the fundamental attribution bias, social loafing, and participative decision making. Although these studies amply document country differences, there is a comparative dearth of systematic theory pertaining to the psychological dimensions that contribute to, or account for, these differences. Brockner goes on to demonstrate a number of important benefits associated with explaining between-country differences. The first and perhaps most obvious benefit is a deeper understanding of the origins of the differences themselves. Second, and perhaps less obviously, Brockner proposes that explicating the psychological determinants of between-country differences might contribute to a better understanding of the null results frequently reported in cross-cultural studies. Brockner suggests that, rather than being simply dismissed as unimportant, such null findings might conceal important insights. Third, explicating the psychological determinants of between-country effects may contribute to a deeper understanding of fundamental theoretical processes. And fourth, explicating the psychological determinants of between-country differences may illuminate also within-country variation along important individual dimensions.

Given the remarkable range of contributions described above, and the caliber of the scholars who produced them, we found compiling the twenty-fifth volume of *Research in Organizational Behavior* a true delight. We hope the reader will experience the same delight in reading them.

Roderick M. Kramer
Barry M. Staw
Editors

THE NORMALIZATION OF CORRUPTION IN ORGANIZATIONS

Blake E. Ashforth and Vikas Anand

ABSTRACT

Organizational corruption imposes a steep cost on society, easily dwarfing that of street crime. We examine how corruption becomes normalized, that is, embedded in the organization such that it is more or less taken for granted and perpetuated. We argue that three mutually reinforcing processes underlie normalization: (1) institutionalization, where an initial corrupt decision or act becomes embedded in structures and processes and thereby routinized; (2) rationalization, where self-serving ideologies develop to justify and perhaps even valorize corruption; and (3) socialization, where naïve newcomers are induced to view corruption as permissible if not desirable. The model helps explain how otherwise morally upright individuals can routinely engage in corruption without experiencing conflict, how corruption can persist despite the turnover of its initial practitioners, how seemingly rational organizations can engage in suicidal corruption and how an emphasis on the individual as evildoer misses the point that systems and individuals are mutually reinforcing.

I will never believe I have done anything criminally wrong. I did what is business. If I bent any rules, who doesn't? If you are going to punish me, sweep away the system. If I am guilty, there are many others who should be by my side in the dock (on trial).
 – an architect, convicted of corrupt practices (Chibnall & Saunders, 1977, p. 142).

Research in Organizational Behavior
Research in Organizational Behavior, Volume 25, 1–52
Copyright © 2003 by Elsevier Ltd.
All rights of reproduction in any form reserved
ISSN: 0191-3085/doi:10.1016/S0191-3085(03)25001-2

INTRODUCTION

What comes to mind when you think about criminals and crime? Odds are that you picture a burglar breaking into a home, a pusher dealing drugs, or some related image. Odds are, in short, that you picture a lone individual engaged in street crime (Collins, 1998; Ermann & Lundman, 1996). In fact, Clinard (1979, p. 16) concluded that "Far more persons are killed through corporate criminal activities than by individual criminal homicides," and the U.S. Department of Justice estimates that the economic costs of corporate crime are seven to 25 times greater than that of street crime (Donziger, 1996). As Darley (1996, p. 13) argues, "the typical evil action is inflicted . . . by individuals acting within an organizational context" rather than by "evil actors carrying out solitary actions." Moreover, Edwin Sutherland (1949), who coined the term *white collar crime* and pioneered early research, argued that corporate misdeeds tear the social fabric more so than street crime because they corrode trust in authorities and institutions.

An even more troubling trend in white-collar crime is that these crimes appear increasingly to be perpetrated through the actions of *numerous* employees in the organization as opposed to being the actions of a single misguided individual. A glance at today's headlines illustrates the point. Enron's senior executives are accused of hiding the company's precarious financial position while cashing out their stocks and shredding incriminating documents (Eichenwald & Henriques, 2002), U.S. Catholic Church officials admit that several key administrators systematically covered up the predatory behaviors of pedophile priests (Miller & France, 2002) and Merrill Lynch agreed to pay the State of New York $100 million to settle accusations that its employees gave its investors misleading and over-optimistic research reports about the stock of its investment banking clients (Gasparino & Smith, 2002).

In this paper, we develop a model that explains how corruption becomes normalized in an organization. We define corrupt acts as the misuse of authority for personal, subunit and/or organizational gain (cf. Sherman, 1980). Because we will argue that corruption often becomes institutionalized in organizations, it is important to note that "misuse" refers to societal norms. We focus on relatively severe or "morally intense" (Jones, 1991) forms of corruption (e.g. self-dealing versus sleeping on the job) because these are more difficult to normalize. We include corruption on behalf of the organization (e.g. price-fixing, bribing outsiders to win contracts) and against the organization (e.g. theft, nepotism) (Coleman, 1987), often referred to as corporate/organizational crime and occupational crime, respectively (Clinard & Quinney, 1973).

Our model examines *collective corruption* (Brief, Buttram & Dukerich, 2001) – acts that require cooperation among two or more individuals. Our analysis is confined to the group level (throughout the paper, we use the term *group* to refer to a collective, such as a workgroup, department, or organization): we do not examine individual differences in susceptibility to corruption. Further, we focus largely on groups that are housed within an organization rather than distributed across organizations (as in, for example, bid rigging). Additionally, our interest is not in the antecedents of corrupt acts – the primary focus of much previous research (e.g. Baucus, 1994; Brass, Butterfield & Skaggs, 1998) – but in how such acts become *normalized*, that is, become embedded in organizational structures and processes, internalized by organizational members as permissible and even desirable behavior, and passed on to successive generations of members (cf. Brief et al., 2001; Zucker, 1977).

We propose that there are three pillars that contribute to the normalization of corruption in an organization: (1) *institutionalization*, the process by which corrupt practices are enacted as a matter of routine, often without conscious thought about their propriety; (2) *rationalization*, the process by which individuals who engage in corrupt acts use socially constructed accounts to legitimate the acts in their own eyes; and (3) *socialization*, the process by which newcomers are taught to perform and accept the corrupt practices. As shown in Fig. 1, the three pillars are mutually reinforcing and reciprocally interdependent; once established in an organization, the pillars create a situation where corruption is practiced collectively by employees and may endure indefinitely. Our analysis suggests an answer to the intriguing question of how a person who is a loving parent, thoughtful neighbor and devout churchgoer is able to engage in workplace corruption.

The first three sections of the paper describe each of the pillars in detail. The fourth section focuses briefly on how institutionalization, rationalization and socialization interact to cement normalization. Finally, we discuss the implications of our model for research and practice.

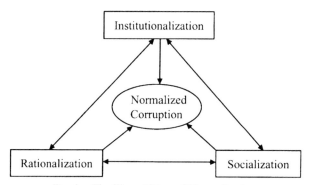

Fig. 1. The Three Pillars of Normalization.

INSTITUTIONALIZING CORRUPTION

In 1996, the Equal Employment Opportunity Commission (EEOC) charged Mitsubishi Motors in the U.S. with creating conditions that led to over 700 women being sexually harassed over a period of several years. According to the EEOC charge, the women had been subjected to groping, sexual graffiti, abusive comments and having lewd photos pasted on their cars. The EEOC further charged that the harassment resulted from the tacit and explicit acts of numerous individuals at all levels in the organization. Additional investigations revealed that the United Auto Workers (UAW), an external agency that could and should have intervened, did not take strong action in response to the repeated complaints that it received from female workers. Further, Mitsubishi's policies required that before any employee filed a complaint, she needed to engage in a lengthy procedure to settle the complaint with the accused individuals; a process that many of the aggrieved employees chose not to go through.

Mitsubishi responded to these accusations by strongly refuting the EEOC allegations. They paid 3,000 workers a day's wages to facilitate them picketing the EEOC offices and set up phone lines on the shop floor to enable workers to call legislators to protest the EEOC's actions. These responses further alienated public opinion and Mitsubishi finally settled the case for $34 million, making this the largest settlement in the legal history of sexual discrimination. This sum was in addition to the private settlements that were paid to individual employees who had sued the company (Elstrom & Updike, 1996; Miller, 1998; Sharpe, 1996; Weimer & Thornton, 1997).

Institutionalized organizational behaviors have been defined as stable, repetitive and enduring activities that are enacted by multiple organization members without significant thought about the propriety, utility, or nature of the behavior (cf. Greenwood & Hinings, 1988; Oliver, 1992; Zucker, 1977, 1988). In institutionalized corruption, the impetus for and apparatus of corruption are external to any one person: corruption is a property of the collective. As the Mitsubishi case illustrates, institutionalized corrupt behaviors can pervade multiple subunits and levels in an organization. They can become an integral part of day-to-day activities to such an extent that individuals may be unable to see the inappropriateness of their behaviors.

Gross (1978, p. 56) argues that "all organizations are inherently criminogenic" – that is, prone to criminality (or at least corruption) – although not inevitably criminal. We view collective corruption as a slippery slope where initial, idiosyncratic corrupt practices become institutionalized over time. As shown in Fig. 2, the institutionalization process appears to consist of three major phases: (1) the initial decision or act; (2) embedding corruption in structures and processes; and (3) routinizing corruption. It should be noted, however, that it is far from inevitable that idiosyncratic corruption will slide into collective corruption: later, under "Implications for Research and Practice," we briefly consider means of reversing normalization.

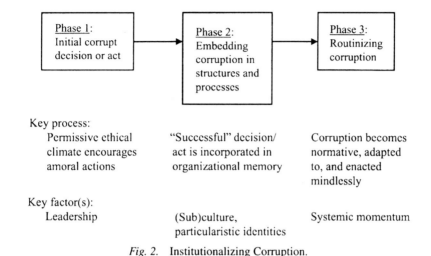

Fig. 2.   Institutionalizing Corruption.

Phase 1: The Initial Decision or Act

Much of the literature on organizational corruption has focused on the genesis of corruption (e.g. Baucus, 1994; Brass et al., 1998; Cohen, 1995; Coleman, 1998; Finney & Lesieur, 1982; Geis & Salinger, 1998; Poveda, 1994; Shover & Bryant, 1993; Szwajkowski, 1985; Yeager, 1986); thus, we will keep our overview brief. This literature argues that the motivation and opportunity to engage in corruption are the product of various environmental (e.g. strong competition, lax legal and regulatory enforcement), organizational (e.g. poor performance, structural complexity) and, to a far lesser extent, personal factors (e.g. cognitive moral development, fear of failing). An implicit assumption seems to be that corruption is usually the product of strong situations that override individual differences or that ordinary people populate the ranks of the corrupt; indeed, Coleman (1998, p. 178) states that "Almost all the studies have agreed on one point: White-collar offenders are psychologically 'normal.' "

In particular, many scholars have linked corruption to a permissive ethical climate at the societal, industry, or organizational levels. Major organizational goals are often tied to resource procurement and financial success and a constellation of values extolled in business is conducive to an amoral and even immoral pursuit of those goals: free enterprise (minimal regulation), individualism, competitive achievement, profitability, efficiency, pragmatism and so on (e.g. Jackall, 1988; Mills, 1956). Brief et al. (2001) argue that belief in the sanctity of the corporation is so strong that managers tend to believe that by serving the corporation's interests they are also serving the public's interests: what's good for Microsoft is good for the country. Thus, ethical issues often are not perceived or are subordinated to or reframed as economic, legal, public relations, or other kinds of "business" issues, leaving managers free to engage in amoral reasoning (Jones & Ryan, 1998). For example, Brenner and Molander (1977, p. 62) surveyed *Harvard Business Review* (*HBR*) readers and found that nearly half agreed that "the American business executive tends not to apply the great ethical laws immediately to work. He is preoccupied chiefly with gain."

According to the rational choice perspective in criminology (Cornish & Clarke, 1986), individuals are thought to engage in "an assessment, however crude or incomplete, of options and the potential risks and payoffs of each" (Shover & Bryant, 1993, p. 153), along with the skills, planning, time needed and so on. Given a permissive ethical climate, an emphasis on financial goals (with commensurate rewards for success), and an opportunity to act amorally or immorally, the ends may soon come to justify the means, leading to a decision to engage in corruption. Further, the leniency and low frequency of formal sanctioning by governments and professional associations often makes corruption economically rational (Braithwaite, 1989; Leaf, 2002): it appears that crime often does pay. Finally, as we argue later under "Rationalizing Corruption," groups often provide self-serving accounts to neutralize the countervailing force of morals and ethics.

To be sure, there are other routes to corruption besides amoral and immoral calculation, including principled disagreement with public policy and laws, managerial incompetence, and the unintended consequences of myriad actors and actions ricocheting within complex systems and contexts. However, we believe, following Vaughan (1992) and others, that amoral or immoral calculation is the most common route – in part because such a calculation is often necessary for a given act of corruption to continue and become institutionalized, regardless of its genesis.

Leadership
Leadership plays a potentially huge role in the institutionalization process. Leaders not only control many of the levers of institutionalization, but are very potent role models for organizational members. Baumhart (1961) and Brenner and Molander (1977) asked *HBR* readers to rank five factors according to their influence on unethical decisions (the 1977 survey included a sixth factor, "society's moral climate," which ranked fifth). In both surveys, the "behavior of superiors" was ranked as the most influential factor, followed by a cluster of factors – "formal policy or lack thereof," "industry ethical climate," and "behavior of one's equals in the company"; tellingly, "one's personal financial needs" came last.

Leaders do not have to actually engage in corruption to serve as role models: rewarding, condoning, ignoring, or otherwise facilitating corruption – whether intentionally or not, or explicitly or not – often sends a clear signal to employees (Baucus, 1994; Ermann & Lundman, 1996). Brief et al. (2001) argue that an emphasis on ends rather than means, supported by high standards and strong rewards (punishments) for attaining (not attaining) them, creates a permissive ethical climate. For example, Sims and Brinkmann (2002) discuss the role of CEO John Gutfreund in helping to foster an unethical climate at Salomon Brothers. Gutfreund focused on and rewarded short-term results, modeled aggressive and Machiavellian behavior, failed to punish employees who broke laws in the pursuit of those results, lied about and covered up ethical and legal lapses, promoted like-minded employees, and fired others capriciously, encouraging conformity.

In addition to serving as role models, leaders – as the legitimate agents of the organization – *authorize* corruption (Kelman, 1973; cf. displacement of responsibility, Bandura, 1999; sanctioning, Brief et al., 2001). As with role modeling, authorizing need not be formal and explicit: a manager who informally encourages or tacitly condones corruption can also be said to be authorizing it. The subordinate, as a designated role occupant, is expected to execute the authorized acts, not to second-guess them: the normative duty to obey is expected to trump personal preferences, particularly in rigidly hierarchical organizations (Hamilton & Sanders, 1992). As illustrated by Milgram's (1974) obedience experiments, the reflexive impulse to obey authority figures – the "habit of obedience" (Hamilton & Sanders, 1992, p. 72) – is so strong and pervasive that most people have a difficult time actively defying orders they do not condone. In any event, because the individuals who perform the corrupt acts "are not the actual agent of their actions, they are spared self-condemning reactions" (Bandura, 1999, p. 196). Further, the relative powerlessness often associated with subordination may induce individuals to abdicate responsibility for moral issues: "'Let the people making the high salaries tackle the difficult ethical decisions' seems to be a widely held view among occupants of lower echelon corporate positions" (Jones & Ryan, 1998, p. 440).

Two final notes regarding leadership and corruption are in order. First, the situational power of office may be complemented (or even supplanted) by the personal power of charisma. The more charismatic the authority figure(s), the greater the identification, trust and reflexive obedience that he or she is likely to engender among subordinates (Conger & Kanungo, 1998). Charisma speaks to a quality of the person, not the mission, and a charismatic leader can use the allegiance of others for benign ends or corrupt ends (Howell, 1988). The cult of personality that arose around Michael Milken enabled him to assemble a force of like-minded disciples at Drexel Burnham Lambert (Stone, 1990).

Second, organizational structures and processes are often contrived to insulate senior managers from blame, thereby further encouraging corruption. For example, a focus on performance goals rather than on means or the use of verbal and general (i.e. ambiguous) orders regarding means, coupled with minimal oversight and documentation, afford the managers "strategic ignorance" (Katz, 1979, p. 297) and therefore "plausible deniability" (Braithwaite, 1989; Browning, 1989, p. 1). Baker and Faulkner (1993) found that top executives involved in two decentralized price fixing networks were less likely to be found guilty than top executives in a centralized price fixing network, and Braithwaite (1984) reports that pharmaceutical firms instituted a "vice-president responsible for going to jail," namely, the only executive who needed to know about corrupt activities. Similarly, isolating subunits allows senior managers to be "willfully blind" (Braithwaite, 1989, p. 351) to corrupt practices (e.g. the independent cells of the Mafia). Thus, the managers can claim that they neither knew of nor approved the corrupt action.

Phase 2: Embedding Corruption in Organizational Structures and Processes

Organizational memory is the metaphor used to describe the process through which an organization acquires, stores and uses the knowledge that is applied to its activities (Anand, Manz & Glick, 1998). In its quest for efficiency, an organization tends to commit a promising activity to its memory (and thus institutionalize it) when it has been performed repetitively in the immediate past (Yates, 1990). Activities stored in organizational memories are often performed through the execution of a series of inter-related routines. The outputs of one routine trigger the initiation of the next routine in the sequence. Thus, entire activities can be performed without any one individual knowing them in their entirety (Levitt & March, 1988; Nelson & Winter, 1982; Weick & Roberts, 1993).

Once a corrupt decision or act produces a positive outcome and is included in organizational memory, it is likely to be used again in the future. When similar issues confront other managers, and if solutions are not readily obvious, answers are sought from the memory because: (1) past decisions and acts are assumed to have been made for rational reasons; and (2) following a precedent helps legitimate the decision and act (Henisz & Delios, 2001; Ocasio, 1999; Simon, 1976). For instance, Ermann and Lundman (1996, pp. 23–24) describe how Gulf Oil laundered and distributed corporate funds illegally to American politicians:

> After the comptroller who helped develop the system left, three other people sequentially occupied his position. None of them had to make any difficult decisions, much less consciously involve themselves in criminal activities. They merely were told that they would receive requests for money . . . Easy to do and easy to live with.

The use of previous unethical decisions is especially significant because individuals often do not consider the contextual issues (including ethics) surrounding the decision or act; the past success of such practices is assumed to validate the process through which it was determined (cf. Miller, 1993). And if the renewed corrupt practice results in a positive outcome an even stronger precedent is set for the future. The organization comes to expect and then *depend* on the payoffs from corruption. In time, goals, budgets, information flows, rewards and punishments and so on may be skewed to support the practices. Eichenwald (2000), for instance, discusses the bureaucratic machinery and processes that evolved to support price-fixing by Archer Daniels Midland and its competitors. The result is institutionalized corruption: personal behaviors become impersonal norms, emergent practices become tacit understandings and idiosyncratic acts become shared procedures. Moreover, the increasingly casual practice of corruption tends to further degrade the ethical climate of the organization. In short, micro and macro practices are mutually reinforcing, encouraging further corruption (Cialdini, 1996; Vaughan, 1992).

Culture
As the repertoire of corrupt practices becomes embedded in the ongoing routines of the organization, a deviant culture (or subculture, in the case of localized corruption) tends to emerge to normalize the corruption. Assumptions, values and beliefs, perhaps drawing on the business values noted above, evolve to rationalize the corrupt practices in ways that neutralize the stigma of corruption. (Later, under "Rationalizing Corruption," we discuss the types of accounts through which this is accomplished.) Indeed, the culture may come to valorize the corruption and promulgate recipes for corruption. For instance, Kappeler, Sluder and Alpert (1994) describe subcultural norms that support police corruption: don't give up another cop; if you get caught, don't implicate anybody else; don't get involved in another cop's affairs; don't trust new cops until they've been checked out; and don't tell anybody more than they need to know.

Deviant (sub)cultures insulate actors from the wider culture with its countervailing norms and beliefs. Indeed, Hollinger and Clark (1983, p. 126) concluded from their study of employee theft that "employee deviance is more constrained by informal social controls present in primary work-group relationships than by the more-formal reactions to deviance by those in positions of authority within the formal organization." Accordingly, a premium is placed on socializing with insiders and on secrecy and obfuscation regarding outsiders (as well as condemning any condemners; Sykes & Matza, 1957). Strong (sub)cultures are more likely to emerge where there is high within-group task interdependence and low between-group interdependence, accountability for performance goals but not means, group-based versus individual-based rewards, member stability and cohesion, peer-based socialization, and physical proximity (e.g. Trice & Beyer, 1993).

How can a group hold a worldview so at odds with the wider culture and not appear to be greatly conflicted by it? The answer may lie in the distinction between *particularism* and *universalism*. An individual develops social identities specific to the social domains, groups and roles – and accompanying subcultures – that he or she occupies (e.g. manager, mother, parishioner, sports fan). Given the diversity of social domains, groups and roles one typically occupies, one's social identities tend to be correspondingly quite diverse. In order not to compromise the utility of identities tailored to particular contexts, individuals often cognitively compartmentalize their identities (Ashforth & Mael, 1989; Settles, Sellers & Damas, 2002). In a real sense, then, to change social domains, groups and roles is to change selves. Derry (1987), for instance, argues that because managers value efficiency and effectiveness, they may use different moral yardsticks at work than at home. The double standard is locally adaptive even as it's morally repugnant from a more generalized perspective.[1] Thus, an individual typically responds to the press of a given context by invoking the localized social identity and culture. As a result, actions tend to be particularistic rather than universalistic; that is, they tend to be tailored to local demands and favor local actors who share one's group membership, identity and culture.

In the case of corruption, this myopia means that an otherwise ethically-minded individual may forsake universalistic or dominant norms about ethical behavior in favor of particularistic behaviors that favor his or her group at the expense of outsiders (Aubert, 1952; cf. ethnocentrism, LeVine & Campbell, 1972; Ryan & Bogart, 1997). Indeed, if a social identity is *chronically* more important to the individual, particularism can metastasize into what Banfield (1958) calls "amoral familism," that is, a tendency to display morality only with regard to one's "family" (ingroup). This tendency to *always* put the ingroup above all others clearly paves the way for collective corruption. Extreme examples include the Mafia and street gangs: members of these groups tend not to see themselves as corrupt but as faithfully serving themselves, their ingroup and perhaps their neighborhood; the wider society exists as a counterpoint to be exploited (e.g. Jankowski, 1991).

In sum, because life is lived in concrete settings, localized social identities and cultures tend to be highly salient. Thus, the individual may bend his or her general commitment to ethics under the press of local circumstances. As Bandura (1999, p. 206) put it, "Most everyone is virtuous at the abstract level."

Beyond the Organization

Corrupt practices within an organization may be disseminated throughout the industry via both micro (e.g. individual mobility) and macro (e.g. imitation) processes (Darley, 1996; Vaughan, 1983; Zucker, 1988) and given impetus by competitive pressure. Industry level corruption is more likely in mature industries, where time and stability facilitate dissemination (Baucus, 1994). Examples abound: Clinard and Yeager (1980) concluded that corporate crime among Fortune 500 companies is most prevalent in the oil, automobile and pharmaceutical industries; Pizzo, Fricker and Muolo (1991) document how a network of individuals spread knowledge of fraudulent techniques throughout the U.S. savings and loan industry; more recently, the U.S. utility industry was accused of indulging in round trip sales (where a firm sells electricity to a dummy firm and buys the same amount of electricity back) to artificially boost revenues (Berman, Angwin & Cummins, 2002). Brenner and Molander (1977, p. 60) asked *HBR* readers, "In every industry there are some generally accepted business practices. In your industry, are there practices which you regard as unethical?" Excluding the "don't know" responses, two-thirds agreed.

Often, an important factor in industry wide corruption is that governing bodies that are responsible for, or have the capacity to monitor, industry behavior may themselves become part of the institutionalized system of corruption (Braithwaite, 1989; Sherman, 1980). As in the example of the UAW's role in the Mitsubishi case described earlier, or as in the case of Arthur Andersen vis-à-vis Enron and Salomon Smith Barney's telecom analysts vis-à-vis Global Crossing (Creswell & Prins, 2002), outside agencies may become co-opted by organizations and develop tacit agreements to turn a blind eye – particularly if the individuals anticipate or have been through the "revolving door" to employment in the industry.[2]

Phase 3: Routinizing

As corrupt practices become institutionalized and repeatedly enacted, they become routinized and habitual. Kelman (1973, p. 46) defines *routinizing* as "transforming the action into routine, mechanical, highly programmed operations." Routinizing neutralizes the salience of corruption in four ways. First, by embedding corruption in *ongoing* processes, routinizing removes discrete (strategic) decision points that might trigger reflective thought and creates a momentum that sustains action without the necessity for thought (Kelman, 1973; Staw, 1980; cf. ritualism, Ashforth & Kreiner, 2002). As an antitrust violator put it, "It was a way of doing business before we even got into the business. So it was like why do you brush your teeth in the morning or something... It was part of the everyday" (Benson, 1985, p. 591). Once corruption is ongoing, it takes more conscious effort to *dis*continue it than to continue it.

Second, to increase efficiency, routinizing tends to break down corrupt acts into specialized tasks that are assigned to separate individuals. The individuals become experts at their jobs and, as noted in the discussion of organizational memory, use the outputs derived from the actions of others as cues to perform their specific tasks (Weick & Roberts, 1993). Often, these tasks become dispersed over multiple subunits and procedures (cf. Argote & Ingram, 2000). The result is that individuals may perform their tasks without knowing how their individual actions, in conjunction with the actions of others, contribute to the enactment of a corrupt practice (cf. normal injustices, Bunderson, 2001). Thus, specialization not only fosters a diffusion of responsibility, it makes it difficult for any individual to comprehend (and easy to deny) the "big picture" (Braithwaite, 1984; Darley, 1992). A test lab supervisor, required to falsify data, said "we're just drawing some curves, and what happens to them after they leave here, well, we're not responsible for that" (Vandivier, 1996, p. 128).

Third, by embedding corruption in a system of *interdependent* processes, routinizing yokes the individual to other role occupants. One is effectively locked in by dense task connections such that the whole sustains each part; one is swept along by the momentum of the *system* (Ashforth & Kreiner, 2002). For instance, an intriguing feature of the infamous Black Sox scandal (where members of the Chicago White Sox threw the 1919 World Series) was the half-hearted commitment of many of the conspirators. Despite their vacillating support, the unfolding events gained a kind of momentum that pulled everyone along to their fate (Asinof, 1963).

Fourth, following Merton's (1968) notion of means-ends displacement, by inducing individuals to focus on the processes, the goals for which the processes were devised become less salient (Brief et al., 2001; Kelman, 1973). Arendt (1965) notes the ease with which the German civil service adapted to handling the paperwork of the Nazi's Final Solution to the Jewish "problem": "Their routine was the same whether the papers referred to furniture shipped to offices (or) Jews shipped to concentration camps" (Silver & Geller, 1978, p. 131).

Thus, routinizing blunts awareness that a *moral issue* – "where a person's actions, when freely performed, may harm or benefit others" (Jones, 1991, p. 367) – is at stake. If a moral issue is not recognized, moral decision-making processes cannot be engaged (Bandura, 1999; Jones, 1991). Thus, morally developed individuals may be induced to voluntarily perform morally unsound actions. Indeed, the casualness of routinized behavior often belies the severity of the consequences: Arendt (1965), writing on the implementation of the Nazi's Final Solution, refers to the "banality of evil."

As routinizing reduces the salience of corrupt practices, corruption comes to be: (1) seen as normative; (2) adapted to; and (3) enacted mindlessly.

Normativeness

By normative, we mean that the practices assume an ought-to patina. Because the practices have been successful and repeatedly enacted, they assume the power of *ritual*, of the correct way to accomplish desirable goals and ward off failure. Thus, the expedient comes to seem necessary; one way of acting comes to seem like the only way; and the instrumental comes to be expressive. In short, the way things are (descriptive) comes to seem like the way things should be (prescriptive). In a review of employee theft, Greenberg (1998, p. 171) concluded that: "In many cases, group norms about theft by employees have become so strongly 'entrenched . . . woven into the fabric of people's lives' (Mars, 1994, p. 17), that to steal is normative whereas to not steal is considered aberrant." Institutionalization enhances legitimacy.

Further, normativeness may pave the way for small corruptions to become large ones. The Knapp Commission (1972), which investigated police corruption in New York City, differentiated between "meat-eaters" who aggressively pursued graft and "grass-eaters" who pursued only relatively petty graft. The commission suggested that the grass-eaters were actually more problematic because their greater numbers produced pressures for conformity and tended to make corruption appear respectable. Much as Zimbardo (1969) found that damage to a car signaled "fair game" for vandals, a sense that corruption is respectable may invite increasingly audacious behavior.

Finally, once corruption is normative, it may accrue *symbolic* rewards, such as status and self-esteem, in addition to the utilitarian rewards, for individuals and groups (Greenberg, 1998). For instance, brokers who arranged fraudulent but profitable deals for Prudential-Bache were accorded high status at the firm (Eichenwald, 1995). Indeed, such individuals may be promoted into positions where they serve as role models and mentors for other employees, thus accelerating the institutionalization process.

Adaptation

Ashforth and Kreiner (2002) discuss two techniques through which the reactions to otherwise aversive stimuli are reduced, thereby enabling adaptation: habituation and desensitization. In *habituation*, repeated exposure to the same stimulus progressively weakens reactions to the stimulus. An investigation of the Tailhook scandal (where women were accosted as they were forced down a gauntlet of Navy officers during a convention) concluded that many officers "saw no reason to stop anything that hadn't been stopped before (at previous conventions)" (Caproni & Finley, 1994, p. 26). In *desensitization*, exposure to different stimuli of increasing aversiveness weakens reactions to the stimuli. The head of a Wall Street investment bank commented on insider trading in the 1980s: "You definitely saw the abuses growing but you also saw the absence of people getting caught, so the atmosphere grew relaxed. There really was a deterioration of caution" (Sethi & Steidlmeier, 1991, p. 112). Through habituation and desensitization, one becomes accustomed to the aversiveness and riskiness of corruption, contributing to the mindlessness discussed below and perhaps carelessness.

Habituation and desensitization tend to be abetted by group contexts. Aversive stimuli – such as perceptions of corrupt activity – foster a desire for social interaction for purposes of sense making, social support and anxiety relief (Rimé, Mesquita, Philippot & Boca, 1991). Following social comparison theory, individuals need to interpret what the stimuli imply (e.g. Is this normal? Should I be worried? What should I do?) and so tend to turn to similarly situated peers, especially those with experience and status (Festinger, 1954; Schachter, 1959). Given social norms to appear in control and to provide reassurance, individuals are inclined to infer that things are not so bad. Thus, social interaction often leads to anxiety relief, particularly when coupled with the rationalizing ideologies and socializing techniques discussed later: anxiety shared is anxiety halved.

Mindlessness
When practices become habits, they tend to become taken-for-granted and enacted mindlessly, that is, with little or no real problem solving or even conscious awareness (Ashforth & Fried, 1988; Brief et al., 2001). Their routinized nature blunts the perceived need to reexamine the premises that gave rise to the practices or the outcomes they produce, creating a certain bureaucratic momentum.

For example, Gioia (1992) discussed his role as a product recall coordinator for Ford at the time of the emerging Pinto crisis. The Pinto had a design defect that often caused the gas tank to explode in rear-end collisions. Gioia notes that the procedural and cognitive scripts used for diagnosing problems, exacerbated by a heavy workload and a muting of emotion (habituation) induced by the ongoing gravity of his job, led him and his colleagues to dismiss the idea of a recall. In a literal sense, they did not see an ethical issue:

> Before I went to Ford I would have argued strongly that Ford had an ethical obligation to recall. After I left Ford I now argue . . . that Ford had an ethical obligation to recall. But, *while I was there*, I perceived no strong obligation to recall and I remember no strong *ethical* overtones to the case whatsoever (p. 388, his emphasis).

In sum, the mindlessness induced by institutionalization may cause individuals to not even notice what might arouse outrage under other circumstances. In a real sense, an organization is corrupt today because it was corrupt yesterday.

Conclusion

Institutionalization is about embedding practices in organizational structures and processes such that they can survive the turnover of generations of employees. As institutionalization sets in, individuals perform the corrupt actions without giving significant thought to the reasons for those actions; indeed the actions may come to seem like the right and only course to take. The actions exist as social knowledge that perpetuates itself: "internalization, self reward, or other intervening processes need not be present to ensure . . . persistence, because social knowledge once institutionalized, exists as a fact, as part of objective reality, and can be transmitted on that basis" (Zucker, 1977, p. 276). Corruption thus becomes resistant not only to change, but to examination.

RATIONALIZING CORRUPTION

An intriguing finding is that *corrupt individuals tend not to view themselves as corrupt*. For example, individuals convicted of white collar crimes tend to acknowledge their errant behavior but nonetheless deny criminal intent and the label of *criminal* (Benson, 1985; Cressey, 1953); in short, unlike many street criminals (Shover, 1996), they resist incorporating a pejorative identity into their self-definition. Indeed, Conklin (1977) entitled his book "Illegal but not criminal," quoting a defendant in the infamous heavy electrical equipment price-fixing conspiracy. By denying the label of corrupt, such individuals avoid the adverse effects of an undesirable social identity.

Further, it appears that most individuals engaged in corrupt acts tend not to abandon the values that society espouses; they continue to value fairness, honesty, integrity and so forth, even as they engage in corruption (Sykes & Matza, 1957). Prior to a group reaching phases 2 and 3 of the institutionalization process described earlier – that is, until the momentum of a corrupted system provides its own seeming legitimacy – how do such individuals pull off this difficult act of willingly engaging in corruption while not perceiving themselves as corrupt and not jettisoning the values that may impede corruption?

Geis and Meier (1979) contend that the answer is that the legal process is lenient on white collar crimes and that offenders hold other highly respectable roles – such as community leader and good provider – that bolster their self-concept. However, given the domain specific nature of many social identities (Ashforth, 2001), it seems likely that this is only a partial answer: the workplace itself is probably the most effective site for maintaining the positive valence of the work-related identities.

We contend that a major part of the answer to the puzzle of how corrupt individuals deny the identity implications of their actions is through the use of *rationalizing ideologies.* These ideologies help distance individuals and groups from the aberrant moral stance implied by their actions and perhaps even forge "a moral inversion, in which the bad becomes good" (Adams & Balfour, 1998, p. 11). Although the beliefs that undergird the ideologies can be used by an individual in isolation, they become far more potent when institutionalized in the collective – when they are a shared resource that all can draw on and mutually affirm (Coleman & Ramos, 1998).

Rationalizing Ideologies

There is a large literature on cognitive defense mechanisms, self-serving biases, ingroup biases, legitimizing myths, neutralization techniques, groupthink, positive illusions and so on (e.g. Chen & Tyler, 2001; Janis, 1983; Johns, 1999; Sykes & Matza, 1957; Taylor, 1989). What these concepts share is the notion that individuals and groups are motivated to resolve the inherent ambiguity that often surrounds action and outcomes in a manner that serves their self-interests. In the case of socially undesirable acts like corruption, this *biased ambiguity resolution* involves reframing the meaning of the acts so as to preserve a salutary social identity (Greenberg, 1998). The rationalizing ideologies negate negative interpretations – and possibly substitute positive ones – by articulating why the specific corruptions are justifiable or excusable exceptions to the general normative rules, or they gerrymander the very boundaries of corruption to exclude those acts. In so doing, individuals and groups engage in uncertainty absorption (March & Simon, 1958), drawing flattering inferences from ambiguous data and then treating the inferences as if they were facts. When the corruption is ongoing, these idiosyncratic social constructions tend to become woven into a self-sealing belief system that routinely neutralizes the potential stigma of corruption; hence our use of the term *rationalizing ideologies.*

We noted earlier that deviant (sub)cultures arise to normalize collective corruption. A large part of what constitutes a (sub)culture is the development of a localized perspective for making sense of the group's role in the wider organization or society. In the case of corruption, the (sub)culture may labor to (loosely) reconcile the pursuit of particularistic goals with the constraint of universalistic values. The outcome of this reconciliation is, of course, rationalizing ideologies. In short, the ideologies serve as *mediatory myths* (Abravanel, 1983), providing a rickety bridge across micro and macro worlds. (It needs to be emphasized that we are referring to ideologies for internal consumption. Judging by the lengths to which group members typically go to hide their activities, it is evident that members usually remain aware of the fact that outsiders would view their behavior as corrupt – although institutionalization, as noted, does tend to dull that awareness.)

Rationalizations are common in everyday life. They are ritualized accounts available to members of a culture to "explain" a variety of untoward acts and outcomes so as to reconcile the acts and outcomes with societal norms (Coleman, 1998; Robinson & Kraatz, 1998; Scott & Lyman, 1968). In the case of corrupt groups, these social resources are simply adapted for local use (indeed, Matza, 1964, argues that in such cases rationalizations are tacit extensions of legally permissible reasons for crimes). Thus, what differs across subcultures is not the types of rationalizations, but the particular applications. Further, rationalizations regarding corruption seldom attack the validity of the universalistic norms; indeed, by attempting to account for lapses from them, they demonstrate *fealty* to the norms (Sykes & Matza, 1957). Rationalizations indicate, however, that the actors are not to be judged by the norms for specific reasons.

To outsiders, rationalizations often sound exactly like what they usually are: patently self-serving attempts to legitimate questionable acts. However, because the rationalizations are intended for internal consumption, the issue is not their objective validity but whether the group accepts them as subjectively valid.[3] Given institutionalization and socialization (described later), there may be few naysayers (or individuals willing to naysay) to puncture the ideological balloon.

Rationalizing ideologies may be prospective or retrospective in nature. Prospective rationalizations are future-oriented and tend to be calculative, providing the actor with a rationale for subsequently engaging in corrupt behavior. Conversely, retrospective rationalizations are past-oriented and tend to be defensive as they are adduced post hoc to make an act appear reasonable (Staw, 1980; cf. pre- and postdecisional accountability, Lerner & Tetlock, 1999). Because prospective rationalizations occur before the actor is committed to a particular course of action, they tend to be more plausible and therefore effective at mitigating prospective dissonance and guilt. In contrast, because retrospective rationalizations must deal with an extant reality and because dissonance and guilt may already have been experienced, the rationalizations may have an element of desperateness to them. The types of rationalizations discussed below can be used prospectively or retrospectively.[4]

There appear to be at least eight types of rationalizations, five of which (No. 2–6) were identified by Sykes and Matza (1957). The eight rationalizations are essentially complementary, and because an ideology is a self-sealing *system* of beliefs, the eight are used in various combinations across groups. Some rationalizations, such as the denial of victim (revenge) and higher loyalty, may go beyond neutralizing the negativity of the corruption to actually *valuing* it. Each rationalization is described below.

Legality

Actors may excuse corrupt practices on the grounds that they are not actually illegal (Gellerman, 1986). Given the lobbying efforts of organizations and industries and the inherent complexity, equivocality and dynamism of organizational life, laws and regulations may not exist, may be dated or unenforced, or their applicability may be questioned. This slippage between behavior and rules provides latitude: as Gellerman (1986, p. 88) put it, "some will conclude that whatever hasn't been labeled specifically wrong must be OK." Gellerman offers the example of E. F. Hutton's 2,000 counts of mail and wire fraud where branch managers frequently drew on uncollected funds, thus generating interest-free money. Because the overdrafts were not specifically proscribed, the managers may have thought they "were simply taking full advantage of what the law . . . permitted" (p. 88).

Indeed, given a sufficiently powerful organization or industry, laws and regulations may be *created* to legitimate unethical behavior. Adams and Balfour (1998) discuss how the German Third Reich enacted laws and decrees to systematically strip Jews of their rights, citizenship and property, facilitating the Jews' eventual destruction. That laws could be used to pave the way to genocide attests to their legitimating power.

Denial of Responsibility

In *denial of responsibility*, actors construe that they have no choice due to circumstances beyond their control such as management orders, peer pressure, dire financial straits, being deceived, existing precedent, that everyone else does it, that they play a small part and so on (cf. defeasibility, scapegoating, Scott & Lyman, 1968; defense of necessity, Minor, 1981; externalization, Greenberg, 1998). For years, Beech-Nut sold adulterated apple juice to the public. Because employees believed that many other companies were also doing it, they concluded that their company was just following the pack (Welles, 1988). Similarly, cattle industry spokespersons justified the use of high levels of hormones in cattle by arguing that it was a standard industry practice (Elsbach, 1994). Denial of responsibility often draws on authorizing and routinizing.

Denial of Injury

Here, actors construe that no one was really harmed, such as when the organization is insured or can easily recover the costs, the actual damage is slight, the organization doesn't appear to care, etc. (cf. minimization, Greenberg, 1998). For example, Horning (1970, Table 1) found that approximately one-third of the employees in an assembly plant thought that their peers did not consider stealing goods to actually be theft. As one employee explained, "They (the employees) wouldn't come into your home and take thirty cents, but they will take from the Company. They figure it's got plenty of money and a few cents don't mean nothing to them" (p. 55). Similarly, Smigel (1956) found greater disapproval of stealing from a small business than from a large one or the government.

A variant of this rationalization is where a given act is rendered less offensive by comparing it to more extreme forms (cf. recalibrating, Ashforth & Kreiner, 1999). A sales manager involved in a price-fixing scandal stated:

> ... since the spirit of such (price-fixing) meetings only appeared to be correcting a horrible price level situation, that there was not an attempt to actually damage customers ... there was no personal gain for me, the company did not seem actually to be defrauding ... So I guess morally it did not seem quite so bad as might be inferred by the definition of the activity itself (Geis, 1996, p. 106).

Thus, the injury should be considered slight because it could have been far worse had the actor been so inclined.

It is easier to deny injury if the offended party does not react. Murphy (1993) and Greenberg (1998) note that organizations that fail to punish employee theft implicitly reinforce the belief that theft does not matter. It is also easier to deny injury when the injury is not visible or is physically or temporally remote (Bandura, 1999). Milgram (1974) found that individuals were less likely to comply with orders to inflict extreme punishment if they could see and hear the resulting suffering. The disturbing implication is that it may not be the corrupt act itself that induces doubt, but whether the resulting suffering is salient.

Denial of Victim
In this fourth form of rationalization, the status of the victim qua victim is refuted. We discern three variants in the literature. The first is that the target deserved their fate due, for example, to past unfairness or corruption on their part (cf. superordination, Greenberg, 1998; attribution of blame, Bandura, 1999). Corruption is a form of revenge. Hollinger and Clark (1983) found that the most common explanation offered by employees for theft of company property was unfair treatment by their employer, and Braithwaite (1989) discusses how corporations may nurse grievances against the U.S. Internal Revenue Service to justify tax evasion. Moreover, although some victims may indeed have contributed to their fate, Tenbrunsel (1998) demonstrated that denial of the victim needs no objective basis. She found that providing an incentive to lie in a negotiation experiment caused the expectation that one's *opponent* would lie. In other words, deception was neatly justified by projecting one's propensity toward corruption onto one's intended victim.

The second variant is that the "victim" volunteered to participate in the act and so is not a victim at all. Some senior officials in the U.S. Catholic Church contended that victims of child abuse in fact invited the sexual advances of

priests (*Boston Globe*, 2002), and police officers who accept gifts or engage in
shakedowns may rationalize that the storeowners are trying to curry favor or are
grateful for police protection (Bahn, 1975).

The third variant is a denial of the victim's individuality through depersonalization (the victim is an interchangeable member of a social category) or of the
victim's very humanity through dehumanization (the victim is an object or of a
lesser species) (Bandura, Underwood & Fromson, 1975; Brief et al., 2001). This
psychological distancing is often abetted by physical and social distance and
makes it easier to deny the impact of corruption on the victims – to practice "moral
exclusion" (Opotow, 1990, p. 1). Depersonalization is evident in accounts of Wall
Street traders who viewed clients not as unique individuals but as suckers asking
to be conned (Lewis, 1990; Partnoy, 1999). The classic example of corporate
dehumanization is the Ford Pinto saga, noted earlier (Gioia, 1992). Recall that
Ford discovered a design defect that often caused the gas tank to explode in
rear-end collisions. Ford performed a cost-benefit analysis in which the forecasted
180 deaths were converted into dollars ($200,000 each), and this bloodless ab-
straction facilitated Ford's decision to forego a recall. Ultimately, hundreds died or
suffered severe burns.

Social Weighting

We view Sykes and Matza's (1957) *condemnation of the condemners* as a subset
of a broader category, *social weighting* (Ashforth & Kreiner, 1999). Social
weighting refers to how much attention and credence one actor gives to the
values and beliefs of another. Condemning condemners involves impugning the
legitimacy of those who would cast the act or actor as corrupt. For instance,
the corrupt may characterize a disliked law as vague, complex, inconsistent,
rarely enforced, punitive, or politically motivated such that enforcement is
capricious or malicious (Lane, 1954). As this example illustrates, condemning
condemners may stem from a rejection of the legitimacy of the law or even the
societal norm itself (cf. defiant neutralization strategies, Robinson & Kraatz,
1998).

A second form of social weighting is *selective social comparisons* (Ashforth
& Kreiner, 1999; Bandura, 1999; Garrett, Bradford, Meyers & Becker, 1989),
analogous to the second form of denial of injury (i.e. extreme comparisons).
Social comparison theory indicates that when actors are experiencing a threat,
downward comparisons with others who appear even worse serve to bolster
the actor against the threat (Gibbons & Gerrard, 1991; Johns, 1999). Because
corruption creates at least a tacit threat to the group's moral identity, the group
is motivated to find examples of others who are even more corrupt and thereby
demonstrate that "we're not so bad." In an article about how longshoremen

collectively engage in pilferage, one commented on another: "He'd take anything – he's even taken baggage – he's nothing more than a thief" (Mars, 1974, p. 224). In the face of a "real" thief, the commentator's own thievery seemed minor.

Appeal to Higher Loyalties
In this sixth type of rationalization, the group construes that universalistic ethical norms have to be sacrificed for more important causes (cf. moral justification, Bandura, 1999). The most common higher cause appears to be group loyalty. As noted in our discussion of particularism, groups often view their own interests as more salient (situationally relevant and subjectively important) than those of other groups or society. The tribe is paramount. Kappeler et al. (1994) note that when police officers are forced to choose between testifying against a colleague and committing perjury, they usually choose the latter and experience remarkably little conflict in doing so, even though they are entrusted with upholding the law. The reason, Kappeler et al. contend, is that they value loyalty to colleagues above loyalty to the justice system. Similarly, in the wake of the Tailhook scandal, one officer said "curbing Navy pilots' sexual feistiness (would) remove the edge (naval aviators) need for combat" (Caproni & Finley, 1994, p. 30).

A less commonly invoked higher loyalty is, ironically, to moral principles. A group may act counter to universal ethical norms if they regard those norms as an obstacle to particular principles or goals. Hunt and Manning (1991) document "normal lies" told by police officers in court to persuade judges to convict defendants that the officers believe are guilty. The law is corrupted in the higher name of "justice": the ends justify the means.

Metaphor of the Ledger
Klockars (1974) identifies a seventh type of rationalization, *the metaphor of the ledger*, where good works (whether actual or anticipated) earn a credit that can be used to offset corrupt acts (Minor, 1981). For example, Dabney (1995) found that the most common rationalization employed by nurses to excuse the theft of supplies and over-the-counter medicines was that the items were a "fringe benefit" that had, implicitly, been earned. Similarly, Rod Kramer (personal communication, November 21st, 2002) notes that CEOs such as Dennis Kozlowski (Tyco) and John Rigas (Adelphia) who used corporate funds for personal ends were often among the most generous in donating corporate funds to charity.

Refocusing Attention
Finally, Ashforth and Kreiner (1999) note that members of so-called "dirty work" occupations may cope with the stigma of their work by shifting attention away from the stigmatized features to the non-stigmatized features. In the case of

corruption, members may willfully deemphasize, compartmentalize, or suppress knowledge of their acts in favor of more normatively redeeming features of their work (cf. instrumental rationalization, Robinson & Kraatz, 1998). Indeed, at the extreme, the behavior may be selectively forgotten such that, in a real sense, it never happened (Wegner, 1989). Senior officials in the U.S. Catholic Church moved pedophile priests from parish to parish as if their pedophilia would somehow not travel with them (*Boston Globe*, 2002).

However, because this rationalization does not deny the inherent corruptness of the act as directly as the previous types of rationalizations, it is less likely to be effective in broaching the particularistic-universalistic divide. Thus, refocusing is likely to be used in combination with one or more other rationalizations.

The Malleability of Language

All eight rationalizations may be abetted by the malleability of symbolism in general and of language in particular. For instance, groups may use an "agentless passive style" (Bandura, 1999, p. 195) (e.g. mistakes were made) and invoke analogies and metaphors (e.g. we're at war), euphemisms (e.g. embezzlers talk of borrowing rather than stealing), labels (e.g. corrupt brokers refer to clients as suckers and saps), and jargon (e.g. referring to illegal dumping as an externality) to dampen the moral implications of their behavior.

The "Payola Scandal" of the 1950s – where disc jockeys were bribed by music companies to air specific records – provides an interesting illustration of the use of malleable language. Congressional investigations revealed that the practice was pervasive. However, disc jockeys never referred to such kickbacks as payoffs. Rather, terms such as "auditioning fees" were used, thus making the corrupt practice appear benign (Rosoff, Pontell & Tillman, 2002). Indeed, given the strong motivation to sanitize corruption, language may take on Orwellian overtones. Vandivier (1996) reports a conversation between himself and another engineer regarding their falsification of critical test data. When Vandivier said they had lied, the engineer responded: "we're not really lying. All we were doing was interpreting the figures the way we knew they should be. We were just exercising engineering license" (p. 135).

One of the most extreme uses of language malleability is found in Lifton's (1986) description of the Nazi doctors who worked at Auschwitz. The doctors who selected prisoners for the gas chambers never used the word *death*; rather, "they called it going on a transport back to camp" (p. 202). Indeed, a prisoner who was a doctor and assisted at the outpatient facilities stated: "I couldn't ask (Dr. Fritz) Klein, 'Don't send this man to the gas chamber,' because I didn't know that he went to the gas chamber. You see, that was a secret. Everybody knows the secret, but it was a secret . . . I suppose that (if asked) he would say, 'Gas chamber? What do you mean?' " (p. 203). Euphemistic language enabled the doctors to engage in denial of the victim.

Denying the Obvious

Ethnographic and journalistic accounts suggest that many instances of collective corruption are doomed from early on to become publicly known and thus fail (Katz, 1979). The very nature of certain forms of corruption, from Prudential-Bache's fraudulent marketing of poor investments (Eichenwald, 1995), to B. F. Goodrich's falsification of aircraft brake test data (Vandivier, 1996), to Bausch and Lomb's booking of false sales (Maremont, 1995), means the fictions the groups are peddling cannot be sustained. Why, then, do individuals agree to participate? Part of the answer, to be sure, lies in the institutionalization and rationalization processes discussed earlier, as well as the socialization processes (particularly incrementalism) discussed later; and part lies in the perceived costs of saying no or of whistle-blowing (e.g. retribution, loss of belonging, sense of disloyalty). But where the ultimate revelation of corruption is *foreseeable* from early on, something more is likely at play. What role might rationalizing ideologies play in this denial of reality?

Kramer and Messick's (1996) review of the framing of organizational dilemmas suggests several common and complementary cognitive tendencies that may encourage what can be termed *suicidal corruption*. Participants may discount the future such that the near-term returns of corruption are weighed more heavily than the distant-term of punishment (cf. self-control, Gottfredson & Hirschi, 1990). And illusions of control and invulnerability may lead participants to credit themselves with more power over events and others' perceptions than is warranted and to ignore very real threats to their machinations. These illusions are evident in the remarks of a senior White House aide reflecting on public revelations of the Watergate break-in:

> Whatever the problems, if any, I felt I could handle them . . . And if I somehow slipped, the most astute politician in the nation, Richard Nixon, would step into the breach. At that point I believed Nixon could accomplish anything . . . Nothing could hurt him now (Janis, 1983, p. 220).

The history of collective cover-ups, from Watergate (Bernstein & Woodward, 1974) to Enron (Eichenwald & Henriques, 2002), suggests that when the dam begins to break, the participants are often unwittingly swept along by events.

We may add one more cognitive tendency to Kramer and Messick's (1996) list: in cases of subtle corruption, an illusion of morality – an unquestioned belief that one's group is inherently ethical (Janis, 1983) – may help a group reduce early doubts about the propriety of its actions. Lee Iacocca, president of Ford at the time of the Pinto, reflected on the car's saga:

> But there's absolutely no truth to the charge that we tried to save a few bucks and knowingly made a dangerous car. The auto industry has often been arrogant, but it's not that callous. The guys who built the Pinto had kids in college who were driving that car. Believe me, nobody sits down and thinks: "I'm deliberately going to make this car unsafe" (Iacocca & Novak, 1984, p. 172).

Iacocca's remarks about *deliberately* putting one's own family members at risk miss the point that *unquestioned* beliefs about the group's inherent morality may inadvertently help foster wrongdoing: by definition, the group must be on the side of the angels.

These positive illusions (Taylor, 1989) are likely to be mutually reinforcing. As one example, the illusion of control may partner with discounting the future to make a near-certain disaster appear to be a distant and manageable possibility. Moreover, Taylor and Gollwitzer (1995) found that when individuals are mulling over a decision (and their commitment is therefore low) their positive illusions are mild, but when individuals are implementing a decision (and commitment is higher) their illusions increase dramatically. Enacting a behavior fosters a strong need to see the behavior in a positive light: doing is believing.

In sum, rationalizing ideologies may incorporate a variety of common cognitive tendencies to tame the anxiety of eventual discovery – and in so doing make discovery that much more likely.

Conclusion

Like the sirens of Greek mythology, the rationalizing ideologies are highly seductive. They offer not only to excuse actors from their misdeeds but to encourage them to forget the misdeeds or reframe them as something necessary and even desirable. In short, they pander to actors' need to believe in their own goodness. What might have originated as a cynical rationalization may, through repeated use, become an article of faith. Rationalizations are particularly potent when they become a property of the group: as individuals socially construct rationalizations, the mutual echo transforms them from self-serving fictions into social facts. Indeed, so potent are the rationalizing ideologies that individuals accused of corruption may be honestly surprised to be seen in such a light (Coleman & Ramos, 1998; Hunt & Manning, 1991).

However, it should be noted that rationalizing ideologies tend to limit some behaviors even as they justify others. By articulating a rationale for why certain acts are justified, rationalizing ideologies may draw a line in the sand: some acts become permissible and some not. Moral boundaries differentiate "legitimate" types, targets and levels of corruption from illegitimate. For example, studies of dockworkers, plant employees, and hotel workers suggest that employee theft is excused through the denials of injury and victim; however, while these rationales may legitimate theft from one's employer, they render theft from individuals less acceptable (Horning, 1970; Mars, 1994).

Rationalizing ideologies are particularly important for newcomers faced with the reality shock of a corrupt group (Minor, 1981). The ideologies provide a *transition bridge* (Ashforth, 2001) from naïve newcomer to corrupted veteran. It is through socialization that newcomers learn the ideologies, and it is to socialization that we now turn.

SOCIALIZING INTO CORRUPTION

How does an otherwise ethically sound person become steeped in corruption? The answer, we contend, lies in the dynamics of socialization. The process of socialization involves imparting to newcomers the values, beliefs, norms, skills, and so forth that they will need to fulfill their roles and function effectively within the group context (Van Maanen, 1976). This process is merely a tool and as such is amenable to a variety of socialization *content* (Ashforth & Saks, 1996), from inculcating corrupt values, beliefs and so on, to inculcating non-corrupt ones. Thus, just as corruption can become institutionalized at the macro level, so it can become internalized at the micro level through socialization.

To be sure, some newcomers are presocialized into corruption through, for instance, previous experience in corrupt occupations, workgroups, organizations, and industries, and through recruitment via personal or social networks. However, given that most newcomers prefer to think of themselves as ethically sound, socialization into corruption tends to consist of relatively strong pressures for change.

In this section, we examine the general role of social influence and three specific avenues to corruption. We argue that socialization processes produce a self-fulfilling prophecy whereby groups intent on corruption produce a workforce that is receptive to corruption.

Social Influence

Sutherland's (1949) classic theory of differential association holds that criminal values, motives, beliefs, behaviors, and techniques are learned through interactions within "intimate personal groups." The theory thus suggests that proximal members of one's role set are more likely to shape learning than distal members (e.g. peers vs.

regulators). (Subsequent scholars have found, however, that differential association is not a *prerequisite* for corruption; e.g. Cressey, 1953). For example, self-reported unethical behavior among marketing managers and ad agency account executives was associated with perceptions of their peers' behavior (Zey-Ferrell & Ferrell, 1982; Zey-Ferrell, Weaver & Ferrell, 1979). Indeed, Zey-Ferrell et al. (1979) found that perceptions of peers' behavior had a greater impact than the respondents' *own* beliefs about what constituted ethical behavior. As Cressey (1986, p. 196) concludes, "White-collar criminals . . . should be viewed as conformists rather than as deviants."

The Social Cocoon
Greil and Rudy's (1984) concept of social cocoon helps explain the strength and dynamics of social influence that corrupts. Cognition, affect and behavior are largely shaped by immediate and pressing concerns – by proximal forces, which are in turn shaped by more distal ones. The socialization of newcomers, then, tends to be mediated by the local context (Ashforth, 2001; O'Reilly & Chatman, 1996). In the case of corruption, groups often create a psychologically (if not physically) encapsulated social cocoon where: (1) veterans model the corrupt behavior and easy acceptance of it; (2) newcomers are encouraged to affiliate and bond with veterans, fostering desires to identify with, emulate and please the veterans; (3) newcomers are subjected to strong and consistent information and ideological statements such that the gray ambiguity of action and meaning is resolved in clear black and white terms (cf. loading the language, Lifton, 1961; mindguards, Janis, 1983); (4) newcomers are encouraged to attribute any misgivings they may have to their own shortcomings (particularly naiveté) rather than to what is being asked of them (cf. doctrine over person, Lifton, 1961); (5) newcomers receive frequent reinforcement for displaying the corrupt behaviors and their acceptance of them; and (6) newcomers are discouraged and possibly punished for displaying doubt, hesitancy, or a tendency to backslide into non-corrupt behavior. The upshot is a "moral microcosm that likely could not survive outside the organization" (Brief et al., 2001, p. 484).

The purpose of the social cocoon is usually not the divestiture of the new-comers' incoming identity of virtuousness but of their attitudes toward particular corrupt behaviors. This is a tricky undertaking because identities undergird values and beliefs and corruption constitutes a strong threat to a virtuous identity. Authorizing, routinizing, and rationalizing are used as a scaffold to support the newcomers' incoming identity of virtuousness, while the three avenues to corruption discussed below (cooptation, incrementalism, and compromise) – in the context of the social cocoon – change the attitudes to specific behaviors that would otherwise be repugnant. At the same time, the group may overlay identity attributes that complement virtuousness by valorizing the newly learned corrupt behaviors (newcomers are, for example, "aggressive," "with it," and "loyal").

There is a strong "as if" or pretend quality to these normalizing machinations (Ashforth & Kreiner, 2002): peers act as if theft, illegal dumping, false advertising and so on are permissible if not desirable. Because newcomers are motivated to neutralize and even value the implications of their incipient corruption, they may tacitly suspend their disbelief and collude in the as-if dramaturgy. The dramaturgical performance is rendered more convincing by the taken-for-granted quality that institutionalization confers: the corrupt acts appear to be routine and unremarkable.

This as-ifness is likely to be amplified by the group context. Research on group polarization suggests that "an initial tendency of individual group members toward a given direction is enhanced following group discussion" (Isenberg, 1986, p. 1141). Group polarization occurs through rational argument and social comparison. In the case of collective corruption, the rationalizing ideologies masquerade as rational arguments and social comparisons are common. As noted earlier, social norms to appear in control and to provide reassurance tend to mitigate newcomers' concerns. A newcomer may reason that: (1) because the acts are routine and the veterans appear to have no qualms; (2) the acts can't be that bad; (3) therefore, I guess my own misgivings are overblown; and (4) I'll go along. The greater the number of members who engage in this self-censorship, the greater the likelihood of pluralistic ignorance where members are unaware of one another's misgivings (Janis, 1983; Myers & Lamm, 1976). The upshot is that groups can often support as-if beliefs that individuals alone cannot (Ashforth & Kreiner, 1999; Hardin & Higgins, 1996). If the beliefs are not subject to a reality check (e.g. public exposure), the group-fed confidence can spiral into arrogance.

Avenues to Corruption

Ashforth (2001, pp. 209–215) argues that there are two routes to identification with an organizational role and its associated prescriptions. The first begins with cognition. Newcomers may partially define themselves in terms of a role because they are attracted to what the role is thought to represent – its goals, values, beliefs, norms, interaction styles, and time horizons – or because they view the role as instrumental to valued goals (e.g. a stepping stone to senior management). In either event, the newcomers are inclined to believe in the role and its prescriptions and so enact the role to express and affirm this affinity. Thus, cognition fosters behavior, which in turn reinforces cognition.

The second route to identification begins with behavior. Newcomers may be unsure or wary of a new role such that identification is low but they may

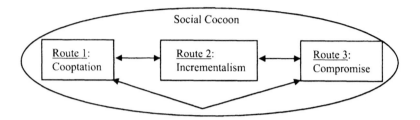

Key process:

Rewards induce
newcomers to change
their attitude toward
the corrupt behavior
(i.e., cognition→
behavior)

Newcomers are induced
to gradually escalate their
corruption, fostering
dissonance and attitude
change (i.e., behavior →
cognition)

In attempting to resolve
dilemmas and other
intractable problems,
newcomers are induced
to engage in corruption,
fostering dissonance and
attitude change (i.e.,
behavior→cognition)

Fig. 3. Socializing into Corruption.

nonetheless be required to learn and enact the role. Given that individuals seek to make sense of and justify their behavior, they are predisposed to find positive qualities in the role and identify with it (cf. honeymoon effect, Fichman & Levinthal, 1991). Further, the more that newcomers perceive their role entry and behavior to be volitional, visible, explicit and irrevocable, the stronger this predisposition (Salancik, 1977). Finally, the act of *doing* the new role psychologically engages the newcomers such that they *think* about and *feel* the role: the abstract and intellectual becomes concrete and visceral (Ashforth, 2001). Thus, behavior fosters cognition, which in turn reinforces the behavior.

As indicated in Fig. 3, these two routes to identification with a role are evident in how newcomers become socialized into corruption. The cognition→behavior route is evident in the process of *cooptation*, whereas behavior→cognition is evident in the processes of *incrementalism* and *compromise*.

Cooptation

In cooptation, newcomers are induced by rewards to skew their attitudes if not their self-conceptions toward certain corrupt behavior (Darley, 2001; Sherman, 1980). Examples abound: financial brokers who, under the guise of advising clients, push offerings with higher commissions; contract researchers who spin their findings to support their sponsors' preferences; HMO doctors who earn cost reduction bonuses by curtailing possibly important medical tests; business and law schools that "game the system" to improve their national rankings; management consultants who push the nostrums their firms are able to provide; journalists who soften their coverage of organizations paying speaking fees; and so on. Latif (2000) found that community pharmacists had lower ethical reasoning scores than first year pharmacy students and other health professionals, and that scores were negatively correlated (though not strongly) with pharmacists' experience. Latif attributed the findings in part to the difficulty of maintaining professional care in the face of financial incentives to stint on care.

Corruption via cooptation is often subtle because the individuals themselves may not realize how the rewards have induced them to resolve the ambiguity that often pervades business issues in a manner that suits their self-interest. Bargh and Alvarez (2001) describe how power tends to non-consciously activate personal goals and biases, guiding information processing and behavior – which the individual then rationalizes in socially desirable terms. Thus, a broker may honestly conclude that the offerings he is rewarded for pushing are in fact the best investments. As Bargh and Alvarez conclude, the road to hell is indeed paved with good intentions.

Incrementalism
Research on the foot-in-the-door phenomenon and the escalation of commitment indicates that small and seemingly innocuous decisions and actions – where each is meant to resolve a pressing issue – can lead one down a road that one would not have taken if the destination had been clear at the outset (Brief et al., 2001; Dillard, 1991; Johns, 1999; Staw, 1997). In terms of corruption, newcomers are initially induced to engage in small acts that seem relatively harmless and volitional as well as possibly visible, explicit and irrevocable. The acts, although small, create some cognitive dissonance (I'm an ethical person, so why did I do that?) that the newcomers can resolve by invoking the rationalizing ideologies that the subculture provides, thereby realigning their attitudes with the acts (I guess it must not be so bad). The realigned attitudes then facilitate an escalation of the behavior and the process continues. Thus, each step up the ladder of corruption enables later ones.

A police officer vividly describes the incremental seduction of corruption:

It may happen like this: The older man (senior police partner) stops at a bar, comes out with some packages of cigarettes. He does this several times. He explains that this is part of the job, getting cigarettes free from proprietors to re-sell and that as a part of the rookie's training it is his turn to "make the butts." So he goes into a Skid Row bar and stands uncomfortably at the end waiting for the bartender to acknowledge his presence and disdainfully toss him two packages of butts. The feeling of pride slips away, and a hint of shame takes hold. But he tells himself this is unusual, that he will say nothing that will upset his probation standing. In six months, after he gets his commission, he will be the upright officer he meant to be ... One thing leads to another for the rookies. After six months they have become conditioned to accept free meals, a few packages of cigarettes, turkeys at Thanksgiving and liquor at Christmas from the respectable people in their district ... So the rookies say to themselves that this is okay, that all the men accept these things, that it is a far cry from stealing and they still can be good policemen... He even may find himself covering in on a burglary call, say to a drug store, and see some officers there eyeing him peculiarly. Maybe at this point the young cop feels the pressure to belong so strongly that he reaches over and picks up something, cigars perhaps. Then he is "in," and the others can do what they wish. (Stern, 1962, pp. 98–99, 100; see also Stoddard, 1968)

Note the iterations of behavior and cognition, as well as the desensitization. The rookie officer was induced to engage in low-grade corruption (behavior) and assuaged his shame by convincing himself that he would desist when he passed probation (cognition). The incremental escalation of corruption (behavior), buoyed by a rationalizing ideology and the desire for acceptance (cognition), reduced the identity threat. Each escalation served as a *rite of incorporation* (Van Gennep, 1960), testing and sanctifying the officer's readiness to partake in more corruption. The image of the "upright officer" was soon forgotten, perhaps willfully so. As Bahn (1975) argues, the small gifts from shopkeepers soon become expected dues and the small luxuries, necessities.

More rigorous research on the acceptance of rationalizing ideologies also supports the notion of incrementalism. Minor (1984), drawing on Hirschi's (1969) "hardening process," found that adult deviant behavior (e.g. shoplifting) softened the moral evaluation of that behavior and enhanced the acceptance of rationalizations for it, which in turn facilitated further deviance. Minor's findings suggest that the rationalizations were initially adduced retrospectively to assuage guilt, but then were available as a prospective ideology to ease future delinquency (Hunt & Manning, 1991). (Minor cautions, however, that the support for the causal model was only moderate.)

Compromise
In the third avenue to corruption, compromise, individuals essentially "back into" corruption through attempts (often in good faith) to resolve pressing dilemmas, role conflicts and other intractable problems (Bird, 1996; Johns, 1999). For instance, politicians accrue power by forming networks, currying favors, and cutting deals, often causing them to support actors and causes they would otherwise avoid (Birnbaum, 1992). As the saying goes, "politics makes strange bedfellows." It thus becomes very difficult for a senior politician to act exclusively according to his or her own ethical principals and preferences.

Bird (1996) provides an example of compromise from a corporate context. A plant manager faced the dilemma of either venting fumes and smoke into the environment, thus exceeding legal limits, or retaining them in the plant and jeopardizing the health of employees. Given the unwillingness of his superiors to address the issue, the manager chose to vent the bad air at night when it was less likely to be detected. Although the conflict afforded some denial of responsibility (what else could I do?), it remains that the individual chose to pollute, thus potentially fostering some dissonance.

As denoted by the double-headed arrows in Fig. 3, cooptation, incrementalism, and compromise are frequently mutually reinforcing. It is often the coopting power of rewards that gives incremental corruption its periodic pushes and may tip the scales of compromise toward one action over another; it is often the seemingly small steps of incrementalism that lead newcomers to become more deeply coopted and compromised; and it is often the sense of being between a rock and a hard place that pushes newcomers to accept rewards that coopt and to continue down an existing path even as the stakes escalate. Sherman (1980) provides an example. Police detectives rely on informants for information about crimes. As a quid pro quo, the police often compromise with informants, overlooking their minor crimes. As the relationships with particular informants solidify, the police may come to depend on them, opening the door to cooptation and overlooking more serious misdeeds. Indeed, the police may shift, incrementally, from passively overlooking minor crimes to actively abetting more serious crimes.

The psychological trajectory of cooptation, incrementalism and compromise means that newcomers may be inadvertently seduced into corruption and may not realize that their actions could be construed as illegal or unethical (at least by outsiders) until they are partly down the slippery slope of corruption. One manager commented:

> ... my ethical standards changed so gradually over the first five years of work that I hardly noticed it, but it was a great shock to suddenly realize what my feelings had been five years ago and how much they had changed (Schein, 1968, p. 8).

By the time such a realization occurs, it may be very difficult to halt the behavior and extricate oneself from the strong situation without suffering stiff psychological, social, financial, and legal costs from guilt, shame, job loss, and so on (Darley, 1992). The temptation to simply continue and cover up one's misdeeds, abetted by the rationalizing ideologies, is very strong and – for many – overwhelming (see, for example, Vandivier, 1996). Thus, what may have been inadvertent now becomes deliberate. Darley (1992, p. 215) asserts that "this is a critical point at which those individuals can become evil actors."

What About Coercion?
Hamilton and Sanders (1992) argue that there are two primary motives for complying with corrupt orders and thus committing "crimes of obedience": loyalty/obligation and fear.[5] Loyalty/obligation is essentially an outcome of the three socialization processes discussed above. Fear, however, tends to follow a different dynamic.

Fear is induced by coercion, the threat of negative consequences such as ostracism and demotion. To be sure, *blatant* coercion facilitates the denial of responsibility and thereby compliance with corrupt directives. Such coercion, however, leaves less room for (perceived) volition, a key precondition for the dissonance reduction process discussed earlier. Newcomers subject to blatant coercion have a sufficient justification for their obedience – to avoid the threat – and thus do not need to realign their attitudes to accommodate the otherwise dissonant behavior. Indeed, blatant coercion may provoke resentment and reactance against the source of coercion and the targeted behavior (e.g. Nail, Van Leeuwen & Powell, 1996). The upshot is a greater likelihood of grudging compliance, whistle-blowing and voluntary turnover (and thus, risk of exposure). Further, coercion may affect behavior only as long as the pressure is applied. For these reasons, blatant coercion tends to be an ineffective means of *sustaining* corruption.

However, more subtle forms of coercion shade grayly into the dissonance inducing processes noted above. The more subtle the coercion (e.g. a manager casually suggests that a subordinate lie to a client), the greater the perceived ambiguity (e.g. does she really want me to do that? Am I expected to? What if I refuse?) and thus the perceived volition if the newcomer complies. Brief et al. (2001, p. 489) add that individuals are motivated to "view themselves as independent actors, not as mere pawns in the workplace." Volition helps commit newcomers to their behavior, thereby triggering attitudinal realignment. Indeed, the dilemmas that foster compromise and the rewards that foster cooptation and incrementalism may be intended by the group to be subtle coercions. In short, the more subtle the coercion, the more likely that initial compliance will metamorphose into acceptance of the otherwise objectionable behavior. Corruption is therefore most difficult to resist when newcomers have only the *illusion* of choice regarding their behavior.

A Self-fulfilling Prophecy

In his classic article, "The people make the place," Schneider (1987; Schneider, Goldstein & Smith, 1995) argues that organizations institutionalize individual predispositions through three complementary practices: attraction (where individuals who perceive a good person-organization (P-O) fit seek employment), selection (where the organization seeks applicants with good P-O fit), and attrition (where members with poor P-O fit are more likely to leave, whether voluntarily or involuntarily).[6] We would add socialization as a fourth complementary process in that it further aligns the values, beliefs, and so forth of newcomers with the group, thus enhancing P-O fit. The result of these four processes is a collection of relatively like-minded individuals.

A corrupt group is likely to be even more homogeneous than a typical group. Because corruption represents deviance from societal values, a corrupt group needs to pay particular attention to attracting, selecting, socializing and retaining to ensure a good P-O fit. However, because groups do not advertise their corruption and it is very difficult to discern an applicant's receptiveness to corruption in a typical interview situation, a premium is placed on indicators of presocialization to corruption, the socialization process itself, and rewards (punishments) for compliance (noncompliance) with the corrupt practices.

For example, Mars (1994) describes how "wolfpacks" (i.e. where theft occurs through organized group efforts; e.g. dockworkers, sanitation workers) attempt to restrict entry to the occupation to family and friends who have been vetted and to allocate status, rewards, and tasks on the basis of seniority and age (thus encouraging conformity to group norms). Ponemon (1992) found that audit managers preferred to promote individuals whose ethical reasoning scores were similar to their own; auditors who progressed from manager to partner positions tended to have lower and more homogeneous levels of ethical reasoning; and auditors whose ethical reasoning scores were either above or below the norm tended to leave the firm.

Because they threaten the integrity of the corrupt subculture, particular attention is paid to individuals who cannot be "turned." Initially, newcomers may be punished in an *inclusionary* manner (e.g. through verbal rebukes, sabotage of tasks), that is, as a means of steering them back into the fold and encouraging compliance with the corruption. If unsuccessful, the punishment usually escalates and becomes *exclusionary* (e.g. through derogatory labels, ostracism), that is, a means of signaling rejection of the newcomer and inducing him or her to quit (cf. reintegrative vs. disintegrative shaming, Braithwaite, 1989). Exclusionary punishment not only pushes the newcomer from the group, it reaffirms the norms and beliefs of the group by clearly drawing the line between acceptable (corrupt) and unacceptable (noncorrupt) behavior. Eichenwald (1995) describes how senior executives at Prudential-Bache systematically marginalized, demoted and fired individuals who objected to the company's questionable practices and rewarded those who went along.

Ambivalence
No matter how tightly wrapped the social cocoon, the newcomer remains a member of society and of other social groups and thus is aware of and has likely internalized general normative beliefs about right and wrong behavior. In short, the amoral familism described by Banfield (1958) is likely to be relatively rare. Thus, there may be an antagonism between one's membership in society with its universalistic attitudes toward corruption and one's membership in a group with its particularistic attitudes.

Of course, as noted, these universalistic attitudes are precisely what the rationalizing ideologies attempt to neutralize and antagonisms may be held at bay by compartmentalizing social domains. However, because the individual is both a member of various tribes and of society, the potential remains for a clash of normative systems – for the particularistic to be evaluated by universalistic standards. The likely upshot is *ambivalence*, a desire to both justify and renounce the corrupt behavior. For instance, a nurse, whose subculture rationalizes theft, attempted to explain her attitude to an outsider, the researcher:

> I steal scrubs. I have a million pairs at home. I cut them off and make shorts. I realize it is a debt but you don't think about it. You think that they won't miss it but you know they do. I mean the scrub loss is $11,000 a month. They take a beating (Dabney, 1995, p. 320).

One can sense her ambivalence as she perhaps sees her behavior through the eyes of an outsider.

As this example illustrates, normative clashes are most likely to occur if circumstances cause social domains to blur, such as when a public accusation of wrongdoing forces a group to explain their actions to outsiders (Chibnall & Saunders, 1977). In the absence of such blurring, the social-psychological compartmentalization of social domains appears to be fairly adept at keeping ambivalence in check.

Conclusion
The socialization of newcomers into institutionalized corruption occurs in a social cocoon, a localized, self-referential world where skewed behaviors and ideologies are presented as normal and acceptable – if not desirable. The newcomers face a strong situation, but one that allows sufficient (perceived) volition to encourage the newcomers to internalize the corrupt behaviors and ideologies as their own. Socialization thus enables corruption to continue despite the inevitable turnover of group members.

INTERDEPENDENCE OF INSTITUTIONALIZATION, RATIONALIZATION, AND SOCIALIZATION

We speculate that each of the three pillars of normalization – institutionalization, rationalization, and socialization – is necessary for corruption to become an ongoing, collective undertaking. In the absence of institutionalization, idiosyncratic acts of corruption would not become embedded in organizational structures and processes and thereby routinized; absent rationalization, it would be very difficult to persuade a collective to engage in corruption; and absent socialization, corruption might die out when the instigators left the group. As touched on earlier, coercion can serve as a crude substitute for rationalization and socialization, but is unlikely to be viable beyond the short term.

We have presented the pillars of normalization as discrete phenomena. However, as shown in Fig. 1, each phenomenon reinforces and in turn is reinforced by the other two. Corruption, like any practice, is said to be institutionalized when it is stable, endures over time, resists change and is transmitted across generations (Oliver, 1992; Zucker, 1977). While we identified the ways in which corruption can become institutionalized, it can endure only when the individuals involved are not prompted by dissonance to seriously challenge established practices. The purpose of the rationalizing ideologies and the social cocoon of socialization that imparts them is to channel one's dissonance into acceptance of corruption or to mute moral awareness such that dissonance never arises. For example, Stevenson (1998) describes how boiler rooms minimize dissonance among telephone operators by creating a game-like atmosphere where attention focuses on the enactment of a salesperson identity and the pursuit of commissions, while the stigma of boiler rooms is projected onto the competition (We're better than them). Thus, socialization and rationalization enable corruption to become more firmly rooted in the group.

Further, socialization practices can themselves become institutionalized and more strongly influence whether newcomers buy into the corruption. According to Jones (1986), *institutionalized socialization* occurs when newcomers experience common indoctrination practices of fixed duration, content, and sequencing, under the auspices of veteran members. Conversely, *individualized socialization* occurs when newcomers are essentially left to sink or swim and represents socialization more by default than design. Jones found that the use of institutionalized socialization increases newcomers' acceptance of organizational activities and role definitions, likely for two reasons. First, when socialization practices are common to all participants, "the interactions among newcomers reinforce the definition of the situation offered by the socialization agent" (p. 264). This leads to common interpretations and less questioning of the status quo. Corruption is more likely to be accepted precisely because it is packaged in a totalizing way that does not encourage dissent. Second, institutionalized socialization can reduce newcomers' efforts to seek additional information beyond what the group provides. Miller and Jablin (1991) note that when newcomers receive inadequate information they try to reduce the uncertainty by engaging in an undirected and unmonitored information search. As a result, they may develop perspectives different from those promoted by the group. However, if a socialization program has been designed to provide answers to commonly asked questions, newcomers are less likely to be inquisitive and more likely to accept the proffered role definitions and practices. Thus, institutionalized socialization may forestall concerns about corrupt practices by providing neatly packaged answers, preferably before the questions themselves arise.

Institutionalization similarly supports rationalization. Institutionalization renders belief systems into seemingly objective accounts of reality, external to any one person (Zucker, 1977). The big lie is thus transformed into the big truth. This process is well illustrated by Lifton's (1986) study of the role of Nazi doctors at Auschwitz. He describes the camp procedures that required Jews to run naked in single files while doctors selected those to be sent to the gas chamber. This and other processes dehumanized the prisoners, allowing doctors to follow the "denial of victim" tactic. Procedures also prescribed the extermination of all residents in a housing block when one resident developed an infectious disease. This allowed doctors to adopt the "appeal to higher loyalties" tactic wherein exterminations were justified as a necessary evil to prevent the spread of disease to the whole camp. Further, Auschwitz doctors were encouraged to develop elaborate outpatient treatment facilities to treat prisoners for minor diseases – even if those prisoners were ultimately destined for the gas chamber. This policy allowed the doctors to focus on the healing part of their work (Lifton called it the healing-killing paradox) and thus use the "refocusing attention" tactic. Institutionalization gave these rationalizations a weight and permanence that rendered them all the more credible.

Finally, socialization and rationalization are mutually reinforcing. The most difficult act of corruption is often one's first act. Rationalizing ideologies serve as a sedative that facilitates the newcomer's first steps down the road to corruption during the socialization process. Similarly, rationalizations are most difficult to accept when they are first proffered. The social cocoon of socialization provides a protective environment for positing beliefs that might cause newcomers to balk under other (unregulated) circumstances. For example, the incremental shaping of corrupt behavior facilitates the incremental acceptance of the big lie.

In sum, just as corruption is insinuated into the fiber and being of the organization through the process of institutionalization, so is it insinuated into the role behavior of individuals through socialization and the sedative of rationalization. As noted, the macro and the micro are mutually reinforcing.

IMPLICATIONS FOR RESEARCH AND PRACTICE

Institutionalization, rationalization, and socialization serve to normalize corruption within the social domain of work and thus help keep doubts and guilt at bay. However, events that blur the line between the particularism of work and the universalism of society may make this clash of normative systems far more salient and cause ambivalence. Conversely, a clear line helps individuals and groups to cognitively segment their micro and macro worlds, allowing them to blithely do what they might loudly renounce in other contexts.

Reversing Normalization

Because of the fundamental attribution error – a tendency to attribute events to individuals rather than situations, particularly if the consequences of the events are severe (Ross, 1977) – it is easy to demonize individuals when wrongdoing is discovered. Indeed, senior managers routinely attempt to blame corruption on a few bad apples (Poveda, 1994; e.g. *Boston Globe*, 2002; Eichenwald, 1995). However, the intertwined processes of institutionalization, rationalization, and socialization conspire to normalize and perpetuate corrupt practices so that the *system* trumps the individual. Even "top managers' ethical standards are not simply their own personal beliefs" (Coleman, 1998, p. 196): a CEO can become as enmeshed in the web of normalization as a middle manager.

That said, our analysis is *not* meant to exempt individuals from personal responsibility for corruption – particularly senior managers, with their relatively greater power and fiduciary responsibility for the organization. Our point is that when bad apples produce a bad barrel through institutionalization, the barrel itself must be repaired: only systemic responses can reverse systemic normalization.

Once corruption sets in, the mutually reinforcing processes of institutionalization, rationalization, and socialization create an unholy trinity that actively resists change. For example, Miceli and Near (2002) found that whistle-blowing was more likely to be effective if the wrongdoing was relatively minor and short-lived – that is, if the organization was less dependent on it. Indeed, whistle-blowing is so uncommon and fraught with career-threatening outcomes, that when three individuals did it in one year, they were named *Time Magazine's* Persons of the Year in 2002.

Specific individuals may recognize that corruption exists but are often powerless to address it; in many cases, the role of such individuals changes over time from: (1) unbending resisters who "protest within the organization about unethical or illegal behavior" to; (2) implicated protestors who "acquiesce when they are ordered to conform," and finally to; (3) reluctant collaborators who "become deeply involved in acts that they privately condemn" (Glazer, 1987, p. 188).

The case of TAP Pharmaceuticals, although not following the trajectory outlined above, is nevertheless a good illustration of the difficulties encountered by insiders trying to act against institutionalized corruption:

> Douglas Durand left his job at Merck Pharmaceuticals to join TAP Pharmaceuticals as their Vice President for Sales. Within a few months of joining TAP, Durand became extremely

concerned about certain practices at TAP – giving doctors a 2% administration fee for prescribing TAP's prostrate cancer drug, Lupron; encouraging doctors to bill Medicaid for the cost of drugs that had been provided to them as free samples; and providing doctors with lavish discounts, gifts, and trips. Durand's efforts to stop these practices were futile. He was told that he did not understand TAP's culture and was kept out of key sales and marketing meetings. His requests for information about unethical practices were routinely ignored. He had been concerned that TAP did not have an in-house legal counsel but found out that TAP employees referred to such individuals as "sales prevention departments." Finally, after several frustrating years, he informed the government. Confronted with overwhelming documentation about its rampant corruption, TAP negotiated a settlement, agreeing to pay a record $875 million in fines (Summarized from Haddad & Barrett, 2002).

As this example shows, it is extremely difficult for inside employees to uproot corruption once it is normalized. As noted, because many of the practices are institutionalized and rationalized away, employees may not believe that they are corrupt and often have strong incentives to continue the behavior. In such situations, it is not uncommon for individuals attempting to eliminate corruption to encounter responses such as "You don't understand the company culture" (Haddad & Barrett, 2002, p. 128) and "We are following market rules" (Berman et al., 2002, A1), or face sanctioning in other forms. For instance, employees who complained about sexual harassment at Mitsubishi America were "shut out of lucrative overtime opportunities or moved to undesirable shifts" (Weimer & Thornton, 1997, p. 74).

The difficulty is further compounded because individuals who have unsuccess-fully tried to disrupt normalized corruption are hesitant to report the corruption to external agencies. Research clearly indicates that whistle-blowers are routinely punished by their employers even as they are lauded by the public (e.g. Miceli & Near, 1992). As Douglas Durand (see example above) stated: "The idea of suing as a whistle-blower intimidated me. Nobody likes a whistle-blower. I thought it would end my career" (Haddad & Barrett, 2002, p. 129).

Given the self-sustaining nature of normalized corruption, overcoming it typically requires the administration of a strong shock – typically from external sources. A common form of such a shock is media exposure. Significant negative exposure creates a socially undesirable image, often galvanizing change. Dutton and Dukerich's (1991) study of the Port Authority showed that as the undesirability of an image increases, employees and top executives are more likely to reinterpret issues and question the appropriateness of actions that had been taken for granted. Additionally, public exposure often results in the forcible intervention of governmental/regulatory agencies that compel a reversal in normalized corruption (Clinard, 1983).

Once top management concludes that corruption has become intolerable, root-ing it out is still a significant challenge. By definition, corruption is normalized when the group's structure, processes, and employee mental models act together to perpetuate unethical acts. Rooting out normalized corruption often requires a significant organizational change effort, where "strategies, power, structure, and systems are fundamentally changed into a new alignment" (Tushman & Romanelli, 1985, p. 173). Clearly, such an effort requires the involvement and support of senior executives (Boeker, 1997; Tushman & Romanelli, 1985).

Further, because top managers are part of the corrupt system, subject to many of the same normalizing pressures as others, the literature on organizational change suggests that creating the needed radical change usually requires the involvement of outsiders who have not been part of the system (Boeker, 1997; Tushman & Romanelli, 1985; Zimmerman, 1991). Indeed, after Mitsubishi America acknowledged the prevalence of widespread sexual harassment at its Normal (Illinois) plant, it hired the former Secretary of Labor, Lynn Martin, to look at its human resource management practices and recommend changes (Weimer & Thornton, 1997).

Because of the intransigence of normalized corruption, we strongly believe that corruption is best handled through *prevention* – through proactive means of forestalling corruption rather than reactive means of rooting it out. These means are not unknown (e.g. Lozano, 2000; Treviño, Weaver, Gibson & Toffler, 1999) – although they are practiced unevenly – and thus will be discussed only briefly. First, ethical values and awareness must be inculcated and institutionalized at all levels of analysis (individual, subunit, organization, industry) and incorporated into everyday decision making and action. For example, as noted, socialization processes are amenable to various content. Ethical training, based on a code of ethics that is grounded in specific role-based situations and dilemmas, can foster awareness of ethical issues and thereby forestall amoral calculations and expose the speciousness of rationalizations. Second, individuals at all levels of analysis must know they will be held accountable for means as well as ends, and real sanctions should be promulgated to encourage ethical behavior and discourage corruption. Because veteran peers and managers serve as potent role models, accountability also tends to make such individuals more effective socialization agents. Third, individuals should have access to the confidential advice of ethics officers or other experts regarding emergent ethical dilemmas and ambiguities (e.g. conflicts of interest, gift giving and receiving). Fourth, organizational practices should be made more transparent. For instance, social or ethics audits, inquisitive boards of directors, and confidential hotlines may surface a group's ethics-in-use (versus espoused ethics) and nip incipient normalization in the bud. Fifth, regarding corruption against the organization in particular, organizations tend to get the respect they deserve: human resource management practices that communicate distrust and inequity often provoke retaliation against the organization (Cialdini, 1996). For example, although electronic surveillance may render employee actions more transparent (in line with No. 4 above), such intrusive practices should be used with caution because they may incite corruption against the organization. Conversely, organizations that signal trust may undercut the motivation for corruption.

The above actions need to be enacted with a genuine desire for preventing corruption rather than as an impression management effort. In this context, Mathews (1988) found that firms that had adopted codes of ethics were *more* likely to engage in fraudulent activities. He attributed this finding partly to executives who – while formulating ethical codes and procedures – have been more "concerned with the control of illegal actions by mid- and lower-level employees against the corporation, rather than illegal actions taken on behalf of the corporation" (p. 83).

As a summary statement, Treviño et al. (1999, pp. 131–132) concluded from a study of over 10,000 employees from six large American companies that what helps an organization the most in behaving ethically is "consistency between policies and actions as well as dimensions of the organization's ethical culture such as ethical leadership, fair treatment of employees, and open discussion of ethics."

Future Research

The analysis suggests a number of promising directions for future research. Five examples will suffice. First, given the proposed interdependence between institutionalization, rationalization, and socialization processes over time, it is important that the trajectory of normalization be tracked through careful comparative case analyses. Existing ethnographic and journalistic accounts of such corruption provide telling anecdotes, but lack a systematic examination of how the proposed dynamics unfold over time. Intriguing questions include: Given the anecdotal evidence suggesting that corruption is typically opportunistic and emergent, under what conditions is the normalization process more likely to be proactively managed? Given the breadth of rationalizing ideologies and socialization tactics, how does the form of corruption affect the selection of ideologies and tactics (and vice versa)? And given organized crime, the Holocaust, and terrorist networks, what are the limits – if any – to what can be normalized?

Second, research should examine what kinds of subunits, organizations, and industries (and practices) are most susceptible to normalized corruption. For example, on one hand, a reasonable case could be made that large and diversified firms are most susceptible to normalization (Green, 1997). Such firms encourage senior executives to rely on financial outcomes to control subsidiaries, encourage subsidiaries to "look good" by skirting ethics and laws (Daboub, Rasheed, Priem & Gray, 1995), and have the requisite longevity and bureaucratic infrastructure for institutionalizing corruption and socializing newcomers accordingly. On the other hand, a case could be made that newer and more specialized firms are most susceptible to normalization. In today's business environment, new organizations have emerged to unseat traditional industry leaders – in part by deviating from tradition. Indeed, Vaughan (1983, p. 60) points out that leaders of such organizations operate on the principle that "new organizations only rise rapidly if they have some disrespect for traditional standards." Because new organizations lack the checks and balances that are in place in the older (and more bureaucratic) organizations, their penchant for disregarding tradition may extend to accepted ethical practices. Similarly, specialized firms encourage employees to develop firm-specific skills that may limit employee mobility. This dependence may render employees susceptible to a win-at-all-costs attitude and to rationalizing ideologies for any resulting corruption (cf. Vaughan, 1983).

Third, although we have treated the normalization of corruption on behalf of the organization as equivalent to that of corruption against the organization, there are real differences that should be investigated. For example, identification, commitment, and other attributes that are usually highly valued are likely to predict corruption on an organization's behalf, whereas precisely the opposite – disidentification, etc. – is likely to predict corruption against it (e.g. Murphy, 1993; Schwartz, 1987; see psychological extensions of Merton's (1968) anomie theory of deviance (Cohen, 1995)). Given the organization's obvious opposition to corruption against it, corruption on behalf of the organization is likely easier to normalize. And given that the forms that corruption takes will usually differ (e.g. theft against the organization versus offering bribes on behalf of the organization), so too might the way that corruption plays out. For instance, all employees are likely to have opportunities to exploit the organization, whereas corruption on behalf of the organization may be confined largely to boundary-spanning roles.

Fourth, in focusing on the emergence of collective corruption, our model implies a certain inevitability to events, that initial decisions and acts lead inexorably to institutionalized wrongdoing. Clearly, this is not the case: our model is meant to be probabilistic, suggesting tendencies, not deterministic. Thus, an important research topic is the factors and dynamics that facilitate or retard normalization as well as the potential exit points where individuals and groups can halt the process. Weitzel and Jonsson's (1989) model of organizational decline provides a useful analogy: they discuss five stages where individuals can intervene to stave off dissolution. Given the momentum associated with normalization, the earlier exit points are probably the most promising.

Fifth, the normalization model depicted in Fig. 1 may be profitably applied to other organizational practices and forms that diverge from tradition or what is socially acceptable (though not necessarily corrupt). For example, the model may shed light on the intraorganizational dynamics of religious cults, radical entrepreneurial firms, and organizations offering such "dirty work" as industrial espionage and prostitution.

In closing, collective corruption represents a pernicious blight on society. Normalization is the process that not only enables individuals to leech off society while maintaining a self-image of probity, but embeds and routinizes that behavior in organizations so that it may be practiced on a wider scale and perpetuated indefinitely. As recent scandals from Enron to WorldCom to the U.S. Catholic Church make all too clear, it is vital that the normalization process be better understood so that it may be better prevented.

NOTES

1. An individual also develops a generalized or *global* identity abstracted from his or her diverse social identities and idiosyncratic attributes such as traits. The global identity is both informed by the social identities and informs the selection and enactment of those identities. The upshot is a roughly coherent self-system (Ashforth, 2001; Epstein, 1980). However, a given social identity tends to be more salient *in its particular localized context* than is the global identity because the social identity is usually more situationally relevant and subjectively important (Ashforth, 2001).

2. Even regulatory agencies that are coercive may push organizations further into corruption. If an organization is labeled as corrupt, it may find legitimate opportunities blocked and internalize the social identity of "corrupt" (Ashforth & Humphrey, 1995; Braithwaite, 1989). Thus, "When organizations are treated as irredeemably crooked, they are more likely to become crooked" (Braithwaite, 1989, p. 346). However, these appear to be relatively rare occurrences.

3. Nonetheless, Robinson and Kraatz (1998, p. 207) argue that because "people tend to buy themselves what they sell to others (and vice versa) . . . we expect to find remarkable convergence between internally and externally directed" rationalizations.

4. Some scholars distinguish between neutralization and rationalization, arguing that the former pertains to prospective accounts whereas the latter pertains to retrospective accounts (Green, 1997). Because the rationalizations we review can be used either way, we do not distinguish between neutralization and rationalization.

5. Similarly, Hughes and Coakley (1991) argue that corruption results from being either overintegrated or overcontrolled (little real discretion to say no) regarding the local norms.

6. Although Schneider views this person-based "ASA framework" as contrary to the kind of situationist framework adopted in the current paper, we view the two frameworks as complementary: whether by design or default, people create the situational conditions in organizations that subsequently shape their own behavior and that of others.

ACKNOWLEDGMENTS

We thank Paul Tiedt for his help with the background research and Gary Johns, Rod Kramer, Anne O'Leary-Kelly, Barry Staw, and audience members at presentations at the Australian Graduate School of Management, Tulane University and the University of Arizona for their very helpful comments on earlier drafts of the paper.

REFERENCES

Abravanel, H. (1983). Mediatory myths in the service of organizational ideology. In: L. R. Pondy, P. J. Frost, G. Morgan & T. C. Dandridge (Eds), *Organizational Symbolism* (pp. 273–293). Greenwich, CT: JAI Press.

Adams, G. B., & Balfour, D. L. (1998). *Unmasking administrative evil.* Thousand Oaks, CA: Sage.

Anand, V., Manz, C. C., & Glick, W. H. (1998). An organizational memory approach to information management. *Academy of Management Review, 23,* 796–809.

Arendt, H. (1965). *Eichmann in Jerusalem: A report on the banality of evil* (Rev. ed.). New York: Penguin Books.

Argote, L., & Ingram, P. (2000). Knowledge transfer: A basis for competitive advantage in firms. *Organizational Behavior and Human Decision Processes, 82,* 150–169.

Ashforth, B. E. (2001). *Role transitions in organizational life: An identity-based perspective.* Mahwah, NJ: Erlbaum.

Ashforth, B. E., & Fried, Y. (1988). The mindlessness of organizational behaviors. *Human Relations, 41,* 305–329.

Ashforth, B. E., & Humphrey, R. H. (1995). Labeling processes in the organization: Constructing the individual. In: L. L. Cummings & B. M. Staw (Eds), *Research in Organizational Behavior* (Vol. 17, pp. 413–461). Greenwich, CT: JAI Press.

Ashforth, B. E., & Kreiner, G. E. (1999). "How can you do it"?: Dirty work and the challenge of constructing a positive identity. *Academy of Management Review, 24,* 413–434.

Ashforth, B. E., & Kreiner, G. E. (2002). Normalizing emotion in organizations: Making the extraordinary seem ordinary. *Human Resource Management Review, 12,* 215–235.

Ashforth, B. E., & Mael, F. (1989). Social identity theory and the organization. *Academy of Management Review, 14,* 20–39.

Ashforth, B. E., & Saks, A. M. (1996). Socialization tactics: Longitudinal effects on newcomer adjustment. *Academy of Management Journal, 39,* 149–178.

Asinof, E. (1963). *Eight men out: The Black Sox and the 1919 World Series.* New York: Holt, Rinehart and Winston.

Aubert, V. (1952). White-collar crime and social structure. *American Journal of Sociology, 58,* 263–271.

Bahn, C. (1975). The psychology of police corruption: Socialization of the corrupt. *Police Journal, 48,* 30–36.

Baker, W. E., & Faulkner, R. R. (1993). The social organization of conspiracy: Illegal networks in the heavy electrical equipment industry. *American Sociological Review, 58,* 837–860.

Bandura, A. (1999). Moral disengagement in the perpetration of inhumanities. *Personality and Social Psychology Review, 3,* 193–209.

Bandura, A., Underwood, B., & Fromson, M. E. (1975). Disinhibition of aggression through diffusion of responsibility and dehumanization of victims. *Journal of Research in Personality, 9,* 253–269.

Banfield, E. C. (1958). *The moral basis of a backward society.* New York: Free Press.

Bargh, J. A., & Alvarez, J. (2001). The road to hell: Good intentions in the face of nonconscious tendencies to misuse power. In: A. Y. Lee-Chai & J. A. Bargh (Eds), *The Use and Abuse of Power: Multiple Perspectives on the Causes of Corruption* (pp. 41–55). Philadelphia: Psychology Press.

Baucus, M. S. (1994). Pressure, opportunity and predisposition: A multivariate model of corporate illegality. *Journal of Management, 20*, 699–721.

Baumhart, R. C. (1961). How ethical are businessmen? *Harvard Business Review, 39*(4), 6–8, 10, 12, 16, 19, 156, 158, 160, 163–164, 166, 168, 170–172, 174, 176.

Benson, M. L. (1985). Denying the guilty mind: Accounting for involvement in a white-collar crime. *Criminology, 23*, 583–607.

Berman, D. K., Angwin, J., & Cummins, C. (2002, December 23rd). What's wrong? Tricks of the trade: As market bubble neared end, bogus swaps provided a lift – some $15 billion in barter padded financial results in telecom, web, energy. *Wall Street Journal*, A1.

Bernstein, C., & Woodward, B. (1974). *All the president's men*. New York: Simon and Schuster.

Bird, F. B. (1996). *The muted conscience: Moral silence and the practice of ethics in business*. Westport, CT: Quorum Books.

Birnbaum, J. H. (1992). *The lobbyists: How influence peddlers work their way in Washington*. New York: Times Books.

Boeker, W. (1997). Strategic change: The influence of managerial characteristics and organizational growth. *Academy of Management Journal, 40*, 152–170.

Boston Globe (2002). *Betrayal: The crisis in the Catholic Church*. Boston: Little, Brown.

Braithwaite, J. (1984). *Corporate crime in the pharmaceutical industry*. London: Routledge & Kegan Paul.

Braithwaite, J. (1989). Criminological theory and organizational crime. *Justice Quarterly, 6*, 333–358.

Brass, D. J., Butterfield, K. D., & Skaggs, B. C. (1998). Relationships and unethical behavior: A social network perspective. *Academy of Management Review, 23*, 14–31.

Brenner, S. N., & Molander, E. A. (1977). Is the ethics of business changing? *Harvard Business Review, 55*(1), 57–71.

Brief, A. P., Buttram, R. T., & Dukerich, J. M. (2001). Collective corruption in the corporate world: Toward a process model. In: M. E. Turner (Ed.), *Groups at Work: Theory and Research* (pp. 471–499). Mahwah, NJ: Erlbaum.

Browning, L. D. (1989). *Managing blame in the Iran-Contra affair: The role of plausible deniability*. Paper presented at the annual meeting of the Academy of Management, Washington, DC.

Bunderson, J. S. (2001). Normal injustices and morality in complex organizations. *Journal of Business Ethics, 33*, 181–190.

Caproni, P. J., & Finley, J. A. (1994). *When organizations do harm: Two cautionary tales*. Paper presented at the annual meeting of the Academy of Management, Dallas.

Chen, E. S., & Tyler, T. R. (2001). Cloaking power: Legitimatizing myths and the psychology of the advantaged. In: A. Y. Lee-Chai & J. A. Bargh (Eds), *The Use and Abuse of Power: Multiple Perspectives on the Causes of Corruption* (pp. 241–261). Philadelphia: Psychology Press.

Chibnall, S., & Saunders, P. (1977). Worlds apart: Notes on the social reality of corruption. *British Journal of Sociology, 28*, 138–154.

Cialdini, R. B. (1996). Social influence and the triple tumor structure of organizational dishonesty. In: D. M. Messick & A. E. Tenbrunsel (Eds), *Codes of Conduct: Behavioral Research into Business Ethics* (pp. 44–58). New York: Sage.

Clinard, M. B. (1979). *Illegal corporate behavior*. Washington, DC: National Institute of Law Enforcement and Criminal Justice.

Clinard, M. B. (1983). *Corporate ethics and crime*. Beverly Hills, CA: Sage.

Clinard, M. B., & Quinney, R. (1973). *Criminal behavior systems: A typology* (2nd ed.). New York: Holt, Rinehart and Winston.

Clinard, M. B., & Yeager, P. C. (1980). *Corporate crime.* New York: Free Press.

Cohen, D. V. (1995). Ethics and crime in business firms: Organizational culture and the impact of anomie. In: F. Adler & W. S. Laufer (Eds), *Advances in Criminological Theory, Vol. 6: The Legacy of Anomie Theory* (pp. 183–206). New Brunswick, NJ: Transaction.

Coleman, J. W. (1987). Toward an integrated theory of white-collar crime. *American Journal of Sociology, 93,* 406–439.

Coleman, J. W. (1998). *The criminal elite: Understanding white-collar crime* (4th ed.). New York: St. Martin's Press.

Coleman, J. W., & Ramos, L. L. (1998). Subcultures and deviant behavior in the organizational context. In: P. A. Bamberger & W. J. Sonnenstuhl (Eds), *Research in the Sociology of Organizations* (Vol. 15, pp. 3–34). Stamford, CT: JAI Press.

Collins, M. D. (1998). Criminality in the corporate organization. In: R. W. Griffin, A. O'Leary-Kelly & J. M. Collins (Eds), *Dysfunctional Behavior in Organizations* (Vol. 2, pp. 1–20). Stamford, CT: JAI Press.

Conger, J. A., & Kanungo, R. N. (1998). *Charismatic leadership in organizations.* Thousand Oaks, CA: Sage.

Conklin, J. E. (1977). *"Illegal but not criminal": Business crime in America.* Englewood Cliffs, NJ: Prentice-Hall.

Cornish, D. B., & Clarke, R.V. (Eds) (1986). *The reasoning criminal: Rational choice perspectives on offending.* New York: Springer-Verlag.

Cressey, D. R. (1953). *Other people's money: A study in the social psychology of embezzlement.* New York: Free Press.

Cressey, D. R. (1986). Why managers commit fraud. *Australian and New Zealand Journal of Criminology, 19,* 195–209.

Creswell, J., & Prins, N. (2002, June 24th). The emperor of greed. *Fortune, 145*(13), 106–108, 110, 112, 114, 116.

Dabney, D. (1995). Neutralization and deviance in the workplace: Theft of supplies and medicines by hospital nurses. *Deviant Behavior, 16,* 313–331.

Daboub, A. J., Rasheed, A. M. A., Priem, R. L., & Gray, D. A. (1995). Top management team characteristics and corporate illegal activity. *Academy of Management Review, 20,* 138–170.

Darley, J. M. (1992). Social organization for the production of evil. *Psychological Inquiry, 3,* 199–218.

Darley, J. M. (1996). How organizations socialize individuals into evildoing. In: D. M. Messick & A. E. Tenbrunsel (Eds), *Codes of Conduct: Behavioral Research Into Business Ethics* (pp. 13–43). New York: Sage.

Darley, J. M. (2001). The dynamics of authority influence in organizations and the unintended action consequences. In: J. M. Darley, D. M. Messick & T. R. Tyler (Eds), *Social Influences on Ethical Behavior in Organizations* (pp. 37–52). Mahwah, NJ: Erlbaum.

Derry, R. (1987). Moral reasoning in work-related conflicts. In: W. C. Frederick (Ed.), *Research in Corporate Social Performance and Policy* (Vol. 9, pp. 25–49). Greenwich, CT: JAI Press.

Dillard, J. P. (1991). The current status of research on sequential-request compliance techniques. *Personality and Social Psychology Bulletin, 17,* 283–288.

Donziger, S. R. (Ed.) (1996). *The real war on crime: The report of the National Criminal Justice Commission.* New York: HarperPerennial.

Dutton, J. E., & Dukerich, J. M. (1991). Keeping an eye on the mirror: Image and identity in organizational adaptation. *Academy of Management Journal, 34,* 517–554.

Eichenwald, K. (1995). *Serpent on the rock*. New York: HarperBusiness.

Eichenwald, K. (2000). *The informant: A true story*. New York: Broadway Books.

Eichenwald, K., & Henriques, D. B. (2002, February, 10th). Enron buffed image to a shine even as it rotted from within. *New York Times*, pp. 1, 26–27.

Elsbach, K. D. (1994). Managing organizational legitimacy in the California cattle industry: The construction and effectiveness of verbal accounts. *Administrative Science Quarterly, 39*, 57–88.

Elstrom, P., & Updike, E. H. (1996, May 6th). Fear and loathing at Mitsubishi. *Business Week*, No. 3474, p. 35.

Epstein, S. (1980). The self-concept: A review and the proposal of an integrated theory of personality. In: E. Staub (Ed.), *Personality: Basic Aspects and Current Research* (pp. 81–132). Englewood Cliffs, NJ: Prentice-Hall.

Ermann, M. D., & Lundman, R. J. (1996). Corporate and governmental deviance: Origins, patterns, and reactions. In: M. D. Ermann & R. J. Lundman (Eds), *Corporate and Governmental Deviance: Problems of Organizational Behavior in Contemporary Society* (5th ed., pp. 3–44). New York: Oxford University Press.

Festinger, L. (1954). A theory of social comparison processes. *Human Relations, 7*, 117–140.

Fichman, M., & Levinthal, D. A. (1991). Honeymoons and the liability of adolescence: A new perspective on duration dependence in social and organizational relationships. *Academy of Management Review, 16*, 442–468.

Finney, H. C., & Lesieur, H. R. (1982). A contingency theory of organizational crime. In: S. B. Bacharach (Ed.), *Research in the Sociology of Organizations* (Vol. 1, pp. 255–299). Greenwich, CT: JAI Press.

Garrett, D. E., Bradford, J. L., Meyers, R. A., & Becker, J. (1989). Issues management and organizational accounts: An analysis of corporate responses to accusations of unethical business practices. *Journal of Business Ethics, 8*, 507–520.

Gasparino, C., & Smith, R. (2002, May 8th). Merrill arrives at framework for possible deal to end inquiry. *Wall Street Journal*, C1.

Geis, G. (1996). The heavy electrical equipment antitrust cases: Price-fixing techniques and rationalizations. In: M. D. Ermann & R. J. Lundman (Eds), *Corporate and Governmental Deviance: Problems of Organizational Behavior in Contemporary Society* (5th ed., pp. 98–117). New York: Oxford University Press.

Geis, G., & Meier, R. F. (1979). The white-collar offender. In: H. Toch (Ed.), *Psychology of Crime and Criminal Justice* (pp. 427–443). Prospect Heights, IL: Waveland Press.

Geis, G., & Salinger, L. S. (1998). Antitrust and organizational deviance. In: P. A. Bamberger & W. J. Sonnenstuhl (Eds), *Research in the Sociology of Organizations* (Vol. 15, pp. 71–110). Stamford, CT: JAI Press.

Gellerman, S. W. (1986). Why "good" managers make bad ethical choices. *Harvard Business Review, 86*(4), 85–90.

Gibbons, F. X., & Gerrard, M. (1991). Downward comparison and coping with threat. In: J. Suls & T. A. Wills (Eds), *Social Comparison: Contemporary Theory and Research* (pp. 317–345). Hillsdale, NJ: Erlbaum.

Gioia, D. A. (1992). Pinto fires and personal ethics: A script analysis of missed opportunities. *Journal of Business Ethics, 11*, 379–389.

Glazer, M. (1987). Whistleblowers. In: M. D. Ermann & R. J. Lundman (Eds), *Corporate and Governmental Deviance: Problems of Organizational Behavior in Contemporary Society* (3rd ed., pp. 187–208). New York: Oxford University Press.

Gottfredson, M. R., & Hirschi, T. (1990). *A general theory of crime.* Stanford, CA: Stanford University Press.

Green, G. S. (1997). *Occupational crime* (2nd ed.). Chicago: Nelson-Hall.

Greenberg, J. (1998). The cognitive geometry of employee theft: Negotiating "the line" between taking and stealing. In: R. W. Griffin, A. O'Leary-Kelly & J. M. Collins (Eds), *Dysfunctional Behavior in Organizations* (Vol. 2, pp. 147–193). Stamford, CT: JAI Press.

Greenwood, R., & Hinings, C. R. (1988). Organizational design types, tracks and the dynamics of strategic change. *Organization Studies, 9*, 293–316.

Greil, A. L., & & Rudy, D. R. (1984). Social cocoons: Encapsulation and identity transformation organizations. *Sociological Inquiry, 54*, 260–278.

Gross, E. (1978). Organizational crime: A theoretical perspective. In: N. K. Denzin (Ed.), *Studies in Symbolic Interaction* (Vol. 1, pp. 55–85). Greenwich, CT: JAI Press.

Haddad, C., & Barrett, A. (2002, June 24th). A whistle-blower rocks an industry. *Business Week*, No. 3788, pp. 126, 138, 130.

Hamilton, V. L., & Sanders, J. (1992). Responsibility and risk in organizational crimes of obedience. In: B. M. Staw & L. L. Cummings (Eds), *Research in Organizational Behavior* (Vol. 14, pp. 49–90). Greenwich, CT: JAI Press.

Hardin, C. D., & Higgins, E. T. (1996). Shared reality: How social verification makes the subjective objective. In: R. M. Sorrentino & E. T. Higgins (Eds), *Handbook of Motivation and Cognition* (Vol. 3, pp. 28–84). New York: Guilford Press.

Henisz, W. J., & Delios, A. (2001). Uncertainty, imitation, and plant location: Japanese multinational corporations, 1990–1996. *Administrative Science Quarterly, 46*, 443–475.

Hirschi, T. (1969). *Causes of delinquency.* Berkeley, CA: University of California Press.

Hollinger, R. C., & Clark, J. P. (1983). *Theft by employees.* Lexington, MA: Lexington Books.

Horning, D. N. M. (1970). Blue-collar theft: Conceptions of property, attitudes toward pilfering, and work group norms in a modern industrial plant. In: E. O. Smigel & H. L. Ross (Eds), *Crimes Against Bureaucracy* (pp. 46–64). New York: Van Nostrand Reinhold.

Howell, J. M. (1988). Two faces of charisma: Socialized and personalized leadership in organizations. In: J. A. Conger, R. N. Kanungo & Associates, *Charismatic Leadership: The Elusive Factor in Organizational Effectiveness* (pp. 213–236). San Francisco: Jossey-Bass.

Hughes, R., & Coakley, J. (1991). Positive deviance among athletes: The implications of overconformity to the sport ethic. *Sociology of Sport Journal, 8*, 307–325.

Hunt, J., & Manning, P. K. (1991). The social context of police lying. *Symbolic Interaction, 14*, 51–70.

Iacocca, L., & Novak, W. (1984). *Iacocca: An autobiography.* Toronto: Bantam Books.

Isenberg, D. J. (1986). Group polarization: A critical review and meta-analysis. *Journal of Personality and Social Psychology, 50*, 1141–1151.

Jackall, R. (1988). *Moral mazes: The world of corporate managers.* New York: Oxford University Press.

Janis, I. L. (1983). *Groupthink: Psychological studies of policy decisions and fiascoes* (2nd ed.). Boston: Houghton Mifflin.

Jankowski, M. S. (1991). *Islands in the street: Gangs and American urban society.* Berkeley, CA: University of California Press.

Johns, G. (1999). A multi-level theory of self-serving behavior in and by organizations. In: R. I. Sutton & B. M. Staw (Eds), *Research in Organizational Behavior* (Vol. 21, pp. 1–38). Stamford, CT: JAI Press.

Jones, G. R. (1986). Socialization tactics, self efficacy, and newcomer's adjustments to organizations. *Academy of Management Journal, 29*, 262–279.

Jones, T. M. (1991). Ethical decision making by individuals in organizations: An issue-contingent model. *Academy of Management Review, 16,* 366–395.

Jones, T. M., & Ryan, L. V. (1998). The effect of organizational forces on individual morality: Judgment, moral approbation, and behavior. *Business Ethics Quarterly, 8,* 431–445.

Kappeler, V. E., Sluder, R. D., & Alpert, G. P. (1994). *Forces of deviance: Understanding the dark side of policing.* Prospect Heights, IL: Waveland Press.

Katz, J. (1979). Concerted ignorance: The social construction of cover-up. *Urban Life, 8,* 295–316.

Kelman, H. C. (1973). Violence without moral restraint: Reflections on the dehumanization of victims and victimizers. *Journal of Social Issues, 29*(4), 25–61.

Klockars, C. B. (1974). *The professional fence.* New York: Macmillan.

Kramer, R. M., & Messick, D. M. (1996). Ethical cognition and the framing of organizational dilemmas: Decision makers as intuitive lawyers. In: D. M. Messick & A. E. Tenbrunsel (Eds), *Codes of Conduct: Behavioral Research Into Business Ethics* (pp. 59–85). New York: Sage.

Lane, R. E. (1954). *The regulation of businessmen: Social conditions of government economic control.* New Haven, CT: Yale University Press.

Latif, D. A. (2000). Ethical cognition and selection-socialization in retail pharmacy. *Journal of Business Ethics, 25,* 343–357.

Leaf, C. (2002, March 18th). White collar criminals: They lie, they cheat, they steal, and they've been getting away with it for too long: Enough is enough. *Fortune, 145*(6), 60–64, 68, 70, 72, 76.

Lerner, J. S., & Tetlock, P. E. (1999). Accounting for the effects of accountability. *Psychological Bulletin, 125,* 255–275.

LeVine, R. A., & Campbell, D. T. (1972). *Ethnocentrism: Theories of conflict, ethnic attitudes, and group behavior.* New York: Wiley.

Levitt, B., & March, J. G. (1988). Organizational learning. In: W. R. Scott & J. Blake (Eds), *Annual Review of Sociology* (Vol. 14, pp. 319–340). Palo Alto, CA: Annual Reviews.

Lewis, M. (1990). *Liar's poker: Rising through the wreckage on Wall Street.* New York: Penguin Books.

Lifton, R. J. (1961). *Thought reform and the psychology of totalism: A study of "brainwashing" in China.* New York: Norton.

Lifton, R. J. (1986). *The Nazi doctors: Medical killing and the psychology of genocide.* New York: Basic Books.

Lozano, J. M. (2000). *Ethics and organizations: Understanding business ethics as a learning process.* Dordrecht, The Netherlands: Kluwer.

March, J. G., & Simon, H. A. (1958). *Organizations.* New York: Wiley.

Maremont, M. (1995, October 23rd). Blind ambition: How the pursuit of results got out of hand at Bausch & Lomb. *Business Week,* No. 3447, pp. 78–82, 86, 90–92.

Mars, G. (1974). Dock pilferage: A case study in occupational theft. In: P. Rock & M. McIntosh (Eds), *Deviance and Social Control* (pp. 209–228). London: Tavistock.

Mars, G. (1994). *Cheats at work: An anthropology of workplace crime.* Aldershot, England: Dartmouth.

Mathews, M. C. (1988). *Strategic intervention in organizations: Resolving ethical dilemmas.* Newbury Park, CA: Sage.

Matza, D. (1964). *Delinquency and drift.* New York: Wiley.

Merton, R. K. (1968). *Social theory and social structure* (Rev. ed.). New York: Free Press.

Miceli, M. P., & Near, J. P. (1992). *Blowing the whistle: The organizational and legal implications for companies and employees.* New York: Lexington Books.

Miceli, M. P., & Near, J. P. (2002). What makes whistle-blowers effective? Three field studies. *Human Relations, 55,* 455–479.

Milgram, S. (1974). *Obedience to authority: An experimental view.* New York: Harper & Row.

Miller, D. (1993). The architecture of simplicity. *Academy of Management Review, 18,* 116–138.

Miller, J. P. (1998, June 12th). Mitsubishi will pay $34 million in sexual-harassment settlement. *Wall Street Journal,* B4.

Miller, L., & France, D. (2002, March 4th). Sins of the fathers. *Newsweek, 139*(9), 42–46, 48–49, 51–52.

Miller, V. D., & Jablin, F. M. (1991). Information seeking during organizational entry: Influences, tactics, and a model of the process. *Academy of Management Review, 16,* 92–120.

Mills, C. W. (1956). *The power elite.* New York: Oxford University Press.

Minor, W. W. (1981). Techniques of neutralization: A reconceptualization and empirical examination. *Journal of Research in Crime and Delinquency, 18,* 295–318.

Minor, W. W. (1984). Neutralization as a hardening process: Considerations in the modeling of change. *Social Forces, 62,* 995–1019.

Murphy, K. R. (1993). *Honesty in the workplace.* Pacific Grove, CA: Brooks/Cole.

Myers, D. G., & Lamm, H. (1976). The group polarization phenomenon. *Psychological Bulletin, 83,* 602–627.

Nail, P. R., Van Leeuwen, M. D., & Powell, A. B. (1996). The effectance versus the self-presentational view of reactance: Are importance ratings influenced by anticipated surveillance? *Journal of Social Behavior and Personality, 11,* 573–584.

Nelson, R. R., & Winter, S. G. (1982). *An evolutionary theory of economic change.* Cambridge, MA: Belknap Press.

Ocasio, W. (1999). Institutionalized action and corporate governance: The reliance on rules of CEO succession. *Administrative Science Quarterly, 44,* 384–416.

Oliver, C. (1992). The antecedents of deinstitutionalization. *Organization Studies, 13,* 563–588.

Opotow, S. (1990). Moral exclusion and injustice: An introduction. *Journal of Social Issues, 46*(1), 1–20.

O'Reilly, C. A., & Chatman, J. A. (1996). Culture as social control: Corporations, cults, and commitment. In: B. M. Staw & L. L. Cummings (Eds), *Research in Organizational Behavior* (Vol. 18, pp. 157–200). Greenwich, CT: JAI Press.

Partnoy, F. (1999). *F.I.A.S.C.O.: The inside story of a Wall Street trader.* New York: Penguin Books.

Pizzo, S., Fricker, M., & Muolo, P. (1991). *Inside job: The looting of America's savings and loans.* New York: HarperPerennial.

Ponemon, L. A. (1992). Ethical reasoning and selection-socialization in accounting. *Accounting, Organizations and Society, 17,* 239–258.

Poveda, T. G. (1994). *Rethinking white-collar crime.* Westport, CT: Praeger.

Rimé, B., Mesquita, B., Philippot, P., & Boca, S. (1991). Beyond the emotional event: Six studies on the social sharing of emotion. *Cognition and Emotion, 5,* 435–465.

Robinson, S. L., & Kraatz, M. S. (1998). Constructing the reality of normative behavior: The use of neutralization strategies by organizational deviants. In: R. W. Griffin, A. O'Leary-Kelly & J. M. Collins (Eds), *Dysfunctional Behavior in Organizations* (Vol. 1, pp. 203–220). Stamford, CT: JAI Press.

Rosoff, S. M., Pontell, H. N., & Tillman, R. H. (2002). *Profit without honor: White-collar crime and the looting of America* (2nd ed.). Upper Saddle River, NJ: Prentice-Hall.

Ross, L. (1977). The intuitive psychologist and his shortcomings: Distortions in the attribution process. In: L. Berkowitz (Ed.), *Advances in Experimental Social Psychology* (Vol. 10, pp. 173–220). New York: Academic Press.

Ryan, C. S., & Bogart, L. M. (1997). Development of new group members' in-group and out-group stereotypes: Changes in perceived group variability and ethnocentrism. *Journal of Personality and Social Psychology, 73,* 719–732.

Salancik, G. R. (1977). Commitment and the control of organizational behavior and belief. In: B. M. Staw & G. R. Salancik (Eds), *New Directions in Organizational Behavior* (pp. 1–54). Chicago: St. Clair Press.

Schachter, S. (1959). *The psychology of affiliation: Experimental studies of the sources of gregariousness.* Stanford, CA: Stanford University Press.

Schein, E. H. (1968). Organizational socialization and the profession of management. *Industrial Management Review, 9*(2), 1–16.

Schneider, B. (1987). The people make the place. *Personnel Psychology, 40*, 437–453.

Schneider, B., Goldstein, H. W., & Smith, D. B. (1995). The ASA framework: An update. *Personnel Psychology, 48*, 747–773.

Schwartz, H. S. (1987). Anti-social actions of committed organizational participants: An existential psychoanalytic perspective. *Organization Studies, 8*, 327–340.

Scott, M. B., & Lyman, S. M. (1968). Accounts. *American Sociological Review, 33*, 46–62.

Sethi, S. P., & Steidlmeier, P. (1991). *Up against the corporate wall: Modern corporations and social issues of the nineties* (5th ed.). Englewood Cliffs, NJ: Prentice-Hall.

Settles, I. H., Sellers, R. M., & Damas, A., Jr. (2002). One role or two? The function of psychological separation in role conflict. *Journal of Applied Psychology, 87*, 574–582.

Sharpe, R. (1996, July 10th). Divided ranks: Women at Mitsubishi say union fell short on sexual harassment. *Wall Street Journal*, A1.

Sherman, L. W. (1980). Three models of organizational corruption in agencies of social control. *Social Problems, 27*, 478–491.

Shover, N. (1996). *Great pretenders: Pursuits and careers of persistent thieves.* Boulder, CO: Westview Press.

Shover, N., & Bryant, K. M. (1993). Theoretical explanations of corporate crime. In: M. B. Blankenship (Ed.), *Understanding Corporate Criminality* (pp. 141–176). New York: Garland.

Silver, M., & Geller, D. (1978). On the irrelevance of evil: The organization and individual action. *Journal of Social Issues, 34*(4), 125–136.

Simon, H. A. (1976). *Administrative behavior: A study of decision-making processes in administrative organization* (3rd ed.). New York: Free Press.

Sims, R. R., & Brinkmann, J. (2002). Leaders as moral role models: The case of John Gutfreund at Salomon Brothers. *Journal of Business Ethics, 35*, 327–339.

Smigel, E. O. (1956). Public attitudes toward stealing as related to the size of the victim organization. *American Sociological Review, 21*, 320–327.

Staw, B. M. (1980). Rationality and justification in organizational life. In: B. M. Staw & L. L. Cummings (Eds), *Research in Organizational Behavior* (Vol. 2, pp. 45–80). Greenwich, CT: JAI Press.

Staw, B. M. (1997). The escalation of commitment: An update and appraisal. In: Z. Shapira (Ed.), *Organizational Decision Making* (pp. 191–215). Cambridge, England: Cambridge University Press.

Stern, M. (1962). What makes a policeman go wrong? An ex-member of the force traces the steps on way from law enforcement to violating. *Journal of Criminal Law, Criminology and Police Science, 53*, 97–101.

Stevenson, R. J. (1998). *The boiler room and other telephone sales scams.* Urbana, IL: University of Illinois Press.

Stoddard, E. R. (1968). The informal "code" of police deviancy: A group approach to "blue-coat crime". *Journal of Criminal Law, Criminology and Police Science, 59*, 201–213.

Stone, D. G. (1990). *April fools: An insider's account of the rise and collapse of Drexel Burnham.* New York: Donald I. Fine.

Sutherland, E. H. (1949). *White collar crime*. New York: Dryden Press.

Sykes, G. M., & Matza, D. (1957). Techniques of neutralization: A theory of delinquency. *American Sociological Review, 22*, 664–670.

Szwajkowski, E. (1985). Organizational illegality: Theoretical integration and illustrative application. *Academy of Management Review, 10*, 558–567.

Taylor, S. E. (1989). *Positive illusions: Creative self-deception and the healthy mind*. New York: Basic Books.

Taylor, S. E., & Gollwitzer, P. M. (1995). Effects of mindset on positive illusions. *Journal of Personality and Social Psychology, 69*, 213–226.

Tenbrunsel, A. E. (1998). Misrepresentation and expectations of misrepresentation in an ethical dilemma: The role of incentives and temptation. *Academy of Management Journal, 41*, 330–339.

The Knapp Commission report on police corruption (1972). New York: George Braziller.

Treviño, L. K., Weaver, G. R., Gibson, D. G., & Toffler, B. L. (1999). Managing ethics and legal compliance: What works and what hurts. *California Management Review, 41*(2), 131–151.

Trice, H. M., & Beyer, J. M. (1993). *The cultures of work organizations*. Englewood Cliffs, NJ: Prentice-Hall.

Tushman, M. L., & Romanelli, E. (1985). Organizational evolution: A metamorphosis model of convergence and reorientation. In: L. L. Cummings & B. M. Staw (Eds), *Research in Organizational Behavior* (Vol. 7, pp. 171–222). Greenwich, CT: JAI Press.

Vandivier, K. (1996). Why should my conscience bother me? Hiding aircraft brake hazards. In: M. D. Ermann & R. J. Lundman (Eds), *Corporate and Governmental Deviance: Problems of Organizational Behavior in Contemporary Society* (5th ed., pp. 118–138). New York: Oxford University Press.

Van Gennep, A. (1960). *The rites of passage*. M. B. Vizedom & G. L. Caffee (Trans.). Chicago: University of Chicago Press.

Van Maanen, J. (1976). Breaking in: Socialization to work. In: R. Dubin (Ed.), *Handbook of Work, Organization, and Society* (pp. 67–130). Chicago: Rand McNally.

Vaughan, D. (1983). *Controlling unlawful organizational behavior: Social structure and corporate misconduct*. Chicago: University of Chicago Press.

Vaughan, D. (1992). The macro-micro connection in white-collar crime theory. In: K. Schlegel & D. Weisburd (Eds), *White-Collar Crime Reconsidered* (pp. 124–145). Boston: Northeastern University Press.

Wegner, D. M. (1989). *White bears and other unwanted thoughts: Suppression, obsession, and the psychology of mental control*. New York: Viking.

Weick, K. E., & Roberts, K. H. (1993). Collective mind in organizations: Heedful interrelating on flight decks. *Administrative Science Quarterly, 38*, 357–381.

Weimer, D. A., & Thornton, E. (1997, September 22nd). Slow healing at Mitsubishi: It's clearing up sex-harassment charges, but ill will lingers. *Business Week*, No. 3545, pp. 74, 76.

Weitzel, W., & Jonsson, E. (1989). Decline in organizations: A literature integration and extension. *Administrative Science Quarterly, 34*, 91–109.

Welles, C. (1988, February 22nd). What led Beech-Nut down the road to disgrace. *Business Week*, No. 3037, pp. 124–126, 128.

Yates, J. (1990). For the record: The embodiment of organizational memory, 1850–1920. *Business and Economic History, 19*, 172–182.

Yeager, P. C. (1986). Analyzing corporate offenses: Progress and prospects. In: J. E. Post (Ed.), *Research in Corporate Social Performance and Policy* (Vol. 8, pp. 93–120). Greenwich, CT: JAI Press.

Zey-Ferrell, M., & Ferrell, O. C. (1982). Role-set configuration and opportunity as predictors of unethical behavior in organizations. *Human Relations, 35*, 587–604.

Zey-Ferrell, M., Weaver, K. M., & Ferrell, O. C. (1979). Predicting unethical behavior among marketing practitioners. *Human Relations, 32*, 557–569.

Zimbardo, P. G. (1969). The human choice: Individuation, reason, and order versus deindividuation, impulse, and chaos. In: W. J. Arnold & D. Levine (Eds), *Nebraska Symposium on Motivation* (Vol. 17, pp. 237–307). Lincoln, NE: University of Nebraska Press.

Zimmerman, F. M. (1991). *The turnaround experience: Real-world lessons in revitalizing corporations.* New York: McGraw-Hill.

Zucker, L. G. (1977). The role of institutionalization in cultural persistence. *American Sociological Review, 42*, 726–743.

Zucker, L. G. (1988). Where do institutional patterns come from? Organizations as actors in social systems. In: L. G. Zucker (Ed.), *Institutional Patterns and Organizations: Culture and Environment* (pp. 23–49). Cambridge, MA: Ballinger.

FAIR MARKET IDEOLOGY: ITS COGNITIVE-MOTIVATIONAL UNDERPINNINGS

John T. Jost, Sally Blount, Jeffrey Pfeffer
and György Hunyady

ABSTRACT

*Public opinion research indicates that most people espouse egalitarian
ideals and acknowledge substantial income inequality in society, but they
consistently perceive the economic system to be highly fair and legitimate.
In an attempt to better understand this paradox by considering the cognitive
and motivational bases of ideological support for the free market system, we
draw on and integrate a number of social psychological theories suggesting
that people want to believe that the systems and institutions that affect
them are fair, legitimate, and justified. We have developed an instrument
for measuring* fair market ideology, *and we have found in several samples
that its endorsement is associated with self-deception, economic system
justification, opposition to equality, power distance orientation, belief in a
just world, political conservatism, right-wing authoritarianism, and scandal
minimization. We also present evidence that people evince a system-justifying
tendency to judge profitable companies to be more ethical than unprofitable
companies. In addition, results from an experimental study we conducted in
Hungary indicate that support for the free market system is strongest among
people who score high in self-deception under conditions of system threat,*

Research in Organizational Behavior
Research in Organizational Behavior, Volume 25, 53–91
© 2003 Published by Elsevier Ltd.
ISSN: 0191-3085/doi:10.1016/S0191-3085(03)25002-4

suggesting the presence of a (non-rational) defensive motivation. Finally, we discuss several organizational and societal implications of the tendency to idealize market mechanisms and to view market-generated outcomes as inherently fair.

1. INSTITUTIONAL PERSISTENCE AS AN IDEOLOGICAL PROCESS

The cultural persistence of existing institutional forms is a topic of recognized importance in organizational sociology (e.g. Hannan & Carroll, 1992; Meyer & Rowan, 1977; Pfeffer, 1981; Van Maanen & Schein, 1979; Zucker, 1977), but it is also a theme that invites social psychological analysis (see also Jost & Major, 2001). Institutional entities like the free market system and specific institutional-ized practices – such as raising prices as consumer demand increases and product supply decreases – survive, at least in part, because people accept them as legiti-mate and therefore protect and sustain them over time. Perceptions of legitimacy, in turn, depend upon ideological factors. One's ideological beliefs, values, and goals, for example, affect the likelihood of judging existing institutional forms and practices to be fair, legitimate, and just and therefore deserving of continued support (e.g. Jost & Banaji, 1994; Major, 1994; Pratto, Sidanius, Stallworth & Malle, 1994).

There are also demonstrable links between ideological orientations and preferences for specific justice principles, such as between liberalism and equality on one hand, and conservatism and equity on the other (e.g. Rasinski, 1987; Rasinski & Tourangeau, 1991). With regard to organizational decision-making, managers with politically liberal orientations have been shown to prefer equal across-the-board pay cuts as a cost-cutting measure, whereas managers who adopt authoritarian and economically conservative orientations are more likely to opt for layoffs (Tetlock, 2000).[1] The notion that ideological beliefs are consequential in organizational settings is consistent with the fact that when people intervene in organizations, they act on the basis of implicit or explicit theories of individual, group, and organizational behavior (Pfeffer, 1981; Salancik & Brindle, 1997; Weick, 1995). Ideologies are complex belief systems that incorporate, among other things, people's theories about human nature, their philosophies concerning the appropriate use of social power, status, and authority, and their moral and pragmatic convictions concerning the maximization of social and economic wel-fare. Indeed, beliefs and values such as these provide a cognitive and motivational basis for people's enduring commitments to cultural institutions, as well as their active participation in work organizations.

Although ideological belief systems have received scant attention in research on organizational behavior, there is a fairly extensive body of literature in political psychology that addresses the nature of ideology, its antecedents, and its consequences for judgment and behavior (see Jost, Glaser, Kruglanski & Sulloway, 2003a for a review). In this chapter, we adopt a psychological approach to understanding the bases of ideological support for the free market system. More specifically, we focus on the cognitive and motivational underpinnings of "fair market ideology," defined as the tendency to view market-based processes and outcomes not simply as efficient, but as inherently fair, legitimate, and just (see also Blount, 1995, 2000).[2]

2. FAIR MARKET IDEOLOGY: A PARADOX

Our interest in analyzing the social psychological bases of fair market ideology arises in part from a desire to understand a paradox brought on by the conjunction of two more or less concurrent developments in U.S. society: (a) a relatively steep increase in economic inequality caused by market forces (e.g. Frank & Cook, 1995; Weinberg, 1996); and (b) a strong consensual faith in the legitimacy of the market system (e.g. Gilens, 1999; Shiller, 2000). By almost any metric – including the *gini* index of income concentration – the distribution of wealth in society has grown increasingly skewed in favor of the affluent over the past two decades (e.g. Blinder, 1987; Marshall, 2000; Weinberg, 2002). As of the late 1990s, the richest 1% of Americans controlled almost half of the country's total financial wealth, and the top 20% possessed 94% of the nation's net wealth (Wolff, 1996). Income inequality has also risen steeply within business organizations (e.g. Crystal, 1991). In 1980, for example, C.E.O.'s earned approximately 40 times the salary of the average worker; by 1998, the ratio had risen to more than 400 to 1 (e.g. Cassidy, 1999). More recent estimates place the figure at nearly 500 to 1 (Crystal, 2002).

Did these unprecedented increases in wage dispersion over the last twenty years stimulate widespread perceptions of market unfairness and a spike in labor union involvement in a country that is famous for espousing egalitarian ideals? No, the evidence suggests that it did not. On the contrary, public opinion research indicates that most people continue to perceive the economic system to be highly fair and legitimate – despite growing inequality.

In 1998, the most recent year for which these data are available, the Gallup Organization conducted a national telephone survey of 5,001 adults concerning perceptions of the fairness of the American economic system as a whole. Despite the magnitude of economic inequality that existed both in the sample and the

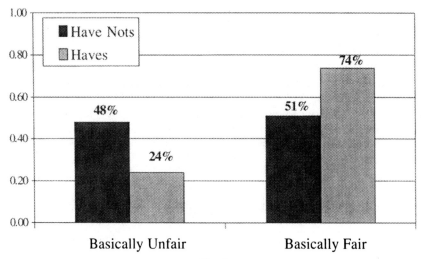

Fig. 1

Percent Believing that the U.S. Economic System is "Basically Flair" vs. "Basically Unfair" (as a Function of Respondent Classification). *Note*: These data are based on responses (*N* = 5,001) to the 1998 Gallup Poll "Have and Have-Nots: Perceptions of Fairness and Opportunity" and reported by Ludwig (1999). "Haves" and "Have Nots" are
self-designated classifications.

population at large, survey results documented an impressive degree of consensus
surrounding belief in the fairness of the economic system (Ludwig, 1999). A
relatively strong majority (68%) agreed that "the economic situation in the United
States is basically fair," and only 29% believed the system to be unfair (see
Fig. 1). Surprisingly – at least in light of prevailing assumptions in social science
concerning self-interest and self-serving patterns of attribution, a majority (52%)
of respondents in the lowest S.E.S. group (many with household incomes below
$15,000/year) believed that the system was fair. When asked whether disparities
between the rich and the poor in the U.S. are "an acceptable part of our economic
system" or "a problem that needs to be fixed," 45% overall (and 37% of the lowest
S.E.S. group) reported that they found the situation to be acceptable. The point
to be made here is not that economic self-interest exerts *no* effect on perceptions
of fairness. As can be seen in Fig. 1, a larger percentage of high-income than
low-income respondents agree that the economic system is fair. What is striking,
however, is the relatively large number of self-designated "have-nots" who accept
the fairness and legitimacy of the economic system.[3]

A finding reported by Tyler and Lind (2002) suggests that overall perceptions of market fairness are linked more to faith and trust in authorities than to justice-based scrutiny of outcomes. They found in a random-digit telephone survey conducted with a sample of 502 U.S. respondents that people were significantly more likely to agree that, "All things considered, the economic system in the United States is fair" to the extent that they also held favorable attitudes toward Congress and were more in favor of governmental intervention (pp. 53–57). This is somewhat surprising, given that genuine faith in market forces should be associated with the desire for less (not more) governmental intrusion. Thus, the belief in the fairness of market exchange seems to have more to do with general faith in the system than with a specific understanding of economic principles.

Social scientists have often puzzled over the popular perception that the American economic system is intrinsically fair, despite widespread awareness of inequality (e.g. Fong, 2001; Gilens, 1999; Hochschild, 1981; Kluegel & Smith, 1986; Lane, 1959; Verba et al., 1987). Such findings are difficult to square with prevailing theories of individual and collective self-interest (see Jost, Banaji & Nosek, 2004). They also raise problems for many other sociological and psychological theories of injustice and rebellion, most notably social comparison and relative deprivation theories, which predict that recognition of disadvantageous inequality should foster perceptions of unfairness and participation in social change (e.g. Gurr, 1970; Pettigrew, 1967; Tajfel & Turner, 1986; Walker & Smith, 2002).

In seeking to understand how and why people believe so strongly in the fairness of economic institutions that disfavor them, researchers have sometimes revisited Marxian concepts of dominant ideology and false consciousness (e.g. Glazer, 2002; Hochschild, 1981; Jost, 1995; Kluegel & Smith, 1986; Tyler & McGraw, 1986; but see Tyler, 2001, for a different view). To the extent that these largely sociological accounts make substantive contact with psychological themes, they explain rigid adherence to fair market ideology as at least partially due to self-deception and system justification, the latter of which is defined as the social psychological "process by which existing social arrangements are legitimized, even at the expense of personal and group interest" (Jost & Banaji, 1994, p. 2). A number of different but convergent research programs that we see as highly relevant to understanding the cognitive-motivational basis of fair market ideology all lead to the conclusion that people are motivated to believe that the systems and institutions that affect them are fair, legitimate, and justified. This insight moves us somewhat closer to a satisfying psychological analysis of the paradox presented by consensual endorsement of fair market ideology.

3. COGNITIVE-MOTIVATIONAL UNDERPINNINGS OF FAIR MARKET IDEOLOGY: A THEORETICAL INTEGRATION

In this section, we review and integrate several social psychological contributions that pertain either directly or indirectly to the cognitive-motivational bases of fair market ideology. These include research programs on the belief in a just world (Lerner & Miller, 1978), the illusion of control and unrealistic optimism (Taylor & Brown, 1988), economic system justification (Jost & Thompson, 2000), and political conservatism as motivated social cognition (Jost et al., 2003a). These accounts differ from one another in important ways, but taken together they suggest that beliefs concerning the inherent fairness of the economic system may involve elements of self-deception, system justification, and ideological socialization.

3.1. The Belief in a Just World

According to Lerner and Miller's (1978) formulation of just world theory, there is a universal human need to believe that outcomes are fair and just and that people "get what they deserve and deserve what they get." The basic argument is that living in an unpredictable, uncontrollable, and capriciously unjust world would be unbearably threatening, and so we cling defensively to the illusion that the world is a just place (Lerner, 1980). When people are confronted with cases of injustice, the belief in a just world is threatened, and people seek to restore it through conscious and non-conscious means (e.g. Hafer, 2000; Kay & Jost, 2003).

Several instruments have been developed for measuring individual differences in the tendency to believe in a just world (BJW), both in relation to one's own outcomes and to the outcomes of others in general (e.g. Lipkus, Dalbert & Siegler, 1996; Rubin & Peplau, 1973). Research has established that people who score high on BJW are more likely than others to trust existing institutions and authorities and to derogate victims and members of underprivileged groups (e.g. Olson & Hafer, 2001; Rubin & Peplau, 1975).[4] Although just world theory has not been applied previously to the perception of economic systems *per se*, it has been used to understand psychological responses to economic inequality. Specifically, people who lack the opportunity for prosocial helping and people who score high on BJW scales tend to blame the poor and credit the rich for their respective fates (e.g. Furnham & Procter, 1989). In the research we have conducted, we expected that individual differences in the motivation to believe in a just world would be associated with the tendency to believe that market-based outcomes and procedures are inherently fair and legitimate. That is, higher BJW scores should predict endorsement of fair market ideology.

3.2. Illusion of Control, Unrealistic Optimism, and Self-Deception

In considering potential arguments for the inherent fairness of economic markets, Sen (1985, p. 3) discussed Friedman and Friedman's (1980) "claim that the market makes people 'free to choose,' a freedom that might be seen to be valuable in itself (whether or not it also helps in other ways, such as the protection of the interests of the consumers)." Sen noted that, "If that freedom is shown to be 'illusory,' then the case for the market mechanism would be dis-established" (p. 5). In commenting on "market mystification," Ollman (1998) similarly underscored the importance of the lay belief that: "despite all the competition and individual decisions involved in buying and selling, a surprising equilibrium gets reached, so that the market not only appears to be just – because no one interferes with our choices – it also appears to work" (p. 84). Thus, the notion (illusory or otherwise) that the free market presents individuals with the opportunity to control their own fates seems to play some role in perceptions of economic fairness.

Research in social psychology suggests that people greatly value individual freedom of choice (Brehm & Brehm, 1981), that the perception of control is crucial to fairness judgments (Lind & Tyler, 1988), and that people often exaggerate the extent to which they have control over randomly determined outcomes (Langer, 1975). There is also evidence that people prefer to accept personal responsibility for unfavorable outcomes than to acknowledge that some events are beyond their personal control (e.g. Lerner, 1980; Miller & Porter, 1983). Kluegel and Smith (1986, pp. 13–14), too, have argued that the "illusion of control" supports the ideological belief that economic inequality is fair and legitimate.

It has also been suggested that poor people might embrace fair market ideology in part because they are unrealistically optimistic about the future and expect to become rich one day (Candiotti, 1998). As a general rule, people do tend to overestimate the extent to which good things are likely to happen to them and to underestimate the extent to which bad things are likely to happen to them (e.g. Weinstein, 1980). More than half a century ago, Katona (1951) observed that approximately twice as many people expected that good (vs. bad) economic times were coming, and although perceptions may fluctuate with objective economic circumstances to some degree, the tendency to see the economy through rose-colored glasses is relatively robust. For instance, the economic optimism index fell below 50% in only 1 of the 30 months between February 2001 and July 2003, despite major corporate scandals and severe economic downturns during this time period (see Investor's Business Daily/Christian Science Monitor, 2003).

Unrealistic optimism in the economic domain seems to be especially common among less educated respondents (Robison, 2003) and may contribute to the phenomenon of investor overconfidence'(Shiller, 2000). Taylor and Brown (1988) argued that both the illusion of control and unrealistic optimism are "positive illusions," that is, adaptive forms of self-deception that facilitate coping with environmental stress and uncertainty.[5] Paulhus (1984) has developed a scale for measuring "self-deceptive enhancement," which gauges the individual propensity to embrace positive illusions. If support for fair market ideology is indeed related to the illusion of control, unrealistic optimism, and other positive illusions, then we would expect that its endorsement would be positively correlated with self-deception. Such a demonstration would be particularly novel because of the fact that general beliefs concerning the legitimacy of the economic system are quite removed from the specific kinds of self-related beliefs typically investigated by self-deception researchers.

3.3. System Justification Theory

Jost and Banaji's (1994; Jost et al., 2004) system justification theory integrates previous research and further elaborates on the theme that people are motivated to perceive existing social, economic, and political arrangements as inherently fair, legitimate, and justifiable. Research examining the theory has demonstrated, among other things, that people tend to rationalize the status quo by enhancing the subjective value of anticipated outcomes, even if they were initially defined as unattractive (Kay, Jimenez & Jost, 2002). Other studies have shown that people develop and use stereotypes to justify inequality in organizations and in society (e.g. Baron & Pfeffer, 1994; Jost & Major, 2001; Operario & Fiske, 2001) and misremember arbitrary reasons given for the existence of inequality among groups as increasingly legitimate over time (Haines & Jost, 2000). System-justifying tendencies are conservative in their consequences and may stem, at least partially, from epistemic and existential needs to manage uncertainty and threat (e.g. Jost et al., 2003a; Kramer, 2001; Lind & van den Bos, 2002).

Jost and Thompson (2000) developed an Economic System Justification (ESJ) Scale to measure individual differences in the propensity to defend and justify the existing economic system, with its attendant degree of inequality. Items from the

Table 1. Items from the Economic System Justification (ESJ) Scale.

1. If people work hard, they almost always get what they want
2. The existence of widespread economic differences does not mean that they are inevitable (R)
3. Laws of nature are responsible for differences in wealth in society
4. It is virtually impossible to eliminate poverty
5. There are many reasons to think that the economic system is unfair (R)
6. Poor people are not essentially different from rich people (R)
7. Most people who don't get ahead in our society should not blame the system; they have only themselves to blame
8. Equal distribution of resources is a possibility for our society (R)
9. Social class differences reflect differences in the natural order of things
10. Economic differences in the society reflect an illegitimate distribution of resources (R)
11. There will always be poor people, because there will never be enough jobs for everybody
12. Equal distribution of resources is unnatural
13. Economic positions are legitimate reflections of people's achievements
14. If people wanted to change the economic system to make things equal, they could (R)
15. It is unfair to have an economic system that produces extreme wealth and extreme poverty at the same time (R)
16. There is no point in trying to make incomes more equal
17. There are no inherent differences between rich and poor; it is purely a matter of the circumstances into which you were born (R)

Note: These items were taken from Jost and Thompson's (2000) Economic System Justification Scale and used in the present research. Because items 5 and 15 from the original scale explicitly addressed fairness issues, they were omitted . . . Responses were given on 9-point scales ranging from 1 ("Strongly Disagree") to 9 ("Strongly Agree"). Items followed by "(R)" were reverse-scored prior to data coding and analyses.

ESJ scale are listed in Table 1. Jost and Thompson found that ESJ scores correlated with ideological "opposition to equality" (see also Kluegel & Smith, 1986). Because it stresses the acceptance of disadvantageous as well as advantageous inequality, ESJ is similar to Hofstede's (1997) more general (and notoriously difficult to measure) construct of "power distance," defined as "the extent to which inequality among persons . . . is viewed as a natural (and even desirable) aspect of the social order" (Brockner et al., 2001, p. 302). Research has demonstrated that for members of advantaged groups (such as European Americans) higher ESJ scores tend to be associated with increased self-esteem and ingroup favoritism, whereas for members of disadvantaged groups (such as African Americans) stronger endorsement of ESJ is associated with decreased self-esteem and increased outgroup favoritism (see Jost & Hunyady, 2002 for a review). This work underscores the fact that people sometimes engage in system justification even at the expense of individual and group self-interest (Jost, 1995; Jost & Burgess, 2000; Jost, Pelham

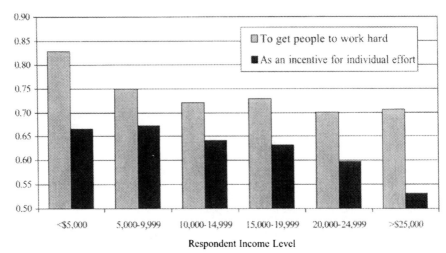

Fig. 2

Percent Agreeing that Large Differences in Income are Legitimate and Necessary (as a Function of Respondent Income). *Note*: These data are based on responses ($N = 2,567$) to the General Social Survey (GSS) between 1983 and 1991 and reported by Jost, Pelham, Sheldon, and Sullivan (2003b, Study 3). Values are combined percentages of respondents who believed that differences in pay were either "absolutely necessary" or "probably necessary" to "get people to work hard" and as "an incentive for individual effort." Income was measured in terms of (self-reported) pre-tax family household income. For both items, regression analyses yielded negative linear effects of family income on the belief that income inequality is legitimate and necessary ($p < 0.01$).

& Carvallo, 2002), suggesting that a broader notion of rationalization and self-deception (i.e. broader than mere self-enhancement) is necessary to understand ideological beliefs. In fact, Jost, Pelham, Sheldon and Sullivan (2003c) found that low-income respondents were even *more* likely than high-income respondents to believe that large differences in pay are necessary to "get people to work hard" and "as an incentive for individual effort." The obtained pattern of results is illustrated in Fig. 2.

According to system justification theory, threats to the legitimacy or stability of the system – as long as they fall short of toppling and replacing the status quo – should evoke defensive ideological responses, leading people to be even more motivated to justify the existing system (see Jost & Hunyady, 2002). We would therefore hypothesize that people will show increased support for fair market ideology following a perceived threat to the social system. To the extent that defensive responses should be especially likely among people who score high on self-deception, we would further predict an interaction between system threat and self-deception.

3.4. Political Conservatism as Motivated Social Cognition

In seeking to understand why most Americans fail to perceive inequality as unfair or illegitimate – that is, to understand "why the dog doesn't bark" – Hochschild (1981) pointed to political orientation. Subsequent research by Verba et al. (1987) confirmed that politically conservative individuals, groups, and party members in Japan, Sweden, and the U.S. were more likely than liberals to believe that the economic status quo is fair and that inequality is an acceptable outcome. For these and other reasons described below, we hypothesized that political conservatism and right-wing authoritarianism would be significant attitudinal predictors of the degree of endorsement of fair market ideology.

Most definitions of political conservatism stress resistance to change and acceptance of inequality (i.e. social differentiation) as core ideological components (e.g. Huntington, 1957; Kerlinger, 1984; Muller, 2001). Defined in this way, conservatism is a prototypical system-justifying ideology, in that it preserves the status quo and provides intellectual and moral justification for maintaining inequality in society. On the assumption that political conservatism could be analyzed as a case of motivated social cognition, Jost et al. (2003a) reviewed theory and research linking a host of psychological variables to endorsement of political conservatism. These variables were selected on the basis of numerous theories of ideological functioning, including theories of right-wing authoritarianism (Adorno, Frenkel-Brunswik, Levinson & Sanford, 1950; Altemeyer, 1996); dogmatism and closed-mindedness (Rokeach, 1960); conservatism as uncertainty avoidance (Wilson, 1973); terror management (Pyszczynski, Greenberg & Solomon, 1997); and system justification (Jost & Banaji, 1994).

Jost et al. (2003a) conducted a meta-analysis of studies conducted between 1958–2002 involving 88 different research samples and 22,818 individual cases. The original studies were carried out in 12 different countries: USA, England, New Zealand, Australia, Poland, Sweden, Germany, Scotland, Israel, Italy, Canada, and South Africa. This corpus of research made it possible to quantitatively assess the strength of hypothesized relations between conservatism and nine specific variables related to epistemic and existential functioning, namely: intolerance of ambiguity; openness to experience; fear of threat and loss; self-esteem; uncertainty avoidance; personal needs for order, structure, and closure; integrative complexity; system instability; and fear of death.

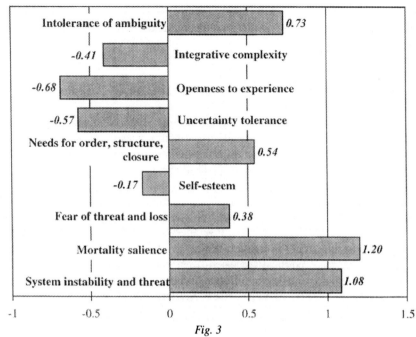

Fig. 3

Cognitive and Motivational Bases of Political Conservation. *Note*: Entries are effect sizes (Cohen's *d*s) for the relation between each cognitive-motivational variable and politi-cal conservatism, as reported in a meta-analysis conducted by Jost, Glaser, Kruglanski and Sulloway (2003a). All effect sizes attained conventional levels of statistical significance (*p* < 0.001).

Results of the meta-analysis indicated that all nine of the hypothesized cognitive-motivational variables were indeed significantly related to political conservatism and the holding of right-wing ideological orientations, although the effect sizes for the different variables ranged considerably (see Fig. 3). The two largest effect sizes were obtained for fear of death (and mortality salience) and system threat (and instability). Moderate effect sizes were also obtained for intolerance of ambiguity, openness to experience, uncertainty avoidance, and personal needs to achieve order, structure, and closure. The weakest effect sizes were obtained for integrative complexity, fear of threat and loss, and self-esteem.

Evidence from the meta-analysis supported the notion that there is a consistent "match" between epistemic and existential needs to manage uncertainty and threat and the specific contents of conservative ideologies (see also Jost, Glaser,

Kruglanski & Sulloway, 2003b). This match had been suggested not only by Adorno et al. (1950), but also by Rokeach (1960), who argued that, "If a person's underlying motivations are served by forming a closed belief system, then it is more likely that his motivations can also be served by embracing an ideology that is blatantly anti-equalitarian. If this is so, it would account for the somewhat greater affinity we have observed between authoritarian belief structure and conservatism than between the same belief structure and liberalism" (p. 127). After 50 years of cumulative research, the evidence consistently indicates that there are, indeed, a number of cognitive and motivational differences between proponents of conservative vs. liberal ideologies, including ideologies pertaining to perceptions of the economic system. To the extent that conservatism is a belief system that provides justifications for economic inequality under capitalism, it should also be associated with endorsement of fair market ideology.

3.5. Summary of Theoretical Propositions

In our research, we have sought to investigate the prevalence of fair market ideology and its cognitive and motivational underpinnings. We enumerate several propositions below that summarize and integrate our theoretical arguments. These may be stated as follows:

(1) *Ceteris paribus*, people living under a free market system will tend to believe that common business practices and market-driven procedures and outcomes are fair, ethical, and legitimate; that is, in general people will endorse a fair market ideology.[6]
(2) People who score high on each of the following cognitive, motivational, and ideological variables will endorse fair market ideology more strongly than will people who score low on each of these variables:
  (a) Belief in a Just World (BJW)
  (b) Economic System Justification (ESJ)
  (c) Opposition to Equality (OEQ)
  (d) Power Distance
  (e) Self-Deception
  (f) Political Conservatism (vs. Liberalism)
  (g) Right-Wing Authoritarianism (RWA)
(3) To the extent that people endorse fair market ideology, they will also be more likely to minimize ethical concerns in response to scandals.
(4) *Ceteris paribus*, business people will be motivated to believe that profitable companies are ethical companies.

(5) In general, people will show increased support for the economic system following a threat to the legitimacy of the system, especially when they are relatively
high in self-deception.

4. EMPIRICAL EVIDENCE BEARING ON THE COGNITIVE-MOTIVATIONAL UNDERPINNINGS OF FAIR MARKET IDEOLOGY

In this section, we summarize several related research programs bearing on the
above propositions. First, we describe the development and validation of an
instrument for measuring the tendency to assume that market-driven procedures
and outcomes are fair. In doing so, we investigate strengths of association
between scores on the fair market ideology scale and measures of belief in a
just world, economic system justification, opposition to equality, power distance,
political conservatism, right-wing authoritarianism, self-deception, and scandal
minimization. Second, we relay the results of an experimental study designed
to assess the system-justifying tendency for people to assume that profitable
companies are more ethical than unprofitable companies. Third, we summarize
data from an experimental investigation pertaining to ideological support for
the free market system and its relation to self-deception and system threat in the
context of the transition from socialism to capitalism in Hungary.

4.1. The Development of a Fair Market Ideology (FMI) Scale

In order to demonstrate that a tendency exists to believe that the existing
free market system is fair, ethical, and legitimate and to measure individual
differences in this tendency, we developed a 25-item Fair Market Ideology (FMI)
Scale. The first 15 items tap perceptions that the free market system is fair on
largely procedural grounds; the last 10 items focus on the perceived fairness
of market-driven outcomes. A complete list of the FMI items is presented in
Table 2, along with scaling and scoring instructions. For the 25-item version of
the scale, reliability is very good, with α's ranging from 0.83 to 0.89. We have
found that using a smaller subset of the scale items (either 6- or 15-item versions)
is acceptable in terms of reliability (α's ranging from 0.61 to 0.78), and obviously
more efficient with regard to time and space savings during data collection.

To date, we have administered either long or short versions of the FMI scale
to seven different respondent samples from 2000 to 2003. Sample and scale
descriptive statistics, including scale reliabilities, are presented in the top panel of

Table 2. Items from the Fair Market Ideology (FMI) Scale.

1. The free market system is a fair system
2. Common or "normal" business practices must be fair, or they would not survive
3. In many markets, there is no such thing as a true "fair" market price (R)
4. Ethical businesses are *not* as profitable as unethical businesses (R)
5. The most fair economic system is a market system in which everyone is allowed to independently pursue their own economic interests
6. Acting in response to market forces is *not* always a fair way to conduct business (R)
7. The free market system is an efficient system
8. The free market system has nothing to do with fairness (R)
9. Acting in response to market forces is an ethical way to conduct business
10. In free market systems, people tend to get the outcomes that they deserve
11. The fairest outcomes result from transactions in which the buyers pay the "fair" market price
12. Profitable businesses tend to be more morally responsible than unprofitable businesses
13. Regulated trade is fair trade (R)
14. Economic markets do *not* fairly reward people (R)
15. Whatever price a buyer and seller agree to trade at is a fair price
16. When a company raises the prices that it charges its customers for its goods, because management has obtained market research which suggests that its customers are willing to pay more, it is . . . [unfair/fair]
17. When a professional athlete receives a raise because a raise has been received by another league player of comparable ability, but none the other team members receive comparable raises, it is . . .
18. The fact that scarce goods tend to cost more in a free market system is . . .
19. When a company downsizes in order to reduce its costs to be more competitive with rival companies, it is . . .
20. When concessions at airports and concerts charge higher prices for beverages because they know that their customers have no alternatives, it is . . .
21. The fact that wealthier people live in bigger homes and better neighborhoods than poorer people who cannot afford to pay the same prices is . . .
22. When a company lays off higher-cost employees in the U.S. and replaces them with lower wage workers in a foreign country in order to make higher profits, it is . . .
23. The fact that housing prices in Palo Alto, California are four to six times those for comparable houses in Chicago is . . .
24. The fact that more educated employees tend to earn higher wages than less-educated employees is . . .
25. The fact that some working families can afford to hire more household help than others is . . .

Note: Items 1–15 emphasize issues of procedural or systemic fairness. Responses were given on 11-point scales ranging from −5 ("Completely Disagree") to 5 ("Completely Agree"). Items followed by "(R)" were reverse-scored prior to data coding and analyses. Items 16–25 emphasize issues of outcome fairness. Responses were given on 11-point scales ranging from −5 ("Completely Unfair") to 5 ("Completely Fair").

Table 3. Fair Market Ideology: Scale Reliabilities and Correlations with Other Variables.

	Sample 1 (n = 89)	Sample 2 (n = 100)	Sample 3 (n = 92)	Sample 4 (n = 357)	Sample 5 (n = 108)	Sample 6 (n = 115)	Sample 7 (n = 112)
Fair Market Ideology (FMI) scale							
Coefficient α	0.83	0.88	0.68	0.78	0.61	0.78	0.89
No. of items	25	25	15	15	6	6	25
Mean	2.23***	1.77***	1.09***	0.70***	−0.04	−0.65***	1.43***
SD	0.99	1.20	1.15	1.27	1.27	1.75	1.22
Correlations between FMI scores and other variables							
Conservatism	0.26*	0.40***	0.37***		0.25**	0.39***	
ESJ	0.44***	0.49***				0.36***	
Self-deception			0.24*	0.20***	0.33***		0.31***
BJW (self)			0.25*				0.38***
BJW (others)			0.18[a]				
Power distance				0.19***			
OEQ					0.29**		0.57***
RWA					0.27**		
Scandal minimization						0.36***	

Note: Significance levels (asterisks) for mean FMI scores refer to statistical differences from zero, as indicated by one-sample *t*-tests. Correlations are bivariate Pearson *r*s. Missing numbers indicate that information was not available for that sample. ESJ = Economic System Justification; BJW = Belief in a Just World; OEQ = Opposition to Equality; RWA = Right-Wing Authoritarianism.

[a] $p < 0.10$.
* $p < 0.05$.
** $p < 0.01$.
*** $p < 0.001$.

Table 3. Sample 1 was comprised of 89 weekend (part-time) MBA students (aged 28–40) from the University of Chicago. They completed the 25-item version of the FMI Scale, along with 15 items from Jost and Thompson's (2000) Economic System Justification (ESJ) Scale, omitting the 2 items that explicitly mentioned "fairness" ($\alpha = 0.69$; see items listed in Table 1), and a single-item measure of political orientation in which participants were asked to locate themselves on a scale ranging from 1 ("Extremely Liberal") to 10 ("Extremely Conservative"). The same materials were administered to Sample 2, which consisted of 100 2nd year (full-time) MBA students who were taking a negotiations course at the University of Chicago ($\alpha = 0.75$ for the ESJ Scale). Mean scores on items 1–15 (procedural/systemic fairness) were found to correlate very highly with overall scores on the 25-item scale in Sample 1 ($r = 0.86$) and Sample 2 ($r = 0.92$). The two subscales (procedural/systemic and outcome fairness) were also reasonably strongly intercorrelated for Sample 1 ($r = 0.48$) and Sample 2 ($r = 0.65$).

Sample 3 was comprised of 92 1st year (full-time) MBA students from the University of Chicago. They completed the first 15 items of the FMI Scale (i.e. the procedural/systemic subscale), as well as the single-item measure of political orientation. In addition, Sample 3 filled out items adapted from Lipkus et al.'s (1996) Belief in a Just World (BJW) Scale, which distinguishes between BJW in relation to self ($\alpha = 0.85$) and to others in general ($\alpha = 0.78$) and Paulhus' (1984) Self-Deceptive Enhancement (SDE) 20-item Scale ($\alpha = 0.64$). A subset of participants from Sample 3 ($n = 42$) also completed 9 items from the outcome fairness subscale (items 16–22 and 24–25) five weeks later. Scores on the procedural/systemic subscale at time 1 did correlate with scores on the outcome fairness subscale at time 2, $r = 0.39, p < 0.02$.

Sample 4, which included 357 1st year (full-time) MBA students from Stanford University, also completed the 15-item version of the FMI Scale. In addition, Sample 4 filled out the SDE scale ($\alpha = 0.67$) and a 6-item scale designed to measure the construct of "Power Distance," including the following items: (1) "Inequality in society should be minimized"; (2) "There should be an order of inequality in this world in which everybody has a rightful place: high and low are protected by this order"; (3) "Power holders are entitled to privileges"; (4) "Other people are a potential threat to one's power and can rarely be trusted"; (5) "The way to change a social system is to redistribute power"; and (6) "A few people should be independent; most should be dependent." It seems that our attempt to come with a highly reliable measure of power distance fared no better than the attempts made by our predecessors (e.g. Brockner et al., 2001; Hofstede, 1997). The α coefficient for this scale (0.46) was the lowest of all the scales we administered.

Sample 5 consisted of 108 Boston University undergraduate students who completed a shortened 6-item version of the FMI scale (items No. 1, 2, 6, 10, 12, and

14). These items were selected because they had correlated especially well with overall FMI scores from the 25-item scale in previous samples. In addition, participants completed a two-item measure of political orientation, the self-deception scale, all 17 items from the ESJ scale, 7 items measuring "Opposition to Equality" (OEQ) that were taken from Kluegel and Smith (1986, pp. 106–107), and 20 items from Altemeyer's (1996) "Right-Wing Authoritarianism" (RWA) Scale.

Sample 6 was comprised of 115 adults recruited for mass-testing sessions on the campus of Stanford University. Most (but not all) participants were undergraduate students. In addition to a single-item measure of political orientation, participants completed the 6-item version of the FMI scale. We also constructed and administered a questionnaire for measuring scandal minimization in relation to two core events that had been in the news at the time of the data collection: (a) alleged ethical violations and accounting irregularities at the Enron Corporation under the leadership of Kenneth Lay; and (b) the reluctance of the Bush-Cheney administration to share documents with the public concerning meetings with Enron executives and other campaign contributors. For each of these two events, participants were asked: (1) "How concerned or unconcerned are you about alleged ethical violations at Enron/the privacy maintained by the Bush-Cheney administration?" Responses were given on a scale ranging from 0 ("Not at all concerned") to 9 ("Extremely concerned") and reverse-scored prior to averaging; (2) "How fair or unfair do you think the actions of Enron officials/the Bush-Cheney administration were?" Responses were given on a scale ranging from 0 ("Extremely unfair") to 9 ("Extremely fair"); (3) "How justifiable or unjustifiable do you think the actions of Enron officials/the Bush-Cheney administration were?" Responses were given on a scale ranging from 0 ("Extremely unjustifiable") to 9 ("Extremely justifiable"). An overall index of scandal minimization was calculated for each participant by averaging across responses to the three items (unconcerned, fair, and justifiable) perceived in relation to each of the two core events ($\alpha = 0.77$).

Sample 7 was the only MBA sample tested after the long string of much publicized corporate scandals in 2001–2003. Participants were 112 full-time MBA students at the Stern School of Business at New York University. In the fall of 2003, they completed the full 25-item FMI Scale ($\alpha = 0.89$), the 7-item OEQ Scale ($\alpha = 0.80$), and the BJW Scale that enabled us to distinguish between perceptions of self ($\alpha = 0.83$) and others ($\alpha = 0.79$).

4.2. Social Psychological Predictors of Fair Market Ideology

Based on several social psychological theories, we anticipated that people (especially those pursuing business careers) would generally endorse fair market ideology by assuming that common business practices and market-driven procedures and outcomes are fair, ethical, and legitimate (Proposition 1). This expectation was supported in all four tests involving MBA samples – regardless of whether students were surveyed at the beginning, middle, or end of their graduate training programs. As can be seen in Table 3, mean FMI scores for Samples 1–4 and Sample 7 were significantly greater than zero at the $p < 0.001$ level. Despite the fact that neoclassical economic theory disavows any necessary connection between the free market as an efficient means for exchanging goods and services and procedural or distributive justice, MBA students tended to believe that market-based exchanges are inherently fair, even after the accumulation of corruption cases at Enron, Arthur Andersen, Worldcom, and others (see also Blount, 2000). This belief was not shared by either of the non-MBA samples. Mean FMI scores for Sample 5 did not differ from zero, and mean FMI scores for Sample 6 differed from zero in the negative direction: These participants endorsed an ideology in which the free market system was perceived as significantly *un*fair.[7]

In terms of non-rational social psychological predictors of the degree of endorsement of fair market ideology across people in general, we hypothesized that FMI scores would be associated with each of the following variables: belief in a just world, economic system justification, opposition to equality, power distance orientation, self-deception, political conservatism, and right-wing authoritarianism (Propositions 2(a)–(g)). Correlational results for all 7 samples are summarized in Table 3. Political conservatism predicted FMI scores in all 5 of the samples in which it was measured, with *r*s ranging from 0.25 to 0.40. Economic system justification scores predicted FMI scores in all 3 of the samples in which it was measured, with *r*s ranging from 0.36 to 0.49. Self-deception, too, predicted FMI scores in all 3 of the samples in which it was measured, with *r*s ranging from 0.20 to 0.33. Belief in a just world scores correlated with FMI scores in Samples 3 and 7, with no consistent differences obtained for personal (or self-related) versus global (or other-related) BJW. Other attitudinal predictors of FMI scores included power distance, $r(357) = 0.19$ (although this result should be interpreted with caution, given the low reliability of the power distance scale); opposition to equality, $r(108) = 0.29$ and $r(112) = 0.57$; and right-wing authoritarianism, $r(108) = 0.27$. Thus, Propositions 2(a)–(g) each received at least some empirical support.

Only one of the samples contained a sufficient number of variables in the same study to allow for an adequate comparison of the relative strengths of the various predictors, controlling for one another. A simultaneous regression was conducted on the data for Sample 5. Results indicated that the strongest unique predictors were self-deception, $\beta = 0.31$, $t(102) = 3.59$, $p < 0.001$, and economic system justification, $\beta = 0.24$, $t(102) = 2.08$, $p < 0.05$. After controlling for these variables, none of the remaining variables (conservatism, opposition to equality, or right-wing authoritarianism) retained statistical significance.

The fact that the hypothesized correlations attained statistical significance suggests that our measure of fair market ideology possesses convergent validity. That is, participants' scores on both short and long forms of our scale were indeed predicted by other variables that were theorized to be conceptually related. At the same time, none of the relations were so strong as to suggest conceptual redundancy between fair market ideology and constructs previously investigated by other researchers. Most zero-order correlations were moderate in magnitude (ranging from 0.18 to 0.57 overall).

We also predicted that people who are especially likely to endorse fair market ideology would be more likely to minimize ethical concerns in response to scandals (Proposition 3). This was investigated in the context of reactions to the Enron scandal and to alleged conflicts of interest involving the Bush/Cheney administration. As can be seen in Table 3, FMI scores in Sample 6 significantly predicted the tendency to engage in scandal minimization, $r(115) = 0.36$, $p < 0.001$. The positive association between FMI and scandal minimization was weaker in magnitude but retained significance after controlling for political conservatism, partial $r(112) = 0.23$, $p < 0.02$. These findings suggest that believing in the inherent fairness of the free market system has less to do with genuine fairness concerns than it does with defending existing institutions and authorities, including both corporate and political actors.

4.3. Ethical Inferences Derived from Profitability Information: An Experimental Study

On the assumption that fair market ideology would be relatively common and manifold in its consequences for judgment, we hypothesized that people would also be motivated to believe that profitable companies are ethical companies (Proposition 4), insofar as such a link would imply that the free market system produces not only efficient outcomes but also morally just outcomes. We conducted an experimental study to investigate this possibility, which is consistent with some formulations of just world theory, especially the notion that people would derogate losers and lionize winners (e.g. Lerner & Miller, 1978). Data concerning the alleged magnitude (large vs. small) and direction of profitability (gain vs. loss) of named and unnamed companies were presented to 343 MBA students. Ratings of the fairness and ethicality of those companies were obtained, and we looked for evidence bearing on the rationalization hypothesis that profitable (gaining) companies would be seen as more ethical than losing companies, especially when gains (vs. losses) were large in magnitude.

In order to manipulate perceived company performance, research participants were presented with data allegedly showing the 1-year and 5-year profitability of 12 different companies. Specifically, participants were given information for each company about annual growth rate in earnings per share, relative to the average growth rate of earnings per share for all companies listed in the S & P 500. Positive percentages were said to indicate that the company had outperformed the market average, and negative percentages were said to indicate that the company had underperformed the market average. Three companies on the list were presented as having posted relatively large losses (averaging −13% over the previous year and the previous 5 years), and three other companies were described as having posted relatively small losses (averaging −4% over the previous year and the previous 5 years). Three more companies were presented as having posted relatively small gains (averaging 4% over the previous year and the previous 5 years), and three others were described as having achieved relatively large gains (averaging 13% over the previous year and the previous 5 years). Companies from each of these four categories were interspersed throughout the list to avoid suspicion and to minimize experimental demand characteristics.

Because we were interested in potential differences between abstract vs. concrete judgments of ethicality in relation to profitability as well as the malleability of ethicality judgments of specific companies, we also manipulated whether companies were named or unnamed. That is, half of the participants read data and made judgments about hypothetical or unnamed companies (Company A, B, C, D, etc.), and the other half read and made judgments about actual companies (Woolworth, Gillette, Toys R Us, Caterpillar, etc.).[8] Thus, the final experimental design was a 2 (Hypothetical vs. Real Company Names) × 2 (Company Profit vs. Loss) × 2 (Large vs. Small Magnitude of Change) mixed factorial design, with the last two factors manipulated in a within-subjects fashion.

For each of the 12 companies (hypothetical or real), participants were asked for their "beliefs and perceptions about how ethical this company is in terms of general business practices, fair employee treatment, responsibility to consumers, and environmental consideration." Responses were given on 9-point scales ranging from 1 ("Not at all ethical") to 9 ("Extremely ethical"). Mean ratings of ethicality as a function of whether companies were seen as posting gains or losses and whether those gains or losses were large or small are graphed in Figs. 4 and 5 for named and unnamed companies, respectively.

A mixed model analysis of variance revealed that several main and interaction effects attained statistical significance. A huge main effect of performance indicated that, as hypothesized, companies that were believed to be profitable were judged to be more ethical ($M = 5.49$) than were companies that were believed to be losing earnings ($M = 4.93$), $F(1, 328) = 53.81, p < 0.001$. A main effect of magnitude indicated that companies with small changes from the status quo (whether losses

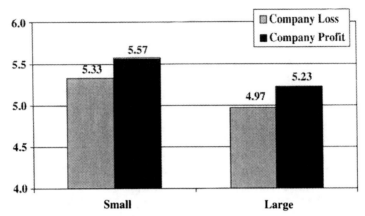

Fig. 4. Ratings of Ethicality as a Function of Company Performance (Profit vs. Loss) and Magnitude of Changes (Large vs. Small) When Actual Company Names Were Used.

or gains) were judged to be more ethical ($M = 5.34$) than were companies with larger changes from the status quo ($M = 5.08$), $F(1, 328) = 23.04, p < 0.001$.

A two-way interaction involving company performance and magnitude was observed, $F(1, 328) = 10.97, p < 0.001$. Companies posting large losses were judged to be significantly less ethical ($M = 4.72$) than companies posting smaller losses ($M = 5.13$), according to a paired samples test, $t(333) = 6.05, p < 0.001$. Companies posting large and small gains, however, were seen as equally ethical

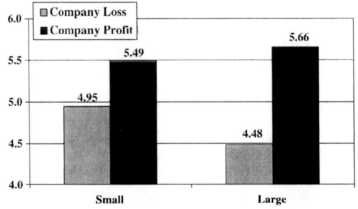

Fig. 5. Ratings of Ethicality as a Function of Company Performance (Profit vs. Loss) and Magnitude of Changes (Large vs. Small) When Hypothetical Company Names Were Used.

($Ms = 5.44$ and 5.53, respectively), $t(334) = 1.33, p = 0.19$. Thus, participants might have assumed that large losses resulted from companies' having been caught engaging in unethical behavior, but participants did not generally appear to assume that large gains were ill gotten.

An interaction involving company performance and name type was also observed, $F(1, 328) = 16.33, p < 0.001$). Companies posting losses were judged to be significantly less ethical when hypothetical names were used ($M = 4.71$) than when actual company names were used ($M = 5.13$), according to an independent samples pairwise comparison, $t(330) = 3.05, p < 0.01$. Companies posting gains, however, were seen as equally ethical whether hypothetical ($M = 5.57$) or actual company names were used ($M = 5.40$), $t(331) = 1.34, p = 0.18$.

Finally, the analysis yielded a three-way interaction involving company performance, magnitude, and name type, $F(1, 328) = 9.93, p < 0.002$). For purposes of interpretation, we conducted separate 2 (Profit vs. Loss) × 2 (Large vs. Small) repeated measures analyses of variance on ratings of actual vs. hypothetical company names. When actual company names were used, participants exhibited two main effect tendencies to rate profitable companies as more ethical than losing companies, $F(1, 171) = 12.93, p < 0.001$, and to rate companies with smaller changes from the status quo as more ethical than companies with larger changes (whether gains or losses), $F(1, 171) = 34.82, p < 0.001$ (see means in Fig. 4). No interaction between performance and magnitude was observed. When hypothetical company names were used, however, the analysis yielded a main effect tendency to again rate profitable companies as more ethical than losing companies, $F(1, 157) = 38.51, p < 0.001$, as well as a two-way interaction effect indicating that this tendency was more pronounced when the magnitude of profits and losses was large rather than small, $F(1, 157) = 14.66, p < 0.001$ (see means in Fig. 5).

For both abstract ratings of unnamed companies and specific ratings of named companies, therefore, we found evidence that people tended to rate companies as more ethical when they were perceived as gaining earnings per share than when they were perceived as losing earnings per share. This supports the rationalization hypothesis that people would seek to legitimize market-based outcomes by drawing (unwarranted) ethical inferences about corporations on the basis of their profitability information (Proposition 4). These inferences were more pronounced when gains and losses were larger rather than smaller, but only when hypothetical company names were used. When actual company names were used, we also found that people judged companies with smaller deviations from the status quo to be more ethical than companies with larger deviations from the status quo (in either direction). This finding is consistent with the notion (expressed also in Proposition 1) that, as part and parcel of fair market ideology, people tend to believe that common business practices and outcomes are more fair, ethical, and legitimate than are uncommon business practices and outcomes. Having demonstrated reasonably consistent support for various manifestations of fair market ideology among different samples in the U.S., we turned our attention in the final study to an investigation of attitudes toward the free market in Hungary.

4.4. Free Market Ideology in Hungary as a Function of Self-Deception and System Threat

For much of the second half of the 20th century, most Central and Eastern European countries operated under centralized state planning systems associated with socialist and/or communist governments. Hungary, like neighboring countries such as Poland and the Czech Republic, experienced a relatively abrupt transition from socialism to capitalism beginning around 1989, providing a useful context for investigating the social psychological shift of allegiances from one system to another (e.g. Csepeli, Örkény & Székelyi, 2000; Hunyady, 1998; Stark, 1996). Because today's Hungarian adults (especially older adults) have lived under two very different social and political systems, they have been exposed to ideological justifications for communism and capitalism. We were intrigued by the opportunity to expand our research agenda by examining the cognitive-motivational bases of Hungarians' attitudes toward the free-market economic system.

Because of their relatively recent history, we expected that it would be possible to alter Hungarian respondents' degree of support for the current economic system by inducing threats either to the legitimacy of the current status quo or to the relatively recent system that preceded it. Specifically, we had proposed that people would show increased support for the free market system following a threat to that system, especially to the extent that they are relatively high in self-deception (Proposition 5).

To assess this hypothesis, we conducted an experimental study in which participants were exposed either to a threat to the socialist system or a threat to the free market system or to a control condition with no system threat. In addition, we measured participants' levels of self-deception. Research participants were 242 adult students (108 men, 134 women, ranging in age from 18–30) majoring in law, engineering, medicine, sciences, forestry, or the humanities who were interviewed confidentially in the cities of Budapest ($n = 121$) or Szeged ($n = 121$) in early 2001. Trained interviewers read the questions aloud and recorded participants' responses.

Embedded in the context of the survey was an experimental manipulation of system threat. In one condition, participants ($n = 82$) were exposed to a brief passage that posed an ideological threat directed at the former socialist system. More specifically, they read a Hungarian translation of the following statement:

> Many people believe that the socialism of the Kádár era (prior to the reforms of 1989) was immoral and dishonest, and they cannot understand why anyone would ever support it. Specifically, *some people believe that the lack of freedom and opportunity under socialism cannot be defended or justified in any way.*

In a second condition, participants ($n = 80$) were exposed to a threat directed at the newer free market system. This passage was as follows:

> Many people believe that the market economy of today (following the reforms of 1989) is immoral and corrupt, and they cannot understand why anyone would ever support it. Specifically, *some people believe that the lack of equality and justice under a free market system cannot be defended or justified in any way.*

As part of the cover story used in both experimental conditions, participants were given the opportunity to provide a few reactions to these statements. A control condition was also included in which participants ($n = 80$) were not presented with any system-threatening message. Following the experimental manipulation of system threat, participants' degree of ideological support for the free market system was measured using an 8-item scale; items are listed in Table 4 ($\alpha = 0.66$). We also administered a Hungarian translation of Paulhus' (1984) 20-item Self-Deceptive Enhancement (SDE) Scale, so that we could compare the responses to system threat of people who scored high vs. low in self-deception.[9]

Table 4. Items from the Free Market Ideology Scale Used in Hungarian Research.

1. There is greater social and political freedom to express ideas under the era of this free market economy
2. A socialist system guarantees an acceptable living standard by providing economic security to its citizens (R)
3. There is a greater danger of corruption and exploitation in a market economy (R)
4. There is less freedom because of the strong ideological and political pressures exerted by a socialist system
5. A market economy leads to increased poverty and a lack of social security for its citizens (R)
6. Socialism leads to a lowered personal ambition and a lack of work motivation
7. The economic opportunities under a free-market system are superior to those under other types of systems
8. Under socialism, it is possible for more people from the lower classes to gain respect and social mobility through talent and education (R)

Note: Interview respondents completed a Hungarian translation of this scale, indicating their strength of agreement or disagreement on a scale ranging from 1 ("Strongly Disagree") to 15 ("Strongly Agree"). Items followed by "(R)" were reverse-scored prior to data coding and analyses. Thus, higher mean scores indicate stronger support for free market ideology.

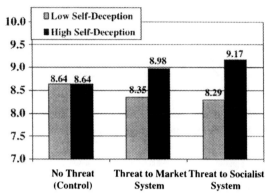

Fig. 6.   Support for Free Market Ideology in Hungary as a Function of System Threat and
Self-Deception.

A regression analysis was conducted to assess the effects of system threat (a
categorical variable) and self-deception (as a continuous variable) on support for
the free market system. For ease of illustration and interpretation, we have graphed
means in Fig. 6 as a function of experimental condition and whether participants
were high or low in self-deception on the basis of a median split, but the continuous
variable was used for significance-testing. The analysis yielded a main effect of
self-deception, $\beta = 0.66$, $t(238) = 3.99$, $p < 0.001$, indicating that people who
scored higher on SDE were more likely to express support for the capitalist status
quo (and to reject the former socialist system) than were participants who scored
lower on SDE; the marginal means for this comparison, based on a median split,
were 8.43 and 8.93, respectively. There was also a two-way interaction between
self-deception and system threat condition, $\beta = -0.47$, $t(238) = 2.86$, $p < 0.005$.
As can be seen in Fig. 6, both types of system threat led high SDE (but not low SDE)
participants to show enhanced support for the free market system, relative to the
control condition. Results therefore supported Proposition 5. People who scored
higher in self-deception defended the status quo from attack by countering the
threat to the free market system, but they showed assimilation (rather than contrast)
to the anti-socialist message, expressing increased support for the free market
system in this condition as well. It is at least conceivable that older generations of
Hungarians (many of whom were supporters of the socialist system) might have
responded differently.

These findings again suggest that a broader conceptualization of self-deception
and rationalization is needed to understand cases that go beyond mere self-
enhancement, as suggested also by Kay et al. (2002). Self-deception seems
to be more closely related to the ideological defense of the status quo and to
the holding of specific political and economic attitudes than previous research

on self-deception would have predicted (e.g. Paulhus, 1984; Taylor & Brown, 1988). In addition, our findings suggest that there is a motivational (or "hot") component to "cold" beliefs concerning the appropriateness and justness of existing economic institutions. Endorsement of free market ideology in Hungary (as well as in the United States) has a non-rational component that is empirically linked to defensive motivational responses. At this point, however, it is difficult to say whether self-deception and system threat predict support for the free market system in particular or support for the status quo in general (i.e. either a centralized or market economy). Future research in countries with active socialist systems is needed to distinguish between these two possibilities (see also Jost et al., 2003a, b).

5. IMPLICATIONS FOR ORGANIZATIONAL DECISION-MAKING AND BEHAVIOR

Although economists would not claim that markets are inherently fair, just, or morally legitimate, we have found substantial evidence that ordinary actors, especially those who are seeking careers in business, do see fairness as a property of the free market system. We have summarized research from a wide range of sources demonstrating that people living under market economies tend to believe that market-based processes and outcomes are inherently fair and just. Our survey and experimental studies address the prevalence of fair market ideology as well as its cognitive-motivational basis. People who are especially prone to endorse fair market ideology are also more likely to believe in a just world, engage in self-deception, accept power distance, endorse economic system justification, oppose equality, and to be politically conservative and even authoritarian. We have also shown that business school students (before and after the recent rash of corporate scandals) judged profitable companies to be more ethical than unprofitable companies, presumably because of the system-justifying assumption that the market rewards ethical behavior and punishes unethical behavior. In the context of a transitional economic system in Hungary, we have also demonstrated in an experimental study that ideological support for the free market is increased when self-deception is high and the legitimacy of the system is threatened.

We turn now to a consideration of the implications of these findings for work organizations. An implicit but important distinction that we make is between market or market-based mechanisms of individual and corporate decision-making, resource allocation, etc. on one hand and the *moral* attributes that people frequently associate with these mechanisms on the other. From a purely economic point of view, it is a fallacy to believe that market mechanisms are themselves imbued with fairness or morality, simply because they operate in the context of market exchange

(Blount, 1995, 2000). In the remainder of this chapter, we consider, somewhat spec-
ulatively, three potentially deleterious organizational consequences of adhering to
fair market ideology. Specifically, we address the possibilities that endorsement
of fair market ideology will exacerbate tendencies to: (a) encourage competitive,
self-interested behavior while hindering the operation and development of
alternative ideological schemes, including those that emphasize cooperation and
investment in the public interest; (b) justify market-based decision logics even
when there are problems, errors, or shortcomings associated with the application of
such logics; and (c) assume that market-driven outcomes are necessarily positive
and attribute poor outcomes to individual managers rather than to environmental
or systemic factors, thereby delaying the implementation of structural changes to
the status quo.

5.1. Fair Market Ideology Encourages Competitive Self-Interest and Discourages Cooperation and Public Investment

The belief that free markets are inherently fair is widely held in the Western
world and has been making incursions into other regions, as our Hungarian study
demonstrates. Market-based systems now enjoy the kind of taken-for-granted
legitimacy that is described by institutional theories of cultural persistence (e.g.
Zucker, 1977). As a result of the increasing dominance of fair market ideology,
other ways of reasoning, other logical schemes, and other values are unlikely
to be seriously considered, even if they would be preferable on moral grounds
(e.g. Sen, 1985). The debate over health care in the United States provides a
vivid illustration. The prevailing assumption is that health care needs will be met
through market mechanisms, as employers choose to offer health insurance in
order to recruit and retain their personnel. Skeptics note that market mechanisms
in the absence of governmental intervention have thus far contributed to the rising
numbers of uninsured people, even among those who are employed. The current
Bush administration is seeking to change Medicare and prescription drug benefit
plans to make them more responsive to market forces, which may well result in
substantially higher cost burdens faced by the elderly and other groups that are in
need of regular medication. Conspicuously absent from this debate are alternative
ideas about public commitment to providing health care for all citizens and the
fairness and necessity of need-based allocation systems, in large part because fair
market ideology dominates public policy discussions.

These trends are consistent with the observations made by a number of
prominent scholars over the past 20 years that neoclassical economics, with its
assumption of universal self-interest, encourages and legitimates competitive,

self-interested behavior and discourages other conceptions of moral obligation (e.g. Etzioni, 1988a; Frank, 1988; Frank & Cook, 1995; Fukuyama, 1995). Psychological evidence indicates that the framing of a situation does have dramatic effects on the degree to which competitive versus cooperative behavior is elicited (e.g. Allison, Beggan & Midgley, 1996; Larrick & Blount, 1997). Even more specifically, studies of resource dilemmas show that market and business frames cue more selfish behavior than do other decision frames (Blount White, 1994; Pillutla & Chen, 1999; Tenbrunsel & Messick, 1999). Fair market ideology provides a powerful rationale for acting in a competitive, self-interested manner and for eschewing cooperative behavior and investment in public resources. Selfishness, according to the ideology, is not only rational; because it conforms to the underlying assumptions of a market-based system, it is actually fair!

5.2. Fair Market Ideology Justifies Over-Reliance on Market-Based Decision Logics

March (1995) argued that managers and other decision-makers approach complex decisions by asking: "What kind of situation is this? What are the appropriate rules to apply?" Answers to these questions, which depend upon contextual features present in the situation, prescribe a set of rules for how each kind of decision "should" be handled (see also Messick, 1999; Pillutla & Chen, 1999). In business settings, it is reasonable to assume that situational cues will often trigger a market context (Tenbrunsel & Messick, 1999), especially among people who are likely to idealize the market system and to embrace fair market ideology. Modal responses are likely to include: "Let the market decide – it knows best!" and "We're willing to pay market value." These ways of framing the decision imply that the value of a service, product, or a person can be captured perfectly (and fairly) through the process of market-based exchange. Of course, this is not always the case, and market reactions are often seriously flawed.

To take one example, companies' stock prices often rise after the announcement of layoffs and other restructuring moves, but there is little or no evidence that layoffs help companies' performance in the long run and there is substantial evidence that layoffs can adversely affect companies, particularly when they are handled without special attention to issues of substantive fairness (e.g. Folger & Skarlicki, 2001). Similarly, stock prices typically drop when a company's workers are successfully unionized, and they rise when a company decertifies collective bargaining organizations, but the evidence suggests that unionization is unrelated to profitability and other measures of economic performance (e.g. Freeman & Medoff, 1984). And because of time and energy constraints, it is often difficult to obtain an accurate picture of market price ranges, especially in labor markets. The belief that a true (and fair) market price exists may lead people to engage in satisficing (rather than optimizing) strategies and to overweight a single reference price as representative of market conditions (Babcock, Wang & Loewenstein, 1996; Blount, Thomas-Hunt & Neale, 1996). Adopting an ideology in which the market is idealized can cause managers to misapply market-based decision logics and to feel justified using faulty approximations of "market value," often using these approximations as standards of fairness, which they certainly are not.

5.3. Fair Market Ideology Exacerbates Attributional Errors and Leads to System Undercorrection

To the extent that fair market ideology is both a cause and a consequence of unrealistic optimism and a general tendency to idealize the free market system, people who embrace it are likely to hold highly favorable economic expectations (e.g. GDP will grow, stock prices will increase, and we will all get wealthier), and they are not likely to anticipate market-based losses. When such losses inevitably do occur, they will evoke strong negative reactions, particularly among adherents to fair market ideology, and they will lead to attributions of blame and perhaps even suspicions of individual (not systemic) impropriety. Ideological factors might therefore exacerbate common attributional biases in organizations, including the tendency to blame managers – rather than underlying market dynamics – for poor corporate performance, and the tendency to praise managers for strong performance (Heath, Larrick & Klayman, 1998). Attributional biases in favor of individual rather than systemic causes could result in disproportionately large (and therefore unfair) punishments such as job loss when results fall below expectations as well as extravagantly large bonuses and other disproportionate individual rewards when results exceed expectations.

Faith in the inherent justice of market forces and the tendency to blame individuals for bad news could also lead people to deny the existence of corruption in the system and to avoid taking corrective action. In commenting on the public's apparent willingness to overlook relatively strong evidence of business scandals in recent years, including market manipulation in the California energy industry, Krugman (2002) marveled at the degree to which the system has managed to escape blame: "Maybe our national faith in free markets is so strong that people just don't want to talk about a case in which markets went spectacularly bad. But I'm still puzzled by the lack of attention, not just to the disaster, but to hints of a cover-up. After all, this was the most spectacular abuse of market power since the days of the robber barons – and the feds did nothing to stop it." Shiller (2000), too, has suggested that public faith in the goodness of corporations and business people may be excessive and may contribute to "irrational exuberance" in the economic domain. Fair market ideology might therefore lead people to minimize systemic problems and to delay the necessary implementation of structural changes to the status quo.

6. CONCLUDING REMARKS

To the limited extent that fairness considerations have entered into theories of economics, the role of fairness has been conceptualized mainly as a "constraint on profit-seeking" (Kahneman, Knetsch & Thaler, 1986). It has been used to explain, for example, why employers typically fail to cut wages during periods of high unemployment and why suppliers rarely take full advantage of their monopolistic power in pricing popular entertainment and sporting events (e.g. Akerlof, 1970; Okun, 1981; Solow, 1980). Economic actors, from this perspective, frequently eschew potentially lucrative opportunities in order to avoid the perception that they are acting unfairly. The point vividly made by Kahneman et al.'s (1986) now infamous "snow shovel problem" is that customers (and other constituencies) are highly sensitive to perceived injustice, and their sensitivity inhibits the operation of market forces (see also Bazerman & Neale, 1995; Bies, Tripp & Neale, 1993; Loewenstein, Thompson & Bazerman, 1989; Rabin, 1993).

Much as the expression of doubt can emerge only in a larger context of belief, our view is that specific complaints about injustice occur in relation to a background in which most aspects of market exchange are perceived as fair and legitimate. By calling attention to perceptions of unfairness in economic exchange (the figure), previous researchers have implicitly moved us closer to appreciating how much is taken for granted as fair (the ground). In this chapter, we have focused our attention on cognitive-motivational bases of the tendency to assume that the free market system yields inherently fair outcomes. Our goal, it should now be clear, is not to contradict the notion that people are concerned about potential unfairness, but rather to initiate a figure-ground reversal in addressing issues of fairness in relation to market mechanisms.

Focusing on the extent to which the economic system enjoys relatively widespread legitimacy enables an even greater appreciation of the power of the status quo to affect fairness judgments.[10] Most theoretical explanations for status quo biases have stressed purely cognitive factors, as suggested by Kahneman and Tversky's (1979) prospect theory. Etzioni (1988b) has observed critically that "these approaches do not deal with the intrusion of emotions and values into inferences and decision-making; indeed they explicitly reject these factors"

(p. 168). Future studies are needed to clarify the role (if any) of emotions and values in specific cases of anchoring on the status quo. Our research program has addressed the question of what leads people to support the status quo in a much broader, institutional sense. Results thus far suggest that belief in the fairness of existing economic markets and market mechanisms is indeed linked to self-deception, political ideology, and other defensive motivational responses.

NOTES

1. There is another, more basic sense in which managerial action is routinely ideological. As Pfeffer (1981) argued: "it is the task of management to provide explanations, rationalization, and legitimation for the activities undertaken in the organization" (p. 4). On this view, managers develop explicit system-justifying ideologies to appease workers, customers, and other important stakeholders and to maintain organizational legitimacy.
2. Classic economic theory dictates that when impediments to free trade are removed, the system of market exchange is highly efficient and aids in the creation of wealth. Despite these advantages, economists are usually careful not to claim that there is anything inherently fair, just, or morally legitimate about market procedures and outcomes. In fact, it is rare for economists to even address the "moral standing of the market," as Sen (1985) put it. When buyers and sellers converge on a market-clearing price that is driven by their individual preferences, wealth creation may be maximized, but fairness simply does not enter into the evaluation.
3. It is conceivable that recent business scandals involving Enron, Arthur Andersen, Worldcom, and others may have (at least temporarily) caused an increase in generalized perceptions of the fairness of the economic system, although these events seem not to have had much effect on other indicators of economic optimism and consumer confidence (see Investor's Business Daily/Christian Science Monitor Poll, 2003).
4. An unresolved theoretical issue is whether the belief in a just world is motivated by a deep-seated, genuine commitment to the cause of justice (Dalbert, 2001), or whether it is better conceptualized as a defensive form of justification on behalf of the system (Jost & Hunyady, 2002). The fact that scores on the belief in a just world scale correlate negatively (rather than positively) with political involvement, social activism, and support for affirmative action seems more consistent with the latter interpretation than the former (e.g. Nosworthy, Lea & Lindsay, 1995; Rubin & Peplau, 1973). Our investigation of scandal minimization also addresses this general issue in relation to fair market ideology.
5. Dalbert (2001) has also interpreted the belief in a just world as a positive illusion, further tightening theoretical connections among constructs of self-deception and justice perceptions.
6. We also considered the possibility that this tendency would be particularly pronounced for people pursuing business careers.
7. The expression of "unfair market ideology" is interesting in its own right and reminds one of the *New Yorker* cartoon in which one worker says to another, "There it is again – the invisible hand of the marketplace giving me the finger!"

8. To minimize the direct influence of specific company reputations on ethicality judgments, the same company names were presented to some participants as profitable and to other participants as losing earnings. We collapsed across this counterbalancing order prior to conducting statistical analyses.

9. No reliable effects of experimental condition were obtained on SDE scores.

10. In research described in this chapter, we have shown that small changes (and no changes) away from a neutrally defined reference point (i.e. the status quo) are judged to be fairer than larger changes (see also Azzi & Jost, 1997). Ariely, Loewenstein and Prelec (2003) have similarly demonstrated that in the absence of objective informational standards, people are willing to pay higher prices (and accept stiffer penalties) to the extent that these outcomes are consistent with previously established anchors – even when those anchors were established arbitrarily.

ACKNOWLEDGMENTS

This work was funded in part by the Radcliffe Institute for Advanced Study at Harvard University, the Graduate School of Business at Stanford University, the Graduate School of Business at the University of Chicago, and the Stern School of Business at New York University. We thank Deborah Gruenfeld, Peter Henry, Orsolya Hunyady, Rick Larrick, George Loewenstein, and Michael Morris for helpful advice concerning the planning and implementation of empirical research described here. We are also grateful to Agnish Chakravarti, Kathie Koo, Tibor Palfai, Oliver Sheldon, and Jojanneke van der Toorn for assistance at various stages with data collection, entry, or analysis. Finally, we credit Rod Kramer and Barry Staw with improving the chapter by providing characteristically insightful and constructive feedback.

REFERENCES

Adorno, T. W., Frenkel-Brunswik, E., Levinson, D. J., & Sanford, R. N. (1950). *The authoritarian personality*. New York: Harper.

Akerlof, G. (1970). The market for lemons: Qualitative uncertainty and the market mechanism. *Quarterly Journal of Economics, 84*, 488–500.

Allison, S. T., Beggan, J. K., & Midgley, E. H. (1996). The quest for 'similar instances' and 'simultaneous possibilities': Metaphors in social dilemmas research. *Journal of Personality and Social Psychology, 71*, 479–497.

Altemeyer, R. A. (1996). *The authoritarian specter*. Cambridge, MA: Harvard University Press.

Ariely, D., Loewenstein, G., & Prelec, D. (2003). Coherent arbitrariness: Stable demand curves without stable preferences. *Quarterly Journal of Economics, 118*, forthcoming.

Azzi, A. E., & Jost, J. T. (1997). Votes without power: Procedural justice as mutual control in majority-minority relations. *Journal of Applied Social Psychology, 27*, 124–155.

Babcock, L., Wang, X., & Loewenstein, G. (1996). Choosing the wrong pond: Social comparisons that reflect a self-serving bias. *Quarterly Journal of Economics, 111*, 1–19.

Baron, J. N., & Pfeffer, J. (1994). The social psychology of organizations and inequality. *Social Psychology Quarterly, 57*, 190–209.

Bazerman, M. H., & Neale, M. A. (1995) The role of fairness considerations and relationships in a judgment perspective of negotiation. In: K. Arrow, R. Mnookin, L. Ross, A. Tversky & R. Wilson (Eds), *Barriers to Conflict Resolution*. New York: Norton.

Bies, R. J., Tripp, T. M., & Neale, M. A. (1993). Procedural fairness and profit seeking: The perceived legitimacy of market exploitation. *Journal of Behavioral Decision Making, 6*, 243–256.

Blinder, A. (1987). *Hard heads, soft hearts: Tough-minded economics for a just society*. Reading, MA: Addison-Wesley.

Blount, S. (1995). When social outcomes aren't fair: The effect of causal attributions on preferences. *Organizational Behavioral and Human Decision Processes, 63*, 131–144.

Blount, S. (2000). Whoever said that markets were fair? *Negotiation Journal, 16*, 237–252.

Blount, S., Thomas-Hunt, M. C., & Neale, M. A. (1996). The price is right – Or is it? A reference point model of two-party price negotiations. *Organizational Behavioral and Human Decision Processes, 68*, 1–12.

Brehm, S., & Brehm, J. W. (1981). *Psychological reactance: A theory of freedom and control*. New York: Academic Press.

Brockner, J., Ackerman, G., Greenberg, J., Gelfand, M. J., Francesco, A. M., Chen, Z. X., Leung, K., Bierbrauer, G., Gomez, C., Kirkman, B. L., & Shapiro, D. (2001). Culture and procedural justice: The influence of power distance on reactions to voice. *Journal of Experimental Social Psychology, 37*, 300–315.

Candiotti, S. (1998, October 20th). Americans see growing economic gap. Retrieved on 3/10/2003 from http://www.cnn.com/US/9810/20/economic.gap/

Cassidy, J. (1999, September 13th). Wall Street follies: A new study shows America's fat cats getting fatter. *The New Yorker, 32*.

Crystal, G. (1991). *In search of excess*. New York: Norton.

Crystal, G. (2002, December 2nd). Executive excess. Retrieved on 8/4/2003 from http://www.pbs.org/newshour/bb/business/july-dec02/ceo1_12-02.html

Csepeli, G., Örkény, A., & Székelyi, M. (2000). *Grappling with national identity: How nations see each other in Central Europe*. Budapest: Akadémiai Kiadó.

Dalbert, C. (2001). *The justice motive as a personal resource: Dealing with challenges and critical life events*. New York: Plenum Press.

Etzioni, A. (1988a). *The moral dimension: Toward a new economics*. New York: Free Press.

Etzioni, A. (1988b). Toward a new paradigm. In: P. J. Albanese (Ed.), *Psychological Foundations of Economic Behavior* (pp. 165–172). New York: Praeger.

Folger, R., & Skarlicki, D. P. (2001). Fairness as a dependent variable: Why tough times can lead to bad management. In: R. Cropanzano (Ed.), *Justice in the Workplace: From Theory to Practice* (pp. 97–118). Mahwah, NJ: Erlbaum.

Fong, C. (2001). Social preferences, self-interest, and the demand for redistribution. *Journal of Public Economics, 82*, 225–246.

Frank, R. H. (1988). *Passions within reason*. New York: Norton.

Frank, R. H., & Cook, P. J. (1995). *The winner-take-all society: Why the few at the top get so much more than the rest of us*. New York: Penguin Books.

Freeman, R. B., & Medoff, J. L. (1984). *What do unions do?* New York: Basic Books.

Friedman, M., & Friedman, R. (1980). *Free to choose: A personal statement*. Harmondsworth: Penguin Books.

Fukuyama, F. (1995). *Trust: The social virtue and the creation of prosperity*. New York: Free Press.

Furnham, A., & Procter, E. (1989). Belief in a just world: Review and critique of the individual difference literature. *British Journal of Social Psychology, 28*, 365–384.

Gilens, M. (1999). *Why Americans hate welfare: Race, media, and the politics of antipoverty policy*. Chicago, IL: University of Chicago Press.

Glazer, N. (2002, February 11th). *Why Americans don't care about income inequality*. Paper presented at the John F. Kennedy School of Government, Harvard University.

Gurr, T. R. (1970). *Why men rebel*. Princeton, NJ: Princeton University Press.

Hafer, C. L. (2000). Do innocent victims threaten the belief in a just world? Evidence from a modified Stroop task. *Journal of Personality and Social Psychology, 79*, 165–173.

Haines, E. L., & Jost, J. T. (2000). Placating the powerless: Effects of legitimate and illegitimate explanation on affect, memory, and stereotyping. *Social Justice Research, 13*, 219–236.

Hannan, M. T., & Carroll, G. (1992). *Dynamics of organizational populations: Density, legitimation, and competition*. Oxford: Oxford University Press.

Heath, C., Larrick, R. P., & Klayman, J. (1998). Cognitive repairs: How organizational practices can compensate for individual shortcomings. In: B. Staw et al. (Eds), *Research in Organizational Behavior* (Vol. 20). Greenwich, CT: JAI Press.

Hochschild, J. L. (1981). *What's fair? American beliefs about distributive justice*. Cambridge, MA: Harvard University Press.

Hofstede, G. H. (1997). *Cultures and organizations: Software of the mind*. New York: McGraw-Hill.

Huntington, S. (1957). Conservatism as an ideology. *American Political Science Review, 51*, 454–473.

Hunyady, G. (1998). *Stereotypes during the decline and fall of communism*. New York: Routledge.

Investor's Business Daily/Christian Science Monitor Poll (2003, July 7th-12th). Retrieved on 8/4/2003 from http://www.pollingreport.com/consumer.htm

Jost, J. T. (1995). Negative illusions: Conceptual clarification and psychological evidence concerning false consciousness. *Political Psychology, 16*, 397–424.

Jost, J. T., & Banaji, M. R. (1994). The role of stereotyping in system-justification and the production of false consciousness. *British Journal of Social Psychology, 33*, 1–27.

Jost, J. T., Banaji, M. R., & Nosek, B. A. (2004). A decade of system justification theory: Accumulated evidence of conscious and unconscious bolstering of the status quo. *Political Psychology*, forthcoming.

Jost, J. T., & Burgess, D. (2000). Attitudinal ambivalence and the conflict between group and system justification motives in low status groups. *Personality and Social Psychology Bulletin, 26*, 293–305.

Jost, J. T., Glaser, J., Kruglanski, A. W., & Sulloway, F. (2003a). Political conservatism as motivated social cognition. *Psychological Bulletin, 129*, 339–375.

Jost, J. T., Glaser, J., Kruglanski, A. W., & Sulloway, F. (2003b). Exceptions that prove the rule – Using a theory of motivated social cognition to account for ideological incongruities and political anomalies: Reply to Greenberg and Jonas (2003). *Psychological Bulletin, 129*, 383–393.

Jost, J. T., & Hunyady, O. (2002). The psychology of system justification and the palliative function of ideology. *European Review of Social Psychology, 13*, 111–153.

Jost, J. T., & Major, B. (Eds) (2001). *The psychology of legitimacy: Emerging perspectives on ideology, justice, and intergroup relations*. New York: Cambridge University Press.

Jost, J. T., Pelham, B. W., & Carvallo, M. (2002). Non-conscious forms of system justification: Cognitive, affective, and behavioral preferences for higher status groups. *Journal of Experimental Social Psychology, 38*, 586–602.

Jost, J. T., Pelham, B. W., Sheldon, O., & Sullivan, B. N. (2003c). Social inequality and the reduction of ideological dissonance on behalf of the system: Evidence of enhanced system justification among the disadvantaged. *European Journal of Social Psychology, 33*, 13–36.

Jost, J. T., & Thompson, E. P. (2000). Group-based dominance and opposition to equality as independent predictors of self-esteem, ethnocentrism, and social policy attitudes among African Americans and European Americans. *Journal of Experimental Social Psychology, 36*, 209–232.

Kahneman, D., Knetsch, J. L., & Thaler, R. H. (1986). Fairness as a constraint on profit seeking: Entitlement in the market. *American Economic Review, 76*, 728–741.

Kahneman, D., & Tversky, A. (1979). Prospect theory: An analysis of decision under risk. *Econometrica, 47*, 263–291.

Katona, G. (1951). *Psychological analysis of economic behavior*. New York: McGraw-Hill.

Kay, A., Jimenez, M. C., & Jost, J. T. (2002). Sour grapes, sweet lemons, and the anticipatory rationalization of the status quo. *Personality and Social Psychology Bulletin, 28*, 1300–1312.

Kay, A. C., & Jost, J. T. (2003). Complementary justice: Effects of poor but happy and poor but honest stereotype exemplars on system justification and implicit activation of the justice motive. *Journal of Personality and Social Psychology*, forthcoming.

Kerlinger, F. M. (1984). *Liberalism and conservatism: The nature and structure of social attitudes*. Hillsdale, NJ: Erlbaum.

Kluegel, J. R., & Smith, E. R. (1986). *Beliefs about inequality: Americans' view of what is and what ought to be*. Hawthorne, NJ: Aldine de Gruyter.

Kramer, R. M. (2001). Identity and trust in organizations: One anatomy of a productive but problematic relationship. In: M. A. Hogg & D. J. Terry (Eds), *Social Identity Processes in Organizational Contexts* (pp. 167–180). New York: Psychology Press.

Krugman, P. (2002, September 27th). In broad daylight. *New York Times* (electronic version).

Lane, R. E. (1959/2003). The fear of equality. Reproduced In: J. T. Jost & J. Sidanius (Eds), *Political Psychology: Key Readings*. New York: Psychology Press/Taylor & Francis. (Original work published 1959).

Langer, E. J. (1975). The illusion of control. *Journal of Personality and Social Psychology, 32*, 311–328.

Larrick, R. P., & Blount, S. (1997). The claiming effect: Why players are more generous in social dilemmas than in ultimatum games. *Journal of Personality and Social Psychology, 72*, 810–825.

Lerner, M. J. (1980). *The belief in a just world: A fundamental delusion*. New York: Plenum.

Lerner, M. J., & Miller, D. T. (1978). Just world research and the attribution process: Looking back and ahead. *Psychological Bulletin, 85*, 1030–1051.

Lind, E. A., & van den Bos, K. (2002). When fairness works: Toward a general theory of uncertainty management. *Research in Organizational Behavior, 24*, 181–223.

Lind, E. A., & Tyler, T. R. (1988). *The social psychology of procedural justice*. New York: Plenum Press.

Lipkus, I. M., Dalbert, C., & Siegler, I. C. (1996). The importance of distinguishing the belief in a just world for self versus for others: Implications for psychological well-being. *Personality and Social Psychology Bulletin, 22*, 666–677.

Loewenstein, G. F., Thompson, L., & Bazerman, M. H. (1989). Social utility and decision making in interpersonal contexts. *Journal of Personality and Social Psychology, 57*, 426–441.

Ludwig, J. (1999). Economic status: Americans assess opportunity, fairness, and responsibility. Retrieved on 5/1/2003 from http://www.globalpolicy.org/socecon/inequal/poll-usa.htm

Major, B. (1994). From social inequality to personal entitlement: The role of social comparisons, legitimacy appraisals, and group memberships. *Advances in Experimental Social Psychology, 26*, 293–355.

March, J. G. (1995). *A primer on decision making.* New York: Free Press.

Marshall, R. (Ed.) (2000). *Back to shared prosperity: The growing inequality of wealth and income in America.* London: M. E. Sharpe.

Messick, D. M. (1999). Alternative logics for decision making in social settings. *Journal of Economic Behavior and Organizations, 39*, 11–28.

Meyer, J. W., & Rowan, B. (1977). Institutionalized organizations: Formal structure as myth and ceremony. *American Journal of Sociology, 83*, 340–363.

Miller, D. T., & Porter, C. A. (1983). Self-blame in victims of violence. *Journal of Social Issues, 39*, 139–152.

Muller, J. Z. (2001). Conservatism: Historical aspects. In: N. J. Smelser & P. Baltes (Eds), *International Encyclopedia of the Social and Behavioral Sciences* (pp. 2624–2628). Amsterdam: Elsevier.

Nosworthy, G. J., Lea, J. A., & Lindsay, R. C. L. (1995). Opposition to affirmative action: Racial affect and traditional value predictors across four programs. *Journal of Applied Social Psychology, 25*, 314–337.

Okun, A. (1981). *Prices and quantities: A macroeconomic analysis.* Washington, DC: Brookings Institute.

Ollman, B. (1998). Market mystification in capitalist and market socialist societies. In: B. Ollman (Ed.), *Market Socialism: The Debate Among Socialists* (pp. 81–121). New York: Routledge.

Olson, J. M., & Hafer, C. (2001). Tolerance of personal deprivation. In: J. T. Jost & B. Major (Eds), *The Psychology of Legitimacy: Emerging Perspectives on Ideology, Justice, and Intergroup Relations* (pp. 157–175). New York: Cambridge University Press.

Operario, D., & Fiske, S. T. (2001). Causes and consequences of stereotypes in organizations. In: M. London (Ed.), *How People Evaluate Others in Organizations* (pp. 45–62). Mahwah, NJ: Erlbaum.

Paulhus, D. L. (1984). Two-component models of socially desirable responding. *Journal of Personality and Social Psychology, 46*, 598–609.

Pettigrew, T. F. (1967). Social evaluation theory: Convergences and applications. In: D. Levine (Ed.), *Nebraska Symposium on Motivation* (Vol. 15, pp. 241–311). Lincoln: University of Nebraska Press.

Pfeffer, J. (1981). Management as symbolic action: The creation and maintenance of organizational paradigms. *Research in Organizational Behavior, 3*, 1–52.

Pillutla, M. M., & Chen, X. (1999). Social norms and cooperation in social dilemmas: The effects of context and feedback. *Organizational Behavior and Human Decision Processes, 78*(2), 81–103.

Pratto, F., Sidanius, J., Stallworth, L. M., & Malle, B. F. (1994). Social dominance orientation: A personality variable predicting social and political attitudes. *Journal of Personality and Social Psychology, 67*, 741–763.

Pyszczynski, T., Greenberg, J., & Solomon, S. (1997). Why do we need what we need? A terror management perspective on the roots of human social motivation. *Psychological Inquiry, 8*, 1–20.

Rabin, M. (1993). Incorporating fairness into game theory and economics. *American Economic Review, 83*, 1281–1302.

Rasinski, K. (1987). What's fair is fair – or is it? Value differences underlying public views about social justice. *Journal of Personality and Social Psychology, 53*, 201–211.

Rasinski, K., & Tourangeau, R. (1991). Psychological aspects of judgments about the economy. *Political Psychology*, *12*, 27–40.

Robison, J. (2003, May 6th). Does less educated mean more optimistic? Retrieved on 5/22/2003 from http://www.gallup.com/poll/tb/finanComme/20030506b.asp?Version=p

Rokeach, M. (1960). *The open and closed mind*. New York: Basic Books.

Rubin, Z., & Peplau, L. A. (1973). Belief in a just world and reactions to another's lot: A study of participants in the national draft lottery. *Journal of Social Issues*, *29*, 73–93.

Rubin, Z., & Peplau, L. A. (1975). Who believes in a just world? *Journal of Social Issues*, *31*, 65–89.

Salancik, G. R., & Brindle, M. C. (1997). The social ideologies of power in organizational decisions. In: Z. Shapira (Ed.), *Organizational Decision-Making* (pp. 111–132). New York: Cambridge University Press.

Sen, A. (1985). The moral standing of the market. *Social Philosophy & Policy*, *2*, 1–19.

Shiller, R. J. (2000). *Irrational exuberance*. New York: Broadway Books.

Solow, R. M. (1980). On theories of unemployment. *American Economic Review*, *70*, 1–11.

Stark, D. (1996). Recombinant property in East European capitalism. *American Journal of Sociology*, *101*, 993–1027.

Tajfel, H., & Turner, J. C. (1986). The social identity theory of intergroup behavior. In: S. Worchel & W. G. Austin (Eds), *The Psychology of Intergroup Relations* (pp. 7–24). Chicago: Nelson-Hall.

Taylor, S. E., & Brown, J. D. (1988). Illusion and well-being: A social psychological perspective on mental health. *Psychological Bulletin*, *103*, 193–210.

Tenbrunsel, A. E., & Messick, D. M. (1999). Sanctioning systems, decision frames and cooperation. *Administrative Science Quarterly*, *44*, 684–707.

Tetlock, P. E. (2000). Cognitive biases and organizational correctives: Do both disease and cure depend on the ideological beholder? *Administrative Science Quarterly*, *45*, 293–326.

Tyler, T. R. (2001). Procedural strategies for gaining deference: Increasing social harmony or creating false consciousness? In: J. M. Darley, D. M. Messick & T. R. Tyler (Eds), *Social Influences on Ethical Behavior in Organizations* (pp. 69–87). Mahwah, NJ: Erlbaum.

Tyler, T. R., & Lind, E. A. (2002). Understanding the nature of fraternalistic deprivation: Does group-based deprivation involve fair outcomes or fair treatment? In: I. Walker & H. Smith (Eds), *Relative Deprivation: Specification, Development, and Integration* (pp. 44–68). New York: Cambridge University Press.

Tyler, T. R., & McGraw, K. M. (1986). Ideology and the interpretation of personal experience: Procedural justice and political quiescence. *Journal of Social Issues*, *42*, 115–128.

Van Maanen, J., & Schein, E. (1979). Toward a theory of organizational socialization. *Research in Organizational Behavior*, *1*, 209–264.

Verba, S., Kelman, S., Orren, G. R., Miyake, I., Watanuki, J., Kabashima, I., & Ferree, G. D., Jr. (1987). *Elites and the idea of equality: A comparison of Japan, Sweden, and the United States*. Cambridge, MA: Harvard University Press.

Walker, I., & Smith, H. J. (Eds) (2002). *Relative deprivation: Specification, development, and integration*. Cambridge, UK: Cambridge University Press.

Weick, K. E. (1995). *Sensemaking in organizations*. Thousand Oaks, CA: Sage.

Weinberg, D. H. (1996, June). Are the rich getting richer and the poor getting poorer? *Current Populations Reports* (pp. 60–191).

Weinberg, D. H. (2002, August 22nd). A brief look at postwar U.S. income inequality. Retrieved on 8/04/2003 from http://www.census.gov/hhes/income/incineq/p60asc.html

Weinstein, N. D. (1980). Unrealistic optimism about future life events. *Journal of Personality and Social Psychology*, *39*, 806–820.

White, S. B. (1994). Testing an economic approach to resource dilemmas. *Organizational Behavior and Human Decision Processes, 58,* 428–456.

Wilson, G. D. (Ed.) (1973). *The psychology of conservatism.* London: Academic Press.

Wolff, E. N. (1996). *Top heavy: The increasing inequality of wealth in America and what can be done about it.* New York: New Press.

Zucker, L. G. (1977). The role of institutionalization in cultural persistence. *American Sociological Review, 42,* 726–743.

INTERPERSONAL SENSEMAKING AND THE MEANING OF WORK

Amy Wrzesniewski, Jane E. Dutton and Gelaye Debebe

ABSTRACT

In this paper, we present a model of interpersonal sensemaking and describe how this process contributes to the meaning that employees make of their work. The cues employees receive from others in the course of their jobs speak directly to the value ascribed by others to the job, role, and employee. We assert that these cues are crucial inputs in a dynamic process through which employees make meaning of their own jobs, roles, and selves at work. We describe the process through which interpersonal cues and the acts of others inform the meaning of work, and present examples from organizational research to illustrate this process. Interpersonal sensemaking at work as a route to work meaning contributes to theories of job attitudes and meaning of work by elaborating the role of relational cues and interpretive processes in the creation of job, role and self-meaning.

INTRODUCTION

Individuals are motivated to make meaning of the information and context around them (Baumeister & Vohs, 2002). Yet as organizational scholars, we do not yet understand a great deal about how the meaning of work in people's lives is created. We know quite a bit about job attitudes and other specific measures of reactions to work (Locke & Latham, 1990; Loscocco, 1989; Staw, Bell &

Research in Organizational Behavior
Research in Organizational Behavior, Volume 25, 93–135
ISSN: 0191-3085/doi:10.1016/S0191-3085(03)25003-6

Clausen, 1986; Withey & Cooper, 1989), but we know much less about how these concepts inform the meaning of work more generally, and how that meaning is created. This gap in understanding is significant, as the meaning people make of their work is tied to their attitudes about the work they do (e.g. Lodahl & Kejner, 1965; MOW, 1987; Roberson, 1990; Vecchio, 1980) and their overall well-being (Campbell, Converse & Rodgers, 1976). Indeed, insofar as meaning and satisfaction are linked (Wrzesniewski, McCauley, Rozin & Schwartz, 1997), there may be individual performance implications of work meanings.

In this chapter, we present a model of interpersonal sensemaking around the social cues employees attend to at work to make the argument that the meaning of work is significantly affected by the interpersonal episodes that employees have with others on the job. We see this model as building upon and complementing earlier research on job attitudes, sensemaking, and the role of relationships in organizations by proposing a process model for understanding how meaning is composed and altered at work. Our theory of interpersonal sensemaking attempts to address a concern that models of individual behavior in work organizations do not do justice to the relational nature of experiences at work (e.g. Bradbury & Lichtenstein, 2000; Gersick, Bartunek & Dutton, 2000; Kahn, 1998; Sandelands & Boudens, 2000).

Indeed, most treatments of the meaning of work and job attitudes specify relationships of individual values (Nord, Brief, Atieh & Doherty, 1990), needs (Alderfer, 1972), and characteristics of the job (Hackman & Oldham, 1976, 1980) with commitment to (Loscocco, 1989; Meyer & Allen, 1997; Morrow & Wirth, 1989), satisfaction with (Arvey, Bouchard, Segal & Abraham, 1989; Judge, Thoresen, Bono & Patton, 2001), and engagement in (Kahn, 1990; Rothbard, 2001) the job and the organization. However, most often the role of other people on the job is ignored in favor of properly specifying the relationship between self and work. While understanding how individual-level meanings of work are constituted between the self and job is critical to our theories of work meaning, this only presents part of the picture. Most every person engaged in work is interacting with other people, whether they are coworkers, supervisors, subordinates, clients, customers, or others in the organizational environment. Indeed, relationships with others form the social fabric and context of a job (Baron & Pfeffer, 1994).

The role of others at work has been partially specified in Salancik and Pfeffer's (1978) influential work on social information processing, where their theory depicts coworkers as having influence over job attitudes through the information and cues they give about their feelings and thoughts about the tasks of the job. However, the cues deemed relevant are ones that convey information only about the task. This focus underspecifies the range of meaning discerned from interpersonal cues. As well, a social information processing perspective is mainly concerned with the cue itself, and less able to explain how the meaning of the cue gets determined. Further, the impact of the full spectrum of interaction partners at work is not understood, especially with respect to the role they may play in employees' understanding of the meaning of their work. Thus, our field suffers from a shallow understanding of the role of others at work, one that this chapter attempts to deepen.

Another shortcoming of traditional research on job attitudes and the meaning of work is its emphasis on the relationship between predictors and outcomes, with relatively less attention paid to the *processes* through which job attitudes and meanings are created in real time at work. While recent research on work emotion has attempted to bridge this gap in understanding (e.g. Waldron, 2000), there are opportunities for exploring and understanding what lies in the black box between inputs and outcomes related to work meaning. Although it is difficult to specify the steps that employees travel through to come to an understanding of their work and how they think, feel, and behave in it, it is a worthy goal, for it brings more light to questions about how the same work and same contexts come to be experienced so differently across employees (e.g. Wrzesniewski et al., 1997). Thus, this paper takes as a starting point the assumption that the role of others in the construction of the meaning of work is an important one, and that others are key contributors to the process through which work meaning is created or destroyed.

Our recent work involves looking at how employees come to understand the meaning of their work as well as what the job consists of (e.g. Wrzesniewski & Dutton, 2001). The ways employees craft their jobs and think about the role of work in their lives (Wrzesniewski et al., 1997) differs greatly both between and within jobs. We have studied the ways in which employees engage in their work, and the role of other people in the organization (defined broadly) in the course of the day's work. We discovered in this research the critical role played by others in the organization in the valuing and devaluing of the work that employees do, the roles employees hold, and the people employees are. Consistent with Bartel (2003), our research suggested that employees draw from a wide variety of different individuals in the organizational context to come to an understanding of who they are at work. We found that in the course of doing their jobs, employees are continuously exposed to cues that convey others' appraisals of their worth and the worth of their roles and jobs. This dynamic took the form of a process through which employees discerned and read the interpersonal cues sent by others that revealed others' evaluations of them. These evaluations, in turn, had a direct and indirect impact on the meaning employees made of their jobs, roles, and selves in the organization. In this chapter we describe and illustrate this process, and suggest how it influences employees' work meanings.

A Review of the Meaning of Work

The general meaning of work is derived from several sources, including features of the person as well as characteristics of the work itself (Arvey, Bouchard, Segal & Abraham, 1989; Hackman & Oldham, 1980; Kohn & Schooler, 1982; Staw et al., 1986; Staw & Ross, 1985). Most research on the meaning of work explores the centrality of the role of work (Debats, Drost & Hanson, 1995; Lodahl & Kejner, 1965; Paullay, Alliger & Stone-Romero, 1994) and the history of the role of work (see Brief & Nord, 1990 for a comprehensive review). Indirectly, the sociological literature on identity and roles (Stryker, 1994; Stryker & Serpe, 1994) has addressed the meaning of work by commenting on the relative salience of the work domain relative to other life domains. Finally, theories of identity and social processes in shaping identity suggest that identity is partially comprised of the set of group memberships one has (e.g. Roccas & Brewer, 2002). For those with many overlapping ingroups, more simplified identity structures are created. Likewise, when one's ingroup memberships do not overlap, identity becomes more complex and differentiated. Thus, the structure of identity groups to which one belongs has implications for the identity one creates in the work organization.

An ongoing debate in the meaning of work literature centers on whether work meaning is determined internally (i.e. within the individual) or externally (i.e. by the job and wider environment). In this paper, we take the perspective that work meaning results from both – the meaning of the job, the role, and the self in the job all constitute work meaning. We describe how work meaning is created based on cues derived from interactions with others. In addition, our view extends the debate by describing how employees take cues from others that help them discern the meaning of their job, role, and self, and use these cues to shape their interaction patterns with organization members and outsiders they encounter in the organizational context.

Some organizational scholars (e.g. Hackman & Oldham, 1980) have looked at job meaning in terms of how skill variety applied to the job, the level of control employees have over completion of the task (task identity), and the impact of the job on others (task significance) contribute to the meaning that employees give to the job (Hackman & Oldham, 1980). The meaning that is inferred from these job elements involves the overall value or worth of the job in the organizational context. In fact, job design researchers have argued that people implicitly seek to understand the meaningfulness of their work in terms of whether it is broadly worthwhile and valuable. Others have argued job meaning results from employees' comparative appraisals of their inputs to and outputs from the job relative to others (Adams, 1963). Finally, others have argued that job meaning results from the influential information offered by other employees about their experience of the tasks that create the work (Salancik & Pfeffer, 1978).

Because the meaning of work is largely constituted *at* work, with others, it becomes a living social account that employees make of their experience at work. This is in contrast to views of work meaning that are more fixed and based on objective judgments made about stable characteristics of the job (Hackman & Oldham, 1980) or views of stigmatized work that emphasize the role of others in the community in shaping work meaning (e.g. Perry, 1978). Thus, our view of meaning treats it as a socially constructed product that is dynamic and fluid.

The Importance of Others at Work

Our chapter also aims to elaborate the role of others at work in the construction of work meaning. The interaction space at work is vast, comprised of interactions, cues and signals that are both executed and interpreted by those on the scene. At work, employees attend to and interpret what others do to them and what they do to these others. This view of the importance of others at work is echoed by Hughes (1950), who stated that the others we encounter at work "do the most to make our life sweet or sour (p. 321)."

Research on the role of others in the creation of work meaning often paints employees as passive recipients of social cues from the work environment, as opposed to active interpreters of what qualifies as a cue and how each cue should be read. In contrast, our perspective assumes that employees actively compose work meaning by what they notice and how they interpret the actions of others at work. Our perspective also assumes that employees seek out social situations in which their view of the meaning of their job, role, and selves is reinforced by the cues they are likely to receive in those settings or interactions. Our perspective imbues employees with a greater sense of agency and proactivity in how they construct work meaning. This more active construction of how employees make meaning at work fits with perspectives of employees at work that see them as having some degree of control and power in how they shape their work worlds (e.g. Bartel, 2003; Black & Ashford, 1994; Wrzesniewski & Dutton, 2001). It also fits with other sensemaking approaches that portray employees as agentic, actively shaping the content and outcomes of the interpretive process (Drazin, Glynn & Kazanjian, 1999). Finally, such a view reinforces the idea that individuals are motivated to seek out interactions and interaction partners who reinforce their view of themselves (Swann, 1987); since an understanding of the place that one's job and self holds in an organizational context clearly involves aspects of identity, this creates a powerful dynamic for shaping the kinds of contexts employees compose for themselves at work.

Recent research bridges the gap between self and other in explaining the sources of work meaning. For example, Sandelands and Boudens (2000) argue that the job attitudes literature overvalues the role of job tasks and rewards at the expense of the ties between employees and others. In their reanalysis of work narratives collected by Terkel (1972), Garson (1975), and Hamper (1986), they conclude that, "While people occasionally talk about their desire for meaningful work, this desire is not, as theories of satisfaction would have it, born of a concern for personal growth or 'self-actualization' (Argyris, 1957; Maslow, 1954)" (p. 49). Rather, they argue that employees want meaning through connection to others. They study employees' work narratives, and offer the statement of one of Terkel's (1972) informants, an assistant professor of occupational therapy, on working with others:

> Until recently, I wasn't sure how meaningful my work was. I had doubts.
> A surgeon does a really beautiful job. That's meaningful to him immediately.
> But it's not the kind of sustaining thing that makes a job meaningful. It must
> concern the relationship that you have with the people you work with (Terkel, 1972, p. 494).

The authors conclude that when people talk about their work, they talk primarily about other people (Sandelands & Boudens, 2000). This finding reinforces the importance of understanding the relational underpinnings of how others matter to the meaning employees make of their work.

While the role of others in self narratives of work meaning provides understanding of global work assessments, it ignores *how* micro-assessments done in the moment affect attitudes. Researchers are starting to fill this gap by considering the role of aggregated micro-level experiences in determining global work assessments (Côté & Moskowitz, 1998; Fisher, 2000). This research aims to understand how the whole set of experiences employees have unite to create the degree of satisfaction and fit they feel with their work.

This research complements arguments that coworkers and others matter for work meaning, but through different paths than interpersonal sensemaking. For example, earlier work has treated others at work as sources of fun (e.g. Roy, 1959), learning (e.g. Orr, 1996), or resources (e.g. Emerson, 1976), but has not focused on the active sensemaking of what the actions of others are saying about an employee's worth at work.

In this paper, we present a model that highlights the experience of employees in interaction with others at work in shaping the meaning of work. In particular, we pay attention to the interpersonal context and its role in helping individuals compose the meaning of their work and themselves in the organizational context,

THE NATURE OF WORK MEANING

Work meanings capture an important part of how employees understand their experience in organizations. We define work meaning as employees' understandings of *what* they do at work as well as the *significance* of what they do. Both aspects of work meaning are related to an employee's beliefs about the function work serves in life (Roberson, 1990), which is affected by the social context in which employees live (Brief & Nord, 1990). Our assumption is that employees are motivated to derive a sense of meaning from their endeavors (Frankl, 1963), including their work (Pratt & Ashforth, 2003; Shamir, 1991). Borrowing from symbolic interactionism, we assume that meaning is not fixed, but is an ongoing production that both reflects and shapes patterns of action (Blumer, 1966). We assume employees engage in continuous sensemaking to discern what meaning their work holds for them, and further, that they act upon their relational setting at work in a motivated fashion to shape the contact with others and the experiences they are likely to have (Wrzesniewski & Dutton, 2001).

Traditionally, studies of work meaning have emphasized the contextual and motivational dimensions of sensemaking (Becker, 1970; Fine, 1996; Friedson, 1970). In organizational settings, individuals are more likely to engage in sensemaking when they encounter problematic experiences at work (Weick, 1995). Furthermore, this process is not a rational and linear one; it is motivated to achieve something, perhaps even redefining and altering the meaning of problematic features of work (Fine, 1996). For example, Fine (1996) demonstrated how restaurant chefs used occupational rhetorics to craft their work as an art form and themselves as artists, thereby constructing themselves as professionals and emphasizing the skilled aspects of work. As our illustration of the process of constructing of job- self- and work-meaning later in this paper demonstrates, interpersonal sensemaking is motivated by the desire to reclaim, for oneself and for others, the value in one's work, and by extension in one's personhood.

The Structure of Work Meaning

We focus on three major facets of the broad domain of work meaning: the meaning of one's job, one's role, and the self at work. Together, the understandings employees come to of how they matter in the work they do and the part they play in the organization combine to map the domain of meaning at work. In Table 1, we map the terrain of work meaning by considering the content and evaluation of job meaning, role meaning, and self meaning at work. Our assumption is that we can usefully describe job meaning, role meaning, and self meaning by looking

AMY WRZESNIEWSKI, JANE E. DUTTON AND GELAYE DEBEBE

Table 1. Work Meaning.

	Job Meaning at Work	Role Meaning at Work	Self Meaning at Work
Content			
What is it?	Characteristics of tasks and activities that one does at work	Characteristics of one's role(s) at work	Characteristics one imputes to the self while at work
Evaluation			
What is the value of it?	Interpreted value of the job and its tasks/activities	Interpreted value of the role(s) at work	Interpreted value of self in the job

through two lenses: content of meaning and evaluation of meaning. Each of these lenses provides a snapshot of the socially constructed meaning of this facet of the work. For example, the content of job meaning refers to the specific tasks and activities that an employee believes compose the job. Thus, job content captures what an employee does and the characteristics ascribed to these activities and tasks by the employee. The evaluative component of job meaning addresses the question of the value of these activities and tasks that an employee believes compose the job. The content of role meaning addresses the perceived position in the social structure an employee holds in the organization (Ashforth, 2001), while the evaluative component of role meaning addresses the perceived value of this position in the organization. Finally, the content of self meaning at work addresses the question of "What are my qualities or characteristics as a person carrying out a particular job?" The evaluative component of self-meaning addresses the issue of the value or worth of the employee's personal qualities in the job.

Job Meaning
There are two kinds of meaning around jobs – the meaning of the tasks and activities themselves (i.e. content), and the meaning of the evaluation of those tasks and activities. While any job has a formal job description, all employees have discretion to craft a job to include or exclude certain tasks (Wrzesniewski & Dutton, 2001), and to impute certain meanings to those tasks. As a result, job meaning is fluid and constructed in doing the work. For example, the task of cleaning a floor does not have an inherent meaning. It acquires meaning through the execution of the task, and the employee's interaction with others that imbue the task with meaning. As such, the cleaning of a floor can become a dirty, devalued, degrading task, or it can become an important, valued task that highlights the criticality of one's job for the achievement of the organization's mission. Thus, the meaning of any job is not fixed.

We propose that two aspects of job meaning are composed in the course of any workday. First, through work, employees discern a sense of what the content of their job is, and understand the tasks and activities that they do as part of the work. For example, knowing that a teacher creates lessons, grades papers, and encourages students is all part of understanding the content of the job of teacher. Usually, job content is rather unambiguous to employees, though there may be liberties taken to alter the content of the job (Morrison, 1994; Wrzesniewski & Dutton, 2001). Second, job meaning also refers to an employee's evaluation of the job. The worth of the job is affected by an employee's personal values, preferences and passions as well as by features of the social context. We focus on the latter category to explore how employees construct, read, interpret, and proactively create the social context in which they perform their work. This social context creates the backdrop against which job meaning (and work meaning in the aggregate) is born. In this paper, we focus on how the interpersonal cues that emerge from this backdrop affect the worth of the job as well as other facets of work meaning.

Role Meaning
Role meaning describes the understanding employees have of what their position in the formal social structure at work is (Ashforth, 2001), and how they evaluate that position. We define a role as Ashforth (2001) does, "a position in a social structure (p. 4)" but also note the impact of others' expectations and the fluid negotiations between employees and others in determining what form the role takes (Graen & Scandura, 1987; Kahn, Wolfe, Quinn, Snoek & Rosenthal, 1964). Thus, our sense of roles includes both structural aspects of the position, and social aspects of the expectations others have of the employee in the position.

We propose that at least two aspects of role meaning are composed during the course of the work day. First, at work, employees get a sense of what the content of their roles are in the organization. For example, the content of an employee's role simply answers questions about whether they are a clerk, a CEO, a floor washer, or a teacher. Second, employees acquire a better understanding of the evaluation of their work role through their experiences at work. Such evaluations help them to understand the worth and value of their role – whether the worth of the role is positive (worthy and valuable), or negative (worthless and valueless). For example, many organizations have institutionalized the role of mentor as part of what defines the work of many different employees (e.g. Murrell, Crosby & Ely, 1999). In some organizations, this role includes many duties and obligations, and the way that the employee and others regard the role infuses it with significance and worth. In other organizations, this role has less responsibility associated with it and people in this role have limited formal or informal authority. In the latter case, role holders are likely to feel that the role has limited value. Of course, whom one regularly interacts with at work will affect the kinds of cues, and meaning, one can impute to the role. For example, a mentor in an organization that gives the role little responsibility who spends a great deal of time and energy with mentees and receives cues that the mentoring work is valuable and worthy is likely to protect against decrements in role meaning.

Self Meaning

Self meaning at work describes the self-understanding that employees acquire about themselves when at work. Some researchers refer to self meaning as self identity, referring to the qualities that employees impute to themselves (Gecas, 1982; Schenkler, 1985), as well as the more elaborated self-narratives that describe who they are (Gergen & Gergen, 1988). Rosenberg (1979) took a broad view when he defined self-concept as "the totality of an employee's thoughts and feelings that have reference to himself as an object" (Rosenberg, 1979, p. 7). There has been a flurry of interest in self meaning and identity at work over the last 15 years (Ashforth & Mael, 1989; Hogg & Terry, 2000; Whetten & Godfrey, 1998). This research reminds us that that self is partially a social product of what happens to employees at work.

We propose that at least two aspects of self-meaning are work products. First, an employee comes to understand, at a very basic level, what the content of his or her self is on the job – am I someone who is careful, fast, and expert at work? Second, an employee acquires a self-understanding about evaluations of the self at work. This self at work may be infused with positive value and worth or with negative value and diminished worth. For example, Lynch (2000) studied women who suffered violence and abuse at home, but at work found new sources of personal meaning and significance for themselves as employees because of the way they were treated by others, and how they came to understand the value of their work to their employers.

The content and evaluation of the self involve negotiations of one's identity in interactions with others (Swann, 1987). Employees' self understandings grow from a process in which they present themselves, and through interacting, learn if their views of themselves are reinforced or validated by others (e.g. Bartel, 2003; Swann, 1987). Accordingly, how the self is evaluated and what the content of the self consists of is a somewhat fluid and socially constructed process. Later, we address how pressures for positive and consistent self-appraisals affect the interpersonal sensemaking process.

In the next section, we describe a model of interpersonal sensemaking at work that specifies the role of interpersonal cues from others in helping employees make meaning of their jobs, roles, and selves at work. We begin to describe the model by focusing on cues employees notice on the job and how these cues are interpreted to have meaning for the work they do.

AN INTERPERSONAL SENSEMAKING
MODEL OF WORK MEANING

Our model addresses how interpersonal cues generated and received on the job shape work meaning. The model assumes the centrality of interpersonal acts at work and how the traces from these acts shape understandings of work, role and self meaning. In terms of Weick's sensemaking framework (1995), our model focuses on the intrasubjective elements in the process. In short, we wish to describe how employees create their own realities at work through their sensemaking around the cues they receive, and their tendency to seek out certain kinds of cues in the construction of the meaning of their work. Since the intrasubjective elements of sensemaking are the foundation for intersubjective or collective sensemaking, our assumption is that this portrayal of interpersonal sensemaking is a good starting point for describing and understanding how this process shapes work meaning.

In Fig. 1 we present our conceptual model, which is built on the premise that employees attend to interpersonal cues generated by themselves and others on the job and engage in sensemaking to determine how others evaluate their job, their role, and them at work. The cues and the interactions that produce them give rise to a pattern of interpersonal sensemaking that creates and alters the meaning of work. The sensemaking process begins with an employee noticing another person's actions. It proceeds as the employee makes sense of the cues from these actions, and then imputes job, role and self meaning from this interpretive effort. We discuss the elements of this model in more detail below.

Interpersonal Cues

As shown in Fig. 1, the process of interpersonal sensemaking begins with an employee at work noticing some kind of action or behavior of another person or group. We call this noticed action an interpersonal cue. Cues can be direct or subtle. For example, an employee who is struggling to meet a deadline who is given helpful material from a coworker is likely to notice this as a rather direct interpersonal cue. Likewise, something as small as a glance between coworkers across a conference table during a work meeting is also a cue. Whether an interpersonal cue involves a direct interaction or a behavior that is only an interaction trace, it provides *cues* that are important to sensemaking. Interpersonal cues are defined as behaviors of an individual in context that are noticed by another person. Symbolic interaction researchers call these cues "lines of action" and argue that individuals "engage in constant interpretation of each other's ongoing lines of action" (Blumer, 1966, p. 538, cited in Prus, 1996, p. 69). Cues are meaningful chunks of other's behavior

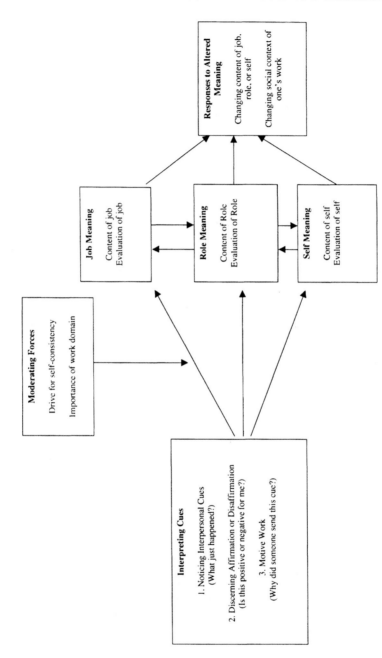

Fig. 1. Interpersonal Sensemaking in the Creation of Meaning at Work.

that carry signal value for understanding how others view us. They are the bits that compose what some researchers call reflected appraisals. From the original idea of a reflected self from William James (1890) to more contemporary developments of the idea of the looking glass self (elaborated by Cooley, 1902 and reviewed by Tice & Wallace, 2002), there is an important assertion that people appraise how others see them by reading cues. These cues vary in how diagnostic they are, meaning the "extent to which a cue gives information about conditions that can serve as a basis for a later judgment" (Dutton, Ashford, Lawrence & Miner-Rubino, 2002, p. 355).

In work organizations, interpersonal cues can be direct and explicit, such as a request made of an employee by another person on the job, or they can be subtle and indirect, such as non-verbal gestures. For example, in Tepper's work on abusive bosses, he provides disturbing accounts about the directness with which some supervisors convey disdain to their subordinates: "What did I tell you the first day?" "Your thoughts are nothing." "If you were in my toilet bowl I wouldn't bother flushing it." "My bath mat means more to me than you." "You don't like it here, leave" (Tepper, 2000, p. 178). But in many organizations, the interpersonal cues are much less direct, thus requiring employees to select which cues to read to interpret what the cue means. In a study of university staff's experience of being valued and devalued at work, Beth, an administrative assistant, described a situation where she assembled a piece of work and asked her boss if he would like to check it over before she sent it out. She conveyed that her boss "did not check it because (he) was confident enough that (she) had done (the work) for so long" and trusted her work (Dutton, 2003). In this example, the boss's cues were quite subtle. While he did not directly tell his subordinate, Beth, about his confidence in her, the granting of autonomy was a powerful cue that Beth experienced as affirmative and diagnostic of his belief that her job was important and that she was doing it competently.

In another example, the cue is even more indirect, and meaning is distilled from one small gesture. In this case, one employee leaves a sent fax in the office machine, and another takes it and returns it to the owner's mailbox. When the employee finds the fax in his mailbox, if he knows that someone has gone through the effort to put it there, the gesture carries weight in how he thinks others regard him, his job and perhaps his role. This example illustrates how minute cues may be and yet still carry diagnostic weight in their impact on the meaning of work. Thus, while one employee may "pick up" a particular cue, another may fail to notice it at all.

A core argument is that employees engage in motivated sensemaking around interpersonal cues. Employees engage in a process of choosing which cues to attend to and interpret, and make sense of the cues in ways that may help to reinforce views of their job, their role, and their selves. A cue represents a behavior that is treated as meaningful by an employee. Whether or not others intend their cues to be interpreted in a particular way is less relevant for discerning the effect of a cue on work meaning. Rather, what matters are the cues employees attend to and how these cues influence the kind of meaning that people make of their work. In this sense, once a cue has been picked up by an employee, the sensemaking process that ensues is an intrapsychic one, and while the employee attends to the social context in which the cue was received, its meaning is constructed alone. Of course, once this process occurs, employees may introduce social processes directly into the cue-receiving and interpreting process by engaging in interactions and with partners that may help to reinforce their desired meaning of the work they do. In the next section, we elaborate the details of the interpersonal sensemaking process.

The Process of Interpretation

Interactions at work produce cues that activate interpretation processes. As shown in Fig. 1, the interpretation process is composed of three elements: noticing, discerning affirmation or disaffirmation, and doing motive work. While we isolate each element and describe the interpretive process as a sequential flow, in most cases, this process happens quickly and with limited conscious thought. However, to understand how work meaning is affected by interpersonal sensemaking, exploring each element of the process affords a different insight. We discuss each element in the process in more detail below.

Noticing Interpersonal Cues

While employees' behaviors generate continuous sensemaking material, only a subset of cues gets noticed, and even fewer are interpreted as meaningful. Noticing an interpersonal cue involves attending to and bounding some chunk of social life at work. As Weick (1995) suggests, it is often swift and automatic, with people barely aware that they have actually sliced or extracted some cue for further notice. For example, Chris Low, a long-time staff member in the legal department at a local pharmaceutical firm, tells of a recent encounter in which the cue interpretation was both swift and powerful. Her company's vice-president had come in to talk to her boss for a quick briefing on a legal issue that was essential to a merger deal that was being negotiated. Chris had met the company vice president on several occasions and had done several small assignments for the Vice President's assistant. Chris and her boss were standing side by side in the law library when the Vice President came to see Chris's boss. The Vice President interrupted them without apology and proceeded to grill her boss with questions. He never acknowledged Chris, nor apologized for the interruption. Chris explained that while she did not think her boss had noticed this encounter, the Vice President's actions left an indelible impression on her.

We assume that interpersonal cues at work are noticed in routine or non-routine situations. Routine noticing happens when, through planned and recurring interactions, individuals are regularly exposed to bounded bits of interpersonal behavior. There are many routine situations in organizations that promote interactions. Some of these situations are formal, such as meetings, or report-in sessions. Other situations, such as impromptu coffee breaks, are informal. Taken-for-granted norms and behavioral expectations that are automatically observed govern each of these situations with very little reflection (Garfinkel, 1967). If behavior is consistent with taken-for-granted expectations, it is not noticed. For example, at the start of a meeting, it is often customary for participants to chat about how things are going and use the few minutes before the meeting begins for a casual catch-up period in which bonds are informally renewed. Behavior that is consistent with these expectations is not noticed, while behavior departing from expectations, even if it is subtle, such as avoiding the initiation or return of greetings, is noticed. This behavior would then activate the interpersonal sensemaking process.

Non-routine cues are likely to be noticed because they are vivid, surprising, or extreme in some way (Fiske & Taylor, 1991). Unexpected events or actions taken by others command attention and become important inputs for further interpretation, and can occur in the midst of routine or non-routine events. For example, in Randy Hodson's (1991) work on experiencing dignity at work, he singles out a quote from Ruth Cavendish's (1982) participant observer study of women in an electronics factory to show how coworkers can create alternative realities that allow people to survive and thrive in harsh work conditions. One of the women she studied described what it was like to receive an unexpected cue from a coworker: "I was talking to Anna after returning from a two-week sick leave without pay, when she stuffed a ten pound note in my trouser pocket so quickly that I wasn't even sure what it was. She was giving it to me because I would be short, having lost two week's wages" (Cavendish, 1982, p. 67).

In this example, the direct cue from Ruth's coworker Anna stands out as an unexpected and generous gesture, thus capturing Ruth's attention. In our theory of interpersonal sensemaking at work, this act is noticeable because it is non-routine, thus becoming a catalyst to sensemaking about what this act means, and providing one among several threads of understanding that form the weave of the meaning of work.

Discerning Affirmation and Disaffirmation
After noticing a cue, the second step in the interpersonal sensemaking process involves an employee's interpretation of whether a cue is affirming or disaffirming.

The basic question that one answers when determining if a cue is affirming or disaffirming is whether a cue conveyed by the other is positive or negative. Interpretation that a cue is positive implies a person believes the noticed behavior communicates regard, care, competence, worth or any attribute that implies that the act confirms the employee's existence and endows the employee with some form of significance. Interpretation that a cue is negative registers disconfirmation of an employee's significance as it says the noticed behavior conveys disregard, lack of caring or value, incompetence or some other derogatory attribute.

The idea that employees interpret interpersonal cues as affirming or disaffirming fits the assumption that people appraise situations using a coarse-grained judgment of whether a situation is positive, negative or neutral (Lazarus & Folkman, 1984). This appraisal functions to help organisms survive in the environment; to the extent that an appraisal is automatic and helps one decide how to act, it has adaptive value for survival (Lazarus, 1991). In social settings individuals have learned to make quick judgments about whether someone is friend or foe, dangerous or not dangerous, helpful or not helpful. A remnant of this basic appraisal is that clues that come to us from others' actions are assessed with a very simple logic – does this affirm or disaffirm who I am as a person? In a work setting, this affirmation and disaffirmation interpretation often implicates others' judgments about the job, the role or the self at work. For example, Konner (1987) describes the general sense of disaffirmation he felt when, in his medical residency training, his supervising resident would use his on-call room in the middle of the night to dictate, for hours, her discharge notes. The on-call room was the only place where he could sleep, and he experienced the practice as abusive, noting that, "She made certain that I would not get any sleep unless she did, too" (Konner, 1987, p. 271).

A wide range of interpersonal cues at work registers affirmation and disaffirmation. Beyond signaling presence, cues that affirm may include interpersonal acts where someone enables an employee's performance at work through providing resources, offering emotional support, simply listening, being polite, conveying trust, including them in group activities, or offering help. All of the acts have in common the idea that they communicate that the employee exists and is significant in some way (Dutton, 2003). Cues that disaffirm, of course, do the opposite. They are read as disaffirming an employee's significance, and may include cues that deny their existence, withhold assistance or support, or actions that harm their efforts at work. At work, interpersonal acts of this kind are common. For example, studies of incivility at work provide some startling findings: 90% of respondents in a recent poll believed that incivility at work is a serious problem, while more than half of respondents in front-line positions surveyed in another poll indicated that they had experienced acts of mistreatment at work during the past three years.

Finally, one-third of more than 600 nurses surveyed experienced verbal abuse during their previous five days of work (Pearson, Andersson & Porath, 2000).

Work on social cognition suggests that people at work may be more influenced by negative or disaffirming cues rather than positive or affirming cues (e.g. Peeters & Czapinski, 1990). There are several logics that explain the importance of disaffirming cues; they are sometimes seen as a result of expectancy violations (Olson, Roese & Zanna, 1996), and other times depicted as due to our systems' hard-wiring to be more vigilant about negative than positive stimuli (e.g. Pratto & John, 1991). Both imply individuals at work might be more attentive to disaffirming than affirming cues. However, if one considers the hedonic principle and people's basic desire to seek pleasure, this would suggest an explicit bias in the search for and attention to affirming cues at work. Thus, psychology gives us competing arguments about whether affirming or disaffirming cues would be more important in affecting work meaning. However, whether any cue shapes meaning depends on inferences about the intentions of those who authored the act or made the move. Borrowing from Mills (1940), we call this part of interpersonal sensemaking "motive work." Such work involves, among other things, a process of discerning others' motives, and is the last step of our proposed model.

Doing Motive Work
The final step in the process of interpretation involves making sense of why someone acted the way that they did. When people notice others' cues, it is in part because they depart from a set of expectations they have for interaction, which creates the need to come up with a plausible explanation for the cue. Motive work in the context of interpersonal sensemaking answers a simple question: did the person or group who authored the act or made the move intend to do what they did? We propose that the answer to this question either increases or decreases the effect of the affirmation/disaffirmation judgment on the meaning of work. Figuring out someone's motives helps people know whether a behavior, move, or act is diagnostic of another's beliefs and feelings and whether the act is likely to be repeated.

Our assertion that attributions of intent or motive work is part of interpersonal sensemaking fits with work that has been done on meaning making in close relationships. For example, Bradbury and Fincham (1990) present evidence suggesting that individuals first code interaction events as either positive or negative, then engage in motive work that serves to increase or decrease the impact of the event. Thus, the positive or negative nature of the cue is primary in the process, but the impact of the cue can change as a result of the motives that are attributed. For example, if an employee is accustomed to having a coworker bring back an extra cup of coffee for her after a regular work break and, one day, this gesture is not made, the initial reaction would likely be that this is a disaffirming act (i.e. "Why didn't my coworker bring coffee, as is our routine?"). However, motive work suggests that the impact of this cue can change as a result of the motives attributed to the sender. If the employee knows that the coffee was forgotten because the coworker is overloaded and stressed, the cue's impact is minimized.

For example, in the story of Chris described above, the meaning of the interpersonal cue from the vice president would have been quite different if Chris felt that the vice president was completely overwhelmed by the merger situation, and so was "forgetting himself" in the way he was acting toward others. This interpretation could have resulted in Chris having no reaction to the cue, or feeling sympathy for the vice president. However, because Chris seemed to feel as though the cue was unnecessary and volitional, her sensemaking resulted in feeling devalued.

Attribution theory supports the importance of motive work in interpersonal sensemaking by assuming that people try to interpret the world in order to control it (Kelly, 1955). Our model of interpersonal sensemaking assumes employees are effortful thinkers about the motives for others' acts, and that the outcomes of motive work provide information that allows employees to understand and predict others' future behavior, and to act more effectively (Swann, 1984).

However, while motivation to infer motives is strong in close relationships (Bradbury & Fincham, 1990), it is less clear that employees would want to engage in motive work around every noticed cue that deviated from their expectations. In fact, the degree to which a cue is noticed, coded as affirming or disaffirming, and interpreted through the imputed motives of others is likely to vary across employee and situation. Motivation to attend to others (that is, to notice and code their cues as affirming or disaffirming) and to infer motives for their actions depends on a number of factors. For example, cues are embedded in organizational structures, which inevitably involve power relations and situated knowledge of the relationship, all of which makes a cue more or less noticeable and diagnostic. Thus, the structural positions of the cue sender and the cue receiver should influence cue interpretation, as structural position is also associated with status (Fiske, 1992). Research has supported the notion that those with more power attend less to others and are more likely to engage in stereotyping (Fiske & Depret, 1996; Keltner, Gruenfeld & Anderson, 2003; Lee & Tiedens, 2001). This suggests that in the interpersonal sensemaking process, the positions of the players involved matter for how motivated each will be to notice cues in the first place, and engage in motive work around them.

The issue of status and attention in organizations works both ways, however. Research on stigmatized work has suggested that in the face of the threats implied by doing "dirty work" (Ashforth & Kreiner, 1999), employees may protect themselves by selectively attending to outsiders who are providing cues about the worth and meaning of their work. Thus, the weight, attention, and processing given to interpersonal cues may depend on the motivation of employees to moderate the impact of the stigma or status of their work on the meaning of what they do.

Another factor that is likely to affect motive work is the relationship of the interaction partner to the employee. For example, if the interaction partner is from one's occupational group or department, it is possible that the motive work will be done with a motivation towards giving a more forgiving interpretation to a negative cue. Weber (1994) has demonstrated that people tend to make kinder attributions for the motives and intentions of members of their own groups relative to members of other groups, attributing negative behavior to external or temporary causes when a group member is the target of motive work. Thus, both the *presence* and the *kind* of motive work that employees engage in are likely to differ depending on the source of the cue.

In short, motive work allows employees to conclude if an interpersonal cue is strongly or weakly affirming or disaffirming. The final link in the process reveals how this affirmation or disaffirmation affects work meaning.

Linking Interpersonal Sensemaking to Work Meaning
The last step in the process specifies how interpreting a cue as affirming or disaffirming translates into changes in work meaning. While we have specified the broad domain of work meaning at the outset of this chapter, interpersonal sensemaking has its major impact on how employees evaluate their jobs, roles and selves at work in light of the imputed evaluations of others. Specifically, the motive work that occurs around the cues others send at work acts to translate a bounded bit or pattern of behavior into relevant information about what others think about one's worth. This is a motivated process, in which employees strive to understand the behavior of others in light of their power relative to them, and the presence or absence of a common group membership with them. The impact of employees' motivated processing and interpretation of cues on the outcome of the sensemaking cannot be underemphasized, for it shapes their understanding of their work context and their place in it, but also acts as a guide for their future behavior in interactions with others, as we will describe later.

The cues that are interpreted at work are sources of information that speak directly to others' evaluation of the value or significance of an employee's job, role, and self in the organization. Specifically, the cues employees receive at work carry in them others' evaluations of the worth and competence that an employee exhibits at work. Thus, interpersonal cues at work register at the level of evaluation of job, role and self in the model we have proposed. The relationship between work meaning and the three sources of meaning that comprise it is a simple one; each source of meaning contributes directly to work meaning, and each affects the other (see Fig. 1). For example, receiving evaluative information via interpersonal cues about the worth of one's job in the organization is likely to have an impact on more than just job meaning. The job is subordinated into a larger role one plays in the organization, and the role is subordinated into the self, creating a nesting of the meanings that are affected by interpersonal cues. Chief among the three meanings that comprise work meaning is self-meaning, for it strikes at the very heart of one's identity and worth as a human being. Thus, self meaning is a repository for job and role meaning, as the information conveyed about job and role ultimately has an impact upon the self. In Fig. 1, the boldfaced arrows indicate this nesting of meaning.

Because individual meaning is derived in part from a need for a sense of self-worth (Baumeister & Vohs, 2002) and self-esteem (Rosenberg, 1979), information from others that speaks *directly* to their evaluation of the worth and competence of what an employee does or who an employee is at work may be relevant as an input to the meaning making process. Indeed, Gecas (1982) argues that worth and competence are essential parts of how individuals evaluate themselves (e.g. Gecas, 1971). We build from the assumptions that people have a strong desire to view their self-definitions in positive terms (Turner & Tajfel, 1986), and that employees assess their worth and competence through the reflected appraisals of others. Given that the cues employees read from others are often diagnostic about worth, competence and other indicators of value, the role of interpersonal cues in the creation of work meaning is likely to be significant.

Our view is consistent with a symbolic interactionist perspective on the self, in which who we are and what we do (and, we would argue, the meaning we make of who we are and what we do) is co-constituted in interaction with others (Cooley, 1902). Through interpersonal cues, employees are granted or denied "a manifest sense of confirmed worth as a human being" (Margolis, 1999, p. 27). Thus, a cue from another that is interpreted to carry weight and have significance will have an impact on the meaning one makes of the job, role, and self at work. It is through this process of reading, interpreting, and incorporating cues about others' assessments of one's value at work that the very evaluation employees make of themselves is affected.

When the process of interpersonal sensemaking strikes at the very heart of the evaluation of job, role, and self meaning, it has the potential to shape the content of these elements as well. Employees can begin to alter the content of the job, the role, and the self at work after integrating others' statements about the value of each into the meaning they make of these elements. For example, in Konner's (1987) story of the abusive head medical resident, the repeated nature of her disaffirming cues eventually led him to approach her, stating, "Look . . . I am trying to pass the course. That means I need a grade of Satisfactory. So why don't you tell me exactly what I have to do to get a grade of Satisfactory? Because I don't intend to do any more than that" (Konner, 1987, p. 270). Konner explained, "What I intended and in fact carried out was minimalism in relation to (her) hazing" (p. 271). What Konner truly carried out was a curtailing of the content of his job, his role, and the characteristics of himself that he brought to his medical internship.

The evaluations others make of the worth of one's job, role, and self help employees to shape the content of all three in response. The interactions that produce cues are the source of affirming or disaffirming evaluations that carry significance for employees. As in the example described above, the impact of interpersonal cues on the meaning employees make of their jobs, roles, and selves can lead employees to change the content of what they do and who they are in the work context. This effect of interpersonal sensemaking speaks directly to the dynamic nature of the model we have proposed. In the next section, we consider how the content of what one does at work can be shaped by the interpersonal sensemaking process, and how employees shape contexts at work to affect the kinds of interactions they are likely to have.

Creating Content and Contexts
The experience of receiving evaluative information about the worth of one's job, role, or self is powerful. Its impact strikes at the core of the self and its worth in the organization. We assume that employees need a secure and stable sense of self-meaning (Erez & Earley, 1993; Schwalbe & Mason-Schrock, 1996), and desire to see themselves in a positive light (Jones, 1973). It is through interpersonal episodes at work that employees come to know the content of who they are. As Ashforth and Kreiner (1999) state: "Through social interaction and internalization of collective values, meanings and standards, individuals come to see themselves somewhat through the eyes of others and construct more or less stable self-definitions" (p. 417).

Employees have the ability to affect how they compose the tasks of their jobs, as well as who they come into contact with on the job (Wrzesniewski & Dutton, 2001). Thus, it is possible to shape the content of what one does in response to the messages one receives about one's worth to bring the two into line to create a coherent experience. For example, if employees get the message that others see certain elements of their job as more worthwhile and valuable than others, a pressure is exerted on the employees to engage in more of this activity, or to emphasize these aspects of the job or role in their interactions with others. This desire for positive regard may lead employees to two different ways of altering the work context. First, as mentioned in the example above, employees may begin to engage in tasks, role behaviors, and presentation of aspects of themselves that have been positively evaluated by others in the past. Second, employees may learn to seek out contexts in which the interactions they have with others reinforce the valued aspects of their jobs, roles, and selves. Thus, through a dual process of shaping how they do their work and building the social context in which they work, employees have at least some ability to influence the context from which they receive interpersonal cues.

However, there are several factors that are likely to affect whether employees are motivated to reshape the content and context of their work in order to win positive evaluations from others. First, while employees are motivated to hold positive images of themselves (Jones, 1973), employees are also motivated to see their reflected selves as consistent with their own understanding of themselves in order to achieve a coherent sense of self (e.g. Swann, 1990, 1999; Swann, Rentfrow & Guinn, 2002). This drive for self-consistency can lead people to prefer that others see them as they see themselves, even when this means that the view will be negative (Swann et al., 2002). Thus, motivation to create and seek out opportunities for receiving affirming interpersonal cues is likely to be moderated by the need for self-consistency.

Second, the drive to receive affirming cues may be influenced by the relationship between the employee and the work. The model we have proposed addresses the domain of work to the exclusion of interpersonal sensemaking in other life domains. While we have made the argument that all employees will attend to and be influenced by interpersonal cues at work, the power of these cues will vary according to the significance of the domain of work for the employee. Not all individuals imbue their work lives with the same significance (Wrzesniewski, et al., 1997), and may not derive the full measure of their self worth from that context. As Crocker and Park (2003) note, people have contingencies of self worth, or domains in which they have staked their self-esteem, so that their worth depends on their perceived successes or failures in those domains. The domain of work is not a focus of self worth for all employees, thus, the centrality and significance of work will affect the impact of cues on the meaning made of the work, as well as the effort made to seek opportunities for receiving affirming cues.

In the next section, we consider the impact of interpersonal cues on the work meanings of employees in a specific context: that of cleaning in hospitals. We describe how the cues cleaners received were noticed, interpreted as affirming or disaffirming, and finally, how their interpretations of the cues altered both their evaluation and the content of their work.

INTERPERSONAL SENSEMAKING IN ACTION: THE CASE OF HOSPITAL CLEANERS

Our insights about interpersonal sensemaking were shaped by a study we did of the work experiences of cleaners in a large Midwestern hospital setting. The study involved face-to-face interviews with a randomly selected sample of 29 cleaners from the population of 237 cleaners in the department. We interviewed cleaners from different shifts and units, who had different levels of contact with nurses, doctors, patients and visitors. We used random sampling to secure a representative group of cleaners from different shifts, departments, and type of cleaning job (e.g. patient rooms, public areas). The interviews explored a number of themes, including the nature of a cleaner's job, how they perform their job, their relationships with others in the workplace, and whether and how these others facilitate or hinder the performance of their job.

The cleaners told three types of stories that illustrate how interpersonal cues contribute to the meanings that employees make about their jobs, roles, and selves. The first type of story pertained to interactions that they interpreted as conveying affirmation for them and for the work they performed. The second story type pertained to interactions that they interpreted as conveying disaffirmation through an expressed lack of appreciation or even disgust for the job the cleaner performs, the role the cleaner has in the hospital and for the cleaner as a person. The third story type depicted interactions where others' cues were equivocal and contained elements of affirmation and disaffirmation. We provide examples of each story type to illustrate the model of interpersonal sensemaking. Despite the different meanings that result from these story types, the interpersonal sensemaking employed in all three situations revealed a basic similarity in process elements. The key elements of the model are related to these stories in Table 2.

An Affirming Story

Our first story describes an interaction that conveys affirmation of and appreciation for the cleaner and his job. After providing a brief description of the story, we analyze it in light of the elements of our theoretical model. The quote below describes positive interactions between Jason and the patients whose rooms he cleans daily.

> Usually every morning I have to knock on the door. If the patient is able to speak, I say "housekeeping" and a few of them can't speak cause of Ortho and so I'll just say "housekeeping, is it okay if I clean your room?" . . . and if they can talk they say "yes" and I'll just talk to some of them that want to talk. Just somebody to talk to. They've been sitting there, or if they don't get a visitor. (They may say) "How ya doing today?" "Is it nice out?" "Is it cold?" (We have) just (a) normal conversation. Every now and then one might say, "Well I'm glad to see your smiling face." It depends on who we are . . . how you carry yourself. (Some patients cannot respond but even in this situation) you just don't bust in nobody's room. You knock and knock. Then I'll announce, "Housekeeping" and every now and then I can tell "Err err err," you know cause they can't say, "Hey, come on in" or nothing.

Table 2. Illustrations of the Interpersonal Sensemaking Process.

Interpersonal Sensemaking	Affirming Stories	Disaffirming Stories	Ambivalent Stories
Interaction	The exchange between cleaners and patients when the cleaner is cleaning the patient's room	Doctors and nurses making messes that they do not clean up	Patient's visitor who accuses cleaner of not cleaning a room
Noticing	Assessing a patient's ability and desire to talk by the things he or she says	Doctors and nurses "throw something on the floor and just . . . look at it" passively as if they did not have a responsibility for picking up what they dropped	Visitor's son, the patient, was in a coma and paralyzed after fighting with a black man. The visitor was anxious over his son's condition
Motive work	Patients who wished to talk, did so because they wished to have social interaction	"Taking advantage" of the cleaner's job as "housekeeper" Cleaning messes was below them	The father may have been angry at black men in general, because of his son's experience
Job meaning	Patients are interested in what the cleaner does	"I don't think they (doctors and nurses) value our jobs . . . like they should"	Visitor's reactions did not convey meaning about how he viewed Luke's job
Role meaning	Patients' interest and appreciation for what the cleaner does at the hospital	Sense that doctors and nurses do not value cleaners' position	Visitor's reactions did not convey meaning about how he viewed Luke's role
Self meaning	Patients' interest and appreciation for a job well done makes the cleaner feel "right"	They (the doctors and nurses) do not really respect us	Visitor's reactions did not convey meaning about how he viewed Luke

This story aptly illustrates how the meaning cleaners make of their interactions with patients are colored by the cleaner's belief that the patient's responses to them are motivated by their desire for social interaction. Thus, Jason described how patients typically want to talk and will say affirming things to him in the course of his day (e.g. "Well I'm glad to see your smiling face"). He then described the possible motives of the patients in starting up conversations by reasoning "they've been sitting there," or because they may be lonely "if they don't get a visitor." Jason pointed out that he assesses the patient's motives by paying attention to the cues provided. Specifically, he notices those actions or gestures that tell him about a patient's condition, and why they may or may not want to engage in conversation

For instance, he points out that he tries to ascertain whether a patient can speak as well as whether the patient shows an interest in talking by offering a greeting once he is in the room. Although he did not explicitly state what this interpersonal interaction meant for the meaning of his job, his role, and himself, this next quote from Hudson describes the meaning of his interactions with patients. Many cleaners described similar meanings made from cues picked up in interactions with patients.

> With patients . . . they really like you to sit and talk with them and just be social. I like that. I think everybody likes to be social . . . I haven't met one (patient that) is bad, and the visitors too. They're interested in what you do, even though it is just housekeeping. They're interested. I guess you appreciate that. Makes you feel alright. And they say thank you a lot.

In this excerpt, Hudson describes the work meaning that results from his interactions with patients and the affirming cues he receives from them. Hudson points out that his job is appreciated by patients who convey an interest in what he does as well as offer gratitude for a job well done. The cues he notices are positive, and his motive work (i.e. "I think everybody likes to be social") suggests a reason for the cues that does not diminish their impact. The cues he receives speak directly to the patients' evaluation of the worth and competence of his job and role in the hospital. Hudson's comment, that the interaction "makes you feel alright," suggests that with respect to self meaning, he feels that he is valued by patients who express thanks. According to our model of interpersonal sensemaking, we would not be surprised to find that he goes out of his way to interact with patients in the course of the work day, thus shaping the content of his job (i.e. the tasks he focuses on) and the social context in which he does his work.

A Disaffirming Story

In contrast to the affirming stories, cleaners also told disaffirming stories. One such story was about how others' actions made a cleaner's job more difficult. In the excerpt below, Bertie describes the problem of others making "messes" that they do not clean up themselves.

> I don't think they (doctors and nurses) value our jobs as much as they should. They take advantage of, you know, our jobs as being housekeepers and (expect us to) pick up after them. I've sat there and watched doctors and nurses throw something on the floor and just, you know, look at it, like 'She'll pick that up.' You know, the housekeeper or somebody will pick it up. (They're) too lazy to pick up after themselves, they leave trash all over the place. So one of the things that I would say about nurses and doctors, is that they don't really respect us. It's in keeping their own environment clean. I'm not going to be sitting in this mess. (Since) they gotta sit in it, I would think they would want to clean it up, but they don't. I think they're pretty messy people – for professional people.

While cleaners appeared to forgive patients and visitors who did not pick up after themselves, nurses and doctors were judged by a different standard. When others do not clean up and leave a mess, many cleaners spoke of this as a negative event or cue. However, the impact of the cue varied greatly, and depended upon who made the mess, and their capacity for cleaning it. For example, cleaners often did motive work that excused patients and visitors for making more work for the cleaner. Cleaners often cited health or emotional reasons as an explanation for why a patient or visitor might leave a mess. In contrast, nurses and doctors were held to a different standard, as is clear from Bertie's story. The cues given by nurses and doctors who left messes were similarly negative, but acquired more of a negative impact in light of motive work. Because they are viewed as able-bodied and responsible for their own messes, when nurses and doctors left work for a cleaner, it was interpreted as a more negative cue. The underlying motive imputed for this behavior was one of "taking advantage" of the cleaner's job as "housekeeper." Bertie considered the possibility that professional staff acted this way because of the assumptions they had about cleaners. That is, "doctors and nurses throw something on the floor, and just, you know, look at it, like 'She'll (the cleaner) pick that up.'" Their "just looking at it," conveyed an assumption that cleaning was for the cleaner and was beneath them. Bertie's attention to the behavior of nurses and doctors, and her motive work around their cues is consistent with research findings that those with relatively less power will attend more to the actions of others and will work to actively process their meaning (Keltner et al., 2003).

These acts sent very strong messages and had a negative impact on work meaning. The evaluation of worth that is carried in the cues that doctors and nurses send in these interactions strike directly at the meaning that Bertie makes of her job, role, and self. As she points out, "I don't think they (doctors and nurses) value our jobs like they should." This suggests that the meaning of both her job and her role, or position in the hospital, is viewed as having little worth. While Bertie does not articulate her view of the worth of her job and role, her statement suggests that the cues of others have an impact on her. This impact moves to the level of self meaning as well, as evidenced by her statement that the doctors and nurses "don't really respect us."

An Ambivalent Story

Luke is an African-American man who had been a cleaner at the hospital for 15 years when he told a story about how he handled an accusation that he had not cleaned a patient's room. The interview excerpt below describes a negative story, but the work meaning that is constructed cannot be described as wholly negative but is rather ambivalent, or mixed. In his interpretation of the cues he received, Luke takes into account mitigating factors that shape his motive work around the story. His motive work alters his interpretation of the other's negative act and thereby leads Luke to construct an ambivalent work meaning.

> Luke: "And there was this other guy who snapped at me. I kind of knew the situation about his son. His son had been here for a long time and . . . from what I hear, his son had got into a fight and he was paralyzed. That's why he got there, and he was in a coma and he wasn't coming out of the coma . . . and I heard how he got that way. He had got into a fight with a black guy and the black guy really, well, you know, because he was here. Well, I guess his father felt a little angry toward blacks and I went and cleaned his room. His father would stay here every day, all day, but he smoked cigarettes. So, he had went out to smoke a cigarette and after I cleaned the room, he came back up to the room. I ran into him in the hall, and he just freaked out . . . telling me I didn't do it. I didn't clean the room and all this stuff. And at first, I got on the defensive, and I was going to argue with him. But I don't know. Something caught me and I said, 'I'm sorry. I'll go clean the room.' "

> Interviewer: "And you cleaned it again?"

> Luke: "Yeah, I cleaned it so that he could see me clean it . . . I can understand how he could be. It was like six months that his son was here. He'd be a little frustrated, and so I cleaned it again. But I wasn't angry with him. I guess I could understand."

In the above excerpt, Luke discerned a negative, disaffirming cue in the accusation by the father that he did not clean the room. The cue was so negative, in fact, that Luke considered arguing with him in order to stand his ground. However, it was motive work that led Luke to interpret the cue differently, and reverse the course of the interpersonal sensemaking process. Specifically, Luke interpreted the father's accusation against a backdrop of motive work that considered the fact that the patient's condition was the result of a fight with another black man. Given these factors, Luke did not view the father's cues as being directed at him or his work. Instead, he reasoned that the father's reaction towards him had more to do with the fact that Luke was also black. Based on this motive work, Luke did not impute a negative evaluation of the meaning of his job, his role, or himself. Instead, he pointed out that he was not angry with the father, but instead could understand his accusation. While Luke does not explicitly describe a change in the meaning of his job, role, or self as a result of this interaction, one senses from the story that the meaning he makes of his work more generally is unchanged after this interaction. Using an interpersonal sensemaking process lens to interpret the story, we can understand how and why this interaction would likely have little impact, even though it is quite negative in tone.

Writing Context Back In

Our treatment of the interpersonal sensemaking process has been largely silent about the role of context in the creation of work meaning. However, we recognize the critical role that contextual factors play in the process. In fact, while context is often treated as a direct input (Salancik & Pfeffer, 1978) or moderator (Dutton et al., 2002; Wrzesniewski & Dutton, 2001) of sensemaking processes at work, context can be theorized as an input, moderator, and outcome of the process we have described. Thus, we see three different ways that organizational context can be written back into our model of interpersonal sensemaking at work.

The ubiquitous role that context plays in shaping the interpersonal sensemaking process is apparent. Earlier, we described how contextual factors such as position or status in the organizational structure, power, stigma of the job, and shared group membership with the interaction partner all influence the likelihood that a cue will be processed, and the amount of motive work that will be done to make sense of the cue. However, the outcomes of sensemaking have implications for the content and social context employees create at work. These actions have the potential to shape the context of the entire organization. For example, if employees receive cues that convey affirmation and worth when they engage in particular parts of their jobs or aspects of their roles, they may be more likely to seek out these situations. Carried out over time, this could potentially mean engaging more often with certain occupational groups in the organization, or in more visible job tasks. Interdependencies and social ties that may have been unintended could result as employees craft the task and relational boundaries of their jobs and create new social structures and norms for behavior in the workplace. For example, in the cleaning study described earlier, it was understood in the interviews that management was not aware of cleaners' relationships with patients and visitors, even as cleaners took significant steps to alter their work days to engage in the often affirming interactions they had with these groups.

Indeed, it is the relational context of the organization that gets created through interpersonal sensemaking processes, which in turn feeds how employees make sense of what is happening to them in their work interactions. This view represents an addition to traditional views of context that focus more on structural features and their impact on the organization. Just as structural position, group membership, and power influence the interpersonal sensemaking process, the relational landscape more generally acts as an important contextual force that also shapes the process. As Emmons (2003) notes, an organization's culture, norms, and shared values about interpersonal treatment affect which acts people notice and how they make sense of them. For example, organizations that repeatedly make salient the enabling actions of others in helping employees to carry out their work are likely to promote heightened attention to noticing how others help each other at work (e.g. Hoffer Gittell, 2003). In Hoffer Gittell's (2003) study of Southwest Airlines, she finds that in a culture in which a lot of attention is paid to noting how everyone is dependent on everyone else to meet organizational objectives, and power is given to people to reward each other for task enabling, a positive spiral results. At Southwest, employees are more likely to notice enabling, affirming acts, which then creates a sense of gratitude, which then encourages prosocial behavior and positive emotion, creating a positive interpersonal dynamic, and reinforcing the organizational culture, as well as the relational landscape at work.

Norms for interpersonal treatment are a powerful contextual variable to specifically illustrate how context can operate in our model. Interpersonal sensemaking around the cues of others at work takes place against the backdrop of the organizational context. While there are myriad variables that capture context (e.g. departmental structure, culture, nature of work task), we focus our attention on norms for interpersonal treatment at work, for it represents a baseline condition that people use in work settings to form expectations about how they are likely to be treated by others (Bies & Moag, 1986). Norms exist for how employees treat each other in the workplace (Robinson & O'Leary-Kelly, 1998). Thus, norms for interpersonal treatment function as input, moderator, and outcome of the interpersonal sensemaking process at work. For example, interpersonal treatment norms function as an input condition insofar as they create a set of preconditions regarding what will demand notice. When an employee discerns that a norm for treatment has been violated, the cue is more likely to be noticed for its discrepancy with how people are normally treated in a setting (Peeters & Czapinski, 1990). In addition, norms for interpersonal treatment may be used as a standard that shapes how affirming or disaffirming a cue is interpreted to be. For example, if a work context treats exchange of casual greetings between employees who meet in the halls as a norm, then departing from this norm (whether it be in the form of a bear hug or a cold stare) is interpreted as affirming (or not) and motivated (or not), more or less strongly as a result of the norms that exist. Through both these means, norms for interpersonal treatment shape work meaning by how they affect noticing and interpreting cues.

Finally, the way employees read interpersonal cues, and the resulting changes in the meaning and content of their jobs, roles, selves at work, affects the context as well. If employees interpret the cues they receive at work as affirming, increasing the sense of significance and value of the work, this has implications for the norms of interpersonal treatment. If employees experience enhanced work meaning through more affirmative interpersonal sensemaking, then the norm for interpersonal treatment may create a higher shared standard for how respectful and other-regarding interpersonal treatment is expected to be. The ironic twist in this development is that if people do not change their behavior in accord with this norm, people may experience more disaffirmation in interpersonal sensemaking. Thus, employees constitute, in part, the context they find themselves in (Cappelli & Scherer, 1991). How they create that context, particularly around treatment norms, is an outcome of and input to the sensemaking process.

DISCUSSION

In this paper, we articulated a theoretical framework of interpersonal sensemaking. Our goal was to elucidate the interpersonal foundations of the process of constructing work meaning. This theoretical framework is built on the premise that employees at work attend to the interpersonal cues generated by others on the job and engage in a process of sensemaking to determine how others evaluate their job, their role, and themselves at work. In previous sections we described how the sensemaking process begins with an employee noticing another person's actions. It proceeds as the employee makes sense of the cues from these actions by discerning affirmation or disaffirmation and contemplating the motivations for the other's actions. In this process, the employee imputes significance to the other's actions and constructs job, role, and self meaning. These meanings, in turn, help to shape the content of the job, role and self as well as the context that the employee creates at work, creating opportunities for repeated engagement in situations and with interaction partners that yield affirming cues that convey worth.

Our theory contributes to three areas of the organizational studies literature. These are the job attitudes, sensemaking, and relationships at work literatures. In particular, the interpersonal sensemaking framework enriches the job attitudes literature by illuminating the interpretive process involved in arriving at global assessments of one's work. Attending to this interpretive process enables us to recognize the zone of variability in job attitudes. Specifically, it allows us to understand how individual job attitudes vary by interaction through a process of discerning affirmation and disaffirmation of interpersonal cues. With respect to the sensemaking literature, the interpersonal sensemaking framework elaborates the intrapersonal process of sensemaking. This gives us insight into how positive, negative, or ambivalent work meanings arise. Further, the theory suggests how these intrapersonal processes give rise to interpersonal outcomes by shaping the social contexts employees seek out and create in the face of affirming and disaffirming cues. Finally, our theory elaborates the relationships at work literature enabling us to see how meaning is shaped through much more than intended actions and by many more means than have been previously considered. Each of these contributions is elaborated below.

Elaborating the Job Attitudes Literature

The interpersonal sensemaking model enriches the job attitudes literature by highlighting the social and interpretive process involved in creating work meaning. By describing this process, we learn how interactions shape job attitudes. Attending to these processes brings into view dynamics that are important in the construction of job meaning and also raises new questions about approaches that may promote positive job attitudes in organizations.

The interpretive process involved in constructing work meaning is implicit in the job enlargement, job enrichment, and job characteristics perspectives, all of which are important lenses on job attitudes. Each of these perspectives, however, relegate this process to the background and treat as foreground the objective features of a job and how these affect global measures of job attitudes. The job enlargement perspective is concerned with increasing the number of tasks an employee performs as part of his or her job while maintaining the level of difficulty and responsibility of the tasks (Griffin, 1982; Griffin & McMahan, 1995). Job enrichment involves increasing the level of responsibility and control that employees have over their jobs by assigning tasks involving greater responsibility and difficulty (Griffin, 1982). The job characteristics perspective focuses on articulating the core dimensions or characteristics of tasks that make a job intrinsically motivating (Hackman & Oldham, 1976). In all these perspectives, the goal is to increase employee intrinsic motivation with the hope that this will produce positive thoughts and feelings about work and translate into better performance, and lower absenteeism and turnover. An important assumption in these perspectives is that if organizations were to manipulate objective features of the job, then positive thoughts and feelings about the job, measured by employees' global assessments of their jobs, and high motivation will follow. These, in turn, would translate into important organizational outcomes such as high performance, low absenteeism, and low turnover.

However, in their model of social information processing, Pfeffer and Salancik (1978) argued that another important factor shaping job attitudes is social information. Of the three perspectives on job attitudes discussed above, Hackman and Oldham (1976) also raise, but do not elaborate, this issue. These scholars argue that employees who perceive their jobs as having the core dimensions that make a job intrinsically motivating experience a psychological state of meaningfulness of their work. The social information processing perspective goes further to suggest that employees' perceptions and responses to their jobs are shaped by social information, that is, information about their jobs from others on the job.

At its core, the social information processing perspective on work meaning focuses on the evaluations employees make about the tasks they do on the job. Other employees become important in their expression of views about work tasks, which become direct inputs to the attitudes that the employee will have toward the task. While the social information processing perspective does address the importance of others for understanding job attitudes, the interpersonal sensemaking model departs from this research vein in several important respects.

First, rather than focus on task information, our model privileges the centrality of social interactions around a wide variety of information, ranging from the degree to which an employee is respected, to whether the employee is included in social interactions at work or is viewed as a valuable member of the organizational enterprise. Such a broad relational focus moves beyond a simple task focus in understanding how others matter for the meaning made of work. As well, a social information processing perspective treats cues as unambiguous and clear, without need for interpretation or motivated cognitive processing. This is likely a result of the model's bounded nature in focusing primarily on the tasks involved in the work.

Second, our model focuses explicitly on the judgment of the motives of individuals who send cues to employees, while social information processing treats cues as unproblematic. In such a view, the cue is divorced from the relationship between sender and employee; thus, the manner in which the cue is delivered, who delivered it, and how is immaterial. In contrast, our model assumes that the relationship between a cue sender and an employee creates an important part of the context against which the cue is interpreted. Our perspective considers such relational concerns as pivotal in understanding the impact of others' cues on the meaning of work.

Third, a social information processing perspective focuses on the task attitude outcomes of the interaction, rather than considering implications of employees coming to view the work they do as relatively impoverished, motivating, exciting, valuable, or any number of other things. Our model of interpersonal sensemaking addresses the potential consequences for individual meaning of receiving information about work tasks, but also about the role one holds and the self one occupies at work. Thus, while social information processing details the meaning of the task, our perspective includes that as well as the deeper work and self meanings that imbue the work.

Fourth, our model offers an important insight concerning the variability of job meaning. Although there is some stability in job attitudes shaped by individual differences (Staw & Ross, 1985), employees operate within a zone within which variation is possible. That is, employees' job attitudes vary within their personal zones as they encounter different types of interactions in the flow of a work day. While social information processing largely treats the employee as a passive reader of direct task cues, our model reveals the dynamic process through which employees enact their social context at work to receive cues that contribute to work meaning.

Elaborating the Sensemaking Literature

As indicated above, our model elaborates the elements of the process of intrapersonal sensemaking. The noticing of interpersonal cues gives rise to a process of intrapersonal sensemaking wherein the employee attempts to assign meaning to an equivocal situation. This process involves discerning the affirmation or disaffirmation of a cue and doing motive work. The interpersonal sensemaking framework shows that meaning arising from this process is not neutral. In particular, through the processes of affirmation, disaffirmation, and motive work, the interpersonal sensemaking model gives us insight into how positive, negative, or ambivalent meanings arise from a process of intrapersonal sensemaking. As our illustrations from the accounts of cleaners show, positive meanings arise when others' actions are seen as affirming one's self, job, and role and when others' motives support this interpretation. Negative meaning arises when others' actions disaffirm one's self, role, and job and when others' motives support this interpretation. Finally, ambivalent meaning arises in situations where others' motives counteract the disaffirmation or affirmation of a given act. The meaning employees make of the cues they receive, and the impact the cues have, are influenced by a number of contextual and relational factors shown in Fig. 1, and have the potential to reshape the content that employees include in their jobs, roles, and selves at work as well as the contexts they are motivated to create for themselves to sustain viable work meaning in the eyes of others encountered on the job.

In particular, employees may be motivated to make sense of their work in patterned ways. For example, employees in low status jobs (Meara, 1974; Riemer, 1979) may be especially motivated to impute value to their work and selves. Indeed, this was the case with the hospital cleaners, who often encountered interpersonal cues that challenged the worth of their jobs and themselves. While the process of constructing work meaning occurs at all status levels, its prevalence in low status jobs are likely to yield different motivations and work meanings.

Elaborating the Role of Others at Work

An interpersonal sensemaking lens reveals the importance of others for understanding how employees construct the meaning of their job, their role, and themselves at work. The model offers several insights into understanding the relational context of employees at work.

First, the model reminds organizational researchers that employees shape others' meaning through more than intended actions. The importance of noticing cues in the interpersonal sensemaking process is that it filters in and filters out intended and unintended actions of others that in turn shape how people interpret their work. Thus, organizational researchers need to consider how the intended and unintended actions of structurally linked colleagues at work (bosses, subordinates, unit colleagues, customers) as well as chosen colleagues (e.g. friends of customers, co-located colleagues from different organizations) all play a role in composing work meaning by offering (intentionally or not) cues that are treated as signals of affirmation or disaffirmation. Theories of work meaning need to reflect this situated relational view (Eide, 2000). Where organizational scholars are interested in the meaning of work for predicting employees' actions, their health, their effectiveness or any other outcome, our model suggests that they need to consider a wider set of players on the relational scene at work that play an often invisible role in composing work meaning.

Second, an interpersonal sensemaking lens suggests others at work make both positive and negative contributions to work meaning, through means that organizational scholars usually do not consider. In particular, it suggests that, through small and seemingly insignificant actions, others can alter the meaning that employees make of the work (as job, role and self-at-work). Rather than seeing others as dispensers of material resources (e.g. in the mentoring or developmental relationships literature (e.g. Kram, 1985)), as nodes in structural networks (e.g. Baker, 2000), or as models to imitate (e.g. Ibarra, 1999), interpersonal sensemaking depicts others as providers of symbolic moves that are the raw materials in creating work meaning.

Elaborating the Meaning of Work

An interpersonal sensemaking perspective aligns with theories of job design that argue others at work help to determine the experienced meaningfulness of jobs (Hackman & Oldham, 1976) and that other people provide social and informational cues about the task that shape how people view their jobs (Salancik & Pfeffer, 1978; White & Mitchell, 1979). However, our perspective suggests that the interpersonal cues that shape work meaning may be much more explicitly social or interaction-based than those implied by a social information processing perspective on job design. Rather than seeing others at work providing cues that job incumbents passively receive and interpret, we argue that employees actively notice, interpret, and seek out cues in the course of daily interaction that convey evaluation and worth. An interpersonal sensemaking perspective suggests that a wider group of individuals play a role in providing social cues about jobs than research has yet considered. Further, it suggests that employees actively interpret and remember what people do or do not do towards them in their jobs. Most importantly, an interpersonal sensemaking perspective suggests that there is a close coupling between the way others make employees feel about the value of their work and how they feel valued as individuals. Thus the design of jobs, and the interactions it implies, shape the meaning of the work. Meaning of work scholars must attend to this dynamic, interactional process that helps to determine work meaning (Brief & Nord, 1990).

The addition of an interpersonal sensemaking perspective to understanding the meaning of work makes at least two contributions to this literature. First, our perspective changes the focus of determinants of the meaning of work from elements within the employee or within the job to the social interplay between employees and others encountered on the job. Thus, research that aims to understand work meaning must attend to the social context in which the work is carried out to fully understand the elements that directly contribute to work meaning.

Second, our perspective suggests that the evaluation and content of work meaning as well as the social context employees create are altered through work interactions. The implications of this process are serious, for we suggest that employees can change the content of their jobs, roles, and selves (e.g. Wrzesniewski & Dutton, 2001) as a result of interpersonal sensemaking at work. Thus, while work meaning has been viewed as a static state to be measured, our view treats work meanings as dynamic. At the extreme, our model suggests that the creation, alteration, and destruction of meaning at work occur in concert with others on a daily basis.

Looking to the Future

An interpersonal sensemaking perspective on work meaning affords many opportunities for future research. We have described the micro-processes that create work meaning through interaction traces. This theoretical advance lays bare the essence of what happens between individuals at work to affect the evaluation, worth, and content of jobs, roles, and selves. However, we have largely portrayed the process of interpersonal cue interpretation and its effect on work meaning as an individual phenomenon, describing how employees notice, interpret, and make meaning of the cues they receive from others. Our hope is that the process we describe opens new territory in research on work meaning, sensemaking, and the role of others at work, and will be useful to elaborating our current theories and research in these areas. While we are describing a social dynamic, the model we have elaborated is not fully social; that is, we take social cues of others into our model, but then describe an individual-level process that unfolds as a result, and offer predictions about how individuals will create and engage their social context at work as a result. As such, we have elaborated one side of the social phenomenon through which work meanings are created. We would encourage organizational behavior theorists to elaborate and test the dynamics that unfold between people at work in situ.

For example, researchers cannot observe and interpret cues themselves, but can use observational and interview techniques to surface employees' reactions to the cues they read from others in the course of their work day. Coding of cues (e.g. "Did you notice anything in the interaction?" "Was that (dis)affirming?" "What do you make of it?"), paired with changes in preferences for or behavioral patterns in interacting with categories of others (e.g. those from higher structural or power positions, those from outside of one's ingroup) may yield evidence for the dynamic unfolding of the shaping of interaction and task patterns on the job as a result of the cues employees read and interpret.

Another fruitful direction for future research would be to consider the impact of interpersonal cues as they combine from a variety of sources to inform an employee of others' evaluations of the job, role, and self. Our model considers the individual impact of each cue, but patterns of cues are likely to be an important consideration as well. For example, if employees are flooded with affirming cues from one set of interaction partners while being ignored or disaffirmed by another group, what is the overall effect of the cue pattern? Future research into these patterns would be valuable for learning if cues are simply aggregated or are chunked in different ways. Exciting possibilities abound with respect to experience sampling methods (Larson & Csikszentmihalyi, 1983), in which individuals report their interactions, affective states, and actions in real time, so that a flow of their activities and responses can be established. By determining who employees encounter on the job and the typical cues they receive in such interactions (ranging from whether the employee was acknowledged by a glance or not, to whether the exchange was respectful and validating), researchers can begin to determine the weight given to such cues and their effects for shaping meaning and experienced worth.

Finally, we have not considered the role of time in the interpersonal sensemaking process. The cues that employees receive early in their organizational and occupational tenure carry greater weight in the creation of work meaning. Also, the length of time an employee has been with a particular workgroup or department may change the effect of interpersonal cues (Polzer, Milton & Swann, 2002). Repeated measures designs, whether in interviews or surveys, can reveal the role that the passage of time plays in the kinds of cues and interaction partners that are attended to, and the kinds of motive work that is (or is not) done on their behalf. Thus, the unfolding of the meaning-making process over time is a rich future area for study.

CONCLUSION

This chapter offers an interpersonal sensemaking perspective on the meaning of work. We argue that the meaning of work is composed, in part, of the evaluations conveyed by a diverse set of people encountered at work. The interpersonal dynamics that unfold between people at work create a powerful context in which work meanings are composed. Our ability to understand the process through which this happens gives us access to the deeper meaning of the lived experience of employees at work. Thus, in this chapter, work meaning is treated as an emergent feature of the social scene at work. We have attempted to reveal the rich relational underpinnings of what have long been treated as individual processes. While this process model celebrates the role of others at work, it also celebrates the role of employees themselves for the active part they play in creating work meaning through interpersonal sensemaking. This characterization of the social context creates rich opportunities for understanding the role of others at work in ways that have not been previously considered.

ACKNOWLEDGMENTS

We appreciate the cooperation and generous gift of time from study participants and hospital management who helped immensely in scheduling interviews and with other details of the study. In efforts to maintain confidentiality, we have disguised the name of the hospital and the study participants. We wish to thank the William Russell Kelly Chair for its financial support, and the Document Processing Department for their timely and accurate transcription services. We also thank Loc Nguyen for her support in preparing this document. Jane Dutton also benefited from support from the Institute for Research on Women and Gender. A special thanks to Sue Ashford, Blake Ashforth, Wayne Baker, Caroline Bartel, Jean Bartunek, Joy Beatty, Michael Belzer, Mary Ceccanese, Rob Faulkner, Martha Feldman, Joyce Fletcher, Peter Frost, Jennifer Hartwell, Wei He, Robert Holmes, Ronit Kark, Gail Keenan, Rod Kramer, Brenda Lausch, Lora Lempert, Tammy Maclean, Joshua Margolis, Deb Meyerson, Jean Baker Miller, Susan Mohrman, Ellen O'Connor, Greg Oldham, Naomi Olson, Terri Orbuch, Leslie Perlow, Joseph Porac, Michael Pratt, Bob Radin, Huggy Rao, Lloyd Sandelands, Brent Schmitt, Myeong-Gu Seo, Barry Staw, Charlie Vanover, Jim Walsh, Karl

Weick, Katherine Williams, and Michele Williams for their individual comments. Several of you read this several times, and we greatly appreciate your fresh insights each time. We appreciate the feedback we received from presentations at ICOS (University of Michigan), Organizational Psychology (Michigan), Carnegie-Mellon University, McGill University, University of British Columbia, University of Illinois, University of Southern California and Wayne State University. Portions of this paper were presented at the 1996 and 1998 meetings of the Academy of Management.

REFERENCES

Adams, J. S. (1963). Toward an understanding of inequity. *Journal of Abnormal and Social Psychology, 67*, 422–436.

Alderfer, C. P. (1972). *Existence, relatedness, and growth.* New York, NY: Free Press.

Argyris, C. P. (1957). *Personality and organization: The conflict between system and the individual.* New York, NY: Harper & Row.

Arvey, R. D., Bouchard, T. J., Segal, N. L., & Abraham, L. M. (1989). Job satisfaction: Environmental and genetic components. *Journal of Applied Psychology, 74*(2), 187–192.

Ashforth, B. E. (2001). *Role transitions in organizational life: An identity-based perspective.* Mahwah, NJ: Lawrence Erlbaum.

Ashforth, B. E., & Kreiner, G. E. (1999). How can you do it?: Dirty work and the challenge of constructing a positive identity. *Academy of management Review, 24*, 413–434.

Ashforth, B. E., & Mael, F. (1989). Social identity theory and the organization. *Academy of Management Review, 14*, 20–39.

Baker, W. (2000). *Achieving success through social capital.* San Francisco, CA: Jossey-Bass.

Baron, J. N., & Pfeffer, J. (1994). The social psychology of organizations and inequality. *Social Psychology Quarterly, 57*(3), 190–209.

Bartel, C. (2003). Ambiguous organizational memberships: Implications for members' identification and coordinated organizational action. Working Paper.

Baumeister, R. F., & Vohs, K. D. (2002). The pursuit of meaningfulness in life. In: C. R. Snyder & S. J. Lopez (Eds), *The Handbook of Positive Psychology* (pp. 608–628). New York: Oxford University Press.

Becker, H. S. (1970). The nature of a profession. In: H. S. Becker (Ed.), *Sociological Work Method and Substance* (pp. 87–103). Chicago: Aldine.

Bies, R., & Moag, J. (1986). Interactional justice: Communication criteria of fairness. In: R. Lewicki (Ed.), *Research on Negotiation in Organizations* (pp. 43–55). Greenwich, CT: JAI Press.

Black, J. S., & Ashford, S. J. (1994). Fitting in or making jobs fit: Factors affecting mode of adjustment of new hires. *Human Relations, 48*(4), 421–437.

Blumer, H. (1966). Sociological implications of the thought of George Hubert Mead. *American Journal of Sociology, 71*, 535–548.

Bradbury, H., & Bergmann Lichtenstein, B. M. (2000). Relationality in organizational research: Exploring the space between. *Organization Science, 11*(5), 551–564.

Bradbury, T. N., & Fincham, F. D. (1990). Attributions in marriage: Review and critique. *Psychological Bulletin, 107*(1), 3–33.

Brief, A. P., & Nord, W. R. (Eds) (1990). *Meanings of occupational work: A collection of essays.* Lexington, MA: Lexington Books.

Campbell, A., Converse, P., & Rodgers, W. (1976). *The quality of American life: Perceptions, evaluations, and satisfactions.* New York, NY: Sage.

Cappelli, P., & Scherer, P. D. (1991). The missing role of context in OB: The need for a meso level approach. In: L. L. Cummings & B. M. Staw (Eds), *Research in Organizational Behavior* (pp. 55–110). Greenwich, CT: JAI Press.

Cavendish, R. (1982). *Women on the line.* London: Routledge & Kegan Paul.

Cooley, C. H. (1902). *Human nature and the social order.* New York, NY: C. Scribner's Sons.

Côté, S., & Moskowitz, D. S. (1998). On the dynamic covariation between interpersonal behavior and affect: Prediction from neuroticism, extraversion, and agreeableness. *Journal of Personality and Social Psychology, 75,* 1032–1046.

Crocker, J., & Park, L. E. (2003). Seeking self-esteem: Construction, maintenance, and protection of self-worth. In: M. Leary & J. Tangney (Eds), *Handbook of Self and Identity* (pp. 291–313). New York: Guilford Press.

Debats, D. L., Drost, J., & Hansen, P. (1995). Experiences of meaning in life: A combined qualitative and quantitative approach. *British Journal of Psychology, 86*(3), 359–376.

Drazin, R., Glynn, M. A., & Kazanjian, R. K. (1999). Multilevel theorizing about creativity in organizations: A sensemaking perspective. *Academy of Management Review, 24*(2), 286–307.

Dutton, J. E. (2003). *Energizing your workplace: Building and sustaining high quality connections at work.* San Francisco, CA: Jossey-Bass.

Dutton, J. E., Ashford, S., Lawrence, K. A., & Miner-Rubino, K. (2002). Red light, green light: Making sense of the organizational context for issue selling. *Organization Science, 13*(4), 355–369.

Eide, D. (2000). Learning across interactions: Which 'voices' matter where? Paper presented at the EGOS colloquium. Helsinki School of Economics and Business Administration.

Emerson, R. M. (1976). Social exchange theory. *Annual Review of Sociology, 2,* 335–362.

Emmons, R. (2003). Acts of gratitude in organizations. In: K. Cameron, J. Dutton & R. Quinn (Eds), *Positive Organizational Scholarship: Foundations of a New Discipline.* San Francisco: Berrett-Koehler.

Erez, M., & Earley, P. C. (1993). *Culture, self-identity, and work.* New York: Oxford University Press.

Fine, G. A. (1996). Justifying work: Occupational rhetorics as resources in restaurant kitchens. *Administrative Science Quarterly, 41,* 90–115.

Fisher, C. D. (2000). Mood and emotions while working: Missing pieces of job satisfaction? *Journal of Organizational Behavior, 21,* 185–202.

Fiske, S. T., & Taylor, S. E. (1991). *Social cognition.* New York, NY: McGraw-Hill.

Frankl, V. E. (1963). *Man's search for meaning.* New York: Simon & Schuster.

Friedson, E. (1970). *Professional dominance: The social structure of medical care.* New York: Atherton.

Garfinkel, H. (1967). *Studies in ethnomethodology.* Englewood Cliffs, NJ: Prentice-Hall.

Garson, B. (1975). *All the livelong day: The meaning and demeaning of routine work.* Garden City, NY: Doubleday.

Gecas, V. (1971). Parental behavior and dimensions of adolescent self-evaluation. *Sociometry, 34,* 466–482.

Gecas, V. (1982). The self-concept. *Annual Review of Sociology, 8,* 1–33.

Gergen, K. J., & Gergen, M. M. (1988). Narrative and the self as relationship. In: L. Berkowitz (Ed.), *Advances in Experimental Social Psychology* (Vol. 21, pp. 17–56). San Diego: Academic Press.

Gersick, C. J. G., Bartunek, J., & Dutton, J. E. (2000). Learning from academia: The importance of relationships in professional life. *Academy of Management Journal, 43*(6), 1026–1044.

Graen, G. B., & Scandura, T. A. (1987). Toward a psychology of dyadic organizing. *Research in Organizational Behavior, 9*, 175–208.

Griffin, R. W. (1982). *Task design: An integrative approach.* Glenview, IL: Scott Foresman.

Griffin, R. W., & McMahan, G. C. (1995). Motivation through job design: Prospects for the future. In: J. Greenberg (Ed.), *Organizational Behavior: The State of the Science* (pp. 23–43). Mahwah, NJ: Lawrence Erlbaum.

Hackman, J. R., & Oldham, G. R. (1976). Motivation through the design of work: Test of a theory. *Organizational Behavior and Human Performance, 16*, 250–279.

Hackman, J. R., & Oldham, G. R. (1980). *Work redesign.* Reading, MA: Addison-Wesley.

Hamper, B. (1986). *Rivethead: Tales from the assembly line.* New York, NY: Warner Books.

Hodson, R. (1991). *Dignity at work.* Cambridge, MA: Cambridge University Press.

Hoffer Gittell, J. (2003). *The southwest airlines way: Using the power of relationships to achieve high performance.* New York: McGraw-Hill.

Hogg, M. A., & Terry, D. J. (2000). Social identity and self-categorization processes in organizational contexts. *Academy of Management Review, 25*, 121–140.

Hughes, E. C. (1950). Work and the self. In: J. H. Rohrer & M. Sherif (Eds), *Social Psychology at the Crossroads* (pp. 313–323). New York: Harper.

Ibarra, H. (1999). Provisional selves: Experimenting with image and identity in professional adaptation. *Administrative Science Quarterly, 44*, 764–791.

James, W. (1890). *Principles of psychology.* New York, NY: Dover.

Jones, S. C. (1973). Self and interpersonal evaluations: Esteem theories versus consistency theories. *Psychological Bulletin, 79*, 185–199.

Judge, T. A., Thoresen, C. J., Bono, J. E., & Patton, G. K. (2001). The job satisfaction-job performance relationship: A qualitative and quantitative review. *Psychological Bulletin, 127*, 376–407.

Kahn, W. A. (1990). Psychological conditions of personal engagement and disengagement at work. *Academy of Management Journal, 33*(4), 692–724.

Kahn, W. A. (1998). Relational systems at work. In: B. M. Staw & L. L. Cummings (Eds), *Research in Organizational Behavior* (pp. 39–76). Greenwich, CT: JAI Press.

Kahn, R. L., Wolfe, D. M., Quinn, R., Snoek, J. D., & Rosenthal, R. A. (1964). *Organizational stress.* New York, NY: Wiley.

Kelly, G. A. (1955). *The psychology of personal constructs: A theory of personality* (Vol. 1). New York, NY: Norton.

Keltner, D., Gruenfeld, D. H., & Anderson, C. (2003). Power, approach, and inhibition. *Psychological Review, 110*, 265–284.

Kohn, M. L., & Schooler, C. (1982). Job conditions and personality: A longitudinal assessment of their reciprocal effects. *American Journal of Sociology, 87*(6), 1257–1286.

Konner, M. (1987). *Becoming a doctor: A journey of initiation in medical school.* New York, NY: Penguin.

Kram, K. (1985). *Mentoring at work: Developmental relationships in organizational life.* Glenville, IL: Scott Foresman & Co.

Larson, R., & Csikszentmihalyi, M. (1983). The experience sampling method. In: H. T. Reis (Ed.), *Naturalistic Approaches to Studying Social Interaction.* San Francisco, CA: Jossey-Bass.

Lazarus, R. S. (1991). *Emotion and adaptation.* New York, NY: Oxford University.

Lazarus, R. S., & Folkman, S. (1984). *Stress, appraisal and coping.* New York, NY: Springer.

Lee, F., & Tiedens, L. (2001). Is it lonely at the top? Independence and interdependence of power-holders. In: B. Staw & R. Sutton (Eds), *Research in Organizational Behavior* (Vol. 23, pp. 43–91).

Locke, E. A., & Latham, G. P. (1990). Work motivation and satisfaction: Light at the end of the tunnel. *Psychological Science, 1*, 240–246.

Lodahl, T. M., & Kejner, M. (1965). The definition and measurement of job involvement. *Journal of Applied Psychology, 49*, 24–33.

Loscocco, K. A. (1989). The instrumentally oriented factory worker. Myth or reality? *Work and Organization, 16*(1), 3–25.

Lynch, S. M. (2000). *The relationship between women's paid work experiences and multiple aspects of the self in the context of partner violence.* Doctoral dissertation, University of Michigan.

Margolis, J. D. (1999). *Dignity in organizations.* Working Paper, University of Michigan Business School, Ann Arbor, MI.

Maslow, A. (1954). *Motivation and personality.* New York, NY: Harper.

Meara, H. (1974). Honor in dirty work: The case of American meat cutters and Turkish butchers. *Sociology of Work and Occupations, 1*, 259–283.

Meyer, J. P., & Allen, N. (1997). *Commitment in the workplace: Theory, research, and application.* Thousand Oaks, CA: Sage.

Mills, C. W. (1940). Situated actions and vocabularies of motive. *American Sociological Review, 5*, 904–913.

Morrison, E. W. (1994). Role definitions and organizational citizenship behavior: The importance of the employee's perspective. *Academy of Management Journal, 37*, 1543–1567.

Morrow, P. C., & Wirth, R. E. (1989). Work commitment among salaried professionals. *Journal of Vocational Behavior, 34*, 40–56.

MOW International Research Team (1987). *The meaning of working.* New York: Academic Press.

Murrell, A. J., Crosby, F., & Ely, R. (1999). *Mentoring dilemmas: Developmental relationships within the multicultural organization.* Mahwah, NJ: Lawrence Erlbaum.

Nord, W. R., Brief, A. P., Atieh, J. M., & Doherty, E. M. (1990). Studying meanings of work: The case of work values. In: A. P. Brief & W. R. Nord (Eds), *Meanings of Occupational Work: A Collection of Essays* (pp. 21–64). Lexington, MA: Lexington Books.

Olson, J. M., Roese, N. J., & Zanna, M. P. (1996). Expectancies. In: E. T. Higgins & A. W. Kruglanski (Eds), *Social Psychology: Handbook of Basic Principles* (pp. 211–238). New York: Guilford Press.

Orr, J. (1996). *Talking about machines: An ethnography of a modern job.* Ithaca, NY: IRL Press.

Paullay, I. M., Alliger, G. M., & Stone-Romero, E. F. (1994). Construct validation of two instruments designed to measure job involvement and work centrality. *Journal of Applied Psychology, 79*(2), 224–228.

Pearson, C. M., Andersson, L. A., & Porath, C. L. (2000). Assessing and attacking workplace incivility. *Organizational Dynamics*, Fall, 123–137.

Peeters, G., & Czapinski, J. (1990). Positive-negative asymmetry in evaluations: The distinction between affective and informational negativity effects. *European Review of Social Psychology, 1*, 33–60.

Perry, S. E. (1978). *San Francisco scavengers: Dirty work and the pride of ownership.* Berkeley, CA: University of California Press.

Polzer, J., Milton, L. P., & Swann, W. B. (2002). Capitalizing on diversity: Interpersonal congruence in small work groups. *Administrative Science Quarterly, 47*, 296–324.

Pratt, M. G., & Ashforth, B. E. (2003). Fostering meaningfulness in working and meaningfulness at work: An identity perspective. In: K. Cameron, J. E. Dutton & R. E. Quinn (Eds), *Positive Organizational Scholarship.* San Francisco: Berrett-Koehler.

Pratto, F., & John, O. P. (1991). Automatic vigilance: The attention-grabbing power of negative social information. *Journal of Personality and Social Psychology, 61*, 380–391.

Prus, R. (1996). *Symbolic interaction and ethnographic research: Intersubjectivity and the study of lived experience.* Albany, NY: State University of New York Press.

Riemer, J. W. (1979). *Hard hats: The work world of construction workers.* Beverly Hills, CA: Sage.

Roberson, L. (1990). Functions of work meanings in organizations: Work meanings and work motivation. In: A. P. Brief & W. R. Nord (Eds), *Meanings of Occupational Work: A Collection of Essays* (pp. 107–134). Lexington, MA: Lexington Books.

Robinson, S. L., & O'Leary-Kelly, A. M. (1998). Monkey see, monkey do: The influence of work groups on the antisocial behavior of employees. *Academy of Management Journal, 41*, 658–672.

Roccas, S., & Brewer, M. (2002). Social identity complexity. *Personality and Social Psychology Review, 6*, 88–106.

Rosenberg, M. (1979). *Conceiving the self.* New York, NY: Basic Books.

Rothbard, N. P. (2001). Enriching or depleting? The dynamics of engagement in work and family roles. *Administrative Science Quarterly, 46*, 655–684.

Roy, D. (1959). Banana time: Job satisfaction and informal interaction. *Human Organization, 18*, 158–168.

Salancik, G. R., & Pfeffer, J. (1978). A social information processing approach to job attitudes and task design. *Administrative Science Quarterly, 23*, 224–253.

Sandelands, L. E., & Boudens, C. J. (2000). Feeling at work. In: S. Fineman (Ed.), *Emotion in Organizations* (pp. 46–63). London: Sage.

Schenkler, B. R. (1985). Self-identification: Toward an integration of the private and public self. In: R. Baumiester (Ed.), *Public Self and Private Self* (pp. 21–62). New York: Springer-Verlag.

Schwalbe, M. L., & Mason-Schrock, D. (1996). Identity work as group process. In: B. Markovsky, M. J. Lovaglia & R. Simon (Eds), *Advances in Group Processes* (Vol. 13, pp. 113–147). Greenwich, CT: JAI Press.

Shamir, B. (1991). Meaning, self and motivation in organizations. *Organizational Studies, 12*, 405–424.

Staw, B. M., Bell, N. E., & Clausen, J. A. (1986). The dispositional approach to job attitudes. *Administrative Science Quarterly, 31*, 56–77.

Staw, B. M., & Ross, J. (1985). Stability in the midst of change: A dispositional approach to job attitudes. *Journal of Applied Psychology, 70*, 469–480.

Stryker, S. (1994). Identity theory: Its development, research base, and prospect. *Studies in Symbolic Interaction, 16*, 9–20.

Stryker, S., & Serpe, R. T. (1994). Identity salience and psychological centrality: Equivalent, overlapping, or complementary concepts? *Social Psychology Quarterly, 57*(1), 16–35.

Swann, W. B. (1984). Quest for accuracy in person perception: A matter of pragmatics. *Psychological Review, 91*, 457–477.

Swann, W. B., Jr. (1987). Identity negotiation: Where two roads meat. *Journal of Personality and Social Psychology, 53*, 1038–1051.

Swann, W. B., Jr. (1990). To be adored or to be known? The interplay of self enhancement and self verification. In: E. T. Higgins & R. M. Sorrentino (Eds), *Handbook of Motivation and Cognition: Foundations of Social Behavior* (Vol. 2, pp. 408–448). New York: Guilford Press.

Swann, W. B., Jr. (1999). *Resilient identities: Self, relationships, and the construction of social reality.* New York: Basic Books.

Swann, W. B., Jr., Rentfrow, P. J., & Guinn, J. (2002). Self-verification: The search for coherence. In: M. Leary & J. Tangney (Eds), *Handbook of Self and Identity.* New York: Guilford Press.

Tepper, B. J. (2000). Consequences of abusive supervision. *Academy of Management Journal, 43,* 178–190.

Terkel, S. (1972). *Working.* New York, NY: New Press.

Tice, D. M., & Wallace, H. M. (2002). The reflected self: Creating ourselves as (you think) others see you. In: M. R. Leary & J. Tangney (Eds), *Handbook of Self and Identity* (pp. 91–105). New York: Guilford Press.

Vecchio, R. P. (1980). The function and meaning of work and the job: Morse and Weiss (1955) revisited. *Academy of Management Journal, 23,* 361–367.

Waldron, V. R. (2000). Relational experiences and emotions at work. In: S. Fineman (Ed.), *Emotions in Organizations* (pp. 64–83). London: Sage.

Weber, J. G. (1994). The nature of ethnocentric attribution bias: Ingroup protection or enhancement? *Journal of Experimental Social Psychology, 30,* 482–504.

Weick, K. E. (1995). *Sensemaking in organizations.* Thousand Oaks, CA: Sage.

Whetten, D. A., & Godfrey, P. C. (1998). *Identity in organizations: Building theory through conversations.* Thousand Oaks, CA: Sage.

White, S. E., & Mitchell, T. M. (1979). Job enrichment versus social cues: A comparison and competitive test. *Journal of Applied Psychology, 64,* 1–9.

Withey, M. J., & Cooper, W. H. (1989). Predicting exit, voice, loyalty, and neglect. *Administrative Science Quarterly, 34,* 521–539.

Wrzesniewski, A., & Dutton, J. E. (2001). Crafting a job: Revisioning employees as active crafters of their work. *Academy of Management Review, 26,* 179–201.

Wrzesniewski, A., McCauley, C. R., Rozin, P., & Schwartz, B. (1997). Jobs, careers, and callings: People's relations to their work. *Journal of Research in Personality, 31,* 21–33.

THE MESSENGER BIAS:
A RELATIONAL MODEL OF
KNOWLEDGE VALUATION

Tanya Menon and Sally Blount

ABSTRACT

*How do managers value the knowledge that they encounter in organizations?
A rational perspective assumes that managers carefully and accurately cull
the best knowledge from their environments, while a random model situates
managers in a chaotic organization, filled with preferences and solutions
that are temporally matched. This paper develops a third view, a relational
perspective, which describes how social relationships between knowledge
messengers and knowledge receivers affect the way that managers evaluate
new knowledge. We begin by focusing on two key dimensions of relational
perception: social identification and threat appraisals. We then use these
dimensions to derive a typology of six "relational schemas" that are commonly perceived between knowledge messengers and knowledge receivers
at work. Next, we reveal how, holding knowledge content constant, these
relational schemas bias the ways in which managers evaluate new knowledge.
While network research demonstrates that relationships determine which
knowledge managers see, this paper demonstrates that these relationships
also have psychological implications by affecting how managers evaluate the
knowledge that they see.*

Research in Organizational Behavior
Research in Organizational Behavior, Volume 25, 137–186
Copyright © 2003 by Elsevier Ltd.
All rights of reproduction in any form reserved
ISSN: 0191-3085/doi:10.1016/S0191-3085(03)25004-8

INTRODUCTION

Emerson once said that "if a man writes a better book, preaches a better sermon, or makes a better mousetrap than his neighbor, though he builds his house in the woods, the world will make a beaten path to his door (cited in Yule & Keene, 1889)." Despite Emerson's optimism about the inherent value of a good idea, people in modern work organizations often come to discover truth in the reverse: frequently it is the good ideas – rather than the paths towards them – that get beaten down. Subordinates complain that, rather than valuing their good ideas, their managers instead ignore them, actively resist them, or sink them in the mire of organizational politics (Morison, 1966; Smith & Alexander, 1988). Similarly, outside consultants observe that even though clients initially prize their ideas, they often don't implement them (Maister, Green & Galford, 2000; O'Shea & Madigan, 1997).

In addition to failing to leverage good ideas, sometimes managers embrace bad ideas. Consider, only recently, how corporate managers over-invested in dot.com ventures (Czernich & Heath, 2002), and how top-tier stock analysts admired and applauded Enron's financial practices. In each of these situations, organizational actors faced with ideas of uncertain value made investment decisions based on their evaluations of these ideas, and their organizations suffered tremendous losses as a result.

These images of decision makers confusing good knowledge with bad and bad knowledge with good call into question rational models of knowledge transfer, in which managers carefully evaluate each piece of new knowledge that they encounter. Yet, the garbage can model (Cohen, March & Olsen, 1972) veers to the other extreme. This model eliminates the notion of managers as rational decision makers engaged in processes of knowledge valuation and replaces it with a time-dependent matching process, in which actors, problems, and solutions happen to converge in time and space. We posit that while knowledge evaluation is often not rational, neither is it random. Instead, it is often a complex process, where well-recognized, social psychological forces converge to determine the fate of new ideas. Specifically, we propose a "relational model of knowledge valuation," whereby the relationships between actors communicating knowledge and actors receiving those communications produce social psychological forces that moderate how a new piece of knowledge is evaluated.

We start from the premise that organizational work requires organizational members to engage in a variety of relationships with other actors (Kahn, 1998). We then model how the nature of a person's different relationships affects how new knowledge that is conveyed within a relationship is evaluated (Snyder & Stukas, 1999). Our objective is to use social psychological research to demonstrate that predictable differences in knowledge valuation often occur in organizations independent of the actual content of the knowledge that is conveyed.

A Workplace Example

To motivate our approach, we offer the following example drawn from our own workplaces: evaluating the knowledge that we receive about newly minted Ph.D. students on the academic job market. When evaluating job candidates, the knowledge that we receive is abundant, confusing, and ambiguous. While, as professors, we care deeply about the content domain (the candidate could be our future colleague, after all!), our time and energy resources are scarce – given the many and conflicting demands on them. In evaluating each candidate, we cannot claim that the process is perfectly rational, but neither is it random. Instead, it is heavily influenced by the nature of the relationships that surround us.

For example, if we receive a positive letter from a chaired professor at a well-regarded department, we weight that piece of knowledge quite heavily in our decision making, perhaps more heavily than a positive letter from an assistant professor at a less-respected department – even though we know the assistant professor better than the chaired professor. Further, if a rival within our field whom we don't trust writes a positive letter for his student, we confess that we are prone to heuristically dismiss that rival's knowledge. Additionally, if we hear from a well-regarded professor at a competitor school that her group is interested in a particular candidate, we tend to automatically assume that our competitor's knowledge is of high quality. We then use it to push that candidate onto our "short list," even if we have not taken the time to carefully read the file.

As this example illustrates, when we receive knowledge about a job candidate, we associate it with the messenger who conveys it, and that relational context affects how we evaluate the knowledge. It is in this manner that relationships influence knowledge valuation. Perceptions of relational similarity, esteem, rivalry and reputation affect how managers evaluate what other people tell them. Our goal in writing this paper is to elaborate these processes – to examine the mechanisms by which perceptions of relationships systematically bias knowledge valuation.

Construct Definition: Knowledge Valuation

We begin by defining our core construct, knowledge, which we distinguish from data (discrete, objective facts about events) and information (data which informs, shapes, and makes a difference to the recipient) (Davenport & Prusak, 1998). Knowledge is "framed experience, values, contextual information, and expert insight that provides a framework for evaluation and incorporation of new experience and information (Davenport & Prusak, 1998, p. 5)." As this definition implies, knowledge is subjective and complex (Argote & Ingram, 2000; Brown & Duguid, 2000). It is framed by the values and context that surround its creators and its evaluators (Polyani, 1958).

Because knowledge is subjective and complex, the process of evaluating it is nuanced and multidimensional. Here, we consider three dimensions that are particularly relevant to knowledge valuation in organizational settings: its content quality, feasibility, and strategic value.

Content Quality
When people evaluate knowledge based on content quality, they consider whether the knowledge is creative, insightful, logical, relevant, and accurate. Key considerations include: does the knowledge address a relevant problem; is it based on accurate data and information; and is it thoughtfully reasoned? As an example, consider oil speculators who are searching for knowledge that will enable them to value a piece of land accurately. Valuable knowledge, from their point of view, is that which is based upon reliable data regarding the likelihood of finding oil underneath a particular plot of land within a specified time period (Milgrom & Roberts, 1992).

Feasibility
In addition to content quality, managers must also take into account the feasibility of new knowledge; that is, the degree to which it is timely, appropriate, and politically practical (e.g. Borgatti & Cross, 2002; Zmud, 1978). Here, key considerations include: does the knowledge address a problem that other organizational members perceive as needing attention; does the knowledge imply a solution that organizational members can buy into to; and does it take into account important contextual constraints (e.g. time, money, logistical and geographical considerations)? As an example, consider the incessant stream of tips that analysts at the CIA and FBI encounter every day (e.g. from intelligence agents, foreign nationals, other government agencies, and Internet chat rooms) (Tor & Bazerman, 2001). Although a particular tip could contain important knowledge about stopping a planned terrorist attack, there is so much data, information, and knowledge floating about (or "chatter" in intelligence jargon), that many pieces of knowledge are devalued simply because they are costly to track and verify (Hansen & Haas, 2001). Such knowledge could contain potentially valuable content, but it is ultimately devalued because of the feasibility issues surrounding its use.

Strategic Value

Finally, knowledge is sometimes valued, not for its content quality or feasibility, but for its strategic value, i.e. its ability to protect, enhance, and/or advance one's personal status, identity, and reputation within the organization (Burt, 1992; Pfeffer, 1992; Tetlock, 1999). Here, key considerations include: does the knowledge imply a solution that will potentially preserve or even elevate the manager's status (even if the solution is not the most elegant) and does the knowledge have the potential to help the manager accrue scarce resources? As an example, when Robert McNamara and the "whiz kids" joined Ford in the mid-1940s, they used their knowledge of financial modeling to build an alliance with Henry Ford, Jr. This knowledge ultimately allowed them to ascend to power by setting the agendas, strategic direction, and even shaping the culture of the entire company for several decades (Halberstam, 1972). Thus, people often value particular pieces of knowledge highly, not because they are high on content quality, but because, by using them, they can acquire and exert power (Pfeffer, 1992).

Integration

In sum, people in organizations often evaluate knowledge based on characteristics other than just content quality. While managers value knowledge most highly if they judge its content quality, feasibility, and strategic value positively, those judgments do not always coincide. Sometimes, managers value the content quality of a piece of knowledge but consider it infeasible. Alternatively, they may appreciate the feasibility of a piece of knowledge but not its content, or devalue the knowledge quality but see it as strategically useful. Often times these judgments converge based on needs for consistency (Cialdini, 2001), but at other times, managers prioritize a single criterion (i.e. focusing either on content quality, feasibility, or strategic value) as the basis for evaluating a particular piece of knowledge (Tetlock, 1999).

Our task in this paper, therefore, is to examine the complex and contextually nuanced ways in which people evaluate knowledge in organizations. We do this by holding knowledge content constant and focusing on how relationships affect the process of evaluation – both in terms of which criteria are applied (i.e. content quality, feasibility and strategic value) and how they are measured. In addition to controlling for knowledge content, we also assume that knowledge receivers are motivated to acquire new knowledge (Zahra & George, 2002) and have the capacity to absorb it (Cohen & Levinthal, 1990). Tying these points to our example, our goal is to show why it is that if the exact same recommendation letter were written by two different professors, the two letters could be evaluated quite differently. To do this, we first develop a general model of how relationships influence the evaluation of knowledge. Then, we develop a taxonomy of relational schemas and explore how different relationships introduce positive or negative biases in knowledge valuation.

RELATIONAL MODEL OF KNOWLEDGE VALUATION

To build our model, we begin with the premise that relationships exist between actors communicating knowledge ("knowledge messengers") and actors receiving those communications ("knowledge receivers") (Davenport & Prusak, 1998; Krone, Jablin & Putnam, 1987), and we focus on the nature of each relationship as the knowledge receiver perceives it. We use the term "relational schemas" to represent the receiver's perception and construal of his or her relationships with different knowledge messengers (Baldwin, 1992). As Baldwin notes, "people develop working models of their relationships that function as cognitive maps to help them navigate their social world (p. 462)." Once in place, these relational schemas affect how a person, as a knowledge receiver, evaluates knowledge conveyed in different relational contexts. This is because these schemas trigger affective orientations, motivational orientations, and knowledge accessibility perceptions, each of which affect how they encode and process knowledge (Baldwin, 1992; Berk & Andersen, 2000; Berscheid, 1994; A. Fiske, 1991; Snyder & Stukas, 1999).

In examining the effect of relational schemas on knowledge valuation, we take a categorical approach to interpreting a knowledge receiver's relationships. As A. Fiske and Haslam (1996) find, people naturally perceive their relationships with others in terms of a small number of categories or types, as compared to a more complex multi-dimensional approach in which they carefully individuate each relationship (see also A. Fiske, 1991; Haslam, 1994). To date, Fiske and Haslam have identified four broad categories of social relationships (e.g. communal and market-price based). However, to say something meaningful about differences in evaluation within organizational settings in particular, a more fine-grained set of categories is needed.

In this section, we develop a taxonomy that includes six relational schemas that are particularly relevant to organizational settings. Each schema produces affective, motivational, and knowledge accessibility tendencies that affect the cognitive processing associated with knowledge valuation. However, before introducing processes that occur within each specific schema, we describe the general mechanisms by which relational schemas affect knowledge valuation.

Overview of Psychological Mechanisms

We begin with a simplified model of evaluation drawn from the decision theory literature (see Goldstein & Hogarth, 1997, for a review). Figure 1 depicts both the knowledge messenger and the knowledge that he or she conveys. At the top of the

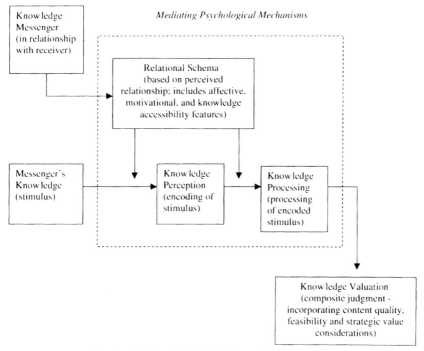

Fig. 1.   Relational Model of Knowledge Valuation.

figure, we show how the knowledge messenger's relationship to the receiver triggers the receiver to apply a relational schema to quickly interpret the messenger's meaning to the self. This schema includes affective, motivational, and knowledge accessibility features.

At the bottom of the figure, we depict how the knowledge that the messenger conveys provides a separate stimulus that is simultaneously perceived, processed, and evaluated by the receiver. As Fig. 1 shows, the application of a specific relational schema influences both knowledge perception (that is, how a new piece of knowledge is encoded as a stimulus) and knowledge processing (that is, how the encoded stimulus is processed to produce an evaluative judgment). Research finds that both stages of evaluation are prone to bias.

Knowledge Perception and Processing
Decision makers tend to simplify complex, nuanced knowledge when they encode it. People often take two types of short-cuts: (a) they focus on only a subset of

attributes, thus over-weighting some attributes of the knowledge while neglecting others and/or; (b) they attach contextual cues such as affect, status, and other traits associated with the messenger, as attributes of the knowledge.

Once a stimulus is encoded, people have multiple ways of processing it. The two most general forms are systematic and heuristic processing (see Chaiken & Trope, 1999, for a review). *Systematic processing* most closely approximates the rational model. It engages the cognitive capacities and capabilities of the receiver. It entails that people process knowledge on the central route, by exerting more mental effort to carefully and diligently assess the attributes of the knowledge (Petty, Cacioppo & Goldman, 1981) and subjecting the knowledge to a "relatively analytic and comprehensive treatment (Chen & Chaiken, 1999, p. 74)." However, systematic processing is cognitively taxing and highly time-consuming. As a result, people often resort to *heuristic processing*, which makes minimal cognitive demands on a person. It entails the activation and application of judgmental shortcuts and "heuristics" that are triggered by cues associated with the knowledge (such as the way that the messenger presents the knowledge), rather than the actual content of the knowledge. Under heuristic processing, people process knowledge using a "peripheral route" where they react to the positive or negative cues that they automatically associate with the knowledge, and then either automatically value or devalue it (Petty & Cacioppo, 1986; Petty, Cacioppo & Goldman, 1981).

The Role of Relational Schemas
Relational schemas color how knowledge is evaluated through their influence on both the encoding and processing stages. In the encoding stage, they can influence which attributes managers attend to – including those that are relevant (e.g. the perceived accuracy of the data underlying the knowledge) and irrelevant (e.g. affective reactions to the messenger). In the processing stage, they influence which evaluation criteria receivers apply (i.e. content quality, feasibility or strategic value), and whether receivers use systematic versus heuristic processing in matching knowledge attributes with their evaluation criteria.

In order to specify the process by which relational schemas moderate knowledge valuation, we focus on three dimensions. Relational schemas trigger affective orientations, motivational orientations, and knowledge accessibility perceptions. We briefly explain each below.

First, relational schemas produce particular *affective orientations* that translate into how receivers encode and process new knowledge. A knowledge messenger naturally elicits affective responses from the receiver that spillover to the receiver's evaluation of the message. For example, managers at a meeting often experience a gut-level positive or negative response to an idea presented by a particular messenger type, even before they hear the actual content. When receivers evaluate messengers (either positively or negatively) based on their perceived relationships with them, these messenger evaluations introduce affective biases into knowledge valuation.

Second, relationships provide motivations. A messenger's relationship to a receiver often involves inherent threats or affirmations, which implicate the receiver's self and/or social identities (Steele, 1988). As a result, motivations to protect or enhance their own identity cloud a receiver's judgments about knowledge. When a messenger's knowledge presents a manager with an opportunity for self-affirmation, for example, the manager gains strategic value by inflating their valuation of its content and feasibility (Menon, Choi & Thompson, 2003). Thus, relational schemas produce *motivational orientations*, as tendencies toward self- or group-protection and self- or group-enhancement are evoked. These orientations influence how receivers encode knowledge, how they select evaluation criteria, and whether they use heuristic processing.

Third, given that knowledge messengers vary in their frequency of contact with receivers, relationships regulate perceptions of *knowledge accessibility*. Knowledge becomes accessible because it is easily acquired; i.e. the messenger is local and willingly communicates that knowledge and/or it is inexpensive in terms of financial search costs. As a consequence of accessibility, the transparency of knowledge varies. For example, knowledge from colleagues travels through rich channels of communication and is more transparent than knowledge from consultants, allowing receivers to elaborate and scrutinize knowledge, and therefore, process it more systematically and deeply. The perceived scarcity (or abundance) of these knowledge flows also influences how knowledge is encoded – making it appear more (or less) valuable (Cialdini, 2001).

In sum, we posit that people often perceive others in terms of relational schemas, and that these schemas bias how people value the new knowledge that they encounter. This is because relational schemas introduce distinct affective, motivational, and knowledge accessibility features that color how people encode, process, and evaluate that knowledge.

Taxonomy of Relational Schemas at Work

We now introduce our taxonomy of relational schemas. Drawing from recent psychological findings on social and relational identities (see Andersen & Chen, in press, for a review), we describe two aspects social perception that are particularly relevant to how receivers perceive relationships in organizations: group-identification and threat appraisals. These two dimensions underlie our six relational schemas.

Group Identification

Group identification reflects a perception of social similarity between the self and another person – that is, a perception of oneness or belongingness with a common human aggregate (Ashforth & Mael, 1989; Brewer & Kramer, 1985; Tajfel & Turner, 1986). Research has long found that people perceive other people based on social categories (Allport, 1954; S. Fiske & Neuberg, 1990; Macrae & Bodenhausen, 2000), and evaluate them based on their categorical similarity or dissimilarity with the self (e.g. Brewer, 1991; Brewer & Gardner, 1996). People make categorical distinctions at work based on many dimensions, such as demographic similarity (e.g. we're all women), shared functional expertise (e.g. we're both in finance), shared product line or organizational affiliations (e.g. we both work for the Saturn division), or shared educational background (e.g. we both have MBAs from Harvard) (Baron & Pfeffer, 1994; Kramer, 1998).

Across different settings, perceptions of a person's social identity shift as different aspects of social identity become salient. For example, in a meeting about maternity policy, a woman may feel most closely identified with the other women in the room. In another meeting about how to allocate capital expenditures across functional departments within her company, she may feel most closely identified with the other marketing executives in the room who are both male and female. Thus, as an actor's perception of his or her social identity shifts across situations, the perception of whether another actor is an in- or out-group member can also change (Brewer, 1991; Brewer & Gardner, 1996; Brewer & Kramer, 1985).

The perception of in- or out-group identification is integral to relational perception, because psychologists have consistently found that people evaluate in-group members more positively than outgroup members (e.g. Festinger, 1954; Goethals & Nelson, 1973; Insko, Smith, Alicke, Wade & Taylor, 1985; Mackie, 1987; Merton, 1957; Siegel & Siegel, 1957). This line of research demonstrates that "in-group favoritism" often occurs unconsciously and heuristically – thus, people automatically favor in-group members and their knowledge (Asch, 1951; Moscovici, 1980; for review see Hewstone, Rubin & Willis, 2002).

Threat Appraisal

While in-group favoritism is a robust finding *in the laboratory*, a core argument of this paper is that relational perception *in the field* is more nuanced. In addition to perceiving the degree to which other actors are similar or different from themselves based on group membership, people also assign trait characteristics to others (Kunda & Thagard, 1996). In the process, they make affective judgments regarding the differences that they perceive between themselves and others (Andersen & Chen, in press; Andersen, Glassman & Gold, 1998; S. Fiske, 1982; Srull & Wyer, 1989; Wyer & Carlston, 1994). People do this to resolve the uncertainty they feel about the motives, intentions, and behaviors of other people (Kramer, 1999a, b).

We use the term personal appraisal to capture this judgment at the individual level. Is the other evaluated positively or negatively; is he an ally or a threat; is she perceived as a friend or foe? Within a social utility approach, this evaluation reflects whether one's own outcomes are experienced negatively (competitor), neutrally, or positively (trusted friend) relative to the other actor's (Loewenstein, Thompson & Bazerman, 1989; Messick & Sentis, 1985). Alternatively, we can interpret this appraisal to incorporate whether a receiver perceives a messenger within a promotion (approach) or prevention (avoid) regulatory focus (see Higgins, 1997 for a review).

Existing research suggests that people base personal appraisals on a variety of factors, including their stereotypes, personal trait inferences (Pavelchak, 1989; Smith & Zárate, 1992), or even transference; that is, if a messenger reminds the receiver of a family member or someone that they used to know (Andersen & Baum, 1994; Berk & Andersen, 2000). Focusing on work contexts, a person can view an actor as a competitor for scarce resources (Kelley & Thibaut, 1978) or a threat to personal welfare (Lazarus & Folkman, 1984). The key point is that in perceiving another actor, a person typically generates an overall judgment regarding the meaning of that actor to self (Kramer, 1999a, b) – either positively (as an ally or friend), neutrally, or negatively (as a threat).

Threat appraisals also occur at the group-level. They relate to how a person or group is appraised in terms of their potential to threaten the in-group. For out-group members, is the out-group that they represent viewed as a competitor for scarce group resources, as a threat to group welfare; or is the out-group viewed neutrally, or even positively, as an ally? These assessments can trigger negative or positive appraisals, which are then attached to messengers representing those groups. In-group members can also present group threats, when others perceive them to be different from other members in terms of their expertise, demographic characteristics, and/or when they violate important group norms. In-group members perceive these differences as threatening their group's identity, solidarity, and status.

Personal and group threat appraisals matter to relational perception because they influence whether messengers are positively or negatively evaluated by the receiver. As we have suggested and will demonstrate shortly, receiver's evaluation of the messenger crucially shapes their evaluation of the knowledge conveyed by that messenger.

Six Schema Types
Building off these two dimensions of relational perception (group identification and threat appraisal), we now introduce our six relational schemas. These are summarized in Table 1. As Table 1 shows, we divide the six types into two subsets,

Table 1.   Taxonomy of Relational Schemas.

	Relationship-Based Evaluation of Messenger		
	Positive/Neutral	Negative (Due to Personal Threat)	Negative (Due to Group Threat)
In-group member	**Colleague**: An insider who is liked or perceived neutrally by the knowledge receiver	**Rival**: An insider who threatens the knowledge receiver's pursuit of personal rewards or sense of safety at work	**Deviant**: An insider who is viewed as diverse or unusual by group members and threatens the group's identity
	Example: A friend in another area of the organization or a fellow work group member	*Example*: A co-worker competing for a promotion or bonus with the knowledge receiver	*Example*: A "black sheep" or outcast within the group
Out-group member	**Advisor**: An outsider with a collaborative relationship with the knowledge receiver	**Intruder**: An outsider who threatens the knowledge receiver's personal status or sense of safety at work	**Enemy**: An outsider who is a member of a group that competes with the knowledge receiver's group
	Example: A consultant, coach, investment banker or management guru	*Example*: A consultant or newly hired manager whose is believed to be hired to "downsize" the organization	*Example*: A member of a competitor firm in the marketplace or of a competing group within the organization

corresponding to three in-group messenger types (top row) and three out-group messenger types (bottom row). Across the columns, we move from schemas that represent messengers who the receiver positively or neutrally evaluates (on the left) to messengers who the receiver negatively evaluates because they represent self- or group-level threats (on the right).

Within the in-group subset, we use the labels colleague, rival and deviant to capture three distinct relational types. The label "colleague" applies to in-group messengers who the receiver evaluates neutrally or positively. These messengers are typically fellow team members and other coworkers and colleagues who the receiver likes, values, and trusts. The label "rival" applies to in-group messengers who are competitors for resources (structurally equivalent actors, e.g. Burt, 1992) or perhaps threats to personal safety (someone who has been known to sabotage the self). Receivers negatively evaluate messengers in this category because they perceive them to threaten their personal outcomes. Finally, we use the term "deviants" to denote in-group members who receivers evaluate negatively because they perceive that deviants threaten the solidarity of their own group. These are the "black sheep," or outcasts, within a group.

Moving to out-group messengers, we use the labels advisor, intruder, and enemy. The label "advisor" refers to out-group members who pose little or no self- or group-threat; such as an executive coach, consultant, or legal counsel (Maister, Green & Galford, 2000). The label "intruder" is similar, in that it applies to members of out-groups whose groups the receiver appraises positively or neutrally relative to their in-group, but who the receiver finds personally threatening. This category is typified by outside consultants who give advice that threatens the receiver's welfare (e.g. they write a report that makes the receiver fear that they will be downsized!). The label "enemy" applies to messengers from out-groups that threaten the in-group (for example, members of a competitor firm that is considered predatory in its practices or another organizational group vying with the in-group for scarce organizational resources).

Integration

In sum, we have identified six different relational types that vary according to whether a messenger is perceived as an in- versus out-group member and the degree to which they are perceived as threatening to the knowledge receiver. Much research has emphasized how knowledge receivers tend to evaluate in-group members positively; however, the degree of threat that the messenger evokes introduces several nuances. Together, these two dimensions bring together a variety of phenomena related to person and group perception. In addition to capturing the general findings of in-group favoritism and outgroup derogation, they also incorporate phenomena such as in-group derogation (both towards internal rivals and diverse group members), and outgroup preferences (both towards neutral experts and competitive threats).

In identifying these six relational schemas, we have thus far assumed that the knowledge messengers have moderate status in relation to the knowledge receivers. That is, we have not addressed the fact that receivers perceive differential status across actors and groups, which influence how they evaluate knowledge messengers. Next, we address this critical issue.

The Moderating Role of Messenger Status

Status and power are central to how people perceive social relationships (see for example, Jones & Pittman, 1982; Keltner, Gruenfeld & Anderson, 2002). These perceptions, which are accorded to both individual messengers and the groups and organizations that they represent, are particularly crucial in organizational settings where hierarchical structures and merit-based cultures naturally elicit perceptions of differential standing among people (Lee & Tiedens, 2001). Power is typically defined as the ability to get something accomplished, and is derived from a person's (or group's) position in informal social networks or from formal titles and authority (Burt, 1992; Pfeffer, 1992). In contrast, status is typically defined as the degree of social esteem that is accorded to one actor by another actor (S. Fiske, 1993; Keltner, Gruenfeld & Anderson, 2002; Ridgeway, 1997). A person (or group) has status when others judge them to be comparatively superior (or inferior) to other people in some important domain (for instance, based on their legitimate position in a formal or informal hierarchy, their unique expertise, or their ranking on social dominance measures, such as age, wealth, education, or physical attractiveness (see, for a review, Y. Chen, Blount & Sanchez-Burks, in press)).

As these definitions imply, status perceptions necessarily incorporate a judgment of deservingness and legitimacy on the part of the perceiver, whereas assessments of power do not. Thus, status is typically accorded to the target by the perceiver, whereas power is bestowed on the target by factors present in the surrounding context. Here, we address the role of status in the knowledge receivers' perception of relationships and valuations of knowledge. Later in the paper, we consider how power, as a contextual variable, also plays a role in knowledge valuation.

Across all relational types, psychological research on source effects predicts that receivers will evaluate messengers more positively, and that this tendency will spill over to the knowledge that they communicate. Simply put, knowledge is evaluated more positively when communicated by messengers with high status, whether it comes from personal or group sources, and denigrated when conveyed by messengers with low status (Hovland, Janis & Kelley, 1953; see Eagly & Chaiken, 1993, for a review). Thus, status represents a critical aspect of relational perception, particularly in organizational settings; and its effect on knowledge valuation is quite clear. As a consequence, in the next two sections, when we examine each of our six relational schemas in depth, we control for the status effect. That is, we assume that knowledge messengers have moderate levels of personal status, and that they represent groups that hold moderate levels of status.

Summary
We began this section of our paper by describing the general process by which relational schemas affect knowledge valuation. We then introduce two dimensions of relational perception (group identification and threat appraisal) that underlie our taxonomy of relational schemas. Next, we derive six relational schema types through which knowledge receivers evaluate messengers. Finally, we describe the moderating role of status perceptions across these categories. We now turn to

our examination of the factors that influence knowledge valuation within each relational schema.

RELATIONAL SCHEMAS: IN-GROUP MEMBERS

In the next two sections of this paper, we examine each of the relational schemas in more depth to uncover how they differentially affect the process of knowledge valuation. In conducting this deeper examination, we consider how the different relational tendencies associated with each schema (i.e. affective, motivational and perceived knowledge accessibility features) affect how evaluation criteria are selected and judgments are formed (i.e. regarding content quality, feasibility and strategic value). We begin with the in-group member schemas: colleagues, who receivers evaluate positively; then rivals and deviants, who they tend to evaluate more negatively. Throughout this section, we will refer to Table 2, which summarizes our analyses of these schemas.

Colleagues

Colleagues are positively regarded acquaintances, close friends, and trusted co-workers who identify with one another and who evoke little or no personal threat. These relational characteristics result in two divergent consequences for knowledge valuation. On one hand, when people encounter a colleague, they feel positive affect towards them and are motivated to enhance their shared social identity. As a result, they heuristically favor knowledge from colleagues and value it for both its content and strategic value. However, knowledge from colleagues also tends to be easily available. Although availability increases the degree to which a receiver perceives the knowledge as feasible, it reduces its salience to the receiver. Even when the receiver attends to the knowledge, its ready availability enables them to subject it to systematic scrutiny which undermines the degree to which they value its content quality. These general relational tendencies are described in detail below.

Positive Affect and Group Enhancement Enhance Valuation
People have been socially and culturally conditioned to experience particular affective reactions to the social groups that surround them (Gaertner & Dovidio, 1986). Specifically, they expect balance from in-group members and experience positive affect when they see them (Heider, 1946; Phillips, 2000). People are also motivated to enhance themselves, and often do so by enhancing in-group members, i.e. creating positive in-group distinctiveness and drawing favorable

Table 2. In-Group Schemas – Relational Tendencies and Knowledge Valuation Implications.

| | Relational Tendencies | | | Knowledge Valuation Implications | | |
	Affective Orientation	Motivational Orientation	Knowledge Accessibility	Content Quality	Feasibility	Strategic Value
Colleague	Positive/neutral	Group enhancement	Available, inexpensive, transparent	Moderate + Positive affect + Group enhancement – Knowledge availability – Knowledge transparency	Moderate + Knowledge availability + Insider's contextual insight – Knowledge salience	Positive + Personal status benefits to valuing in-group knowledge
Deviant	Negative	Group protection	Available, inexpensive, transparent	Negative – Negative affect – Group protection from internal threat – Knowledge transparency	Negative – Deviant's reputation – Knowledge salience	Negative – Personal status benefits to devaluing deviant's knowledge
Rival	Negative	Self protection, interpersonal competition	Available, inexpensive, transparent	Negative – Negative affect – Self protection – Interpersonal competition – Knowledge transparency	Moderate – Negative affect + Knowledge availability	Negative – Personal status benefits to devaluing competitor's knowledge

comparisons with relevant out-groups (Bourhis, Turner & Gagnon, 1997). Rather than engaging in in-depth analysis, receivers often unconsciously, automatically, and heuristically evaluate knowledge communicated by in-group members more positively than knowledge communicated by out-group members (Asch, 1951; Moscovici, 1980; for review see Hewstone, Rubin & Willis, 2002).

Outside of the laboratory, these processes produce the well-known "Not-Invented-Here" syndrome, whereby people assume that a piece of knowledge does not have value unless it originated within the boundaries of the group (Katz & Allen, 1982). This pattern of knowledge valuation is exhibited at American Express, where managers tend to believe that American Express is better than any of its competitors at marketing. Managers report a strong preference toward insider perspectives on marketing, which makes it extremely difficult for a senior outside marketing hire to gain credibility within the organization. Kahn (1998) reports a similar situation at a consulting firm, where partners gave greater weight to the perspectives of insider consultants who were relatively junior, but trained at the firm, than they did to more experienced consultants hired from the outside. In these types of settings, positive knowledge valuation has a strategic value, as a form of ingratiation that enables receivers to be well-liked and gain status in their groups.

Knowledge Accessibility Enhances Feasibility Valuation
Because of colleagues' proximity, their knowledge is abundant and highly accessible, which raises judgments of the feasibility of their knowledge for several reasons (Cyert & March, 1963; O'Reilly, 1982). First, managers often engage in satisficing, whereby they favor local, readily accessible knowledge not because they think that it is the best knowledge based on its content, but simply because it is good enough (March & Simon, 1958). The logic of satisficing is particularly likely to operate when a knowledge receiver is under high levels of time pressure, given that time pressure induces a drive toward closure (De Dreu, Koole & Oldersma, 1999; Kruglanski & Webster, 1996) and more heuristic processing (see Svenson & Maule, 1993; for a review).

Second, a colleague's knowledge appears more relevant, appropriate, and hence more feasible, because the colleague shares a common background and similar taken-for-granted cultural assumptions (Bourdieu, 1980). Knowledge receivers expect that colleagues are more aware of surrounding operational, cultural and political contexts; including, for example, standard operating procedures, power dynamics, and cultural values. Thus, receivers often assume that a colleague's knowledge is particularly relevant, because it incorporates an understanding of context.

Third, a colleague's knowledge is also judged as more feasible when the in-group develops procedures that enable it to efficiently share knowledge with its members. People in groups often develop transactive memory systems whereby members supplement their individual memories (which are often unreliable and subject to natural limits) with other group members as external aids (Moreland, Argote & Krishnan, 1998; Wegner, 1987). Because individual group members share implicit knowledge about who knows what in the group, they do not attempt to become experts in all content areas. As a result of their mutual dependence, members in such groups are more willing to defer to others for knowledge, and are prone to heuristically enhance their valuations of colleagues' knowledge.

Knowledge Accessibility Inhibits Valuation
While knowledge accessibility causes receivers to appreciate the feasibility of knowledge from colleagues, organizational evidence shows that accessibility does not necessarily raise knowledge valuation (Szulanski, 1996; von Hippel, 1994). Here, we question the assumption that identification breeds respect, and describe some reasons why close contact and readily available knowledge reduce evaluations of content quality.

First, while proximity and close contact allow insiders to develop strong identifications with one another (Festinger, Schachter & Back, 1950) and make internal knowledge readily available (March & Simon, 1958; O'Reilly, 1982), the same factors make collegial knowledge more transparent. This transparency enables receivers to more readily see the errors and imperfections of colleagues' ideas (Menon & Pfeffer, 2003; Strickland, 1958). As Strickland notes, the subordinate in close proximity to a boss receives a lower performance evaluation than a subordinate who is more physically removed. Further, whereas managers see both the colleagues' successes and failures, as with most negative pieces of information (Pratto & John, 1991), failures are likely to be more salient. Managers are also likely to attribute these failures to their colleagues' competence, rather than to a variety of external causal factors (such as bad luck, lack of resources, etc.; e.g. Mitchell & Wood, 1980; Ross, 1977). Finally, managers experience spillover, a tendency to extend unrelated negative information about colleagues across domains (deficiencies in interpersonal skills or personal disorganization, for example). Such close-up scrutiny, and the attributional and recall biases that follow from it, are particularly problematic when evaluating colleagues' new ideas, which naturally contain flaws.

A quote from an FBI agent in the months following the World Trade Center attacks illustrates how such attributional biases made it easy to dismiss a colleague, when people knew him at a personal level, with all his quirks and flaws. "If a confidential memorandum comes from a guy out in say, Phoenix, the first thing that goes up the line, is 'That's Harry again. He's like a broken clock twice a day (sic.),' ..." (Hirsh & Isoff, 2002, p. 30). The result is that colleagues elicit an ambivalent reaction (Glick & Fiske, 1996): while people regard them as well-liked friends and acquaintances, they do not necessarily see them as sources of valuable, new knowledge.

Salience is another barrier that inhibits receivers from valuing the highly available knowledge that colleagues communicate. When internal knowledge is abundant, managers become distracted, and fail to identify useful and relevant kernels of knowledge. This problem is widespread in legal and management consulting firms where dispersed teams of professionals generate large amounts of knowledge on an on-going basis. The key constraints in such an environment do not lie in generating the knowledge, but in retaining and tracking it for others to use (Hansen & Haas, 2001; Ocasio, 1997). Note that this salience problem does not reflect the negative valuation of colleagues' knowledge, but the tendency to de facto devalue it by losing track of it.

Summary
In sum, collegial relationships evoke affective and motivational forces that result in a general positive bias towards knowledge from such messengers. The strong identification that develops between colleagues increases positive affect towards them, in-group enhancement motivations, and hence, the valuation of their knowledge. However, other dynamics undermine this positive bias. Specifically, although the availability of knowledge from colleagues promotes perceptions of its feasibility, it also undermines valuation of its content. Available knowledge is often so abundant that it lacks salience, and its flaws are readily scrutinized as well. These conflicting dynamics are summarized in the top row of Table 2. In the end, we suggest that the strength of the motivation to perceive insiders favorably (that is, the degree of in-group favoritism that is present) determines whether a positive bias prevails.

Deviants
We now consider deviants, those in-group members who other group members perceive as group threats. They might threaten the status of a group because they are poor performers, and hence poor exemplars of the group; or they might destabilize the group by questioning or ignoring group norms. They stimulate group conflict by holding unusual positions that do not correspond to the taken-for-granted assumptions of the group, or they foster ill-will by alienating group members with their non-normative behaviors in group meetings. Or, they might simply be diverse on particular demographic characteristics (Williams & O'Reilly, 1998) or newcomers who have not yet been integrated into the group (Gruenfeld, Martorana & Fan, 2000). Whether conscious of their actions or not, deviants disrupt group balance and evoke strong negative reactions from other group members (Heider, 1946; Phillips, 2000).

Consider the specific example of a deviant – the whistle-blower. TAP drugs is a pharmaceutical company which eventually paid a $875 million fine for conspiring with doctors to cheat the government. When a whistle-blower sought to reform the company's unfair practices he found that, "Most of what I did there was resisted, undermined" (Haddad & Barrett, 2002, p. 128). Co-workers at the company countered the threat he posed to their group identity by rejecting his ideas, telling him he didn't understand the company culture, and excluding him from top marketing and sales meetings. Some even hinted that he could become a convenient scapegoat for the company if it were caught.

Negative Affect and Group Protection Inhibit Valuation
As the above example suggests, the robustness of the in-group favoritism effect depends on the characteristics and behaviors of the in-group member in question. Specifically, the interaction of in-group identification and group-threat that the deviant evokes generates negative affect and motivations to protect the group. Thus, in-group members often dislike "black sheep," i.e. insiders who they perceive as deviant, more than they dislike out-group members (Marques, Paez & Abrams, 1998). Further, people also display horizontal hostility, evaluating in-group members who are closer to the mainstream more negatively than more distant outsiders (White & Langer, 1999).

If a receiver dislikes a messenger, or considers her untrustworthy or unattractive, research on source effects predicts that the receiver will tend to automatically evaluate that messenger's arguments less favorably (for reviews, see Chaiken, 1987; McGuire, 1985). Even when a receiver seeks to carefully and objectively consider the new knowledge of a disliked colleague, existing psychological research suggests that a negative bias persists in evaluating deviants' knowledge in terms of content quality (Chaiken & Maheswaran, 1994; Kunda, 1990). Further, the receiver also has group-level motivations to devalue the knowledge's quality (i.e. to defend the group from potential identity and solidarity threats implicit in the deviant's knowledge), and personal motivations to devalue the knowledge strategically (i.e. to maintain or gain status by criticizing the deviant's knowledge).

Knowledge Accessibility Inhibits Valuation
Although the deviant's knowledge is available, that knowledge is not perceived as feasible, because of the negative social implications of using it. Further, the deviant's proximity within the in-group makes the knowledge transparent and open to scrutiny by ingroup members, who happen to be especially motivated to search for its flaws.

This negativity bias is particularly problematic in organizations because deviants are sometimes the most likely to hold unique and diverse perspectives that can benefit the rest of the group. For example, consider the fact that itinerants, people who leave their in-groups and then return to them, produce more unique ideas than others. Yet, their boundary spanning behaviors blur their identities as in-group members and increase the degree to which other group members treat them like black sheep. Their in-groups see them as more argumentative and are less likely to value and use their ideas (Gruenfeld, Martorana & Fan, 2000). Stasser (1999) notes that unique ideas are less likely to be transferred within groups as compared to those which group members share. This has been described as "the common knowledge effect" (Gigone & Hastie, 1996), whereby the effect of a piece of information on group decision making is correlated with the number of people who have it. The tendency to not share unique information in groups results because in-group members look to one another to affirm category boundaries – while deviants, by definition, are insiders who threaten those boundaries (Phillips, 2003).

Summary
Despite the deviant's potential role as an internal innovator and stimulus for change (Sutton, 2002), we predict that even when deviants convey potentially valuable knowledge, others will devalue it heuristically or scrutinize it more carefully than when a well-respected colleague conveys the same knowledge. Whereas people are motivated to affirm knowledge from a colleague, they experience strategic value in downgrading a deviant's knowledge. Thus, as the receiver evaluates a deviant's knowledge, their motivations to reject it lead to assessments of lower content quality and feasibility, as well. These negative implications for valuation of deviants' knowledge are summarized in the middle row of Table 2.

Rivals
We now turn to rivals, who, like deviants, are in-group members who are negatively evaluated by receivers. They can be competitors for resources (such as customers or promotions), threats to personal safety (someone who has been known to sabotage the receiver), or threats to one's identity and sense of competence. In any case, in contrast to deviants, they threaten the receiver, although other in-group members regard them as colleagues or friends. Thus, while the receiver's colleagues favor the rival messenger's knowledge because they are motivated to bolster their group's identity, the receiver's reaction is more ambivalent. The rival relational schema, created by the interaction of in-group identification and personal threat, evokes negative affect, motivations to protect the self, and knowledge availability effects – all of which lead to knowledge devaluation.

Negative Affect and Self Protection Inhibit Valuation

Although receivers are motivated to monitor the knowledge of their rivals as a tool for managing the uncertainties implicit in competition (Pfeffer & Salancik, 1978; Ruscher & Fiske, 1990), they are less motivated to actually value and use that knowledge. This is because they face threats to the self if they use it (Menon, Choi & Thompson, 2003). When a rival has a good idea, the receiver faces a painful upward social comparison, which elicits a host of negative affective responses that increase their defensiveness toward that knowledge (Argyris, 1985). Upward comparisons can increase a receiver's sense of inferiority and insecurity, and constitute a "loss of uniqueness" (Brickman & Janoff-Bulman, 1977, p. 179). These self-threats are particularly high when rival messengers are in-group members, rather than more distant, and therefore less directly threatening, out-group members (Tesser, Millar & Moore, 1988).

Consider the following analysis of the relationship between Clinton and Gore during the 2000 presidential election:

> In Gore's mind, the humiliation (of asking Clinton for help) must be greater than any risk (associated with Clinton's character issues). After being advised to be his own man, Gore is now being told he needs to be Bill Clinton's man... How Gore must resent hearing that he needs this guy to hoist him over the high bar against a lightweight Texas governor. Clinton is everything Gore isn't as a campaigner – bright and charming, with unerring political instincts and a jawbreaker of a punch (Gailey, 2000).

In this example, it is not the negative character issues associated with Bill Clinton that threaten Al Gore (as would be the case if Clinton were construed as a deviant), but his positive attributes (i.e. his knowledge and talents) that evoke threat by posing painful upward comparisons. The threats of social comparison are particularly intense when they occur on a public stage. Here, the pains of social comparison do not only involve private insecurities and emotional heartache – one's reputation, social standing within the group, and even more tangible financial rewards and promotions are also at stake.

The motivation for self-protection and knowledge derogation is strongest when the knowledge communicated by a rival messenger is in a domain that implicates the receiver's self-concept (Tesser, Millar & Moore, 1988). For instance, Bill Clinton's knowledge would be most threatening to Al Gore if he sought to provide Gore with knowledge on the Internet or the environment, and least threatening if he chose to advise Gore on the Arkansas economy. Because status accrues to those who can cope with the critical problems of the organization (Salancik & Pfeffer, 1982), if a receiver evaluates a rival's knowledge positively, they legitimate a direct competitor for rewards and status in the group. Thus, there is also strategic value in underrating a rival's knowledge and conveying the reasons for this devaluation to relevant constituencies in the organization – particularly when the knowledge is in the receiver's own domain of expertise.

Knowledge Accessibility Inhibits Valuation
In order to devalue the knowledge of their rivals, receivers often invoke the façade of objectivity. Because their peers lack the motivation to devalue their rivals' knowledge, receivers must justify their objections carefully. Since the rival's knowledge is internal and often transparent, receivers search for all available evidence to scrutinize and criticize their rivals' knowledge. Thus, even if receivers intend to be even-handed and methodical in evaluating their rivals' knowledge, the negative conclusions that they hope to reach about the content and feasibility of that knowledge often color their evaluations (Kunda, 1990).

Summary
When faced with a rival's knowledge, receivers are personally threatened and motivated by strategic concerns to degrade it, in order to protect their own status. They ask themselves, does this act of learning display my incompetence? Does it confirm the superiority of my direct competitor? And what will the ever-present audience of my peers around me think? The answers to these questions often result in a negativity bias towards rivals' knowledge that is manifested in both private and public derogation. These negative implications are summarized in the bottom row in Table 2.

RELATIONAL SCHEMAS: OUTSIDERS

We now move to the relational schemas associated with out-group members, and examine the affective, motivational, and knowledge accessibility factors that bias receivers' valuations of outsider knowledge. While the finding of in-group favoritism is one of social psychology's most robust (see Hewstone et al., 2002; Mackie & Smith, 1998, for reviews on intergroup bias), the interesting observation from organizational settings is that managers often value external knowledge highly, sometimes to the point of over-valuation (consider the popularity of management gurus). Yet, at other times, as psychological theory would predict, managers shun the intrusion of outsiders into their affairs.

To make sense of these counterintuitive and seemingly contradictory observations, we begin our analysis with advisors, who are positively evaluated outsiders. Next we consider enemies, who like rivals and deviants, are negatively evaluated. Throughout this section, we refer to Table 3, which summarizes our analyses for each of these relational schemas.

Table 3. Out-Group Schemas – Relational Tendencies and Knowledge Valuation Implications.

	Relational Tendencies			Knowledge Valuation Implications		
	Affective Orientation	Motivational Orientation	Knowledge Accessibility	Content Quality	Feasibility	Strategic Value
Advisor	Positive/neutral	Self or group enhancement	Scarce, expensive, moderately transparent	Positive + Positive affect + Self and group enhancement + Knowledge scarcity and expense + Outsider objectivity and access to "best," most current ideas	Negative – Knowledge expense – Outsider's lack of contextual insight – Limited content appropriateness	Positive + Group status benefits to acquiring advisor knowledge + Personal status benefits to providing advisor knowledge to in-group
Enemy	Negative	Group protection, intergroup competition	Scarce, expensive, opaque	Positive (ambivalently) – Negative affect + Group protection from external threat + Intergroup competition + Knowledge scarcity and expense + Acquisition challenge	Negative – Knowledge opacity – Limited contextual appropriateness – Not timely	Positive + Personal status benefits to defending in-group by acquiring enemy knowledge
Intruder	Negative	Self protection	Scarce, expensive, moderately transparent	Negative – Negative affect – Self protection – Knowledge transparency	Negative – Knowledge expense – Outsider's lack of contextual insight	Negative – Personal status benefits to devaluing threatening knowledge

Advisors

We begin with the category of advisors, who are members of out-groups that the receiver perceives as neutral or allied with their in-group. This category includes professional service providers such as consultants, accountants, legal counsel, executive coaches, trainers, and other external brokers of knowledge (Hargadon, 2002). Actors in these roles do not threaten the receiver either at the group- or individual-level – instead, they are valued for their wisdom, insight, discussion, support, and advice. As such, they have the potential to create positive affect and provide knowledge which can foster self and group enhancement.

Positive Affect and Self/Group Enhancement Enhance Valuation
Although advisors lack the positive inducements of in-group favoritism, their knowledge is valued precisely because of their lack of relationship to the in-group. As managers seek to deal with the competitive uncertainties of an ever-changing environment, they crave information and insight into what is "really happening out there." Amid the mire of organizational politics, they seek someone with an unbiased view. As Hayakawa (1953, p. 97) notes, "The great problem in our culture . . . is that of finding disinterested sources of information." As a result of their independence, advisors evade the thorny entanglements of identification and rivalry – remaining seemingly objective, impartial, and detached when advocating controversial views.

As a consequence, managers approach advisor knowledge with a promotion, risk-seeking, positive affect focus (e.g. Higgins, 1997), creating a bias toward positive evaluation – sometimes to the point of absurdity. Consider research on management fads that portrays managers as actively seeking out and embracing ideas of dubious quality from guru advisors (Abrahamson, 1996; Staw & Epstein, 2000; Zbaracki, 1998) or looking to charismatic outsiders as corporate saviors (Khurana, 2002). Similarly, as business school professors, we are all familiar with the experience of inviting an outside business speaker into the classroom and watching the class receive their knowledge enthusiastically. Yet, the same students seemed somewhat less excited when they heard the same ideas from their professor the week before – and the professor is a person with whom they have a closer relationship and more frequent communication.

In the words of Ralph Larsen, former CEO of Johnson & Johnson, "McKinsey is expensive. But what they provide is a fresh look at our thinking and a certain detachment" (Byrne, 2002, p. 76). In encoding terms, this means that the advisor's out-group membership becomes a positive attribute associated with their knowledge, which in turn enhances perceived content quality. This aspect also enhances perceived strategic value. In an effort to imply objectivity, knowledge receivers sometimes cite a well-respected advisor's knowledge to legitimate their decisions to others (Sabatier, 1978). For example, "You heard BCG tell us that this is the best course of action."

Knowledge Inaccessibility Enhances Valuation
In contrast to the inexpensive and plentiful knowledge from colleagues, managers often pay large sums of money for the prized assistance of the advisor, which can further bias their evaluations of its quality and escalate their commitment to it (Cialdini, 2001; Staw, 1981). There are personal and strategic benefits to be gained for the members of management teams who use advisors' knowledge to increase their reputations (Staw & Epstein, 2000). Some managers enhance their status even further by becoming collectors of scarce knowledge (Brown & Duguid, 2000) – pursuing knowledge from multiple outside sources in order to display their intelligence and social connections (Feldman & March, 1981).These strategic benefits often lead to a heuristic overvaluation of advisor knowledge. As many observers have noted, managers often mindlessly embrace the faddish and ill-conceived ideas that advisors circulate in the marketplace (Abrahamson, 1996; O'Shea & Madigan, 1997). Particularly if managers believe that their competitors are evaluating the same advisor's knowledge favorably, they heuristically embrace that knowledge in an effort to stay abreast of the competition (Staw, Sandelands & Dutton, 1981). They do not value this knowledge because they have carefully evaluated it, but because the idea has been socially validated (Abrahamson, 1996; Heath, Bell & Sternberg, 2001).

Managers also use advisors for knowledge flow control and sorting functions – i.e. relying on the advisor's content expertise to highlight good ideas in an environment congested with data and information (Cohen, March & Olsen, 1972; Gergen, 1991). Here, managers embrace the advisor's knowledge as a satisficing strategy (March & Simon, 1958). The receiver, who lacks the time or ability to cull through the ideas in his or her overflowing environment, assumes that the advisor is a thorough information processor, uses them as a decision making aid, and again is prone to embrace their knowledge heuristically (see Chaiken & Trope, 1999; Svenson & Maule, 1993 for reviews).

Knowledge Inaccessibility Inhibits Feasibility Valuation
If managers respect advisors based on the perceived scarcity of their knowledge, they doubt the feasibility of their knowledge for that very reason. Quite simply, the cost and scarcity of advisors' knowledge reduces its practicality. While consultants are often effective brokers of new knowledge, carrying ideas across companies and industries (Hargadon & Sutton, 1997), they can also be seen as out-of-touch editors whose advice disregards the political and cultural context

(Sahlin-Andersson, 1996). Alternatively, they can be seen as brokers of recycled knowledge that is hardly current or unique. Every few years, a new story breaks about consultants who have sold the same knowledge to multiple clients, each time promoting it as unique and newly conceived. Any exposure which calls into question the advisor's value in this manner threatens the advisor's status – moving the advisor from an admired sage to a disregarded charlatan.

Another feasibility issue concerns the kind of knowledge that people seek from advisors. Advisors are often effective only in transmitting certain types of knowledge. According to research in social psychology (e.g. Goethals & Nelson, 1973), in-group members are more influential when communicating knowledge about values, and out-group members are more influential when communicating information about beliefs. This is because people prefer to compare the appropriateness of their feelings, values, and attitudes to those who are similar (Darley & Aronson, 1966; Festinger, 1954), but, according to attribution theory, find the consensus of dissimilar others more convincing when they evaluate the truth of beliefs or judgments (Kelley, 1973). As a result, receivers often find a consultant's consensus on the latest trends in the marketplace (a belief) more convincing than an insider's opinion, but look to their colleagues for norms on the most appropriate ways to prioritize work and family commitments (a value).

Summary
In sum, advisors are often seen as independent messengers who thoughtfully filter through the multitude of knowledge flows that pervade the external environment and produce creative insights from their unique vantage points. They can inject "objective" perspectives into politically-charged work settings, and give receivers opportunities to preempt internal threats and thereby enhance the receiver's self and/or group. They also perform a sorting function by culling out the most important information from the marketplace. However, their knowledge suffers from feasibility concerns when it is too expensive, contextually inappropriate, or appears to be recycled. These mixed implications for the valuation of advisors' knowledge are summarized in the top row of Table 3. As this analysis shows, advisors' knowledge tends to be highly prized by the managers who employ them – just as long as the advisor doesn't espouse a position or behave in a manner that seems politically infeasible or evokes a personal threat.

Enemies
The relational schema of the enemy is created by the interaction between out-group membership and group-level threat. Enemies are members of groups that compete for customers in the external marketplace or for scarce resources within the intra-organizational marketplace. In either form, they introduce an interesting

nuance for the knowledge receiver. Although they are threatening outsiders who evoke negative affect, this affect does not result in stereotyping (Sherif, 1966) or spill over that taints the receiver's evaluation of their knowledge. Instead, the receiver's motivations to protect the in-group and out-compete the enemy lead the receiver to pay a great deal of attention to enemies – forming individuated, highly elaborated impressions of them (Ruscher & Fiske, 1990). Further, the scarcity of the enemy's knowledge makes it even more attractive. Consider the meticulous care with which corporations pursue enemy knowledge – even using wiretaps, bribery, and computer hacking to illegally obtain it. For example, Oracle recently admitted that its detectives had hired janitors to go through Microsoft's trash (Lavelle, 2001). Despite the low feasibility of such knowledge (acquiring fully elaborated knowledge from enemies is often impossible), it is perceived as valuable based on its content and strategic value.

Group Protection and Intergroup Competition Enhance Valuation
An important question is why receivers meet an enemy's threat with knowledge over-valuation while confronting a deviant or rival's threat with knowledge devaluation (Menon, Choi & Thompson, 2002). The answer is that receivers perceive threats from insiders differently than they perceive threats from out-group competitors. First of all, enemies induce vigilance on the group-level, while rivals induce vigilance on the individual-level. When managers perceive an external threat, they do not have the luxury of ignoring or pondering it as they do with an internal rival (Cyert & March, 1963). Threats from enemies seem urgent – more urgent than the potential opportunities that internal knowledge represents. Managers feel time pressure to respond in kind, which induces more heuristic processing and mindless imitation (DiMaggio & Powell, 1983; Haveman, 1993).

Second, because knowledge from rivals represents a threat to the self, receivers are in a prevention mode – focusing on what they stand to lose (Higgins, Rholes & Jones, 1977; Higgins, Roney, Crowe & Hymes, 1994). In contrast, because enemies pose a threat to the receiver's group, their knowledge has fewer direct personal implications for receiver. Receivers can, therefore, more easily maintain a promotion mode when encountering enemy knowledge.

Thus, managers heuristically approach knowledge from their enemies, too willingly embracing what they find. As an example, a recent analysis of the threat that China's high-tech sector posed for the Silicon Valley illustrates how people respond to a threatening enemy by over-estimating their knowledge and competence (and heightening the in-group fear that enemies evoke). An American venture capitalist predicted that China would become "a ferociously formidable competitor for companies that run the entire length of the technology food chain." A Chinese executive describes Fudan University as the next Stanford or Berkeley, and another threateningly states, "We will have the ability to exceed them (Lucent, Ericsson, or Cisco) in 3–5 years" (Einhorn, 2002, p. 84). This dramatic characterization of an apparently invincible new enemy remarkably parallels descriptions of the Japanese as an economic powerhouse in the late 1980s (Thurow, 1993). As a result of their positive assessments of Japanese corporations, managers blindly pursued Japanese management practices in the late 1980s as they sought to match that enemy's achievements – even when idea appropriation involved large costs (Thurow, 1987). In hindsight, Japan was viewed through a simplified lens – albeit one that exaggerated, rather than derogated, the quality of its knowledge.

Knowledge Inaccessibility Enhances Valuation
In contrast to the rival's knowledge which is readily available within the organization, enemy knowledge is closely guarded behind enemy walls. Enemy messengers often don't want to part with their knowledge, while colleagues or rivals readily share, and sometimes even market their knowledge, because they can gain status by doing so. Thus, the elusiveness of enemy knowledge enhances its perceived content quality (Cialdini, 2001). Further, when managers expend considerable effort and financial resources to obtain enemy knowledge, they escalate their psychological commitment to perceiving it as valuable (Staw, 1981). Managers also see strategic benefits in valuing enemy knowledge. By providing scarce knowledge about how to cope with group threats, managers accrue status within the in-group by helping the group to neutralize some of their competitor's fire (Nelson & Winter, 1982; Tushman, 1977).

Knowledge Inaccessibility Inhibits Feasibility Valuation
Because enemy knowledge is scarce and difficult to acquire, valuations of knowledge feasibility can suffer. The knowledge that is communicated by enemies is typically more opaque (i.e. less elaborated), because access and transmission typically occur in very limited timeframes that do not allow for full explanation and exploration. Also, because enemy knowledge tends to be well-guarded, the knowledge frequently lacks timeliness, coming too late to be implemented or incorporated into the in-group's on-going plans. Finally, the fact that enemy knowledge has been developed within a different setting, governed by different norms and operating procedures, means that the knowledge that comes to the receiver is "out-of-context." Here, contextual peculiarities that are group-specific are embedded in the knowledge, and reduce its perceived relevance to the receiver and the in-group.

Summary
In sum, receivers are prone to automatically over-value the quality and strategic value of the knowledge that enemies communicate. Competitive uncertainties,

status-enhancement opportunities, and perceived scarcity all serve to heighten valuation. Even when receivers deeply process enemy knowledge, their competitive motivations to "keep up with the enemy" can implicitly elevate the value of the knowledge. The one area where receivers question the value of enemy knowledge is in evaluations of feasibility, given issues of incompleteness, timeliness, and relevance. These conflicting evaluation tendencies are summarized in the middle row of Table 3.

With enemies, it is important to note that even when the enemy is a respected competitor, the negative affect that managers experience from that competitor often results in ambivalent assessments of the enemy and their knowledge (Glick & Fiske, 1996). Although receivers highly value enemy knowledge for strategic reasons and even try to copy and appropriate it, they still search for opportunities to derogate the enemy and their ideas. For example, in the 1980s, managers considered the Japanese to be formidable competitors with useful production knowledge but often disparaged them for lack of creativity. Such ambivalence enables the receiver to simultaneously gain the benefits of learning from the enemy, while also gaining the psychological benefits of derogating a potential threat who elicits a negative affective response.

Intruders
We finally consider intruders, who on the surface appear to be important sources of new knowledge for the organization. These actors might have initially been advisors (i.e. consultants, accountants, legal counsel, etc.). However, when advisors promote change that feels threatening, the receiver's perception of the advisor can shift from a promotion to a prevention focus (Higgins, 1997), and they recategorize the advisor as an intruder. This transition activates predictable patterns of out-group and personal derogation. Because intruders are outsiders whose relationships are not governed by group norms, the negative consequences for knowledge valuation can be even more devastating than for rivals. The intruder schema, created by the interaction of out-group identification and personal threat, thus evokes negative affect and motivations to protect the self.

Negative Affect and Self Protection Inhibit Valuation
When intruders offer knowledge to in-group members, they find that receivers often respond with the vigor of a parent whose child has been criticized by a stranger. Even if that stranger has valuable insights and intends to be helpful, a parent is unlikely to appreciate an intrusion into their own sphere of jurisdiction. Similarly, intruders evoke negative affect as managers question the intruder's right to comment on the managers' own areas of expertise. Even when the intruder has expertise-based status, which typically heightens the perceived quality of their

knowledge, that expertise personally threatens the receiver's sense of autonomy and competence. As a result, the strategic benefit of denigrating intruder knowledge is high.

Receivers often denigrate the intruder via motivated reasoning, in which they disparage the intruders' expertise and group identity in order to devalue the content quality of the knowledge that they offer (Mackie, Devos & Smith, 2000). For example, they charge consultants with "repackaging what we already knew," being out of touch with the "realities of running a business," and being paid "yes-men" (O'Shea & Madigan, 1997) – sentiments that so many Dilbert cartoons rely upon in order to ridicule consultants.

Knowledge Accessibility Inhibits Valuation
To further detract from the intruder's knowledge, receivers question the feasibility and relevance of the knowledge that intruders carry, since these outsiders lack the in-depth insider view of the organization and its circumstances. And while intruders wear the taint of being an outsider, they actually have the disadvantages of being an insider given that their knowledge is moderately transparent. Their knowledge is scarce in the sense that it is highly valued by the more senior managers who initially paid the fees to hire them, but it is also elaborated enough to be scrutinized at close range by the mid-level managers whom they threaten.

Summary
In sum, because intruders evoke a sense of personal threat, receivers are motivated to protect the self. As a result, receivers respond by derogating intruders, the out-groups that they represent, and the knowledge that they carry. Receivers lack the status-enhancement motive that they have with enemies to embrace their knowledge (Burt, 1992; Tushman, 1977). Instead, receivers respond as they do to rivals: they avoid affirming the knowledge that intruders carry for strategic reasons, while also devaluing it in terms of quality and feasibility. These negative implications for the valuation of intruders' knowledge are summarized in the bottom row of Table 3.

RELATIONAL SCHEMAS IN CONTEXT

In the last two sections, we have examined each of the relational schemas in depth – to uncover the complex ways in which each differentially biases the process of knowledge valuation. These findings are summarized in Tables 2 and 3. As these tables show, each schema is associated with different relational tendencies in terms of affect, motivation, and knowledge accessibility perceptions. These differences have implications for knowledge valuation across multiple criteria: namely, content quality, feasibility and strategic value.

A central observation, gleaned from scanning these tables, is that with the exception of the intruder, the evaluation of outsider knowledge is often preferred in terms of content quality and strategic value. In contrast, insider knowledge is valued most for feasibility. Still, knowledge valuation is quite nuanced, as we have noted. The exact manner in which the biases are enacted within each schema is moderated by context specifics. Further, the degree to which receivers weight content quality, feasibility and strategic value considerations in developing a composite judgment of value also varies across contexts.

In order to make our task tractable, we have controlled for contextual variation and our analysis has, thus far, been quite limited contextually. We have isolated our focus upon the messenger-receiver dyad, i.e. how the knowledge receiver perceives his or her relationship with the knowledge messenger and the effect that perception has on evaluation. In this final section, our goal is to add back some context, because in order to fully appreciate the evaluation tendencies associated with the six relational schemas, we must situate them organizationally (Lant, 1999). To do this, we consider three aspects of context: hierarchical, social and cultural.

Hierarchical Context: The Role of Messenger Power

Although we have argued that knowledge from messengers with high status is highly valued, we have deliberately deferred on the issue of organizational power. This is because the effects of a messenger's organizational power on the valuation of their knowledge are more nuanced than the effects of their high status.

Unlike status, power is contextually conferred by forces within the organization; it is not conferred by the knowledge receiver. Thus, perceptions of power, unlike perceptions of status, do not entail a perception of deservingness or legitimacy in the eyes of the knowledge receiver. If a messenger's power is, in fact, perceived as undeserved or illegitimate, that perception can bias evaluations of content quality negatively, rather than positively. As a result, the implications of power for how a messenger's knowledge is evaluated are determined by the organizational context in which the power is situated, and whether the messenger's power is perceived as legitimate and fair (Tyler, 1998).

Given that powerful people control their own and others' outcomes (Blau, 1955; Fiske, 1993; Lee, 1997), receivers often pay a good deal of attention to knowledge communicated by them. Since high-power actors have the force and resources necessary to realize their ideas, receivers automatically elevate the perceived feasibility of their knowledge and the strategic value to be gained by embracing it. However, if the receiver considers the messenger's power to be illegitimately conferred, receivers pragmatically avow the content quality of knowledge in public, but also seek out contexts in which they can safely devalue it.

For instance, the growing wave of anti-Americanism overseas suggests that, despite the tremendous power that the United States holds internationally, the United States lacks legitimacy. This was most visible in the build-up to the war in Iraq when people around the world were more willing to value Saddam Hussain's assertions, despite his reputation for dishonesty, as compared to U.S. claims of knowledge. A recent political cartoon summarizes the skepticism associated with knowledge from powerful actors. In it, a clenched-fist Donald Rumsfeld states, "Look, we said Saddam *might* have a nuclear program, he *might* have ties to Al Queda, he *might* have bio-weapons . . . and that's what we based our policy on – American might (Wasserman, 2003)!" If the people who hold power are perceived to lack benevolent and trustworthy motives, people engaging in causal attributions about them assume that they are advocating positions that serve self-interested agendas (cf. Blount, 1995).

In environments where people resent the powerful, canny messengers must adjust strategically – often adopting stances that mimic the powerless in order to maximize their credibility. Compare the success of Bill Clinton's egalitarian town meetings (Gladwell, 1998) and Hillary Clinton's listening tour with Al Gore's frequent claims of his expert status. Rather than making Gore appear more credible, these claims led people to construe him as patronizing. This observation signifies the importance of context, as context determines whether the receiver associates power with legitimacy or resentment. Thus, while the effects of messenger status on knowledge valuation are quite straightforward, the effects of a messenger's organizational power on knowledge valuation are more nuanced.

Social Context: The Role of Other Relationships

Our analysis has thus far assumed that the messenger and receiver are involved in a dyadic relationship, and has not considered the broader web of relationships within which the dyad is embedded. Here, we examine this broader relational context.

The Receiver's Relationship to the In-Group

Our analysis has implicitly assumed that the knowledge receiver is embedded within an in-group and a web of group-based relationships. These relationships necessarily shape the meaning and the value of knowledge that the receiver encounters. For instance, if the receiver's in-group is highly cohesive, long-standing, and working in isolation from other groups, strong relationships are likely to develop between members. In such situations, people are particularly likely to succumb to the NIH syndrome, where they see in-group knowledge as superior to that possessed by outsiders (Katz & Allen, 1982; see Hewstone et al., 2002). People in highly cohesive groups are also prone to engage in groupthink, a tendency to confirm in-group ideas heuristically in an effort to get along and keep group interactions fluid (S. Chen, Shechter & Chaiken, 1996). While these internal group dynamics make receivers particularly likely to value knowledge from colleagues, they are also especially likely to reject knowledge from deviants who threaten the group's solidarity. Further, when a highly cohesive, committed team works in isolation, an "us against the world mentality" often emerges (Levy, 2001). The result is an environment in which knowledge from outsiders, such as intruders and advisors, is not only derogated, but actively defended against.

At other times, a knowledge receiver is only loosely tied to his or her in-group. This happens, for example, if the receiver perceives the in-group to be of low status. Here, research evidence suggests that negative status effects can override the tendency to enhance the in-group; and knowledge receivers derogate the knowledge of their own group members (Jost & Banaji, 1994; Jost & Burgess, 2000), and instead favoring outsider knowledge (Boldry & Kashy, 1999). As these examples illustrate, the strength of a receiver's ties to the in-group determine the relative strength of the motivation toward in-group versus out-group favoritism when evaluating new knowledge.

The Messenger's Relationship to Other Actors

Now we consider the effects of the knowledge messenger's relationships with other members of the receiver's in-group, as well as with members of competitive out-groups. Here, both the quantity and quality of those relationships matters. First, the *quantity* of people who are perceived to be tied to a particular messenger (both internally and externally) can influence knowledge valuation by creating perceptions of inevitability and bandwagon effects (Staw & Epstein, 2000); i.e. a tipping point after which the messenger's ideas are accepted immediately and heuristically by the knowledge receiver (Gladwell, 2000).

Second, the *quality* of a messenger's other relationships provides a source of power and status that can give their knowledge greater credibility (or as a liability that makes their knowledge seem less valuable). For example, an intruder's knowledge is normally devalued, but if the intruder is known to have a close relationship with a high-status organizational member, such as the CEO or the receiver's direct supervisor, the receiver views the intruder as a high-status insider (by association). Consequently, their knowledge will be attended to more closely and processed with a positivity bias (Krackhardt, 1992). Alternatively, if the intruder is known to be working closely with the members of a competitor group, receivers view the intruder's knowledge as a form of competitive intelligence, and heuristically value it more highly.

What these observations highlight is that across each of the relational schemas, a receiver modifies the relational schema that is applied to a knowledge messenger if he or she perceives that the knowledge messenger has strong ties to influential in-group members or members of competitive out-groups. Thus, the effects of both in- versus out-group standing and intruder versus enemy status change depending on the receiver's perception of a particular messenger's social network and the receiver's relationships with the in-group.

Cultural Context: Competition Versus Collaboration

Simply put, culture matters in knowledge valuation. An organizational culture is created by the beliefs, values, and norms of behavior espoused by its members; as well as its more formalized human resources practices, systems of evaluation, and economic incentives. Together, both informal and formal mechanisms combine to create environments that are characterized, quite often, by values of cooperation or competition. To the degree that a culture emphasizes one over the other, this influences how relational schemas operate in several ways.

First, the surrounding cultural context determines the degree to which knowledge receivers perceive particular relationships in their environment. The distribution of relational types that members perceive in an organization is thus an outcome of its culture. For example, because members of individualistic, competitive organizational cultures experience high levels of threat and paranoia, they are more likely to perceive one another as rivals, rather than colleagues. These categorization tendencies implicitly reduce the valuation of internal knowledge and diminish the possibilities for learning within the knowledge community (Edmondson, 1999; Kramer, 1999a, b).

Second, the cultural context shapes the degree to which strategic concerns drive knowledge valuation. In more efficiency-driven cultures, the goals of valuation are to determine the content quality and feasibility of new ideas, with relatively little emphasis given to strategic value. In more competitive cultures, the strategic value of new knowledge weighs more heavily in valuation. For example, at Ford,

Robert McNamara used knowledge devaluation as a weapon to enhance the legitimacy and power of his own group and to sabotage other groups. He actively sought to discredit tacit knowledge within manufacturing groups, and replace it with more rational decision procedures and accounting principles that enhanced the power of finance (Halberstam, 1972).

Finally, culture determines the kinds of behaviors that are deemed appropriate with respect to knowledge valuation, and even knowledge acquisition. Receivers can use many methods in order to devalue an idea. For instance, people in more formal or rationalistic cultures attempt to articulate reasons before they devalue an idea, whereas people in conflict-avoidant cultures simply ignore ideas in order to devalue them. In competitive cultures, in addition to strategically devaluing knowledge, people frequently engage in illegitimate tactics, such as idea theft. They value the ideas of normally devalued rivals if they can appropriate credit for those ideas. Consider the case of Maurice Wilkins and Rosalind Franklin, two rival scientists at King's College in England who were attempting to uncover the structure of DNA. Given that Franklin was the lone female scientist in the group, and hence a low-status rival, it would seem that her ideas would have been heuristically devalued. However, once she produced photographs that depicted the double helix structure of DNA, Wilkins was able to illicitly appropriate and share those pictures with two other scientists at Cambridge University without her permission. Those pictures were the critical piece of knowledge necessary for James Watson and Francis Crick's path-breaking discoveries. Franklin died four years before the other three shared the Nobel Prize for medicine, and never received the credit she deserved for her contribution (Watson, 1980).

Summary

As this section demonstrates, the exact manner in which relational schemas bias knowledge valuation does not depend solely on the schema that a knowledge receiver applies to evaluate a knowledge messenger. Context also matters – by influencing both *which* schema is most likely to be applied to a messenger, and *how* different features of that schema influence evaluation. For example, the degree to which content quality, feasibility and strategic value considerations are weighted in developing a composite judgment of value varies across contexts. So does the strength of the receiver's motivations toward in-group favoritism versus derogation, personal and group competition, as well as self- and group-protection. Thus, to fully understand the evaluation tendencies associated with each relational schema, knowledge valuation must be situated within a hierarchical, social, and cultural context.

GENERAL DISCUSSION

We began this paper with the observation that organizational work requires organization members to engage in a variety of relationships. We then identified six relational types, which we argued typify these relationships: colleagues, deviants, rivals, enemies, intruders, and advisors. Next, we examined how each type evokes a relational schema, which can differentially affect how a knowledge receiver evaluates new knowledge conveyed in that relational context. These schemas elucidate the nuanced, interactive ways that group identification and threat appraisals affect valuation of knowledge content, feasibility, and strategic value.

In general, we observe that a manager's identification with colleagues increases the degree to which their knowledge is valued; however, the close contact and availability that fosters identification can decrease salience and the visibility of flaws. In contrast, deviants, rivals, and intruders present threats to group and personal identities, and receivers resist valuing their knowledge. However, when enemies such as competitor firms pose threats to group identity, people monitor and value their scarce knowledge, because their in-groups often reward them for doing so. Finally, advisors are often viewed as independent messengers who are capable of objective detachment, and whose knowledge is prized as a result. These effects demonstrate that the tendency to confuse good knowledge with bad and bad knowledge with good in organizations is not simply the result of randomness. Instead, there are discernable relational patterns present in knowledge valuation that enable these errors.

In applying our framework, it is important to note that an actor's location within a specific category is not static. Relational perceptions are dynamic. In- and out-group perceptions change from situation to situation, as do appraisals of threat versus safety. The same actor can occupy different categories over the course of time. A consultant originally seen as an intruder can become a trusted advisor; a rival can become a colleague; a colleague can become a rival, deviant, or even an enemy. These categories portray general patterns of evaluation that research suggests are common to knowledge receivers, which depend upon how they categorize a particular messenger at a particular point in time. Furthermore, the effect of a particular schema on knowledge valuation is not static. Its effect is moderated by the hierarchical, social, cultural, and even temporal context of the organization within which the receiver-messenger relationship is embedded.

We conclude this paper by considering the connections between our relational model of knowledge valuation and other pertinent literatures. First, we describe how relational schemas introduce specific heuristics and biases into judgment and decision making. Second, we show the ways in which relational models complement rational and random models of decision making. Finally, we outline the connections between relational models and other theories of organizational learning.

Heuristics and Biases Associated with Relational Schemas

Relational schemas are simplifications (Schank & Abelson, 1977) that allow knowledge receivers to quickly interpret the meaning of an actor to the self. In the process of assigning a schema to a knowledge messenger, the receiver assumes specific affective, motivational, and knowledge perception tendencies that are associated with that schema. These tendencies, in turn, color how the receiver encodes and processes knowledge conveyed in that relational context. It is through this process that relational schemas trigger the use of heuristics that bias the process of evaluation (Hastie, 1981; Tversky & Kahneman, 1974). Here, we suggest that these biases take three general forms.

Relational Schemas Lead Decision Makers to Confuse Relationship Cues with Knowledge Attributes

Relationship characteristics can become implicit characteristics associated with the knowledge that messengers carry. When the quality of knowledge is ambiguous, receivers rely on their more elaborated understanding of their relationships with messengers to appraise the quality of messenger knowledge. In this sense, feelings about relationships can often substitute for information about the quality of knowledge. In the process, irrelevant affect, status effects, and in-group dynamics can all spill over to affect the evaluation of ideas. This process is worrisome because, objectively, relationship attributes should have little to do with interpreting the value of ideas. Further, the relational schema that a receiver applies is subject to manipulation. As an example, advertisers often elicit phony relationships in order to evoke particular modes of processing and take advantage of the systematic biases in evaluation that result from them (e.g. the "average Joe" who is classified as an in-group member recommends a beer, the high status advisor promotes a medicine).

Relational Schemas Trigger Self-Serving Motivations

Relationships color how we view ourselves, and in the process, influence a receiver's motivations, goals, and incentives regarding the knowledge that they encounter. These motivations give knowledge meaning, i.e. they contextualize its personal and social importance to the receiver. However, these motivational states also lead to self- and group-serving biases in knowledge valuation. When receivers encounter knowledge from colleagues, they are often motivated to enhance the in-group; when they encounter knowledge from deviants and enemies, they are motivated to protect the in-group; and when they encounter knowledge from rivals and intruders, they are motivated to protect the self. These motivations often result in the valuations of knowledge that protect and benefit the self or group, at the expense of knowledge that benefits the organization as a whole.

Relational Schemas Lead Decision Makers to Overweight the Value of Scarcity
Relationships are channels through which knowledge is encountered and which determine how readily or scarcely knowledge flows. As such, they determine the frequency of contact between messengers and receivers, and hence the quantity and quality of receivers' "knowledge about knowledge." The richness of a channel of communication determines, not only the ways in which knowledge is transferred (Daft & Lengel, 1986; Hansen, 1999), but also its subjective valuation. Often times, the perceived scarcity of knowledge is an important cue with respect to its value – i.e. a piece of knowledge that is rare, that another party conceals, or that is costly to acquire, is indeed more valuable than one that is readily available (Cialdini, 2000). However, this scarcity heuristic is often misleading. When knowledge is conveyed by enemies or advisors, receivers unconsciously make attributions about the idea's quality because they are enticed by its scarcity.

Integration
Relational schemas produce affective, motivational, and knowledge accessibility cues that create heuristics which simplify cognitive processing. As a result, knowledge receivers quickly and adaptively respond to the complex task of making evaluative judgments about ambiguous stimuli. However, the very act of classifying a messenger by applying a relational schema interrupts the act of communication. As Hayakawa explains (1953, p. 33), "The minute you classify, the minute you stop listening so you can say you've heard this stuff before." As a result, relational schemas can result in both Type 1 or Type 2 errors – the quick, unjustified rejection of good knowledge, and the acceptance of bad knowledge, often times, without carefully evaluating it. Many of these errors result from tendencies to confuse relationship cues with knowledge attributes, fall prey to self-serving motivations, and overweight the value of scarcity.

Rationality, Randomness and Relationships
At the start of this paper, we argued that while knowledge valuation is not rational, neither is it random. Instead, it is a complex process, where well-recognized, social psychological forces converge to determine the fate of new ideas. On one hand, rational, random, and relational processes can be viewed as three distinct forms of

managerial decision making that exist in organizations. In reality, the boundaries across these decision making processes are likely to be fuzzy.

First, we suggest that the role that rational, random, and relational processes each play in knowledge valuation depends upon the degree and type of uncertainty present within the evaluation context, as well as the manager's own motivations and capabilities regarding the content of the knowledge. We start with situations where knowledge quality is relatively unambiguous – that is, decision makers have extensive knowledge about a subject, clear criteria for choice, and adequate time with which to decide. Further, the manager is motivated to engage their cognitive resources in processing the knowledge she encounters. In these contexts, relationships are likely to exert little influence, and managers approximate a rational model of valuation.

On the other end of the continuum are situations in which there is a high degree of ambiguity about both the quality of knowledge and the relational context in which it is embedded. These are contexts in which decision makers have little expertise, confused criteria, and a desire to limit their search costs – plus they are not well-acquainted with the knowledge messengers. Here, a more random model of evaluation is likely, because the manager lacks: (a) expertise in the relevant content area; (b) access to a social network that has such expertise; and (c) the motivation to engage in more elaborated processing due to limitations of time, money, or the ability for in-depth cognition.

In middle of this continuum are situations in which knowledge quality is ambiguous, and managerial motivations to expend effort are limited, but the relational context is clear. It is in these contexts that managers rely on their relationships with other actors to guide their processes of knowledge valuation. Therefore, our point is not to argue that rationality and randomness do not exist in organizations, but to suggest that a relational perspective provides a third, quite important, force driving knowledge evaluation.

In addition, we suggest that a relational model elucidates the processes that occur within both of these other lenses. With respect to a rational model, relationships influence when managers use systematic, rational procedures as compared to more heuristic processes. And with respect to a random model, relationships help structure the nature of the matching processes that occur within the organizational "garbage can." Specifically, ideas do not simply circulate within organizations based on temporal processes. The configuration of social relationships in the organization also affects how matches between problems and solutions converge.

Relational Schemas and Theories of Organizational Learning
Finally, we consider the ways in which a relational model can inform theories of organizational learning. In this paper, we have sought to elucidate the psychological

processes that occur after knowledge exposure (e.g. Burt, 1992; Granovetter, 1973) and prior to knowledge transfer, use, and implementation (Argote, 1999; Argote & Ingram, 2000; Bardach, 1977; Pfeffer & Sutton, 2000; Pressman & Wildavsky, 1984). Our key tenet is that valuation mediates the link between knowledge exposure and use. In the process, we have provided a framework for linking highly nuanced, micro-level dynamics (e.g. social identification, threat appraisals, and cognitive decision processes) to organizational-level outcomes such as learning – through their effect on knowledge valuation. As such, we argue that our relational model of knowledge valuation provides a critical step for crossing levels of analysis and integrating other theories of organizational learning.

Consider, for example, the role that knowledge valuation plays in the development of transactive memory systems (Moreland, Argote & Krishnan, 1998; Wegner, 1987). Transactive memory systems assume that people in groups are able to recognize the expertise of different members and segment their work to take advantage of those differences. On one hand, relational schemas can provide heuristics that facilitate the speed with which transactive memory systems develop. This is because relational schemas can simplify the perception and categorization of other actors. On the other hand, relational schemas can introduce biases into how people evaluate knowledge within their groups, and compromise the integrity of the transactive memory systems that develop. For example, if knowledge from particular group members is undervalued, it is more likely to be forgotten as compared to knowledge from more favored group members. Alternatively, people might misattribute the source of ideas based on their valuations, and therefore lose track of them. Specifically, people might mistakenly associate good ideas with particular relationships (colleagues, enemies, advisors) and bad ideas with other relationships (deviants, rivals, intruders).

Consider also the phenomenon of knowledge brokering (Burt, 1992; Hargadon, 2002). Effective knowledge valuation is a prerequisite for effective knowledge brokering. This is because the knowledge broker needs to access knowledge from a variety of sources, and see how different pieces of knowledge are valuable in other contexts (Hargadon, 2002). This process is fundamentally a relational task. If a particular broker finds himself embedded in relationships with other actors whose ideas have a propensity to appear valuable (e.g. enemies and advisors) or worthless (e.g. deviants and rivals), he or she needs to be able to compensate for the relational biases that these relationships induce. Only then is the broker in a position to appreciate the truly good knowledge, and make analogies about its appropriateness and transferability to other contexts (Thompson, Gentner & Loewenstein, 2000).

Conclusion

While organizations are sometimes rational, and at times random – they are also driven by relationships, which both help and hinder the transfer of knowledge. Here, we have argued that a better understanding of relationships, how they are perceived, and how those perceptions influence the evaluation of the knowledge can help us to interpret why bad ideas are sometimes heuristically assumed to be good, and why good ideas are sometimes dismissed as bad.

Specifically, we have introduced a relational model of knowledge valuation. That model proposes that receivers often use relational schemas for quickly interpreting another actor's meaning to the self. These relational schemas, in turn, shape the knowledge receiver's perceptions and thoughts by injecting affective, motivational, and knowledge perception tendencies into the process of evaluating new knowledge. As such, relationships intimately affect the process of knowledge valuation and, consequently, knowledge transfer and learning in organizations.

The fundamental issue for many organizations may not be whether they can produce innovations, but the apparently more mundane concern of whether the managers within them can recognize when an innovation has occurred. In this paper we have taken an important first step toward ameliorating this concern by identifying and labeling discernable patterns in how the messengers who communicate knowledge bias the receivers who evaluate that knowledge.

ACKNOWLEDGMENTS

This research was supported by University of Chicago's Graduate School of Business and New York University's Stern School of Management. We would like to thank our editors, Rod Kramer and Barry Staw, for their thoughtful suggestions which greatly improved our paper. Robert Bernstein, Steve Blader, Reid Hastie, Chip Heath, and Theresa Lant also read drafts of the paper and provided us with many invaluable insights.

REFERENCES

Abrahamson, E. (1996). Management fashion. *Academy of Management Review, 21*, 254–285.
Allport, G. W. (1954). *The nature of prejudice*. Reading, MA: Addison-Wesley.
Andersen, S. M., & Baum, A. (1994). Transference in interpersonal relations: Schema-triggered infer-
        ences and affect based on significant-other representations. *Journal of Personality, 62*, 459–498.
Andersen, S. M., & Chen, S. (in press). The relational self: An interpersonal social-cognitive theory.
        Psychological Review.

Andersen, S. M., Glassman, N. S., & Gold, D. A. (1998). Mental Representations of the self, significant others, and nonsignificant others: Structure and processing of private and public aspects. *Journal of Personality and Social Psychology, 75,* 845–861.

Argote, L. (1999). *Organizational learning: Creating, retaining, and transferring knowledge.* Boston: Kluwer Academic.

Argote, L., & Ingram, P. (2000). Knowledge transfer: A basis for competitive advantage in firms. *Organizational Behavior & Human Decision Processes, 82,* 150–169.

Argyris, C. (1985). *Action science, concepts, methods, and skills for research and intervention.* San Francisco: Jossey-Bass.

Asch, S. E. (1951). Effects of group pressure upon the modification and distortion of judgment. In: H. Guetzkow (Ed.), *Groups, Leadership, and Men.* Pittsburgh, PA: Carnegie Press.

Ashforth, B. E., & Mael, F. (1989). Social identity and the organization. *Academy of Management Review, 14,* 20–39.

Baldwin, M. W. (1992). Relational schemas and the processing of social information. *Psychological Bulletin, 112*(3), 461–484.

Bardach, E. (1977). *The implementation game: What happens after a bill becomes a law.* Cambridge, MA: MIT Press.

Baron, J., & Pfeffer, J. (1994). The social psychology of organizations and inequality. *Social Psychology Quarterly, 57,* 190–209.

Berk, M. S., & Andersen, S. M. (2000). The impact of past relationships on interpersonal behavior: Behavioral confirmation in the social-cognitive process of transference. *Journal of Personality and Social Psychology, 79,* 546–562.

Berscheid, E. (1994). Interpersonal relationships. *Annual Review of Psychology, 45,* 79–129.

Blau, P. M. (1955). *The dynamics of bureaucracy.* Chicago, IL: University of Chicago Press.

Blount, S. (1995). When social outcomes aren't fair. *Organizational Behavior & Human Decision Processes, LXIII,* 131–144.

Boldry, J. G., & Kashy, D. A. (1999). Intergroup perception in naturally occurring groups of differential status: A social relations perspective. *Journal of Personality and Social Psychology.*

Borgatti, S. P., & Cross, R. (2002). A relational view of information seeking and learning in social networks. Working Paper, Boston College.

Bourdieu, P. (1980–1990). *The logic of practice.* Stanford, CA: Stanford University Press.

Bourhis, R. Y., Turner, J. C., & Gagnon, A. (1997). Interdependence, social identity, and discrimination. In: R. Spears, P. J. Oakes, N. Ellemers & S. A. Haslam (Eds), *The Social Psychology of Stereotyping and Group Life* (pp. 273–295). Cambridge, MA: Blackwell.

Brewer, M. B. (1991). The social self: On being the same and different at the same time. *Personality and Social Psychology Bulletin, 17,* 475–482.

Brewer, M. B., & Gardner, W. L. (1996). Who is this 'we'? Levels of collective identity and self representations. *Journal of Personality and Social Psychology, 71,* 83–93.

Brewer, M. B., & Kramer, R. M. (1985). The psychology of intergroup attitudes and behavior. *Annual Review of Psychology, 36,* 219–243.

Brickman, P., & Janoff-Bulman, R. (1977). Pleasure and pain in social comparison. In: R. L. Miller & J. M. Suls (Eds), *Social Comparison Processes: Theoretical and Empirical Perspectives* (pp. 149–186). Washington, DC: Hemisphere.

Brown, J. S., & Duguid, P. (2000). *The social life of information.* Boston, MA: Harvard Business School Press.

Burt, R. S. (1992). *Structural holes.* Cambridge, MA: Harvard University Press.

Byrne, J. (2002). Inside McKinsey. *Businessweek, 3790,* 66–76.

Chaiken, S. (1987). The heuristic model of persuasion. In: M. P. Zanna, J. M. Olson & C. P. Herman (Eds), *Social Influence: The Ontario Symposium* (Vol. 5, pp. 3–39). Hillsdale, NJ: Lawrence Erlbaum; San Diego: Academic Press.

Chaiken, S., & Maheswaran, D. (1994). Heuristic processing can bias systematic processing: Effects of source credibility, argument ambiguity, and task importance on attitude judgment. *Journal of Personality and Social Psychology, 66*, 460–473.

Chaiken, S., & Trope, Y. (Eds) (1999). *Dual process theories in social psychology*. New York: Guilford Press.

Chen, S., Shechter, D., & Chaiken, S. (1996). Getting at the truth or getting along: Accuracy- versus impression-motivated heuristic and systematic processing. *Journal of Personality and Social Psychology, 71*(2), 262–275.

Chen, Y., Blount, S., & Sanchez-Burks, J. (in press). The role of status in group synchronization. In: E. A. Mannix, M. A. Neale & S. Blount (Eds), *Research on Managing Groups and Teams: Time in Groups* (Vol. 6).

Cialdini, R. B. (2001). *Influence*. Needham Heights, MA: Allyn & Bacon.

Cohen, W. M., & Levinthal, D. A. (1990). Absorptive capacity: A new perspective on learning and innovation. *Administrative Science Quarterly, 35*, 128–152.

Cohen, M. D., March, J. P., & Olsen, J. P. (1972). A garbage can model of organizational choice. *Administrative Science Quarterly, 17*, 1–25.

Cyert, R. M., & March, J. G. (1963). *A behavioral theory of the firm*. Englewood Cliffs, NJ: Prentice-Hall.

Czernich, C., & Heath, C. (2002). Towards a theory of variation in idea markets: Attracting eyeballs to websites during the dot-com boom and bust. Working Paper, Stanford University.

Daft, R. L., & Lengel, R. H. (1986). Organizational information requirements, media richness and structural design. *Management Science, 32*, 554–571.

Darley, J. M., & Aronson, E. (1966). Self-evaluation vs. direct anxiety reduction as determinants of the fear-affiliation relationship. *Journal of Experimental Social Psychology, 1*(Suppl.), 66–79.

Davenport, T. H., & Prusak, L. (1998). *Working knowledge: How organizations manage what they know*. Boston, MA: Harvard Business School Press.

De Dreu, C. K. W., Koole, S., & Oldersma, F. L. (1999). Need for cognitive closure and the use of heuristics in negotiation. *Personality and Social Psychology Bulletin, 25*, 348–362.

DiMaggio, P. J., & Powell, W. W. (1983). The iron cage revisited: Institutional isomorphism and collective rationality in organizational fields. *American Sociological Review, 48*, 147–160.

Eagly, A. H., & Chaiken, S. (1993). *The psychology of attitudes*. New York: Harcourt Brace Jovanovich.

Edmondson, A. (1999). Psychological safety and learning behavior in work teams. *Administrative Science Quarterly, 44*, 350–383.

Einhorn, B. (2002). High tech in China: Is it a threat to Silicon Valley? *Businessweek, 3805*, 80–91.

Feldman, M. S., & March, J. G. (1981). Information in organizations as signal and symbol. *Administrative Science Quarterly, 26*, 171–186.

Festinger, L. (1954). Theory of social comparison processess. *Human Relations, 7*, 117–140.

Festinger, L., Schachter, S., & Back, K. (1950). *Social pressures in informal groups: A study of human factors in housing*. NY: Harper.

Fiske, A. P. (1991). *Structures of social life: The four elementary forms of human relations: Communal sharing, authority ranking, equality matching, market pricing*. New York: Free Press.

Fiske, A. P., & Haslam, N. (1996). Social cognition is thinking about relationships. *Current Directions in Psychological Science, 5*, 131–148.

Fiske, S. T. (1982). Schema-triggered affect: Applications to social perception. In: M. S. Clark & S. T. Fiske (Eds), *Affect and Cognition: The 17th Annual Carnegie Symposium on Cognition* (pp. 55–78). Hillsdale, NJ: Lawrence Erlbaum.

Fiske, S. T. (1993). Controlling other people: The impact of power on stereotyping. *American Psychologist, 48*, 621–628.

Fiske, S. T., & Neuberg, S. L. (1990). A continuum of impression formation from category-based to individuating processes: Influences of information and motivation on attention and interpretation. In: M. P. Zanna (Ed.), *Advances in Experimental Social Psychology* (Vol. 23, pp. 1–74). New York: Academic Press.

Gaertner, S. L., & Dovidio, J. F. (1986). The aversive form of racism. In: J. F. Dovidio & S. L. Gaertner (Eds), *Prejudice, Discrimination, and Racism*. Orlando, FL: Academic Press.

Gailey, P. (2000). Clinton's help may be too late for Gore. *St. Petersburg Times*, October 22nd, 3D.

Gergen, K. (1991). *The saturated self: Dilemmas of identity in contemporary life*. New York: Basic Books.

Gigone, D., & Hastie, R. (1996). The impact of information on small group choice. *Journal of Personality and Social Psychology, 65*, 959–974.

Gladwell, M. (1998). The spin myth. *The New Yorker*, July 6th.

Gladwell, M. (2000). *The tipping point: How little things can make a big difference*. New York: Little Brown & Co.

Glick, P., & Fiske, S. T. (1996). The ambivalent sexism inventory: Differentiating hostile and benevolent sexism. *Journal of Personality & Social Psychology, 70*(3), 491–512.

Goethals, G. R., & Nelson, R. E. (1973). Similarity and the influence process: The belief-value distinction. *The Journal of Personality & Social Psychology, 25*, 117–122.

Granovetter, M. (1973). The strength of weak ties. *American Journal of Sociology, 78*, 1360–1380.

Gruenfeld, D. H., Martorana, P. V., & Fan, E. T. (2000). What do groups learn from their worldliest members? Direct and indirect influence in dynamic teams. *Organizational Behavior and Human Decision Processes, 82*, 45–59.

Haddad, C., & Barrett, A. (2002). A whistle-blower rocks an industry. *Businessweek*, 3788, 126–130.

Halberstam, D. (1972). *The best and the brightest*. New York, NY: Random House.

Hansen, M. T. (1999). The search-transfer problem: The role of weak ties in sharing knowledge across organization subunits. *Administrative Science Quarterly, 44*, 82–111.

Hansen, M. T., & Haas, M. R. (2001). Competing for attention in knowledge markets: Electronic document dissemination in a management consulting company. *Administrative Science Quarterly, 46*, 1–28.

Hargadon, A. B. (2002). Knowledge brokering: A network perspective on learning and innovation. In: B. Staw & R. Kramer (Eds), *Research in Organizational Behavior* (Vol. 24, pp. 41–85). Greenwich, CT: JAI Press.

Hargadon, A. B., & Sutton, R. I. (1997). Technology brokering and innovation in a product development firm. *Administrative Science Quarterly, 42*, 716–749.

Haslam, N. (1994). The mental representation of social relationships: Dimensions, laws or categories? *Journal of Personality and Social Psychology, 67*, 575–584.

Hastie, R. (1981). Schematic principles in human memory. In: E. T. Higgins, C. P. Herman & M. P. Zanna (Eds), *Social Cognition: The Ontario Symposium* (Vol. 1). Hillsdale, NJ: Lawrence Erlbaum.

Haveman, H. A. (1993). Follow the leader: Mimetic isomorphism and entry into new markets. *Administrative Science Quarterly, 38*, 593–627.

Hayakawa, S. I. (1953). *Symbol, status, and personality*. New York: Harcourt Brace Jovanovich.

Heath, C., Bell, C., & Sternberg, E. (2001). Emotional selection in memes: The case of urban legends. *Journal of Personality & Social Psychology, 81,* 1028–1041.

Heider, F. (1946). Attitudes and cognitive organization. *Journal of Psychology, 21,* 107–112.

Hewstone, M., Rubin, M., & Willis, H. (2002). Intergroup bias. *Annual Review of Psychology, 53,* 575–604.

Higgins, E. T. (1997). Beyond pleasure and pain. *American Psychologist, 52,* 1280–1300.

Higgins, E. T., Rholes, W. S., & Jones, C. R. (1977). Category accessibility and impression formation. *Journal of Experimental Social Psychology, 13,* 141–154.

Higgins, E. T., Roney, C. J. R., Crowe, E., & Hymes, C. (1994). Ideal versus ought predilections for approach and avoidance: Distinct self-regulatory systems. *Journal of Personality and Social Psychology, 66,* 276–286.

Hirsh, M., & Isoff, M. (2002). What went wrong. *Newsweek,* May 27th, 28–35.

Hovland, C. I., Janis, I. L., & Kelley, H. H. (1953). *Communication and persuasion* New Haven: Yale.

Insko, C. A., Smith, R. H., Alicke, M. D., Wade, J., & Taylor, S. (1985). Conformity and group size: The concern with being right and the concern with being liked. *Personality and Social Psychology Bulletin, 11,* 41–50.

Jones, E. E., & Pittman, T. S. (1982). Toward a general theory of self-presentation. In: J. Suls (Ed.), *Psychological Perspectives on the Self* (Vol. 1, pp. 231–262). Hillsdale, NJ: Lawrence Erlbaum.

Jost, J. T., & Banaji, M. R. (1994). The role of stereotyping in system-justification and the production of false consciousness. *British Journal of Social Psychology, 33,* 1–27.

Jost, J. T., & Burgess, D. (2000). Attitudinal ambivalence and the conflict between group and system justification motives in low status groups. *Personality and Social Psychology Bulletin, 26,* 293–305.

Kahn, W. A. (1998). Relational systems at work. *Research on Organizational Behavior, 20,* 39–76.

Katz, R., & Allen, T. J. (1982). Investigating the not invented here (NIH) Syndrome: A look at the performance, tenure, and communication patterns of 50 R & D project groups. *R & D Management, 121,* 7–19.

Kelley, H. H. (1973). The process of causal attribution. *American Psychologist, 28,* 107–128.

Kelley, H. H., & Thibaut, J. W. (1978). *Interpersonal relations: A theory of interdependence.* New York: Wiley.

Keltner, D., Gruenfeld, D. H., & Anderson, C. (2002). Power, approach, and inhibition. *Psychological Review.*

Khurana, R. (2002). *Searching for a corporate savior: The irrational quest for charismatic CEOs.* Princeton, NJ: Princeton University Press.

Krackhardt, D. (1992). The strength of strong ties: The importance of philos in organizations. In: N. Nohria & R. G. Eccles (Eds), *Networks and Organizations: Structure, Form, and Action* (pp. 216–239). Boston, MA: Harvard Business School Press.

Kramer, R. M. (1998). Paranoid cognition in social systems: Thinking and acting in the shadow of doubt. *Personality and Social Psychological Review, 2,* 251–275.

Kramer, R. M. (1999a). Trust and distrust in organizations: Emerging perspectives, enduring questions. *Annual Review of Psychology, 50,* 569–598.

Kramer, G. (1999b). Social uncertainty and collective paranoia in knowledge communities: Thinking and acting in the shadow of doubt. In: J. Levine, L. Thompson & D. Messick (Eds), *Shared Cognition in Organizations: The Management of Knowledge* (pp. 163–191). Hillsdale, NJ: Lawrence Erlbaum.

Krone, K., Jablin, F., & Putnam, L. (1987). Communications theory and organizational communication: Multiple perspectives. In: F. Jablin, L. Putnam, K. Roberts & L. Porter (Eds), *Handbook of Organizational Communications: An Interdisciplinary Perspective* (pp. 411–421). Newbury Park, CA: Sage.

Kruglanski, A. E., & Webster, D. M. (1996). Motivated closing of the mind: "Seizing" and "freezing". *Psychological Review, 103*, 263–283.

Kunda, Z. (1990). The case for motivated reasoning. *Psychological Bulletin, 108*, 480–498.

Kunda, Z., & Thagard, P. (1996). Forming impressions from stereotypes, traits, and behaviors: A parallel-constraint-satisfaction theory. *Psychological Review, 103*, 284–308.

Lant, T. K. (1999). A situated learning perspective on the emergence of knowledge and identity in cognitive communities. In: R. Garud & J. Porac (Eds), *Advances in Managerial Cognition and Organizational Information Processing* (Vol. 6, pp. 171–194). JAI Press.

Lavelle, L. (2001). The case of the corporate spy. *Businessweek*, 3759, 56–58.

Lazarus, R. S., & Folkman, S. (1984). *Stress appraisal and coping*. New York: Springer-Verlag.

Lee, F. (1997). When the going gets tough, do the tough ask for help? Help seeking and power motivation in organizations. *Organizational Behavior and Human Decision Processes, 72*, 336–363.

Lee, F., & Tiedens, L. Z. (2001). Who's being served? Self-serving attributions in social hierarchies. *Organizational Behavior and Human Decision Processes, 84*, 254–287.

Levy, P. F. (2001). The nut island effect: When good teams go wrong. *Harvard Business Review, 79*, 51–61.

Loewenstein, G., Thompson, L., & Bazerman, M. (1989). Social utility and decision making in interpersonal contexts. *Journal of Personality & Social Psychology, 57*, 426–441.

Mackie, D. M. (1987). Systematic and nonsystematic processing of majority and minority persuasive communications. *Journal of Personality and Social Psychology, 53*, 41–52.

Mackie, D. M., Devos, T., & Smith, E. R. (2000). Intergroup emotions: Explaining offensive action tendencies in an intergroup context. *Journal of Personality and Social Psychology, 79*, 602–616.

Mackie, D. M., & Smith, E. R. (1998). Intergroup relations: Insights from a theoretically integrative approach. *Psychological Review, 105*, 499–529.

Macrae, C. N., & Bodenhausen, G. V. (2000). Social cognition: Thinking categorically about others. *Annual Review of Psychology, 51*, 93–120.

Maister, D. H., Green, C. H., & Galford, R. M. (2000). *The trusted advisor*. New York: Free Press.

March, J. G., & Simon, H. A. (1958). *Organizations*. New York: Wiley.

Marques, J. M., Paez, D., & Abrams, D. (1998). Social identity and intragroup differentiation as subjective social control. In: S. Worchel & J. F. Morales (Eds), *Social Identity: International Perspectives* (pp. 124–141). London, England: Sage.

McGuire, W. J. (1985). Attitudes and attitude change. In: G. Lindzey & E. Aronson (Eds), *The Handbook of Social Psychology* (Vol. 2, pp. 238–241). New York, NY: Random House.

Menon, T., Choi, H., & Thompson, L. (2002). Managerial strategies for surviving organizational vs. market competition: Implications for knowledge valuation. Working Paper, University of Chicago.

Menon, T., & Pfeffer, J. (2003). Valuing internal versus external knowledge: Explaining the preference for outsiders. *Management Science, 49*, 497–513.

Messick, D. M., & Sentis, K. P. (1985). Estimating social and nonsocial utility functions from ordinal data. *European Journal of Social Psychology, 15*, 389–399.

Milgrom, P. R., & Roberts, J. (1992). *Economics, organization and management*. Englewood Cliffs, NJ: Prentice-Hall.

Mitchell, T. R., & Wood, R. E. (1980). Supervisor's response to subordinate poor performance: A test of attributional model. *Organizational Behavior and Human Decision Processes, 25*(1), 123–138.

Moreland, R. L., Argote, L., & Krishnan, R. (1998). Training people to work in groups. In: R. S. Tindale & Colleagues (Eds), *Theory and Research on Small Groups* (pp. 37–60). New York: Plenum Press.

Morison, E. (1966). *Men, machines, and modern times.* Cambridge, MA: MIT Press.

Moscovici, S. (1980). Toward a theory of conversion behavior. In: L. Berkowitz (Ed.), *Advances in Experimental Psychology* (Vol. 13, pp. 209–239). New York: Academic Press.

Nelson, R. R., & Winter, S. G. (1982). The schumpeterian tradeoff revisited. *American Economic Review, 72,* 114–132.

Ocasio, W. (1997). Towards an attention-based view of the firm. *Strategic Management Journal, 18,* 187–206.

O'Reilly, C. A. (1982). Variations in decision makers' use of information sources: The impact of quality and accessibility of information. *Academy of Management Journal, 25,* 756–771.

O'Shea, J., & Madigan, C. (1997). *Dangerous company: The consulting powerhouses and the businesses they save and ruin.* Times.

Pavelchak, M. A. (1989). Piecemeal and category-based evaluation: An idiographic analysis. *Journal of Personality and Social Psychology, 56,* 354–363.

Petty, R. E., & Cacioppo, J. T. (1986). *Communication and persuasion: Central and peripheral routes to attitude change.* New York: Springer-Verlag.

Petty, R. E., Cacioppo, J. T., & Goldman, R. (1981). Personal Involvement as a determinant of argument-based persuasion. *Journal of Personality and Social Psychology, 41,* 847–855.

Pfeffer, J. (1992). *Managing with power: Politics and influence in organizations.* Boston, MA: Harvard Business School Press.

Pfeffer, J., & Salancik, G. R. (1978). *The external control of organizations: A resource dependence perspective.* New York: Harper & Row.

Pfeffer, J., & Sutton, R. I. (2000). *The knowing-doing gap: How smart companies turn knowledge into action.* Boston, MA: Harvard Business School Press.

Phillips, K. W. (2000). The effects of in-group and out-group expectations on beneficial task conflict in groups. Working Paper, Northwestern University.

Polyani, M. (1958). *Personal knowledge: Towards a post-critical philosophy.* Chicago, IL: University of Chicago Press.

Pratto, F., & John, O. P. (1991). Automatic vigilance: The attention-grabbing Power of negative social information. *Journal of Personality and Social Psychology, 61,* 380–391.

Pressman, J. L., & Wildavsky, A. (1984). *Implementation: How great expectations in Washington are dashed in Oakland: Or, why it's amazing that federal programs work at all, this being a saga of the economic development administration as told by two sympathetic observers Who seek to build morals on a foundation of ruined hopes* (3rd ed.). Berkeley: University of California Press.

Ridgeway, C. L. (1997). Where do status value beliefs come from? New developments. In: J. Szmatka, J. Skvoretz & J. Berger (Eds), *Status, Network, and Structure* (pp. 137–158). Stanford, CA: Stanford University Press.

Ross, L. D. (1977). The intuitive psychologist and his shortcomings. In: L. Berkowitz (Ed.), *Advances in Experimental Social Psychology* (Vol. 10, pp. 174–220). New York: Academic Press.

Ruscher, J. B., & Fiske, S. T. (1990). Interpersonal competition can cause individuating processes. *Journal Personality and Social Psychology, 58,* 832–843.

Sabatier, P. (1978). The acquisition and utilization of technical information by administrative agencies. *Administrative Science Quarterly, 23*(3), 396–417.

Sahlin-Andersson, K. (1996). Imitating by editing success: The construction of organizational fields. In: B. Czarniawska-Joerges & G. Sevon (Eds), *Translating Organizational Change* (pp. 61–92). Berlin: Walter de Gruyter.

Salancik, G. R., & Pfeffer, J. (1982). Who gets power – and how they hold on to it: A strategic-contingency model of power. In: M. L. Tushman & W. L. Moore (Eds), *Readings in the Management of Innovation.* Boston: Pitman.

Schank, R. C., & Abelson, R. (1977). *Scripts, plans, goals and understanding.* Hillsdale, NJ: Lawrence Erlbaum.

Sherif, M. (1966). *In common predicament.* Boston, MA: Houghton Mifflin.

Siegel, A. E., & Siegel, S. (1957). Reference groups, membership groups, and attitude change. *Journal of Abnormal and Social Psychology, 55,* 360–365.

Smith, D. K., & Alexander, R. C. (1988). *Fumbling the future.* New York: Morrow.

Smith, E. R., & Zárate, M. A. (1992). Exemplar-based model of social judgment. *Psychological Review, 99,* 3–21.

Snyder, M., & Stukas, A. A. (1999). Interpersonal processes: The interplay of cognitive, motivational, and behavioral activities in social interaction. *Annual Review of Psychology, 50,* 273–303.

Srull, T. K., & Wyer, R. S. (1989). Person memory and judgment. *Psychological Review, 96,* 58–83.

Stasser, G. (1999). The uncertain role of unshared information in collective choice. In: J. Levine, L. Thompson & D. Messick (Eds), *Shared Cognition in Organizations: The Management of Knowledge* (pp. 49–69). Hillsdale, NJ: Lawrence Erlbaum.

Staw, B. M. (1981). The escalation of commitment to a course of action. *Academy of Management Review, 6,* 577–587.

Staw, B. M., & Epstein, L. D. (2000). What bandwagons bring: Effects of popular management techniques on corporate performance, reputation, and CEO pay. *Administrative Science Quarterly, 45,* 523–556.

Staw, B. M., Sandelands, L. E., & Dutton, J. E. (1981). Threat-rigidity effects in organizational behavior: A multi-level analysis. *Administrative Science Quarterly, 26,* 501–524.

Strickland, L. H. (1958). Surveillance and trust. *Journal of Personality, 26,* 200–215.

Sutton, R. I. (2002). *Weird ideas that work: 11 1/2 practices for promoting, managing, and sustaining innovation.* New York: Free Press.

Svenson, O., & Maule, A. J. (Eds) (1993). *Time pressure and stress in human judgment and decision making.* New York: Plenum Press.

Szulanski, G. (1996). Exploring internal stickiness: Impediments to the transfer of best practice within the firm. *Strategic Management Journal, 17,* 27–43.

Tajfel, H., & Turner, J. (1986). Social identity theory of intergroup behavior. In: S. Worschel & W. G. Austin (Eds), *Psychology of Intergroup Relations.* Chicago: Nelson-Hall.

Tesser, A., Millar, J., & Moore, J. (1988). Some affective consequences of social comparison and reflection processes: The pain and pleasure of being close. *Journal of Personality and Social Psychology, 54,* 49–61.

Tetlock, P. E. (1999). Accountability theory: Mixing properties of human agents with properties of social systems. In: J. Levine, L. Thompson & D. Messick (Eds), *Shared Cognition in Organizations: The Management of Knowledge* (pp. 117–137). Hillsdale, NJ: Lawrence Erlbaum.

Thompson, L., Gentner, D., & Loewenstein, J. (2000). Avoiding missed opportunities in managerial life: Analogical training more powerful than individual case training. *Organization Behavior and Human Decision Processes, 82*(1), 60–75.

Thurow, L. (1993). *Head to head: The coming economic battle among Japan, Europe & America.* New York: Warner Books.

Tor, A., & Bazerman, M. (2001). Understanding indirect effects in competitive environments: Explaining decision errors in the Monty Hall game, the acquiring a company problem, and multi-party ultimatums. Working Paper, Harvard Business School.

Tushman, M. L. (1977). Communication across organizational boundaries: Special boundary roles in the innovation process. *Administrative Science Quarterly, 22,* 587–605.

Tversky, A., & Kahneman, D. (1974). Judgment under uncertainty: Heuristics and biases. *Science, 185,* 1124–1131.

Tyler, T. (1998). The psychology of authority relations: A relational perspective on influence and power in groups. In: Kramer & Neale (Eds), *Power and Influence in Organizations* (pp. 251–260). Thousand Oaks, CA: Sage.

von Hippel, E. (1994). Sticky information and the locus of problem solving: Implications for innovation. *Management Science, 40,* 429–439.

Wasserman, D. (2003). Political cartoon from the Boston Globe. Reprinted in *The New York Times,* June 15th, Section 4, 4.

Watson, J. (1980). *The double helix: A personal account of the discovery of the structure of DNA.* New York: Atheneum.

Wegner, D. M. (1987). Transactive memory: A contemporary analysis of the group mind. In: B. Mullen & G. R. Goethals (Eds), *Theories of Group Behavior* (pp. 185–208). New York: Springer-Verlag.

White, J. B., & Langer, E. J. (1999). Horizontal hostility: Relations between similar minority groups. *Journal of Social Issues, 55,* 537–559.

Williams, K. Y., & O'Reilly, C. A. (1998). Demography and diversity in organizations: A review of 40 years of research. In: B. Staw & R. I. Sutton (Eds), *Research in Organizational Behavior* (Vol. 20, pp. 77–140). Greenwich, CT: JAI Press.

Wyer, R. S., & Carlston, D. E. (1994). The cognitive representation of persons and events. In: R. S. Wyer & T. K. Srull (Eds), *Handbook of Social Cognition* (2nd ed.). Hillsdale, NJ: Lawrence Erlbaum.

Yule, S. B., & Keene, M. S. (Eds) (1889). *Borrowings: A compilation of helpful and beautiful thoughts from great authors.* New York: Dodge.

Zahra, S., & George, G. (2002). Absorptive capacity: A review, reconceptualization and extension. *Academy of Management Review, 27*(2), 185–203.

Zbaracki, M. J. (1998). The rhetoric and reality of total quality management. *Administrative Science Quarterly, 43,* 602–636.

Zmud, R. W. (1978). An empirical investigation of the dimensionality of the concept of information. *Decision Sciences, 9,* 187–195.

INTRAGROUP CONFLICT IN ORGANIZATIONS: A CONTINGENCY PERSPECTIVE ON THE CONFLICT-OUTCOME RELATIONSHIP

Karen A. Jehn and Corinne Bendersky

ABSTRACT

In this paper, we review recent empirical work on interpersonal conflict in organizations and, by incorporating past theory and multiple disciplinary views, develop a comprehensive model of the effects of intragroup conflict in organizations from a contingency perspective. We consider: (1) the type of conflicts that exist; (2) the organizational outcome that is predicted or desired; (3) the temporal aspect of group life and conflict; and (4) the circumstances under which conflict occurs and the processes used to manage it that moderate the conflict-outcome relationship. We highlight the final aspect, the moderating factors, by presenting a conflict-outcome moderated (COM) model that delineates types of moderators which influence the conflict-outcome relationship: amplifiers (those variables that amplify the conflict-outcome relationship, strengthening both the positive and negative effects), suppressors (those variables that weaken both the positive and negative effects on outcomes), ameliorators (those variables that decrease negative effects and increase positive effects), and exacerbators (those variables that increase negative effects of conflict and decrease positive effects). We ultimately

Research in Organizational Behavior
Research in Organizational Behavior, Volume 25, 187–1
ISSN: 0191-3085/doi:10.1016/S0191-3085(03)25005-X

present a model of constructive intragroup conflict in organizations delin-
eating the contingencies upon which group success, as it relates to conflict,
is dependent.

INTRODUCTION

Before 1990, much of the organizational literature presumed that conflict was counterproductive. Theorists shyly suggested that conflict might be constructive in organizations under certain circumstances, but empirical studies were lacking. Since then, workplace conflict has become ever more visible in organizations. As organizations experiment with flatter, more decentralized structures, workers are becoming more interdependent and responsible for more decision-making (Dumaine, 1991; Nohria, 1991). These changes mean new types of conflicts may arise among different groups of workers than were experienced in bureaucratically structured organizations (Janssen, Van de Vliert & Veenstra, 1999). The workforce is also becoming increasingly diverse. More women, minorities, foreign nationals, and people with different educational and experiential backgrounds are entering the workforce. This diversity inevitably leads to different kinds of conflicts than were experienced by a more homogenous workforce (Fiol, 1994; Williams & O'Reilly, 1998).

More recent empirical work has begun to consider the potential benefits of organizational conflict rather than focusing only on the negative effects associated with it. A goal of this article is to review recent empirical work and, by incorporating past theory and multiple disciplinary views, to present a contingency perspective of the effects of intragroup conflict in organizations, which highlights the conditions that determine whether conflict is positive or negative to individual and group functioning. We consider: (1) the type of conflicts that exist; (2) the organizational outcome that is predicted or desired; (3) the temporal aspect of group life and conflict; and (4) the circumstances under which conflict occurs and the processes used to manage it that moderate the conflict-outcome relationship. We highlight the final aspect, the moderating factors, by presenting a conflict-outcome moderated (COM) model that delineates types of moderators which influence the conflict-outcome relationship: amplifiers (those variables that amplify the conflict-outcome relationship, strengthening both the positive and negative effects), suppressors (those variables that weaken both the positive and negative effects on outcomes), ameliorators (those variables that decrease negative effects and increase positive effects), and exacerbators (those variables that increase negative effects of conflict and decrease the positive effects).

In this article, we focus on conflict between at least two people, and most often in the group or intergroup setting within organizations. Conflict can be broadly defined as perceived incompatibilities or discrepant views among the parties involved. This broad view of conflict allows us to use a number of different theoretical underpinnings to examine the circumstances surrounding the conflict debate. After reviewing this literature, we develop a conceptualization of intragroup conflict to clarify the effects of conflict on group outcomes.

A MAIN DEBATE: IS CONFLICT GOOD OR BAD?

The conflict debate we identify is whether disagreements within groups and organizations can be constructive or not. In addition to research studies focusing on group and organizational conflict (reviewed below), past theorizing and research from areas such as communication theory (cf. Cloven & Roloff, 1993; Drake & Donohue, 1996; Roloff, 1987), group interaction processes (e.g. Bales, 1958; Gersick, 1988; Gladstein, 1984; Guzzo, 1986; McGrath, 1984), power dynamics in organizations (e.g. Eisenhardt & Bourgeois, 1988; Eisenhardt & Schoonhoven, 1990; Enz, 1988), collective bargaining (cf. Baruch, Bush & Folger, 1994; Bingham, Chesmore, Moon & Napoli, 2000; Chamberlain & Kuhn, 1965), and diversity in groups and organizations (e.g. Wagner, Pfeffer & O'Reilly, 1984; Williams & O'Reilly, 1998) have provided contradictory results as to whether conflict is a help or hindrance in work groups. We incorporate these literatures, as well as research from anthropology, economics, sociology, and political science, to develop a contingency perspective of intragroup conflict in organizations; addressing when, what type, and in what way conflict constructively influences organizational group performance.

Cons: Conflict is a Detriment to Organizational Functioning

Reviews over the past fifty years of organizational research (cf. Coleman, 2003; Coser, 1956; Pondy, 1967, 1992; Thomas, 1976, 1992) suggest that conflict is: (1) ubiquitous in life whenever people interact; and (2) detrimental to organizational functioning. In addition, today's managers and employees still overwhelmingly view conflict as negative and something to be reprimanded, shunned, or immediately resolved (Jehn, 1999; Schwenk, 1990). Organizational conflict research, in general, has shown that group conflict can decrease individual satisfaction and group productivity.

Pondy (1967) assumes that conflict is the negative outcome of a breakdown in the cooperative organizational system, which affects the equilibrium of a high-performing corporation. This is based on March and Simon's (1958) view of conflict as a failure in organizational standard operating procedures. Other scholars argued in the same vein that goal conflicts inhibited the search for information in decision-making processes (Argyris, 1976; Beyer, 1981; Mitroff & Emshoff, 1979). Blake and Mouton (1984) proposed a process model of conflict resolution, which assumes that conflict is the main detriment to group effectiveness. Argyris (1962) also notes that interpersonal problems will produce suboptimal products and Deutsch (1969) theorizes that conflicts decrease goodwill and mutual understanding. Rapoport (1960) describes conflict as non-rational fights motivated by interpersonal aggression, confirming the negative view of interpersonal and organizational conflict. These theoretical views of conflict point out the negative aspects assumed to be associated with organizational conflict.

Empirical research confirmed this negative view of conflict. Wall and Nolan (1986) studied conflict with 375 students in task-oriented groups and noted that satisfaction was significantly lower in groups with conflicts related to equity issues, task-related goals and objectives, and personality differences than in low-conflict groups. In an empirical study of student decision-making teams, Schwenk and Cosier (1993) found that groups with low levels of conflict and high levels of consensus performed better and were more willing to work together again than were low-consensus groups. Evan, in a 1965 study of research and development teams, shows that interpersonal conflicts were correlated with low group-level and individual performance. The nature of his data and analyses leaves the direction of causality ambiguous, however. By examining 42 manufacturing teams, Pelled (1996) found that relationship conflicts within teams decreases perceived productivity. Gladstein's (1984) study of sales teams also demonstrates that intra-group conflicts within teams contribute to lower levels of reported performance and satisfaction.

Scholars from disciplines other than organizational behavior have also studied intragroup and interpersonal conflict, and their work helps us understand the often negative view of conflict that has developed in other areas of study. Anthropologists, for instance, have discussed conflict in the realm of different and often conflicting cultural values and beliefs that are manifested negatively at both the cultural level (e.g. warfare) and the level of individuals interacting with other individuals (e.g. community conflicts; Balkenohl, 1971; see Fry & Fry, 1997, for a review). While culture is most often viewed as a system of mutual expectation and understanding that humans use to interpret interactions (Goodenough, 1983), it is also the basis for intense conflict. Glenn, Johnson, Kimmel and Wedge (1970) incorporate political theories of conflict into anthropological culture theories to explain interactions of individuals from various cultural backgrounds. More recently, the focus of cultural, psychological, and political anthropologists has been on ethnic conflict, which incorporates the context of the conflict (Esman, 1994;

Gurr & Harff, 1994), as well as the identities of the individuals involved in intranational warfare (Eidelson & Eidelson, 2003; Ross, 1997). In particular, Faure (1995) points out that conflict, negotiation, peace, and aggression are defined differently in different cultures and must be understood from the frames of those involved. This view has influenced recent work on intra- and inter-cultural conflict conducted in an anthropologic, inductive framework attempting to rid the work of the North American biases that Faure criticizes (Doucet & Jehn, 1997; Shapiro & Von Glinow, 1999; Tinsley, 2003; Weldon, Jehn, Doucet & Wang, 1996). The general anthropologic view, however, is that conflict is a negative force with the potential for aggression, violence, and ultimately, warfare.

Political science scholars' studies of warfare and strategic use of force tend to promote the view that harmony is optimal and conflict is in direct opposition to a peaceful state of affairs (Boulding, 1962; Schelling, 1960). This research emphasizes strategies to influence an enemy or adversary (Deutsch, 1965; Gamson & Modigliani, 1971; Leng & Wheeler, 1979). A predominant approach that arose from the Cold War experience is the use of deterrence strategies that rely on credible threats of massive punishment (George & Smoke, 1974; Jervis, 1976, 1979; Morgan, 1977; Snyder & Diesing, 1977). For instance, using simulations of the Cuban Missile Crisis, Langlois (1991) developed game theoretic models to determine that a successful deterrence policy begins with restrained responses that become increasingly firm if the opponent refuses to compromise. Another approach has been to use reciprocal actions to induce cooperative behavior. Dimuccio (1998, p. 251) studied policies of appeasement in numerous international crises, and argued that appeasement is an effort to bring about cooperation among adversaries in a normative environment that approximates social exchange. In contrast, Druckman (1990) argues that because antagonists do not necessarily share a normative ideology that includes expectations of reciprocal interaction, such behavior is guided by both sides' calculations of expected utility. He discusses the effectiveness of learning mechanisms, tit-for-tat approaches, and unilateral initiatives to start a cycle of instrumental reciprocal interaction. All of these approaches are based on the assumption that conflict is disruptive and dangerous, and should be eliminated through the strategic use of influence techniques.

Sociologists identify how conflicts can be used to reinforce the power distribution in an organization by framing conflicts as threats to group cohesion (Black, 1990). By defining the terms of a conflict situation and its appropriate resolution, Barley (1991) argues that individuals may have little choice but to acquiesce to a superior's preferences. This has been supported by a number of ethnographic case studies of conflict in organizations that describe conflicts as opportunities for high-powered individuals to assert the means of control over subordinates

(Kolb, 1994; Kolb & Bartunek, 1992; Kunda, 1992; Morrill, 1995). This view of conflicts suggests that they may hinder creativity and risk-taking, which can limit performance gains over time.

Another view of conflict, the simple economic model, focuses on resource and wealth distribution activities (Neary, 1997). Conflict is often viewed in an interest-based competitive game setting, with the major question being one of coordination and equilibria (Knez, 1998). Game theory employs economic analyses of conflicts as competition and defection in complex social behavior (Luce & Raiffa, 1957; see De Dreu, Weingart & Kwon, 2000, for a review of competition and cooperation as it relates to conflict in groups and teams). At another level of analysis, economists also examine the effects of war and peace negotiations (Elster, 1995) and the motivations and outcomes of uprisings and wars (Hirshleifer, 1995). In addition, Fink (1972) proposed conflict resolution strategies using an expected utility model that focuses on violence prevention from an economic viewpoint.

A cognitive perspective, which is closely linked to the economic one, is often taken to investigate decision-making under conditions of conflict (Kahneman & Tversky, 1995). The conflict theory of decision-making is based on situations in which participants have multiple objectives (Cole, Phillips & Hartman, 1977; Radford, Hipel & Fang, 1994; Taylor, 1983). A basic assumption is that rational decision makers always choose an option that optimizes their own outcome, often resulting in a worse one for the other party – hence the conflict potential. Many decision theorists consider situations in which one or both parties have incomplete information and/or the situation is extremely complex, leading them to be imperfectly, or "boundedly" rational (Bennett & Cropper, 1990; Raiffa, 1982; Rudashevskii, 1974). Heckathorn's unified model of decision-making, bargaining, and conflict (1980), suggests that incomplete information is the cause of conflict, which necessitates coming to a mutual decision through bargaining and tactical (and not necessarily amiable) information exchange. Mandel's (1979) perceptual decision-making conflict model suggests that tensions across dyads and within groups are the basic causes of distorted perceptions and conflict, which ultimately result in suboptimal decisions. Various psychological processes have been studied for their effects on generating cognitive biases in the negotiation process, also leading to sub-optimal outcomes. For example, Bazerman (2002) reviews and summarizes biases that emanate from the availability and representative heuristic, and bargaining around particular anchors. The way in which issues are framed and interpreted may cause people in conflict to behave irrationally. These models incorporating decision-making and conflict are based on the premise, as is often the case in negotiation research (see Lewicki, Weiss & Lewin, 1992, for a review of negotiation research, labor relations, and third party interventions), that conflict is negative and needs to be quickly resolved.

Similarly, the classic view of organizational or employment conflict in law is as an adversarial dispute that is handled by the courts or other public adjudicatory procedures, by formal labor negotiations, and recently by alternative dispute resolution processes, such as mediation and arbitration (Block, 1993; Edwards, 1995; Kochan, Lautsch & Bendersky, 2000; McDermott et al., 2000). Conflicts are viewed as violations of contractual agreements or legally-mandated behavior that should be resolved by restoring justice to the aggrieved party(ies) (Dunlop & Zack, 1997; Feullie & Delaney, 1992). Conflict, is therefore narrowly defined and viewed as an inherently negative phenomenon. The legal system in this country is structured to eliminate conflicts through adjudicatory procedures. The relatively recent introduction of alternative dispute resolution (ADR) procedures into the practice of employment law are designed to decrease the time it takes to resolve conflicts and to, thus, reduce legal expenses (GAO, 1997; Lipsky & Seeber, 1998). ADR that is practiced within a legal context is often considered a more efficient means through which conflicts are resolved or eliminated. In most cases (some exceptions will be presented later), conflicts are still viewed as counterproductive, negative interactions.

Family studies research includes views from marital and divorce therapy, family systems approaches, and clinical psychology focusing on family therapy. Marital conflict has been studied in settings as varied as using Prisoner's Dilemma games and videotaping interactions in the laboratory (Knudson, Sommers & Golding, 1980; Santa-Barbara & Epstein, 1974) to Muslim/Jewish relations in cross-national marriages (Lachkar, 1993). Much of the family research regards conflict as discord, abuse, or distress, whether in the marriage (Arellano & Markman, 1995; Christiansen & Shenk, 1991; Eggeman, Moxley & Schumm, 1985; Forehand & McCombs, 1989), throughout the family (Barkley, Guevremont, Anastopoulos & Fletcher, 1992; Siani & Siciliani, 1996), between parent and child, or among siblings (Katz, Kramer & Gottman, 1992). Zuk and Zuk (1989) and Zuk (1988) provide an interesting model of the conflict cycle in families and in therapy consisting of four steps: (1) the dispute; (2) blaming; (3) shame, guilt, or denial; and (4) reparation, reconciliation, or retaliation. This parallels an earlier, more general, dynamic model including owning one's position, attending to the other person, and resolving the conflict (Rollin & Dowd, 1979). In none of these models, though, is conflict seen as a constructive force within the family. However, conflict has been identified by some as a normal, even instinctual (Bernstein et al., 1997), part of the family system.

Communication research on conflict has often focused on an individual's conflict style (Cloven & Roloff, 1993), dominance behavior (Jones & Remland, 1993) or preferred tactic for handling conflict (McCready, Roberts, Bangala, Harris, Kingsley & Krikorian, 1996; Putnam & Wilson, 1982; Rahim & Magner, 1995).

At the dyadic level, investigations of conflict resolution frames in negotiation and bargaining situations have been the focus of interest (Drake & Donohue, 1996). Both of the above views assume that conflict has negative influences and should be resolved. A review of the empirical work on organizational communication from 1979 to 1989 (Wert-Gray, Center, Brashers & Meyers, 1991) indicates that the research focused on three topics, one of which was conflict (the other two areas were culture and superior-subordinate relations). This review reiterated the above claim, that conflict is a negative factor in organizations and the work being done focused on resolution and minimization of interference to the organization.

Also, three streams of marketing research have focused on dysfunctional conflict (Menon, Bharadwaj & Howell, 1996). The first stream focuses on conflict in organizational purchasing behavior and conflict resolution in that setting (Day, Michaels & Perdue, 1988; Sheth, 1973; Strauss, 1962). The second investigates marketing strategic planning and conflicts that occur in the decision making process that interfere with process and performance (Whitney & Smith, 1983). The third focuses on personality conflicts in sales force management teams, similar to Gladstein's (1984) study on team effectiveness (cf. Menon, Bharadwaj & Howell, 1996).

To summarize, multiple disciplines and streams of research have contributed to the view of conflict as a negative interpersonal and organizational force. In the next section, we focus on research pointing to the potential positive effects of conflict within organizations.

Pros: Productive Conflict in Organizations

In contrast to the above theories and empirical work, conflict, under some circumstances, may be beneficial. Based on George Simmel's (1955) essay that viewed conflict as a form of socialization, Coser (1956) suggests that social conflict may have a functional purpose. He argued that conflict serves to establish and maintain the identity and boundaries of groups, acts as a safety valve, increases in-group cohesion, establishes and maintains the balance of power, and creates allies and coalitions. Others view conflict as the means through which groups attempt to define the terms of their interaction and adapt to changing conditions (Morrison & Milliken, 2000; Walton & McKersie, 1965). Deutsch (1973) argued that conflict may enhance creativity by motivating people to solve a problem that might otherwise go unattended, while others observe that some level of task-related conflict improves strategic decisions and creative performance in groups, as well as inhibits groupthink (Amason & Schweiger, 1994; Jehn, 1995; Schweiger, Sandberg & Rechner, 1989). Most of this research has been conducted in the areas of group processes, strategic planning, decision-making, collective bargaining and conflict resolution.

Conflict within teams has been shown to improve decision quality and strategic planning of groups and organizations. In one of the earliest empirical studies of conflict's productivity-enhancing potential, Pelz and Andrews (1966) surveyed 1,311 scientists from universities, industrial laboratories, and government laboratories. They determined that high performing scientists had colleagues who disagreed with them on the strategy for approaching a task. Additionally, groups retained their productive strength over time only when they maintained vigorous interaction and intellectual tension. Eisenhardt and Bourgeois (1988) studied politics in strategic decision making of top executives and found that unchallenged ideas decreased firm performance, suggesting that conflict that challenges the dominant coalition can improve performance. Mitroff, Barabba and Kilmann (1977), in a case study of strategic planning in a large federal agency, found that people who were stuck in current modes of thinking and in current operating constraints of the organization could not effectively solve problems in a group. Exercises instructing employees to create and integrate diverse themes enhanced proactive planning. Additionally, groups of middle and upper-level managers in a longitudinal laboratory setting made higher quality decisions when challenging and conflicting views were presented (Schweiger, Sandberg & Rechner, 1989). Cosier and Rose (1977) studied prediction error by inducing conflict by providing subjects with information about another's view that differed from their own. Subjects in the high conflict condition were able to better predict error in the initial round of four trials (no difference was found in the other three trials) – which was interpreted as improved decision quality. Using a computer-generated model, Cohen (1984) demonstrated that groups with conflicting goals engaged in more effective organizational search and arrived at optimal policies by making fewer erroneous judgments during the decision-making process.

Studies examining organizational conflict at the team-level of analysis have also found positive associations between conflict and performance. In a study of 88 student teams, Jehn (1994) found that task conflicts increased team performance on a ten-week class project. In a follow-up study of organizational teams in a Fortune 500 company, Jehn (1995) found similar results. Groups that had moderate to high levels of task conflicts had higher performing individuals and higher overall group performance (measured by supervisor reports and objective departmentally produced production reports) than did groups with low levels of task conflict. Van de Vliert and De Dreu (1994) also suggest that the stimulation of conflict can increase joint performance in decision-making groups and Tjosvold (1991) theorizes that the right to dissent will lead to cooperative conflict. Nemeth (1987, 1995, 2001) finds that minority dissent stimulates divergent thought processes, which leads people to consider a problem from multiple perspectives, generate more original ideas, and arrive at superior decisions and performance outcomes. Indeed, an edited volume (De Dreu & Van de Vliert, 1997) has been published informing managers how to stimulate conflict within their teams and organizations with the intention of increasing performance.

Task-related management team conflict improves organizational performance and growth through enhanced understanding of various viewpoints and creative options. Bourgeois' (1985) study of top management teams indicates that too little task dissent can interfere with successful strategy making. Organizational growth and decision-quality have been positively linked to the top management teams' constructive conflict (Amason, 1996; Eisenhardt & Schoonhoven, 1990). Research on marketing strategy also agrees with this perspective that divergent views produce better quality ideas and decisions (Anderson & Weitz, 1992; Bucklin & Sengupta, 1993; Lusch, 1976; Rosenberg & Stern, 1970; Rosenbloom, 1973). In addition, marketing researchers suggest that conflict can strengthen the quality of channel relationships (Frazier & Rody, 1991).

The field of industrial relations evolved as a means to manage inherent conflicts of interest between workers and managers that characterize many employment relationships (Dunlop, 1958; Kochan, Katz & McKersie, 1986). From this perspective, conflicts are not only considered to be inevitable, but they are also the means through which power may be redistributed and the opportunistic behaviors of managers kept in check (Chamberlain & Kuhn, 1965). Thus, from the workers' perspective, conflicts are an essential mechanism for bringing attention to their collective interests.

While conflicts are viewed negatively by alternative dispute resolution (ADR) practices conducted in association with formal legal procedures, some forms of ADR have been introduced within organizations as a way to harness the positive potential of workplace disputes through conflict *management* instead of resolution. Conflicts are viewed as inevitable and inherently neutral (i.e. they potentially have both good and bad effects). The *means* through which they are addressed produces the good or bad effects for individuals and organizations (Costantino & Merchant, 1996; Ury, Brett & Goldberg, 1989). For example, one form of ADR, called transformative mediation, focuses on helping the parties gain deeper understanding about one another, which can transform their subsequent interactions to be more open and productive (Baruch, Bush & Folger, 1994). Research on the implementation of transformative mediation in organizations offers some support for potential positive outcomes associated with organizational conflict. For example, Bingham and her colleagues have produced several evaluations of the U.S. Postal Service's transformative mediation alternative to Equal Employment Opportunity Commission adjudicatory procedures (Bingham, Chesmore, Moon & Napoli, 2000; Bingham & Novac, 2000). They found consistent evidence that the mediation program that acknowledged and even embraced certain forms of conflict was preferable to the adjudicatory procedures for both employee complainants and managerial respondents. Not only did the mediation process generate faster resolution at lower costs than the adjudicatory procedures, but also it generated more flexible and creative solutions, and enhanced participant satisfaction with both the process and the outcomes.

In sum, there is theorizing and empirical evidence that conflict can be destructive and that conflict can be beneficial to groups and organizations. In the following sections, we present a contingency perspective that proposes four explanations for this puzzle. After that, we delineate the relationships that lead to high levels of intragroup processing and performance by developing a conflict-outcome moderated (COM) model that includes variables that act like amplifiers, suppressors, ameliorators, and exacerbators of the conflict-outcome relationship.

CONCEPTUALIZING INTRAGROUP CONFLICT

Given the contrasting evidence and complexity surrounding conflict and its effects, it is important to determine whether conflict is always detrimental to organizational functioning, and if it is not, to identify the situations in which conflict is beneficial and on what this is contingent. To do this, we first provide an overview of past typologies and definitions of conflict, followed by our conceptualization of intragroup conflict developed to assist in the creation and prediction of constructive conflict situations within organizational groups. We present a contingency perspective to reconcile the pros and cons of conflict by considering: (1) the type of conflict that exist; (2) the organizational outcome of interest; (3) the temporal aspect of conflict in groups; and (4) the moderators of the conflict-outcome relationship. We highlight the forth aspect, the moderating factors, by presenting a theory of moderation that delineates types of moderators that influence the conflict-outcome relationship (the COM model): amplifiers (which strengthen both the positive and negative effects), suppressors (which weaken both the positive and negative effects), ameliorators (which strengthen positive effects and weaken negative effects), and exacerbators (which strengthen negative effects and weaken positive effects).

A Review of Past Typologies of Conflict

The most frequently used explanation for the conflict-performance relationship is that there are different types of conflict with different performance implications.

For example, conflict researchers have recently found that while relationship conflicts based on personality clashes and interpersonal antagonism are detrimental to group performance and morale, task conflicts are often beneficial (Amason, 1996; Amason & Schweiger, 1994; Jehn, 1995, 1997a, b; Jehn & Mannix, 2001).

Guetzkow and Gyr (1954) make a conceptual distinction between substantive conflict, or conflict based on the substance of the task that the group is performing, and affective conflict, or conflict rooted in the emotional aspects of interpersonal relationships. They suggest that both kinds of conflict may lead to the same overt behaviors (e.g. both would delay a meeting), but that they arise and disappear under different conditions. Substantive conflicts arise from discrepancies over group goals as members of a team try to complete a task and are resolved when individuals are willing to honestly evaluate one another's ideas. Affective conflict is likely to exist when members are focused on their individual satisfaction or their need for status, and will dissipate when members focus on the group needs rather than their individual needs.

Coser (1956) discusses social change efforts based on realistic and non-realistic conflict. Realistic conflicts are social conflicts that develop out of frustration regarding specific demands and expectations. The object of the conflict, in this case, is the source of frustration, or the obstacle to gains. This can be a positive force if it causes individuals to organize their efforts toward change. Non-realistic conflicts, according to Coser, do not focus on goals but on the need for tension release. Non-realistic conflict is unlikely to be creative (Coser's word) and is not often a positive force in social change.

Pondy (1967) delineates three general types of organizational conflict episodes: bargaining conflicts, bureaucratic conflicts, and systems conflicts. Bargaining conflicts are based on differing interests and discrepancies over demands of shared, scarce resources. Bureaucratic conflicts exist because of the vertical hierarchy in organizations and arise because superiors attempt to control subordinates and the subordinates resist. Pondy bases bargaining conflicts in differing interests over shared resources and bureaucratic conflicts in power and personal autonomy issues. Systems conflicts, linked to March and Simon's (1958) administrative issues, reflect lateral conflicts among employees at the same level, which are based on problems of coordination.

Cosier and Rose (1977) characterize two types of conflict, cognitive and goal conflict, to examine decision-making groups and their use of devil's advocacy, dialectical inquiry, and consensus approaches. Cognitive conflicts involve disagreement over interpretation and goal conflicts are interpersonal disagreements focusing on competition for rewards or status. Wall and Nolan (1986) differentiate between relationship focused people-centered conflicts and conflicts about the substantive content of the task. Like Pelz and Andrews (1966), Wall and Nolan explicitly announce that task conflict will result in more productive conflicts than will people conflicts. Wall and Nolan focused their people-centered problems on those that grow out of inequities and issues of unfairness, while task conflicts revolved around alternative solutions and debates that enhanced decision outcomes. When you look closely at the methodology of their empirical study, the people-centered conflicts are operationalized by unequal workloads, struggles over leadership, and personality differences. Task conflicts are conflicts over procedural matters and ideational matters relating to ideas, goals, and values associated with the substantive content of the task.

Pinkley (1990), in one of the first studies to empirically identify disputants' conflict resolution frames, uncovered three dimensions of conflict: relationship versus task, intellectual versus emotional, and win versus compromise. Relationship conflicts focus on interpersonal issues based on problems within the relationship while task conflicts relate to issues of money and property settlement. Disputants who are using intellectual conflict frames focus on the facts of the case while those in emotional frames focus on feelings of jealousy, frustration, and anger. Disputants in the win frame feel that one party was right and the other wrong, while those in the compromise frame feel that mutual agreement was necessary and that both parties caused the conflict.

Priem and Price (1991) built on Cosier and Rose's (1977) distinction between cognitive conflict and goal conflict. They incorporated goal conflict into cognitive conflict and defined cognitive conflict as disagreements that are task related, often about goal differences. They discussed social-emotional conflicts as those that involve interpersonal disagreements in general and more specifically as a consequence of miscommunication and competition.

Defining Conflict: The Relationship/Task Distinction

There is an apparent distinction between task and relationship components in these typologies. We refine and expand the previous categorization of conflict by: (1) delineating emotion as a separate dimension from each conflict type; and (2) identifying process conflict as a unique form of task conflict. Note that in practice, while occurrences of task, relationship and process conflict are often interrelated (i.e. a group with many relationship conflicts may also have a high number of task conflicts), we believe that the conflict types are distinct and that the opportunity for productive conflict from a contingency perspective is found specifically in the ability to distinguish among the conflict types and the factors that influence their impact on group performance. In other words, the impact of conflict on group outcomes depends on, or is contingent upon, the specific type of conflict experienced in the group.

Relationship Conflict

Relationship conflicts exist when there are interpersonal incompatibilities among group members. This type of conflict often includes personality differences as well as differences of opinion and preferences regarding nontask issues (e.g. religion, politics, fashion). While early studies used the concepts of affective or emotional conflict and relationship conflict interchangeably (Guetzkow & Gyr, 1954), a number of more recent studies indicate that the task/relationship dimension of conflict is separate from the intellectual/emotional component (Jehn, 1992, 1997a, b; Pelled, 1996; Pinkley, 1990). In other words, both relationship and task conflicts may be characterized by strong or weak emotional components. In response, researchers have turned to the term "relationship conflict" as a separate dimension from emotional conflict (cf. De Dreu & Weingart, 2003; Jehn, 1995; Jehn & Mannix, 2001).

In a qualitative study, Jehn (1997a, b) found that organizational members discussed "people problems," "personal conflicts," and "interpersonal problems" distinctly from the emotional component of the conflict. While relationship conflicts focused on interpersonal relationships among coworkers, they were not necessarily emotional debates. Jehn also found that task conflicts, while unrelated to personal issues, did sometimes involve emotional components. For example, an employee can have a different preference regarding food, politicians, or livable cities but not release emotion. Granted, many relationship conflicts do evoke emotional responses (as do task conflicts) but to clarify the association between conflict and group performance we choose to separately examine the topic of the conflict (i.e. the group task, the group process, or the group relationships) from the level of emotion involved. We discuss emotion as a moderator of the conflict-outcome relationship later in the presentation of the constructive conflict model.

Task Conflict

While labeled many different things (i.e. cognitive conflict, substantive conflict, content conflict, realistic conflict), task conflicts are consistently defined as disagreements among group members about the tasks being performed. Task conflict pertains to conflicts of ideas in the group and disagreement about the content and issues of the task. Task conflict exists when there are disagreements among group members about the content of the tasks being performed, including differences in viewpoints, ideas, and opinions. Employees often describe these conflicts as "work conflict," "work disagreements," and "task problems." Examples of task conflicts are: "The discussion was about how to correctly calculate relative capacity utilization. We couldn't agree. Everyone had his or her own viewpoint and argued for it." and "Some people were sure that the future strategy should be to focus on the super premium market, while others felt the focus should be the minority market. There were different interpretations of the key issues. We debated a long time." (Jehn, 1994, p. 235; see Jehn, 1997a, b, for more examples). The key concept is that task conflicts are focused on the work or task at hand, in contrast to relationship conflicts which focus on non-task issues.

Process Conflict
A third type of conflict has begun to surface in organizational conflict research (Jehn, 1997a, b; Jehn & Mannix, 2001; Jehn, Northcraft & Neale, 1999; Thatcher, Jehn & Chadwick, 1998) – *process conflict*. Hints of this type of conflict have been present in past theorizing (e.g. Kelley & Thibaut's, 1969 and Rapoport's, 1960 conflicts of resources), but not until recently have researchers incorporated it into their conflict models as a construct separate from task conflict.

Most past research viewed task conflicts as substantive issues or a combination of substantive and process issues, but not as process issues separate from the content of the task (Amason, 1996; Cosier & Rose, 1977; Jehn, 1995; Schweiger, Sandberg & Rechner, 1989). Process conflicts are about the means to accomplish the specific tasks, not about the content or substance of the task itself, but about strategies for approaching the task, as Pelz and Andrews (1966) would say. Examples of such are disagreements about the composite of a team and who should do what, debates about resources, and fights about how to schedule tasks efficiently. When four researchers disagree about data interpretation and the meaning of the results, they are experiencing task conflict. If they argue about who is responsible for writing up the final report and who will make the presentation, they are having a process conflict.

In a multidimensional scaling study of group conflict, Jehn (1992) found that employees often discussed "administrative conflicts." Group members distinguished between conflicts over task content issues (e.g. debates over marketing proposals) and administrative issues such as delegating resources and duties. In an ethnographic study of work groups, Jehn (1997a, b) labeled these "process" conflicts and defined them as conflicts about "how task accomplishment should proceed in the work unit, who's responsible for what, and how things should be delegated." Employees mentioned "reorganization disagreements" "responsibility disagreements" and "disagreeing about utilizing people." In planning sessions, members ordered each other around and fought about capabilities and assignments to duties and workstations. Process conflict is similar to past organizational constructs such as distributive conflict (Kabanoff, 1991) or procedural complexity (Kramer, 1991). In 1991, Kabanoff depicted distributive conflict as political contention about rules that dictate the allocation of material interests, while task conflict refers to the goals and ends of the group. Kramer (1991) examined conflicts based on power differentials in a case study. Procedural complexity included conflicts over group means, such as the exchange of resources and role responsibilities. Pondy's (1967) typology of bargaining conflicts also included process issues such as discrepancies over shared, scarce resources. His systems conflicts were also linked to problems of coordination, which infers issues of delegation and task processing. Wall and Nolan (1986) discuss people-centered problems but operationalize it as conflicts of inequities and issues of unfairness such as unequal workloads (p. 1038). We therefore believe it is critical to examine task and process conflict as separate constructs, in addition to relationship conflict, to more adequately theorize the relationship between group conflict and outcomes.

A CONTINGENCY PERSPECTIVE OF CONSTRUCTIVE CONFLICT IN ORGANIZATIONS

In the prior sections we discussed past theory and empirical work on conflict from multiple disciplinary views. We structured the discussion by examining views that see conflict as a negative process in organizations (the predominant view) and those that view conflict as a potentially positive process. We then reviewed past frameworks regarding types of conflicts in groups and organizations and presented a conceptualization of conflict incorporating and elaborating on the past work. We now discuss the effects of each conflict type (i.e. task, relationship, and process) on group outcomes by specifying the influence that conflict has on individual cognitions, emotions, and attitudes as well as on intragroup dynamics. The processes by which each conflict type influences individuals and the resulting group dynamics is summarized in Fig. 1 and a conflict-outcome moderated model is presented in Fig. 2.

Performance Outcomes

Research has demonstrated that the effect of conflict is different depending on the outcome of interest. Thus, the managerial implications of conflict follow the contingency perspective – the decision to promote or eliminate conflict will depend on what it is that you are concerned about within your organization or team. For example, if you want your employees to be happy interacting with one another, you will probably view all types of conflict as negative. But, if you want to improve group performance, you should consider task conflict as a positive force. In other words, there are trade-offs in the value of conflict across outcomes. We delineate the specific relationships between conflict types and various outcomes in

	Individual Level	Group Level

Relationship Conflict:	Distraction
	Misspent time
	Misspent effort
	Limits cognitive processes
	Decreased ability to
	   assess new information
	Decreases commitment
		Decreases cooperation; goodwill
		Decreases communication and
		   understanding
		Group focus on resolving or
		   retaliation
		Access to new information limited

Task Conflict:	Being challenged increases
	   effort
	Increases divergent cognitive
	   processes
	Enhances task focus
	Increases anxiety and tension
		Increases divergent opinions,
		   interpretations, viewpoints
		Increases critical evaluation and
		   assessment of alternatives
		Increases communication, shared
		   information, problem identification
		Increases group problem-solving

Process Conflict:	Increases claim and blame
	   perspective
	Feel personally attacked
	Unfairness and inequity
	   primed
		Increases re-evaluation of processes
		   and standards
		Increases appropriateness of task
		   and resource assignments

Fig. 1. Individual Reactions to Conflict and Intragroup Interaction Processes.

our model of intragroup conflict (Fig. 2). The most common research outcomes in conflict studies have been objective performance and member morale, including intent to remain in the group and individual satisfaction. These outcomes parallel Hackman's (1987) three criteria of team effectiveness: (1) the productive output of the group meets or surpasses the standards of the customer; (2) the work processes are such that members ability and desire to work together again are enhanced; and (3) employees are satisfied rather than frustrated with the work experience. The first component includes measures of individual and team performance. The second and third components are related to the morale of members and often

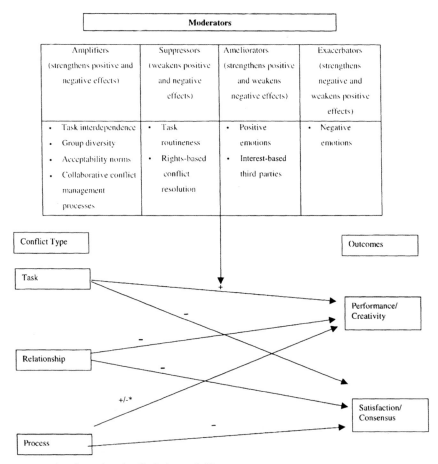

Fig. 2. The Conflict-Outcome Moderated Model.

represented by absenteeism, turnover, and attitudes such as satisfaction and intent to work in the group again. We additionally consider less-studied outcomes, such as creativity and decision consensus, to present a more comprehensive model of intragroup conflict and its effects.

Performance is defined as the output of an individual or team that is depicted in their job description and for which they are rewarded based on performance appraisals. For example, in an assembly line or piece-rate situation, the number of widgets produced determines the worker's performance. Creative outcomes are often the result of work that is not directly rewarded or indicated in the job description. Creativity is the production of ideas, products, or procedures that are: (a) novel or original and (b) potentially relevant for or useful to the organization (Amabile, 1983, 1988; Sternberg & Lubart, 1996). It often involves gathering information from multiple sources, recognizing unusual connections between elements of a problem or situation, and combining them into a practical and useful product (Amabile, 1983; Van de Ven, 1986). While creativity is not usually explicitly required in many organizational jobs, and even less often explicitly measured, it is often valued by customers, peers, and supervisors and can sometimes increase overall organizational performance, especially in organizations that depend on innovative ideas.

While some level of task conflict may generate performance and creativity benefits (discussed in more detail below), it comes at a cost in terms of group member satisfaction and ability to reach consensus. Amason and Schweiger (1994) introduce group consensus as a separate outcome from decision quality. They note that the ultimate consensus formed around a decision is critical to its implementation and that conflict affects both the quality and the consensus of the decision. A team reaches consensus when "its members have a thorough knowledge of and are committed to a particular decision." (1994, p. 241). Group consensus impacts subsequent commitment to implementing group decisions (Amason, 1996; Amason & Schweiger, 1994; Walton, Cutcher-Gershenfeld & McKersie, 1994; Walton & McKersie, 1965). Excessive levels of any type of conflict can erode group consensus and member satisfaction. In other words, even if task conflicts can generate more creative decisions, too much task conflict can hurt their implementation by limiting consensus. It can also suppress members' willingness to work together in the future due to low satisfaction with the group.

In sum, a constructive group outcome is contingent not only on the type of conflict occurring in the group, but also on the outcome desired. For instance, if one is promoting high performance and creativity, it is important to encourage high levels of task conflict but low levels of relationship and process conflict. However, if the goal of the team is to have a highly satisfied group of members willing to work together again and who can efficiently reach consensus, it is beneficial to have a low level of all types of conflict, including task conflict. This creates a dilemma for managers and group leaders attempting to have happy, long-term high-producing creative groups. We theoretically develop the main effect predictions of each type of conflict on each performance outcome in the sections that follow (also see Figs 1 and 2). After that, we utilize the contingency perspective to further develop the conflict-outcome moderated model by introducing four forms of moderation to the conflict-outcome relationship (amplification, suppression, amelioration, and exacerbation) with the goal of identifying the optimal conditions for high-performing teams with satisfied members.

Relationship Conflict and Group Outcomes

Empirical research shows a negative association between relationship conflict, productivity, creativity, consensus building, and satisfaction in groups (Evan, 1965; Gladstein, 1984; Wall & Nolan, 1986). We discuss the reasons for these findings by focusing on mechanisms at two levels of functioning within groups: (1) the individual reactions to conflict; and (2) the group level processes resulting from conflict (see Fig. 1). The experience of conflict influences group members' perceptions, attitudes, emotions, and behaviors, which in turn influence the interaction processes among group members.

Relationship conflicts interfere with task-related effort because members focus on reducing threats, increasing power, and attempting to build cohesion rather than working on the task. According to Deutsch (1969), relationship conflicts decrease goodwill and mutual understanding, which hinders the completion of organizational tasks. Time is often spent on interpersonal aspects of the group rather than on technical and decision-making tasks (Evan, 1965). Pelled (1996) summarizes three ways in which relationship conflict affects group performance. First, relationship conflict limits cognitive processing and reduces the ability of group members to assess new information provided by other members. Second, the interpersonal conflict makes members less receptive to the ideas of other group members, some of whom they may not like or who may not like them. Third, the time and energy that should be devoted to working on the task is used to discuss, resolve, or ignore the often task-irrelevant conflicts.

Another reason that relationship conflict may negatively impact group performance is the threat involved with damaging a working relationship. Studies have suggested that the threat and anxiety associated with relationship conflict tend to inhibit people's cognitive functioning in processing complex information (Roseman, Wiest & Swartz, 1994; Staw, Sandelands & Dutton, 1981) and thus inhibit individual performance. The results of Evan's (1965) study on research and development teams indicated that interpersonal attacks seriously limit group and individual-level performance and productivity. Relationship conflict also negatively effects performance by distracting members from the task at hand. Group members focus their efforts on resolving or ignoring the interpersonal conflicts, rather than concentrating on task completion, which severely limits group productivity (Evan, 1965; Jehn, 1995). Social psychologists suggest that interpersonal negativity such as insulting coworkers, being rude, and breaking promises focuses employees on retaliation and escalation (cf. Gabriel, 1998).

While there has been little research on impediments to creativity in organizations (for an exception, see Amabile, Conti, Coon, Lazenby & Herron, 1996), we propose that relationship conflict will negatively affect creative behavior for three basic reasons. First, the distraction often caused by relationship conflicts can reduce employees' ability to recognize alternative approaches and can prevent them from integrating diverse sources of information into innovative products (Cohen, 1984). Second, discretionary job behavior such as creativity is often excluded from formal organizational reward systems (Van Dyne, Jehn & Cummings, 2001). When employees have interpersonal conflicts and are distracted from their work and less motivated to perform well as a team, they will most likely focus on specified behaviors that they know will be measured and considered in performance reviews. As a result, their creativity is reduced because the effort that they do place on the task-aspect of their job will be focused on measurable objective performance and not on innovation and creativity. The third reason, building on the prior logic, is that the effort used to resolve interpersonal conflicts will detract from the energy and peace of mind often needed to be creative at one's job (Cummings & Jehn, 1999).

Relationship conflict has a relatively obvious negative effect on member morale. This is based on a general dissatisfaction with conflict in personal relationships. For instance, Surra and Longstreth (1990) demonstrated that people who felt conflict with the person they were dating were less satisfied in the relationship than those who didn't. More specifically to the case of conflict in organizations, Wall and Nolan discovered that interpersonal conflicts decreased satisfaction in task groups (1986). A series of organizational team studies (Jehn, 1994, 1995, 1997a, b; Jehn, Northcraft & Neale, 1999) have also consistently found that relationship-based conflicts decreased satisfaction with one's job, task group, and organization.

Relationship conflict can also interfere with consensus building in groups and the implementation of decision outcomes. It can lead team members to disagree with others even if they rationally know that other members have agreed on a high-quality outcome. This often irrational deal breaking arises out of interpersonal issues that stimulate revenge, retaliation, and further escalation of conflict. Amason and Schweiger (1994) propose that relationship conflicts cause members to misinterpret constructive debate as personal criticisms, which inhibits affective acceptance or decision consensus. Guetzkow and Gyr (1954) studied small, face-to-face decision-making groups and found that interpersonal conflicts decreased consensus because members did not attempt to reduce forces hindering agreement, but instead, often belabored the points that inhibited consensus. The individual- and group-level mechanisms that cause the negative impact of relationship conflict on group outcomes are summarized in Fig. 1.

Task Conflict and Group Outcomes

In contrast to relationship conflict, task conflict within a group can be beneficial to performance and creativity, although it can still hurt consensus building and satisfaction. In a number of studies and settings, Jehn and her colleagues have shown that task conflicts at moderate levels can improve team performance (Jehn, 1995; Jehn, Chadwick & Thatcher, 1997; Jehn & Mannix, 2001; Jehn, Northcraft & Neale, 1999; Levine & Jehn, 1999). Disagreements related to the task can improve group decision making, strategic planning, top management team success, and general task performance. For instance, Pelz and Andrews (1966) found that the most productive research and development teams were those that maintained a significant level of intellectual challenge and disagreement over time. Amabile and colleagues also found higher productivity when respondents experienced pressure from challenging work situations (Amabile, 1983, 1988; Amabile, Conti, Coon, Lazenby & Herron, 1996). The increased number of opinions and critical evaluation enhances effectiveness in both laboratory and field settings. Research suggests that task-focused conflict within teams can improve decision quality and strategic planning (Amason & Schweiger, 1994; Cosier & Rose, 1977; Mitroff, Barabba & Kilmann, 1977; Schweiger, Sandberg & Rechner, 1989).

The cognitive, task-focused aspect of conflict enhances the assessment of shared information and deliberate, careful assessment of alternatives (Baron, 1984). The useful give and take among members, the consultative interaction and problem-solving, and the increased information exchanged enhances performance (Menon, Bharadwaj & Howell, 1996; Van de Vliert, Nauta, Euwema & Janssen, 1997). In a longitudinal study, Fiol (1994) showed that when group members had different interpretations of task content issues, the group's learning and accurate assessment of the situation increased. Schwenk and Valacich (1994) showed that evaluating and critiquing the status quo yielded higher quality decisions in work groups because members confronted problems rather than avoiding or smoothing over the issues. Consistent with theories of groupthink and decision making, when members agree with other group members about concepts or actions without presenting dissenting viewpoints, superior alternatives may be overlooked and thus, performance may be suboptimal (Janis, 1982; McCauley, 1998; Peterson, Owens, Tetlock, Fan & Martorana, 1998; Tjosvold, Dann & Wong, 1992; Turner, Pratkanis, Probasco & Leve, 1992). An empirical test of the groupthink model shows that putting pressure on dissenters, self-censorship, and collective justifications increase defective decision-making (Choi & Kim, 1999). In other words, lack of task conflict can lead to an ineffective consensus, or suboptimal decision, among members.

Organizational researchers have also discussed "speaking out and challenging the status quo with the intent of improving the situation" (Le Pine &

Van Dyne, 1998, p. 853) which indicates that task conflict increases the likelihood of creative solutions (see Fig. 1). We suggest that task conflicts will enhance creativity in teams and organizations even more than it does general performance. Research suggests that task conflicts stimulate divergent, rather than convergent, cognitive processes which help members consider problems from new perspectives and produce creative ideas (Nemeth, 1995). Likewise, research on dissent and devil's advocacy suggests that task-based conflicts help members see problems from new angles and arrive at creative ideas (Nemeth, 1987, 1995, 2001). Task conflicts may also increase group members' tendency to scrutinize issues and engage in deep and deliberate processing of relevant information. This can foster learning and the development of highly creative insights (De Dreu & West, 2001).

Task-related conflict, while potentially beneficial to performance and creativity, can still cause anxiety and uncomfortable feelings among group members (Hoffman, 1978; Roloff, 1987). Task-related conflicts may cause tension, antagonism, and unhappiness among group members that can damage both their satisfaction with the work experience and their ability to reach consensus on decision making tasks (the negative main effects of task conflict on group member satisfaction and consensus is represented in Fig. 2). Ross (1989) suggested that a person's normal reaction to disagreement and questioning of one's viewpoints is dissatisfaction, however advantageous the outcome of the confrontation. Baron (1990), in his study of performance evaluations, showed that critical evaluations caused negative affective reactions regardless of the outcome. Even if members realize positive outcomes, the conflictful group process leading to them, including critical evaluation, can cause dissatisfaction (Jehn, 1995). Schweiger, Sandberg and Ragan (1986) provided evidence that people in groups with high levels of consensus about task issues expressed more satisfaction and desire to stay in the group than members in groups with higher levels of dissension regarding the task.

The above discussion of the mechanisms by which task conflict influences group outcomes at the individual and group levels is outlined in Fig. 1. We also provide a summary of the main effects of task conflict on group outcomes in Fig. 2; mainly, that moderate to high levels of task conflict will enhance group performance and creativity (indicated by a "+" on those paths), but will also lessen satisfaction with the group and challenge consensus building (indicated by a "−" on those paths).

Process Conflict and Group Outcomes

The relationship between process conflict and group outcomes is more complicated than the seemingly straightforward effects of task conflict and relationship conflict on group outcomes. We present competing hypotheses resolved by the temporal component of our model, discussed in the next section. In arguing for the positive effects of process conflict on performance, research has shown that process-related debates can increase reevaluation of current processes and standards (see Fig. 1; Hedberg, Nystrom & Starbuck, 1976; Tjosvold, 1991), thus causing changes that upgrade the quality of the product and enhance individual and group performance. In addition, discussions related to task assignment and resource delegation are often necessary to begin and complete a task effectively, as well as to reach consensus. Despite this reasoning, a second line of logic has arisen with the current research on process conflict.

While process conflict may seem closely related to task conflict in that the issues in dispute are somewhat task-focused, Jehn (1997a, b) found that process conflict operated more like relationship conflict in its connection to performance and satisfaction. It may be that while process conflicts are generated by tasks that need to be done, process issues revolve around people. Determining who does something involves an assessment about individuals' abilities, skills, and even values. The process of how issues are delegated is intertwined with one's interpersonal skills. Thus, Jehn (1997a, b) found that small amounts of process conflict that were resolved easily facilitated performance, but for the most part, process conflict had negative effects because of process loss. Three more recent field studies (Jehn & Mannix, 2001; Jehn, Northcraft & Neale, 1999; Thatcher, Jehn & Chadwick, 1998) found that process conflict was negatively related to morale (intent to remain, commitment, satisfaction) and performance (objective group performance, perceived individual and group performance). We predict a similar effect for process conflict and creativity, as group members claim or blame others for ideas (Fig. 1), the personal investment in the creative aspect will cause members to react negatively to process conflicts about the creative process (see Fig. 2).

Furthering the Contingency Perspective: The Temporal Aspect of Conflict

We continue with our contingency perspective of conflict by introducing the role of temporal phases of group or project life. Whether or not conflict is beneficial or detrimental to group functioning and outcomes is dependent on the time in a group's life that the conflict occurs. A dynamic view of conflict helps further the model beyond the main effects of conflict types on different group outcomes (Fig. 2). For instance, it resolves the ambiguous findings about the effects of process conflict on group outcomes by suggesting that process conflict can positively affect performance and creativity only if it occurs at the early stages of a group's lifecycle. We begin with a review of some of the past work on conflict stages as well as the work on group dynamics and phases of group life (see Mannix & Jehn, 2004, for a

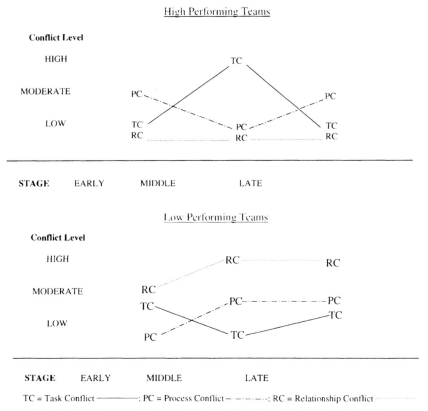

Fig. 3. The Temporal Aspect of Conflict (Based on Jehn & Mannix, 2001).

more thorough review). We then propose a model regarding the temporal aspects of task, relationship, and process conflict in high-performing workgroups (see Fig. 3).

According to Deutsch (1969), conflict has a tendency to escalate and expand, often leaving the initial cause behind and forgotten. Zuk and Zuk (1989) and Zuk (1988) provide an interesting model of the conflict cycle in families consisting of four steps: (1) the dispute; (2) blaming; (3) shame, guilt, or denial; and (4) reparation, reconciliation, or retaliation. This parallels an earlier, more general, dynamic model including owning one's position, attending to the other person, and resolving the conflict (Rollin & Dowd, 1979).

Pondy (1967) provided an early dynamic model of conflict in which he defined conflict as a series of episodes. The first stage involved initial, antecedent conditions (i.e. scarce resources, policy debates), or "latent conflict." This was followed by affective states (i.e. stress, hostility) – what Pondy referred to as "felt conflict," – and cognitive states, "perceived conflict," signifying to the individual that conflict is present. It is at this point that conflict is hypothesized to enter the individual's consciousness. According to Pondy, if the conflict never moves out of the antecedent stage from latent conflict to felt or cognitive conflict, it may never be perceived as conflict by individuals. The manifest stage entails conflict behaviors ranging from passive resistance to overt displays of aggression. The final stage is the conflict aftermath.

Early efforts in the study of groups had an inherently temporal dimension, notably the work on group dynamics and the related study of phases in group problem-solving. Many stage models have been proposed, the key features of which were reviewed and integrated by Tuckman (1965): forming, storming, norming, and performing. More recently, Gersick (1988, 1989) has demonstrated that groups exhibit a "punctuated equilibrium" in which temporal phases emerge as bounded eras within each group, without being composed of identical activities across groups and without the phases necessarily progressing in a hierarchically set order.

Recent empirical work by Jehn and Mannix (2001) examines conflict over time in organizational groups. In a longitudinal study of fifty-one workgroups, they examined the temporal profile of the three conflict types (task, relationship, process) in high and low-performing groups. They found that the effects of the different conflict types varied depending on the stage of the group's development. A general temporal pattern of conflict in high performing groups emerged: low to moderate levels of process conflict in the early stages, moderately high levels of task conflict during the middle and latter stages, and consistently low levels of relationship conflict across all stages. Groups that experienced high task conflict from the beginning, or that started with high levels of task conflict but tapered off over the life of the project were less successful (see Fig. 3).

The temporal model especially helps to explain the effects of process conflict in workgroups. Process conflict at the beginning stages of a group's interaction, when responsibilities and deadlines are decided (Jehn, 1997a, b; Mintzberg, Raisinghani & Theoret, 1976), allows work norms to be agreed upon, accepted, and understood (Tuckman, 1965). In Gersick's (1989) laboratory study, activities of successful groups included process discussions, time-pacing, and resource requirements in the early phases of interaction. In the field, Gersick (1988) also found that high performing teams made decisions about milestones, task responsibilities, and deadlines early; having determined their processes and procedures, the groups were able to then focus on the content of the task. Process discussions and debates that occur early in a group's life, as indicated by the above studies, allow the groups to set up agreed-upon working norms for successful task completion. In addition, group members who are allowed "voice" during these early stages are likely to understand and be committed to the resulting decisions regarding the task (Greenberg & Folger, 1983).

The final stages of the group task often involve formalizing and presenting a specific plan for implementation – another time of increased process conflict (Jehn & Mannix, 2001). Tasks during this completion phase include editing, formatting, and deciding methods of presentation (Gersick, 1988, 1989). Group members need to decide who is most capable of completing various new task assignments such as organizing and presenting the compiled information, decision, or completed product. These adaptations allow the successful team to smoothly move into task completion and implementation (Gersick, 1991).

Relationship conflict is negative whenever it occurs during the lifecycle of the group or project. The negative processes associated with relationship conflict – distraction of members, misspent time and effort, limits to cognitive processing, problems in coordination, communication and group focus – lead to inferior group performance and low satisfaction. Low performing teams have a pattern of relationship conflicts over time that escalates; for example, misspent time and effort is blamed on fellow group members and communication and coordination continue to suffer. Task and process conflicts also increase throughout the group's life, indicating a negative cycle of conflict. By the end of the group's life, the high level of task conflict is associated not with increased communication and problem identification, but with intractable problems related to the task that, at this point, are distracting, dysfunctional and often interconnected with relationship problems. In high-performing groups, relationship conflict was low throughout and task conflict was highest at the midpoint of the group's life. The timing of the task conflict, along with the low levels of relationship conflict, allow groups to capitalize on the constructive aspects of task conflict such as enhanced information sharing, critical evaluation of divergent opinions, and increased task focus. Thus, in addition to the relationship between conflict type and performance outcomes, the contingency perspective suggests that the time in the lifecycle of a group that a certain type of conflict occurs will affect its impact on performance.

A CONFLICT-OUTCOME MODERATED (COM) MODEL: AMPLIFIERS, SUPPRESSORS, AMELIORATORS, AND EXACERBATORS

A recent meta-analysis of studies relating task-conflict to group performance has found little evidence for a direct, positive relationship – suggesting potential moderating variables (De Dreu & Weingart, 2003). We suggest that task characteristics, group diversity, group conflict norms, emotions, and conflict management processes all moderate the relationship between conflict types and outcomes (represented in a table above the main-effects paths in Fig. 2). We develop the COM model to specify the context and mechanisms by which groups can leverage conflict to produce high effectiveness on multiple dimensions. We first introduce the moderation categories of amplifiers, suppressors, ameliorators, and exacerbators as a set of factors that differentially, but predictably, influence the relationship between conflict and group outcomes.

Amplifier moderators strengthen the relationship between conflict and outcomes, regardless of the direction of the main effect. The key here is that amplifier moderators can both increase the positive effects *and* the negative effects of conflict on the outcome, depending on the direction of the main effect. For example, acceptability norms (group norms than encourage an openness and acceptance of disagreement) as an amplifier moderator will increase the positive effect of task conflict on performance, but will *also* increase the negative effect of relationship conflict on performance. Amplifiers do not determine whether the relationship between conflict and a group outcome is positive or negative, therefore, but amplify the already existing direction of the main effect.

Suppressors are on the other side of the coin to amplifiers. They do not determine the direction of the relationship between conflict and group outcomes either, but weaken both the positive and negative effects of conflict on group outcomes. For example, if a group leader works to resolve all conflicts, the negative effects of relationship conflict will be reduced, but the positive effects of task conflict will be inhibited as well.

Similar to more traditional theories of moderation, we propose moderators that act as ameliorators and exacerbators of the main effect relationship. That is, exacerbators cause the conflict to have a negative impact on group outcomes, increasing negative effects and decreasing positive effects. Ameliorators, in contrast, weaken the negative effects and strengthen the positive effects of conflict on outcomes. For instance, positive emotions in a group will lessen the negative effects of relationship conflict but also enhance the positive effects of task conflict in that same group.

This approach to moderation highlights the challenges to managers and group leaders when attempting to manage conflict in work groups: not only can the same kinds of conflicts have both positive and negative effects on different group outcomes, at different points in the group's lifecycle, but the same intervention can also serve to strengthen both the positive *and* negative effects of those conflicts.

Amplifier Moderators

Amplifier moderators increase both the positive and negative effects of conflict on group outcomes. We discuss how task interdependence, group diversity, acceptability norms, and collaborative conflict management processes each make the effects of task conflicts more positive and the effects of relationship and process conflict more negative on group outcomes.

Task Interdependence

Task interdependence exists to the extent that group members rely on each other to perform and complete their individual jobs (Van de Ven, Delbecq & Koenig, 1976). Increased interaction and dependence among members causes conflict to have an intensified effect on individual and group outcomes (Gladstein, 1984; Schmidt & Kochan, 1972). Task interdependence increases the amount and intensity of interaction among members, thus increasing the salience of conflicts that occur within a group to its members. Therefore, it amplifies the positive effect of task conflict while also amplifying the negative effects of relationship and process conflict (see Fig. 2). Task conflict positively influences performance through increased debate and discussion of alternative viewpoints; therefore, the interdependence required by a task will increase collaboration and communication thus amplifying the positive effects of constructive debate and task conflict. In the same way, however, negative effects of relationship and process conflict will be amplified by the necessary interaction required by these interdependent tasks. The negative processes (see Fig. 1) associated with relationship conflict, for instance, will be exaggerated when members are forced to interact regarding task completion in groups with high levels of interdependence.

Group Diversity

Conflicts are often linked to the diversity of work groups (Jehn, Northcraft & Neale, 1999; Pelled, 1996; Pelled, Eisenhardt & Xin, 1999); however, the direct relationship between diversity and performance is weak (Williams & O'Reilly, 1998). While diverse groups are especially well suited for innovation and creative problem solving, workgroups that must incorporate employees with diverse national, cultural, ethnic, linguistic, and experiential backgrounds are also prone to high levels of conflict that can impede performance (Pelled, 1996). Pelled, Eisenhardt and Xin (1999) built on this finding by studying the impacts of different kinds of diversity (functional, tenure, race, gender and age) on task and emotional (similar to relationship) conflict in 45 research and development teams. They found that only functional diversity increased task conflict, which positively affected cognitive task performance. Tenure and race diversity increased emotional conflict, but did not negatively impact performance. In a field study of 98 work groups, Jehn, Northcraft and Neale (1999) also examined situations in which diversity improves workgroup effectiveness, member morale and efficiency, and situations in which diversity hinders effectiveness. They developed a typology of diversity types (informational diversity, demographic diversity, and value/goal diversity) and discovered that the various types of diversity differentially affect the group processes leading to conflict, individual morale, and group effectiveness. Specifically, informational diversity increased task conflict in workgroups, which led to performance improvements. Social category diversity increased relationship conflict, which decreased worker morale and group performance. Value diversity was positively related to all three types of conflicts, but only relationship conflict mediated the relationship between value diversity and performance.

Rather than viewing conflict as a mediator between diversity and group outcomes, as the above research has, we propose group diversity acts as a moderator of the relationship between conflict and group outcomes (see Fig. 2). Specifically, we see diversity as an amplifier of the relationship such that it enhances the positive effect of task conflict in groups (e.g. increasing performance and innovation) but can also increase the negative effects of relationship and process conflicts in groups. For instance, task conflict will be even more beneficial in groups with a variety of educational, cultural, and vocational viewpoints to help reconcile the differences creatively. The various perspectives members bring to group discussions will enhance debates surrounding task content (Hoffman, 1978; Hoffman & Maier, 1961). The critical evaluation possible when members have diverse educational backgrounds, for instance, will lead to high-quality decisions and group products (Jackson, 1992; Jehn, Northcraft & Neale, 1999). However, these same diverse characteristics can amplify the negative impact of relationship conflicts by causing stereotyping that can lead to animosity and misunderstandings (Jehn, Chadwick & Thatcher, 1997; Thatcher, 1999). When relationship conflicts are present among members, differences in race, age, educational perspectives or work experience can lead to negative categorizing and prejudice which increases the negative effect of the already present relationship conflict.

Acceptability Norms
One defining aspect of organizational or group culture that guides actions is the sharing of knowledge and values among group members (Enz, 1988; Sathe, 1983; Schein, 1985). Values are the beliefs held by an individual regarding behavioral choices that influence norms (Enz, 1988; Rokeach, 1973). Group norms, as defined by Bettenhausen and Murnighan (1985), are standards that regulate behavior among group members that are often developed by the members and the leadership of the group. The norms of the group control how group

members perceive conflict and can affect the degree to which conflict influences performance and members' attitudes. Openness norms (i.e. open confrontation, open discussion), which Tjosvold (1991) discusses, encourage people to express their doubts, opinions, and uncertainties. Similarly, Brett (1991), who described effective discussion norms, stated that a very important norm for a group to develop is tolerance of differing viewpoints.

Both the Tjosvold and Brett frameworks regarding norms have as their fundamental component the acceptability of conflict. Therefore, we call this moderator of the conflict-outcome relationship "acceptability norms" and treat it conceptually as having an amplification effect. Norms can encourage an openness and acceptance of disagreement or they can carry the view that conflict is unacceptable in a certain group situation (Jehn, 1995; Pruitt, 1981). For example, members in groups with acceptability norms regarding task conflict will encourage one another to express their doubts, opinions, and uncertainties, which can augment the positive effects of task conflict on performance and innovation. However, when the same acceptability norms encourage speaking out about relationship conflict within a group, it has been shown that the norms increase the negative effects of relationship conflict on performance and satisfaction. For instance, Jehn (1997a, b) found that in groups with acceptability norms about conflict, members discussed problems and openly displayed feelings of conflict. This created a healthy, constructive atmosphere around task conflict, which permitted members to investigate various alternatives and to excel at their complex tasks. However, the acceptability of relationship conflicts was *also* detrimental to the group process as the expression of these conflicts severely interfered with collaboration, task focus, commitment, and satisfaction of group members. While this seems to contradict recommendations by past studies on T-groups and process consultation (Campbell & Dunnette, 1968) which encourage open venting of interpersonal problems, it is consistent with more recent organizational and conflict research which suggests that openly discussing interpersonal conflicts at the workplace can be detrimental (Amason, 1996; Murnighan & Conlon, 1991). Thus, when the norms in a group encourage speaking out about both task and relationship conflicts, acceptability norms act as an amplifier moderator, increasing both the positive and negative effects.

Collaborative Conflict Management Processes

The effects of intragroup conflicts on organizational performance may also depend on how they are managed (De Dreu & Weingart, 2003; Jehn, Northcraft & Neale 1999; Pelled, Eisenhardt & Xin 1999). While it is important to resolve negative forms of conflict as quickly as possible, moderate levels of task conflict should be encouraged and actively managed. Pro-actively managed task conflict allows organizations to benefit from diverse views and improves productivity, decision-making, creativity and innovation (Amason, 1996; Schweiger et al., 1989; Tetlock, Armor & Peterson, 1994). When conflicts are avoided, however, other research demonstrates that it creates complacency about problems and decisions (Janis, 1985; Morrison & Milliken, 2000) and creates an illusion of understanding the reasoning and thinking underlying others' arguments (Tjosvold, Nibler & Wan, 2001).

Recent studies have shown that collaborative conflict management in which efforts are made to maximize the interests of both parties (Blake & Mouton, 1984; Van de Vliert, 1997) – is a prerequisite for task-related conflicts to positively affect group innovativeness. Lovelace, Shapiro and Weingart (2001) studied 43 cross-functional product teams. They found that the impact of task disagreements on team performance and innovativeness was moderated by the extent to which members felt free to express doubts and how collaboratively those doubts were communicated. De Dreu and West (2001) found that minority dissent led to higher innovation only in groups where there was a high level of participatory decision-making. Similarly, Tjosvold and his colleagues have studied the effects of cooperation and competition on constructive controversy in work groups (Tjosvold, 1990, 1998; Tjosvold, Johnson & Johnson, 1984). They found that when group members engaged in constructive discussion and debate over task conflicts they achieved better productivity outcomes than when conflicts were handled competitively. Likewise, De Church and Marks (2001) found that task conflict had a positive effect on productivity and satisfaction only when collaborative, what they call "agreeable," conflict management processes were used.

Interestingly, using collaborative conflict management processes to address relationship conflicts can increase their negative effects on outcomes. It increases the likelihood that time and energy are spent airing negative relationship conflicts, which distracts team members from the work tasks they are assigned (De Dreu & Van Vianen, 2001). Thus, the challenge is to focus collaborative conflict management processes on task-related conflicts while using more rights-based conflict resolution techniques (a suppressor moderator, discussed below, in which a third party determines the outcome of a conflict) to deal with relationship conflict.

Suppressor Moderators

Suppressor moderators have the opposite effect to amplifier moderators, in that they weaken both the positive effects of task conflict and the negative effects of relationship conflict on group outcomes. We discuss how task rountineness and rights-based conflict resolution each function to suppress both the positive and negative effects of conflict in groups.

Routine Tasks

Research has shown that whether or not task conflict is beneficial depends on the type of task the groups performs (Brehmer, 1976; Gladstein, 1984; Jehn, 1995; Van de Ven & Ferry, 1980). Routine tasks have a low level of task variability, which is defined as the amount of variety in methods and repetitiveness of task processes (Hall, 1972). They are generally familiar and are done the same way each time, with predictable results (Thompson, 1967). Researchers argue that conflict about the task will be a hindrance to routine performance because it interferes with efficient processing (Barnard, 1938; Guzzo, 1986; Pelz & Andrews, 1966). When groups consistently perform the same activities in the same way day after day, conflicts that arise about the task may be interruptive, counterproductive, and time consuming for the group and its members. If the task is simple, discussions of task strategy are not necessary, since members can usually rely on standard operating procedures (Gladstein, 1984). Hackman, Brousseau and Weiss (1976) demonstrated that when a group was adequately performing a fairly routine task, substantial debate of task strategy and goals decreased productivity. However, it has been suggested that routineness also inhibits the negative effects of relationship conflict as the conflicts are viewed as a welcome relief to the boredom of the routine task (Jehn, 1995). Members in groups performing routine and often boring tasks stated that the interpersonal problems and issues made their work at least interesting enough to "make it through the day." The relationship problems were viewed as natural consequences of the dull environment (Jehn, 1994) and therefore lessened the negative impact of the relationship conflict on satisfaction and group productivity – members mentioned they went back to their tasks with renewed energy and focus after the petty fighting.

In contrast to routine tasks, nonroutine tasks require problem solving and have a high degree of uncertainty (Van de Ven, Delbecq & Koenig, 1976). According to Ashby's (1956) theory of requisite variety and the information-processing approach (Galbraith, 1973; Tushman & Nadler, 1978), the amount of disagreement and variety in a group needs to match the level of variety in the task for the group to be effective. If the level of task variety and amount of information required to complete the task exceeds the level of variety and number of differing viewpoints among group members, the costs associated with searching for information and evaluating solutions may become unreasonable. Inadequate knowledge or assessment can lead to poor decisions and inferior products.

Nonroutine tasks therefore benefit from diverse ideas of group members. When members feel pressured to agree with other group members about concepts or actions instead of presenting dissenting viewpoints, the group may overlook superior alternatives. Task conflict facilitates critical evaluation and increases thoughtful consideration of criticism and alternative solutions (see Fig. 1), which decreases the groupthink phenomenon (Janis, 1982). Group pressure toward agreement can also squelch the creativity needed to complete nonroutine tasks effectively because members focus on building consensus rather than entertaining innovative ideas. Amason and Schweiger (1994) specified the positive aspect of task conflict as allowing members to identify and discuss diverse perspectives, thus increasing their understanding of the task. For nonroutine performance, this allows a more thorough evaluation of the criteria needed for individuals and groups to make high-quality decisions and create superior products. Putnam (1994) showed that task conflicts helped people identify and better understand the issues involved, and Baron (1991) provided evidence that task conflicts within groups encouraged people to develop new ideas and approaches. Constructive task conflict, therefore, may be ideal when working on nonroutine tasks, but may lead the group to reinvent the wheel when it is working on routine tasks (De Dreu & Weingart, 2003). Thus, the task characteristic of routineness is seen as a suppressor of the relationship between conflict and group outcomes, inhibiting the positive effects of task conflict as well as the negative effects of relationship and process conflict (see Fig. 2).

Rights-Based Conflict Resolution
Unlike collaborative conflict management processes, which encourage proactive efforts to manage but not necessarily resolve conflict, efforts to resolve conflicts through rights-based processes have the effect of suppressing both the positive effects of task conflict and the negative effects of relationship conflict. Rights-based processes are those that rely on some independent, legitimate standard (such as laws, contracts, or social norms) to determine if one side's rights have been violated, in an effort to end a conflict usually through some form of imposed reparations (Ury, Brett & Goldberg, 1989, p. 7). Rights-based conflict resolution processes are generally administered by a third-party; i.e. someone who is not directly involved in the conflict, such as a judge or arbitrator. Unlike collaborative conflict management processes, which elicit effort to generate solutions from the disputing parties themselves that are often creative and have an amplifying effect on the conflict-outcome relationship, rights-based processes neither allow the positive effects of task conflicts to be engaged nor the negative effects of relationship conflicts to occur. The goal of these processes is to basically squelch, or end, all conflict. Rights-based conflict resolution, therefore, acts as a suppressor moderator of the conflict-outcome relationship.

Ameliorator Moderators
Ameliorators lessen the negative effects of conflict while increasing the positive effects. We present positive emotions and interest-based third parties as two variables that moderate the effect of conflict on outcomes in this constructive manner.

Positive Emotions

Emotional experiences, broadly defined, are a complex chain of loosely connected events, beginning with a stimulus and including feelings, psychological changes, impulses to action, and specific goal-directed behavior (Plutchik, 2001). Positive affect – having a generally positive disposition or being in a good mood – smoothes over conflict behavior and can ameliorate the negative effects of conflict and accentuate the positive effects. Emotions such as joy and delight create positive feelings of well-being and satisfaction with the group (Russell, 1978). During experiences of relationship conflict, these feelings can ease the negative effects of conflict. Cooperation, communication, and goodwill will be enhanced, or at least not as damaged, if positive emotions are present in the group environment during a conflict episode.

The benefits of task conflict for group processes – e.g. increasing divergent opinions, interpretations, and viewpoints, and evaluation and assessment of these (Fig. 1) – will be accentuated if there are positive emotions present among group members. Shah and Jehn's (1993) research on friendship in workgroups demonstrated that the positive emotions associated with friendship allowed groups to have more open, constructive task debates resulting in better group decisions and group products. The positive emotion among friends also assisted in lessening the negative effects of relationship and process conflicts within these groups. Morris and Keltner (2000) argue that emotions play an important social-functional role during conflict and negotiations by generating reciprocal emotional responses. Deferential behaviors expressed in response to expressions of anger might temper the anger and resolve the crisis. Positive emotions displayed by one party or group member during a conflict, they would suggest, may be reciprocated with a more positive response from the other party involved in the conflict. Forgas (1998) empirically confirmed this idea. He contrasted positive and negative emotions in negotiations, and found that being in a good mood led to more cooperation and less competition among negotiators.

We present positive emotions as an ameliorator moderator given the above reasoning and research regarding positive group processes; however, recent research has shown some limitations of positive emotions, thus suggesting that this moderator may act as a suppressor under some circumstances. For instance, being in a good mood has been show to lead to superficial processing of information (Bless, Bohner, Schwarz & Strack, 1990), less judgmental accuracy (Sinclair & Mark, 1995), broad categorizations (Isen & Daubman, 1984), and reliance on stereotypes (Bodenhausen, 1993). One study suggests that negotiators in positive moods had the illusion that they performed well, and therefore, failed to learn from their mistakes (Kramer, Newton & Pommerenke, 1993). In another study, Sanna, Parks and Chang (2003) suggest that people construe good moods as indicating that they have achieved their performance goal, leading to behavioral complacency. Thus, positive emotions in situations requiring complex judgments and learning may weaken the positive effects of task conflict on group outcomes.

Interest-Based Third Parties

Both collaborative conflict management processes and rights-based conflict resolution have some beneficial effects (e.g. collaborative conflict management processes increase the positive effects of task conflicts, and right based conflict resolution decreases the negative effects of relationship conflict) but they also have their limitations (e.g. collaborative conflict management processes increase the costs of relationship conflict and rights based conflict resolution limits the benefits of task conflict). A third type of dispute resolution component is interest-based third parties – mediators and organizational ombudsmen – who intervene to assist with the conflict resolution process, but leave decision-making authority about the outcome up to the disputants themselves (Carnevale & Pruitt, 1992). Interest-based third parties are ameliorators in our model because their interest-based process interventions help to both increase the positive effects of task conflicts and decrease the negative effects of relationship conflicts by facilitating effective communication based on parties' interest and delineation of these types of conflict. Specifically, interest-based third parties allow disputants to vent relationship-based aspects of their conflict in private and reframe communication between the disputing parties to emphasize task aspects of the conflict (Cobb, 1993; Rubin, 1980). In a laboratory study comparing mediation tactics, for instance, Esser and Marriott (1995) found that helping parties identify trade-offs among issues was the key to effective mediation. In this manner, the detrimental impact of relationship conflict is effectively suppressed while the beneficial aspect of task conflict is surfaced collaboratively.

Recent research suggests that multi-component dispute resolution systems – in which organizational members have opportunities to select collaborative negotiation processes, interest-based third parties and/or rights-based conflict resolution – are far more effective than any one type of component is by itself (Bendersky, 2003a, b; Rowe, 1997; Ury, Brett & Goldberg, 1989). Thus, the most effective ameliorating mediator of the conflict outcome relationship may in fact be a combination of all three types of dispute resolution components.

Exacerbator Moderator

The fourth type of moderator in our model is an exacerbator. Negative emotions make the effect of task conflict less positive and the effect of relationship conflict more negative on group outcomes.

Negative Emotions

Negative emotions are an important element of conflict and, as noted earlier and discussed below, we treat them as a separate construct from conflict types in the model (see Fig. 2). We present negative emotions as exacerbators of the conflict-outcome relationship. Emotionality refers to the amount of negative affect exhibited and felt during a conflict. Past literature shows that negative affect includes a wide range of negative feelings and emotions (Fiske & Taylor, 1984; Lazarus, 1982; Park, Sims & Motowidlo, 1986; Zajonc, 1984). According to Russell and Fehr (1994, p. 186), "emotion includes anger, which includes rage, annoyance, and all other subcategories of anger." Other negative emotions relevant to the study of conflict are frustration (Guetzkow & Gyr, 1954) uneasiness, discomfort, tenseness, resentment (Stearns, 1972), annoyance, irritation, fury, rage (Russell, 1978), reproach, scorn, remorse, and hatred (Allport, 1937). Behavioral manifestations of negative emotion in conflict episodes include yelling, crying, banging fists, slamming doors, and having an angry tone (Jehn, 1997a, b).

The negative emotion moderator is considered an exacerbator because it is hypothesized to consistently increase the negative influence of all types of conflict on group outcomes. It will decrease the positive effects of task conflict, even causing task conflict to have negative effects on performance and creativity, as well as increasing the already negative effects of relationship and process conflict on group outcomes. One reason for this exacerbating effect is that conflict is often associated with stress and threat, which increase the effect of emotional responses and negative affect (Thomas, 1992). Pinkley (1990), in a study of disputants' interpretations of conflict, found an intellectual vs. emotional dimension of conflict resolution frames. Disputants with emotional frames had feelings such as jealousy, hatred, anger, and frustration. These kinds of negative emotions may lead to irrational decisions and behaviors because emotions overrun and oversimplify rational and instrumental reasoning (see Brief & Weiss, 2002 for a review; Thomas, 1992). For instance, Pillutla and Murnighan (1996) found that anger reactions can lead negotiators to reject offers that are in their best interests as judged by purely economic standards. Similarly, associating a negotiation offer with a disliked counterpart may cause the recipient to reactively devalue the offer; that is, one values an offer that he or she receives from a negatively-viewed counterpart lower than they would objectively value the same offer (Bazerman & Neale, 1983; Ross, 1995). Kelley (1979) explained that a person who is angry or antagonistic simply loses perspective about the task being performed, potentially leading to inaccurate impressions of their counterparts' interests (see also Allred, Mallozzi, Matsui & Raia, 1997). In another study, Baron (1991) found that effective communication and cooperation among group members was reduced when interpersonal conflicts included components of anger and frustration.

While it is easy to imagine the negative emotional component in connection to relationship conflicts, task and process conflicts can also contain high levels of negative emotion that inhibit their positive effects on group outcomes. Jehn (1997a, b) found instances of both *heated* task conflicts and relationship conflicts *void of emotion*. In one instance, a manager became quite angry because his idea did not get selected. He became frustrated and hostile. This emotion was not necessarily aimed at other individuals within the team, but focused on the project, or the task, to which the idea was related. He stated: "I'm not mad at you; I'm angry with the project." In this instance a task conflict was occurring and there was negative emotion involved. Even though the negative emotion was directed at the task conflict discussion, and not at the people involved, the negativity decreased the potential constructive effects of task conflict. In addition, the relationship conflicts void of emotion (e.g. "I just don't like you, that's all. It's no big deal") were much less detrimental than relationship conflicts laden with negative emotion (e.g. "That is the stupidest thing I have ever heard – you are such an idiot I cannot stand to be in the same room with you!"). In sum, negative emotion exacerbates the downsides of conflict – weakening the positive effects of task conflict and strengthening the negative effects of relationship and process conflict.

THE PATH TO CONSTRUCTIVE CONFLICT IN ORGANIZATIONS

In reviewing past empirical and theoretical work on conflict from a multi-disciplinary view, we find the main debate to be whether conflict is beneficial or detrimental in organizational contexts. This literature and more current research led us to conclude that there are four main ways in which to resolve this debate. The general answer to the question of conflict's consequences is that conflict is both detrimental and beneficial depending on multiple factors. The contingency perspective we propose states that, in certain circumstances, conflicts should be encouraged and carefully managed, while in others they should be discouraged or resolved as quickly as possible. More specifically, we propose the following four main factors to respond to this debate and to better specify the complex relationship between conflict and effectiveness: (1) the type of conflict; (2) the consequences desired; (3) the temporal dynamics occurring in the group; and (4) the types of conflict-outcome moderators.

Overview

The first major point of the paper is to separate the types of conflict. Past theories have confounded them, or assumed that all types of conflict function similarly. It is critical for researchers and group leaders to distinguish between the types of conflict and to implement group interventions that pertain to specific types of conflict. Thus, to enhance the functioning of a group and to elicit the most beneficial results from its conflict, a group leader should first be able to distinguish among the types of conflict and to relate this to group members. Research has shown that minimal training on the conflict types and the optimal conflict context can be quite effective in improving group performance (Mannix & Jehn, 2004).

The second main point is that there may be trade-offs across different group outcomes. While task conflicts may improve a groups' productivity and creativity under some circumstances, it can also damage group members' satisfaction and their ability to reach consensus decisions. We consider the optimal path to functional conflict to be the one that maximizes group performance and creativity and minimizes the costs to satisfaction and consensus making. Nonetheless, group leaders need to carefully consider what group outcomes are most important in their particular situation, and tailor the optimal conflict path to address their needs.

The third aspect we discussed in reconciling the debate regarding the benefits and detriments of conflict is the temporal aspect. We briefly discuss the dynamic component of conflict in workgroups which, while quite speculative at this point, is fortunately beginning to receive more attention in group and conflict theorizing and empirical research. We believe that the developmental aspect of group processes and conflict over time is critical to a better understanding of effective conflict handling. When researchers examine conflict over time occurring at different periods in a group's life, they find very different results than what is found in the traditional cross-sectional studies (e.g. Ancona, Goodman, Lawrence & Tushman, 2001; Jehn & Mannix, 2001; Mannix & Jehn, 2004). For instance, process conflict in the early stages of a group's development can be constructive, allowing debates to occur over task assignment and appropriate or fair delegation of duties. However, process conflict in the middle or late stages (which is common) can disrupt and detract from the task focus of the group and often decreases satisfaction and productivity. Therefore, past research on process conflict (and task conflict, as well) has been misleading when researchers aggregate conflict levels over time or examine conflict at only one point in time in a group's life. We see this as one of the main challenges of future research, given the complexity of both group research and longitudinal research, but one well worth confronting for the potential contribution such research could make to increasing our understanding of the dynamic nature of intragroup conflict in organizations.

The next major point of the paper is that in order for the recommended profile of conflict to be constructive (i.e. moderate task conflict starting in the middle of a group's life, low relationship conflict, and moderate early process conflict), there must also be certain moderator conditions present regarding group norms, conflict management, emotions, task characteristics, and diversity. To this end, we presented our COM model, which states that for the optimal level of team effectiveness, the moderators need to be considered specifically with respect to *each type* of conflict. For instance, once a group leader has identified different types of conflict, the group should work to establish norms for acceptable discussions of task conflict (and early process conflict) and norms that discourage relationship conflict at any phase of the group's lifecycle. We also suggest that it is important to consider the suppressing effects of moderators such as task routineness and rights-based conflict resolution on different types of conflict. If one is trying to eliminate or decrease negative relationship conflict in a group, he or she may assume that rights-based conflict resolution will optimize performance. However, in doing so the group will also benefit less from constructive task conflict. Thus, the group should promote collaborative conflict management processes and interest-based third parties for task conflicts, and provide rights-based conflict resolution processes for resolving relationship conflicts. An important point of our model, different from past theories of conflict moderation, is that one needs to first distinguish the type of conflict and differentially apply the moderating effects; otherwise one can unknowingly increase negative effects while intending to enhance constructive conflict. Also note that one also needs to determine the time during the group's life at which the conflict is occurring. For example, process conflict at the early stages of a group's life is beneficial so amplifier moderators should be applied to strengthen the positive effects it can have on group outcomes; however, process conflict in the later stages has negative effects so suppressor moderators are more appropriate at that time. We attempt to simplify these complex relationships among the elements influencing group outcomes by describing a path to constructive conflict in the next section, illustrated in Fig. 4.

The Elements of Constructive Conflict

While past moderation theories of conflict have assumed that the moderating effect treats all conflict relationships similarly, in delineating the COM model, we argue that the key to understanding the influence of conflict in organizational groups is to realize that there are various forms of moderators that will affect the various conflict types differently. This poses quite a challenge for those attempting to manage the process of group conflict because, as noted previously, by attempting

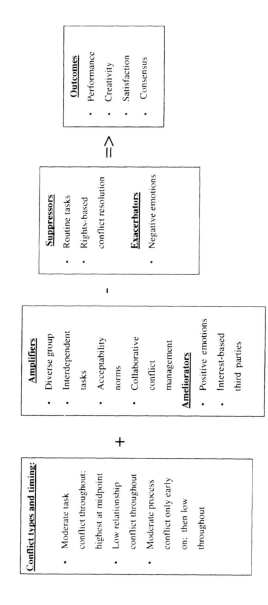

Fig. 4. The Path to Constructive Conflict and Effective Groups.

Note: "+" signifies factors that one should attempt to add or increase. "–" signifies factors that one should attempt to subtract or decrease.

to increase one type of conflict (e.g. constructive task conflict) one can quite unwittingly also amplify the negative effects of dysfunctional relationship or process conflict. Therefore, to help clarify the complexity of these relationships, we summarize the path to constructive conflict in organizational groups in Fig. 4.

In order to have high performance and creativity, without too much loss of satisfaction or consensus-building ability, a group needs to have low levels of relationship conflict throughout its lifecycle, moderate levels of process conflict at the beginning, and moderate levels of task conflict starting in the middle of a group's project or life-cycle – the leftmost box in Fig. 4, titled "Conflict types and timing." Given this optimal, temporal profile of conflict types, a group further benefits from the presence of amplifier and ameliorator moderators; considerable diversity, interdependent tasks, high acceptability norms for task conflicts and early process conflicts, collaborative conflict management processes, interest-based third parties and positive emotions. This is indicated in Fig. 4 by a plus (+) sign, thus "adding" these variables, or increasing levels of these factors, to the constructive conflict profile. The group should not have suppressor moderators, including routine tasks and rights-based conflict resolution processes. The group should also strive to avoid the exacerbating effects of negative emotionality. The undesirability of the suppressor and exacerbator moderators is represented by a minus (−) sign, subtracting them from the profile in Fig. 4.

Further Directions and Future Research

We would like to offer some further suggestions regarding the exacerbator moderator in our model – negative emotions. While it may be the case that relationship conflicts are more often associated with negative emotions, we believe that by separating the effects of conflict type and emotion we provide a more specific and accurate model of conflict processes, thus providing meaningful advice for managers and group leaders. If you can train or encourage individuals to separate the emotion from the conflict, they will be better able to have high performing teams as well as satisfied members. However, this may be unrealistic given the nature of human beings, the time they spend at work, and the challenges and frustrations, especially surrounding conflict, which they experience. Van Maanan (1992) in his study of the police force noted that a constructive way to let off steam outside of the task environment was to engage in after-hours discussions and social events, entirely separated from the workplace. This is similar to the strategy provided in the example of the Japanese businessman criticizing his boss after work in a bar as an acceptable and safe way to vent his frustration. In addition, high levels of trust may reduce the risk of emotionally charged task conflicts being misattributed as relationship conflicts (Simons & Peterson, 2000). So, while it may be unrealistic to ask employees to ignore their emotions, an organization may be able to set up safe places (or contexts) for them to express their emotions in order for the negative impact on group outcomes to be minimized.

One area for future research is the relationship between conflict and diversity in groups. While much research has begun to examine the effects of diversity on conflict and performance in groups and teams (e.g. Kochan, Bezrukova, Ely, Jackson, Joshi, Jehn, Leonard, Levine & Thomas, 2003; Pelled, Eisenhardt & Xin, 1999; cf. Williams & O'Reilly, 1998), it does not consider group diversity as a moderating variable that influences the conflict-outcome relationship. In addition, future research should take a more detailed look at the type of diversity and how it influences conflict within teams (Jehn, Northcraft & Neale, 1999). We suspect that the various types of diversity may have different moderating effects on the conflict-outcome relationship. For instance, informational diversity will be more likely to enhance the positive effects of conflict on performance and creativity than social category diversity. Recent work on social differentiation and demographically-aligned subgroup formation in teams is also relevant for the understanding of constructive conflict in organizational groups. Faultline theory suggests that the existence of subgroups based on demographic characteristics can lead to power dynamics within the group that can increase the negative effects of conflict (Lau & Murnighan, 1998). Recent empirical work demonstrates that faultlines formed by demographic characteristics increase negative effects of conflict (Thatcher, Jehn & Zannutto, 2003) and that demographic alignment which causes coalition formation within groups also impedes the positive effects of task conflict (Bezrukova & Jehn, 2002).

In sum, we hope our contingency perspective and conflict-outcome moderated model inspires future research on intragroup conflict in organizations and other settings. By identifying the effects of different types of conflicts on different outcomes, given certain moderating variables at particular times in a group's life-cycle, we have attempted to consolidate a complex and often contradictory body of work into a comprehensive model of intragroup conflict in organizations. We hope that this categorization can improve the predicative capability of researchers as well as the ability of managers and team leaders to successfully harness conflict's constructive potential in organizations.

REFERENCES

Allport, G. (1937). *Personality: A psychological interpretation.* New York: Holt.
Allred, K., Mallozzi, J., Matsui, F., & Raia, C. (1997). The influence of anger and compassion on negotiation performance. *Organizational Behavior and Human Decision Processes, 70,* 175–187.
Amabile, T. (1983). The social psychology of creativity: A componential conceptualization. *Journal of Personality and Social Psychology, 45,* 357–376.

Amabile, T. (1988). From individual creativity to organizational innovation. In: K. Gronhaug, G. Kaufmann et al. (Eds), *Innovation: A Cross-Disciplinary Perspective* (pp. 139–166). Oslo, Norway: Norwegian University Press.

Amabile, T., Conti, R., Coon, H., Lazenby, J., & Herron, M. (1996). Assessing the work environment for creativity. *Academy of Management Journal, 39*, 1154–1184.

Amason, A. (1996). Distinguishing effects of functional and dysfunctional conflict on strategic decision making: Resolving a paradox for top management teams. *Academy of Management Journal, 39*, 123–148.

Amason, A., & Schweiger, D. (1994). Resolving the paradox of conflict, strategic decision making, and organizational performance. *International Journal of Conflict Management, 5*, 239–253.

Ancona, D. G., Goodman, P. S., Lawrence, B. S., & Tushman, M. L. (2001). Time: A new research lens. *Academy of Management Review, 26*, 645–663.

Anderson, E., & Weitz, B. (1992). The use of pledges to build and sustain commitment in distribution channels. *Journal of Marketing Research, 29*, 18–34.

Arellano, C., & Markman, H. (1995). The managing affect and differences scale (MADS): A self-report measure assessing conflict management in couples. *Journal of Family Psychology, 9*, 319–334.

Argyris, C. (1962). *Interpersonal competence and organizational effectiveness.* Homewood, IL: Dorsey Press.

Argyris, C. (1976). Single loop and double loop models in research on decision making. *Administrative Science Quarterly, 21*, 363–375.

Ashby, W. R. (1956). *An introduction to cybernetics.* London: Methuen & Company Ltd.

Bales, R. R. (1958). Task roles and social roles in problem-solving groups. In: E. Maccoby, T. M. Newcomb & E. L. Hartley (Eds), *Social Psychology* (3rd ed., pp. 437–447). New York: Holt, Rinehart & Winston.

Balkenohl, M. (1971). The origin of psychic disturbances and interhuman conflicts: An anthropological enlightening of personal relations. *Heilpaedagogik, 40*, 174–179.

Barkley, R., Anastopoulos, A., Guevremont, D., & Fletcher, K. (1992). Adolescents with attention deficit hyperactivity disorder: Mother-adolescent interactions, family beliefs and conflicts, and maternal psychopathology. *Journal of Abnormal Child Psychology, 20*, 263–288.

Barley, S. (1991). Contextualizing conflict: Notes on the anthropology of disputes and negotiations. *Research on Negotiation in Organizations, 3*, 165–199.

Barnard, C. (1938). *The functions of the executive.* Cambridge, MA: Harvard University Press.

Baron, R. (1984). Reducing organizational conflict: An incompatible response approach. *Journal of Applied Psychology, 69*, 272–279.

Baron, R. (1990). Countering the effects of destructive criticism: The relative efficacy of four interventions. *Journal of Applied Psychology, 75*, 235–245.

Baron, R. (1991). Positive effects of conflict: A cognitive perspective. *Employees Responsibilities and Rights Journal, 4*, 25–36.

Baruch, Bush, R., & Folger, J. (1994). *The promise of mediation: Responding to conflict through empowerment and recognition.* San Francisco, CA: Jossey-Bass.

Bazerman, M. (2002). *Judgment in managerial decision making* (5th ed.). New York: Wiley.

Bazerman, M., & Neale, M. (1983). Heuristics in negotiation: Limitations to dispute resolution effectiveness. In: M. H. Bazerman & R. Lewicki (Eds), *Negotiations in Organizations* (pp. 51–67). Beverly Hills, CA: Sage.

Bendersky, C. (2003a). Dispute resolution systems: A complementarities modes. *Academy of Management Review, 28*, 643–656.

Bendersky, C. (2003b). *Dispute resolution system effectiveness: Complementarities and mediators.* Academy of Management Meetings, Seattle, WA.

Bennett, P., & Cropper, S. (1990). Uncertainty and conflict: Combining conflict analysis and strategic choice. *Journal of Behavioral Decision Making, 3,* 29–45.

Bernstein, D. A., Clarke-Stewart, A., Roy, E. J., & Wickens, C. D. (1997). *Psychology* (4th ed.). New York: Houghton Mifflin.

Bettenhausen, K., & Murnighan, J. K. (1985). The emergence of norms in competitive decision-making groups. *Administrative Science Quarterly, 30,* 350–372.

Beyer, J. (1981). Ideologies, values and decision making in organizations. In: P. C. Nystrom & W. Starbuck (Eds), *Handbook of Organizational Design* (pp. 166–202). New York: Oxford University Press.

Bezrukova, K., & Jehn, K. A. (2002). *The effects of cross-level conflict: The moderating effects of conflict culture on the group faultlines-performance link.* Academy of Management Meetings, Denver, CO.

Bingham, L., Chesmore, G., Moon, Y., & Napoli, L. (2000). Mediating employment disputes at the United States postal service: A comparison of in-house and outside neutral mediator models. *Review of Public Personnel Administration, XX*(1), 5–19.

Bingham, L., & Novac, M. (2000). Mediation's impact on formal discrimination complaint filing: Before and after the REDRESS program at the United States postal service. Paper presented at the International Association of Conflict Management 13th Annual Meeting, St. Louis, MO.

Black, D. (1990). The elementary forms of conflict management. In: A. S. U. School of Justice Studies (Ed.), *New Directions in the Study of Justice, Law, and Social Control* (pp. 43–69). New York: Plenum.

Blake, R., & Mouton, J. (1984). *The managerial grid.* Houston, TX: Gulf Publishing.

Bless, H., Bohner, G., Schwarz, N., & Strack, F. (1990). Mood and persuasion: A cognitive response analysis. *Personality and Social Psychology Bulletin, 16,* 331–345.

Block, J. (1993). Conflict resolution: A model for effective marital and family relations. *American Journal of Family Therapy, 7,* 61–67.

Bodenhausen, G. (1993). Emotions, arousal and stereotypic judgments: A heuristic model of affect and stereotyping. In: D. Mackie & D. Hamilton (Eds), *Affect, Cognition, and Stereotyping: Interactive Processes in Group Perception* (pp. 13–37). San Diego, CA: Academic Press.

Boulding, K. (1962). *Conflict and defense.* New York: Harper & Row.

Bourgeois, L. J. (1985). Strategic goals, environmental uncertainty, and economic performance in volatile environments. *Academy of Management Journal, 28,* 548–573.

Brehmer, B. (1976). Social judgement theory and the analysis of interpersonal conflict. *Psychological Bulletin, 83,* 985–1003.

Brett, J. (1991). Negotiating group decisions. *Negotiation Journal, 7,* 291–310.

Brief, A. P., & Weiss, H. M. (2002). Organizational behavior: Affect in the workplace. *Annual Review of Psychology, 53*(1), 279–307.

Bucklin, L., & Sengupta, S. (1993). Organizing successful co-marketing alliances. *Journal of Marketing, 57,* 32–46.

Campbell, H. P., & Dunnette, M. D. (1968). Effectiveness of the t-group experience in managerial training and development. *Psychological Bulletin, 70,* 73–104.

Carnevale, P., & Pruitt, D. (1992). Negotiation and mediation. *Annual Review of Psychology, 43,* 531–582.

Chamberlain, N., & Kuhn, J. (1965). *Collective bargaining.* New York: McGraw-Hill.

Choi, J., & Kim, M. (1999). The organizational application of groupthink and its limitations in organizations. *Journal of Applied Psychology, 84,* 297–306.

Christiansen, A., & Shenk, J. (1991). Communications, conflict, and psychological distance in nondistressed, clinic, and divorcing couples. *Journal of Consulting and Clinical Psychology, 59*, 458–463.

Cloven, D., & Roloff, M. (1993). The chilling effect of aggressive potential on the expression of complaints in intimate relationships. *Communication Monographs, 60*, 199–219.

Cobb, S. (1993). Empowerment and mediation: A narrative perspective. *Negotiation Journal, 9*, 245–259.

Cohen, M. D. (1984). Conflict and complexity: Goal diversity and organizational search effectiveness. *The American Political Science Review, 78*(2), 435–451.

Cole, S., Phillips, J., & Hartman, A. (1977). Test of a model of decision processes in an intense conflict situation. *Behavioral Science, 22*, 186–196.

Coleman, P. T. (2003). Characteristics of protracted, intractable conflict: Toward the development of a metaframework – I. *Peace and Conflict: Journal of Peace Psychology, 9*, 1–37.

Coser, L. (1956). *The functions of social conflict*. Glencoe, IL: Free Press.

Cosier, R., & Rose, G. (1977). Cognitive conflict and goal conflict effects on task performance. *Organizational Behavior and Human Performance, 19*, 378–391.

Costantino, C. A., & Merchant, C. S. (1996). *Designing conflict management systems: A guide to creating productive and healthy organizations*. San Francisco, CA: Jossey-Bass.

Cummings, A., & Jehn, K. A. (1999). The role of team leadership in the constructive use of conflict for creativity and change. Leadership Conference, The Wharton School, University of Pennsylvania.

Day, R., Michaels, R., & Perdue, B. (1988). How buyers handle conflicts. *Industrial Marketing Management, 17*, 153–160.

De Church, L. A., & Marks, M. A. (2001). Maximizing the benefits of task conflict: The role of conflict management. *International Journal of Conflict Management, 12*(1), 4–22.

De Dreu, C., & Van de Vliert, E. (Eds) (1997). *Using conflict in organizations*. London: Sage.

De Dreu, C. W., & Van Vianen, A. M. (2001). Managing relationship conflict and the effectiveness of organizational teams. *Journal of Organizational Behavior, 22*(3), 309–328.

De Dreu, C. K. W., & Weingart, L. (2003). Task versus relationship conflict, team performance, and team member satisfaction: A meta-analysis. *Journal of Applied Psychology, 88*, 741–749.

De Dreu, C. K. W., Weingart, L. R., & Kwon, S. (2000). Influence of social motives on integrative negotiations: A meta-analytic review and test of two theories. *Journal of Personality and Social Psychology, 78*, 889–905.

De Dreu, C., & West, M. (2001). Minority dissent and team innovation: The importance of participation in decision making. *Journal of Applied Psychology, 86*(6), 1191–1201.

Deutsch, M. (1965). Producing change in an adversary. In: R. Fisher (Ed.), *International Conflict and Behavioral Science* (pp. 145–160). New York: Basic Books.

Deutsch, M. (1969). Conflicts: Productive and destructive. *Journal of Social Issues, 25*, 7–41.

Deutsch, M. (1973). *The resolution of conflict*. New Haven: Yale University Press.

Dimuccio, R. (1998). The study of appeasement in international relations: Polemics, paradigms and problems. *Journal of Peace Research, 35*(2), 245–259.

Doucet, L., & Jehn, K. (1997). Analyzing harsh words in a sensitive setting: American expatriates in Communist China. *Journal of Organizational Behavior, 18*, 559–582.

Drake, L. E., & Donohue, W. A. (1996). Communicative framing theory in conflict resolution. *Communication Research, 23*, 297–322.

Druckman, D. (1990). The social psychology of arms control and reciprocation. *Political Psychology, 11*(3), 553–581.

Dumaine, B. (1991). The bureaucracy busters. *Fortune* (June 17th), 36–50.

Dunlop, J. T. (1958). *Industrial relations systems.* New York: Holt.

Dunlop, J. T., & Zack, A. (1997). *Mediation and arbitration of employment disputes.* San Francisco, CA: Jossey-Bass.

Edwards, J. (1995). Alternatives to difference scores as dependent variables in the study of congruence in organizational research. *Organizational Behavior & Human Decision Processes, 64,* 307–324.

Eggeman, K., Moxley, V., & Schumm, W. (1985). Assessing spouses' perceptions of Gottman's temporal form in marital conflict. *Psychological Reports, 57,* 171–181.

Eidelson, R. J., & Eidelson, J. I. (2003). Dangerous ideas: Five beliefs that propel groups toward conflict. *American Psychologist, 58,* 182–192.

Eisenhardt, K., & Bourgeois, J. (1988). Politics of strategic decision making in high-velocity environments: Toward a midrange theory. *Academy of Management Journal, 31,* 737–770.

Eisenhardt, K., & Schoonhoven, C. (1990). Organizational growth: Linking founding team, strategy, environment, and growth among U.S. semiconductor ventures, 1978–1988. *Administrative Science Quarterly, 35,* 504–529.

Elster, J. (1995). Strategic uses of argument. In: K. J. Arrow et al. (Eds), *Barriers to Conflict Resolution* (pp. 236–257). New York: Norton.

Enz, C. (1988). The role of value congruity on intraorganizational power. *Administrative Science Quarterly, 33,* 284–304.

Esman, M. (1994). *Ethnic politics.* Ithaca, NY: Cornell University Press.

Esser, J., & Marriott, R. (1995). A comparison of the effectiveness of substantive and contextual mediation tactics. *Journal of Applied Social Psychology, 25,* 1340–1359.

Evan, W. (1965). Conflict and performance in R&D organizations. *Industrial Management Review, 7,* 37–46.

Faure, G. O. (1995). Conflict formulation: Going beyond culture-bound views of conflict. In: B. Bunker, J. Rubin et al. (Eds), *Conflict, Cooperation, and Justice: Essays Inspired by the Work of Morton Deutsch* (pp. 39–57). San Francisco, CA: Jossey-Bass.

Feullie, P., & Delaney, J. (1992). The individual pursuit of organizational justice: Grievance procedures in nonunion workplaces. In: G. R. Ferris & K. M. Rowland (Eds), *Research in Personnel and Human Resources Management* (Vol. 10, pp. 187–232).

Fink, C. (1972). Conflict management strategies implied by expected utility models of behavior. *American Behavioral Scientist, 15,* 837–858.

Fiol, M. C. (1994). Consensus, diversity, and learning in organizations. *Organization Science, 5,* 403–420.

Fiske, S. T., & Taylor, S. E. (1984). *Social cognition.* Reading, MA: Addison-Wesley.

Forehand, R., & McCombs, A. (1989). The nature of interparental conflict of married and divorced parents: Implications for young adolescents. *Journal of Abnormal Child Psychology, 17,* 235–249.

Forgas, J. P. (1998). On feeling good and getting your way: Mood effects on negotiator cognition and bargaining strategies. *Journal of Personality and Social Psychology, 74*(3), 565–577.

Frazier, G. L., & Rody, R. (1991). The use of influence strategies in interfirm relationships in industrial product channels. *Journal of Marketing, 55,* 52–69.

Fry, D. P., & Fry, C. B. (1997). Culture and conflict-resolution models: Exploring alternatives to violence. In: D. P. Fry & K. Bjorkqvist (Eds), *Cultural Variation in Conflict Resolution* (pp. 9–23). Mahweh, NJ: Lawrence Erlbaum.

Gabriel, Y. (1998). An introduction to the social psychology of insults in organizations. *Human Relations, 51,* 1329–1354.

Galbraith, J. (1973). *Designing complex organizations.* Reading, MA: Addison-Wesley.

Gamson, W., & Modigliani, A. (1971). *Untangling the cold war: A strategy for testing rival theories.* Boston: Little, Brown.

General Accounting Office (1997). ADR: Employers experience with ADR in the workplace. Washington, DC: General Accounting Office.

George, A., & Smoke, R. (1974). *Deterrence and American foreign policy: Theory and practice.* New York: Columbia University Press.

Gersick, C. (1988). Time and transition in work teams: Toward a new model of group development. *Academy of Management Journal, 31,* 9–41.

Gersick, C. (1989). Marking time: Predictable transitions in task groups. *Academy of Management Journal, 32,* 274–309.

Gersick, C. (1991). Revolutionary change theories: A multilevel exploration of the punctuated equilibrium paradigm. *Academy of Management Review, 16*(1), 10–36.

Gladstein, D. (1984). A model of task group effectiveness. *Administrative Science Quarterly, 29*(4), 499–517.

Glenn, E., Johnson, R., Kimmel, P., & Wedge, B. (1970). A cognitive interaction model to analyze culture conflict in international relations. *Journal of Conflict Resolution, 14,* 35–48.

Goodenough, W. (1983). Consequences of social living, language, and culture for conflict and its management. *Zygon: Journal of Religion & Science, 18,* 415–424.

Greenberg, J., & Folger, R. (1983). Procedural justice, participation, and the fair process effect in groups and organizations. In: P. B. Paulus (Ed.), *Basic Group Processes* (pp. 235–256). New York: Springer-Verlag.

Guetzkow, H., & Gyr, J. (1954). An analysis of conflict in decision making groups. *Human Relations, 7,* 367–381.

Gurr, T. R., & Harff, B. (1994). *Ethnic conflict in world politics.* Boulder: Westview Press.

Guzzo, R. (1986). Group decision making and group effectiveness in organizations. In: P. S. Goodman (Ed.), *Designing Effective Work Groups* (pp. 34–71). San Francisco, CA: Jossey-Bass.

Hackman, R. (1987). The design of work teams. In: J. Lorsch (Ed.), *Handbook of Organizational Behavior* (pp. 315–342). Englewood Cliffs, NJ: Prentice-Hall.

Hackman, J. R., Brousseau, K., & Weiss, J. (1976). The interaction of task design and group performance strategies in determining group effectiveness. *Organizational Behavior and Human Performance, 16,* 350–365.

Hall, R. (1972). *Organizations, structure, and process.* Englewood Cliffs, NJ: Prentice-Hall.

Heckathorn, D. (1980). A unified model for bargaining and conflict. *Behavioral Science, 25,* 261–284.

Hedberg, B., Nystrom, P., & Starbuck, W. (1976). Camping on seesaws: Prescriptions for a self-designing organization. *Administrative Science Quarterly, 21,* 41–65.

Hirshleifer, J. (1995). Theorizing about conflict. In: D. Hartley & T. Sandler (Eds), *Handbook of Defense Economics* (pp. 166–189). New York: Elsevier.

Hoffman, L. R. (1978). Group problem solving. In: L. Berkowitz (Ed.), *Group Processes.* New York: Academic Press.

Hoffman, L., & Maier, N. (1961). Quality and acceptance of problem solutions by members of homogeneous and heterogeneous groups. *Journal of Abnormal and Social Psychology, 62,* 401–407.

Isen, A., & Daubman, K. (1984). The influence of affect on categorization. *Journal of Personality and Social Psychology, 47,* 473–478.

Jackson, S. (1992). Team composition in organizations. In: S. Worchel, W. Wood & J. Simpson (Eds), *Group Process and Productivity* (pp. 1–12). London: Sage.

Janis, I. L. (1982). *Victims of groupthink* (2nd ed.). Boston: Houghton Mifflin.

Janis, I. L. (1985). Sources of error in strategic decision making. In: J. M. Pennings (Ed.), *Organizational Strategy and Change* (pp. 157–197). San Francisco, CA: Jossey-Bass.

Janssen, O., Van de Vliert, E., & Veenstra, C. (1999). How task and person conflict shape the role of positive interdependence in management teams. *Journal of Management, 25*(2), 117–141.

Jehn, K. (1992). The impact of intragroup conflict on effectiveness: A multimethod examination of the benefits and detriments of conflict. Unpublished doctoral dissertation, Northwestern University.

Jehn, K. (1994). Enhancing effectiveness: An investigation of advantages and disadvantages of value-based intragroup conflict. *International Journal of Conflict Management, 5*, 223–238.

Jehn, K. (1995). A multimethod examination of the benefits and detriments of intragroup conflict. *Administrative Science Quarterly, 40*, 256–282.

Jehn, K. (1997a). The effect of value-based conflict on group performance and satisfaction: Can we be both productive and happy? In: C. de Dreu & E. van de Vliert (Eds), *Optimizing Performance by Stimulating Conflict: Fundamental Issues for Groups and Organizations* (pp. 87–100). Thousand Oaks, CA: Sage.

Jehn, K. (1997b). A qualitative analysis of conflict types and dimensions in organizational groups. *Administrative Science Quarterly, 42*, 530–557.

Jehn, K. (1999). Diversity, conflict, and team performance: Summary of a program of research. *Performance Improvement Quarterly, 12*, 6–19.

Jehn, K., Chadwick, C., & Thatcher, S. (1997). To agree or not to agree: The effects of value congruence, member diversity, member diversity & conflict on workgroup outcomes. *International Journal of Conflict Management, 8*, 287–305.

Jehn, K., & Mannix, E. (2001). The dynamic nature of conflict: A longitudinal study of intragroup conflict and group performance. *Academy of Management Journal, 44*, 238–251.

Jehn, K., Northcraft, G., & Neale, M. (1999). Why differences make a difference: A field study of diversity, conflict, and performance in workgroups. *Administrative Science Quarterly, 44*, 741–763.

Jervis, R. (1976). *Perception and misperception in international politics*. Princeton, NJ: Princeton University Press.

Jervis, R. (1979). Deterrence theory revisited. *World Politics, 21*(2), 289–324.

Jones, T., & Remland, M. (1993). Nonverbal communication and conflict escalation: An attribution-based model. *The International Journal of Conflict Management, 4*, 119–137.

Kabanoff, B. (1991). Equity, equality, power, and conflict. *Academy of Management Review, 16*, 416–441.

Kahneman, D., & Tversky, A. (1995). Conflict resolution: A cognitive perspective. In: K. Arrow, R. Mnookin, L. Ross, A. Tversky & R. Wilson (Eds), *Barriers to Conflict Resolution* (pp. 45–60). New York: W. W. Norton & Company.

Katz, L. F., Kramer, L., & Gottman, J. (1992). Conflict and emotions in marital, sibling, and peer relationships. In: C. U. Shantz & W. W. Hartup (Eds), *Conflict in Child and Adolescent Development. Cambridge Studies in Social and Emotional Development* (pp. 122–149). New York: Cambridge University Press.

Kelley, H. H. (1979). *Personal relationships*. Hillsdale, NJ: Lawrence Erlbaum.

Kelley, H. H., & Thibaut, J. (1969). Group problem solving. In: G. Lindzey & E. Aronson (Eds), *The Handbook of Social Psychology* (2nd ed., Vol. 4). Reading, MA: Addison-Wesley.

Knez, M. (1998). Precedent transfer in experimental conflict-of-interest games. *Journal of Economic Behavior and Organization, 34*, 239–249.

Knudson, R., Sommers, A., & Golding, S. (1980). Interpersonal perception and mode of resolution in marital conflict. *Journal of Personality and Social Psychology, 38*, 751–763.

Kochan, T., Bezrukova, K., Ely, R., Jackson, S., Joshi, A., Jehn, K., Leonard, J., Levine, D., & Thomas, D. (2003). The effects of diversity on business performance: Report of a feasibility study of the diversity research network. *Human Resource Management Journal, 42*, 3–21.

Kochan, T., Katz, H., & McKersie, R. (1986). *The transformation of American industrial relations.* New York: Basic Books.

Kochan, T., Lautsch, B., & Bendersky, C. (2000). An evaluation of the Massachusetts commission against discrimination's alternative dispute resolution program. *Harvard Negotiation Law Review, 5*, 233–278.

Kolb, D. (1994). Negotiation theory: Through the looking glass of gender. *Institute for Conflict Analysis and Resolution, 9*, 1–32, Occasional Paper.

Kolb, D., & Bartunek, J. (1992). *Hidden conflict in organizations: Uncovering behind-the-scenes disputes.* Newbury Park, CA: Sage.

Kramer, R. (1991). Intergroup relations and organizational dilemmas: The role categorization processes. In: L. L. Cummings & B. M. Staw (Eds), *Research in Organizational Behavior* (Vol. 13, pp. 191–228). Greenwich, CT: JAI Press.

Kramer, R., Newton, E., & Pomemrenke, P. (1993). Self-enhancement biases and negotiator judgment: Effects of self-esteem and mood. *Organizational Behavior and Human Decision Processes, 56*, 110–133.

Kunda, G. (1992). *Engineering culture: Control and commitment in a high-tech company.* Philadelphia: Temple University Press.

Lachkar, J. (1993). Parallels between marital and political conflict. *Journal of Psychohistory, 20*, 275–287.

Langlois, J. (1991). Rational deterrence and crisis stability. *American Journal of Political Science, 35*(4), 801–832.

Lau, D., & Murnighan, J. K. (1998). Demographic diversity and faultlines: The compositional dynamics of organizational groups. *Academy of Management Review, 23*(2), 325–340.

Lazarus, R. S. (1982). Thoughts on the relations between emotion and cognition. *American Psychologist, 37*, 1019–1024.

Leng, R., & Wheeler, H. (1979). Influence strategies, success, and war. *Journal of Conflict Resolution, 23*(4), 655–684.

Le Pine, J., & Van Dyne, L. (1998). Predicting voice behavior in work groups. *Journal of Applied Psychology, 83*, 853–868.

Levine, S., & Jehn, K. (1999). *High performing teams: Characteristics of the optimal conflict profile.* Academy of Management Meetings, Chicago, IL.

Lewicki, R., Weiss, S., & Lewin, D. (1992). Models of conflict, negotiation and third party intervention: A review and synthesis. *Journal of Organizational Behavior, 113*, 209–252.

Lipsky, D., & Seeber, R. (1998). The appropriate resolution of corporate disputes: A report on the growing use of ADR by US corporations. Ithaca, Cornell/PERC institute on conflict resolution, 1–40.

Lovelace, K., Shapiro, D., & Weingart, L. (2001). Maximizing cross-functional new product teams' innovativeness and constraint adherence: A conflict communications perspective. *Academy of Management Journal, 24*(4), 779–784.

Luce, R. D., & Raiffa, H. (1957). *Games and decisions: Introduction and critical survey.* New York: Wiley.

Lusch, R. (1976). Channel conflict: Its impact on retailer operating performance. *Journal of Retailing, 52*, 3–12.

Mandel, R. (1979). *Perception, decision making and conflict.* Washington, DC: University Press of America.

Mannix, E., & Jehn, K. A. (2004, forthcoming). Let's norm and storm, but not right now: What to do with phase models of group interaction. In: M. Neale, E. Mannix & S. Blount (Eds), *Research on Managing Groups and Teams*. Greenwich, CT: JAI Press.

March, J., & Simon, H. (1958). *Organizations*. New York: Wiley.

McCauley, C. (1998). Group dynamics in Janis's theory of groupthink: Backward and forward. *Organizational Behavior and Human Decision Processes, 73*, 1–21.

McCready, V., Roberts, J., Bengala, D., Harris, H., Kingsley, G., & Krikorian, C. (1996). A comparison of conflict tactics in the supervisory process. *Journal of Speech & Hearing Research, 39*, 191–199.

McDermott, P., Obar, R., Jose, A., & Bowers, M. (2000). *An evaluation of the equal employment opportunity commission mediation program*. Washington, DC: U.S. Equal Employment Opportunity Commission.

McGrath, J. E. (1984). *Groups: Interaction and performance*. Englewood Cliffs, NJ: Prentice-Hall.

Menon, A., Bharadwaj, S., & Howell, R. (1996). The quality and effectiveness of marketing strategy: Effects of functional and dysfunctional conflict in intraorganizational relationships. *Journal of the Academy of Marketing Science, 24*, 299–313.

Mintzberg, H., Raisinghani, D., & Théorêt, A. (1976). The structure of 'unstructured' decision processes. *Administrative Science Quarterly, 21*, 246–275.

Mitroff, J., Barabba, N., & Kilmann, R. (1977). The application of behavioral and philosophical technologies to strategic planning: A case study of a large federal agency. *Management Science, 24*, 44–58.

Mitroff, I., & Emshoff, J. (1979). On strategic assumption-making: A dialectical approach to policy and planning. *Academy of Management Review, 4*, 1–12.

Morgan, P. (1977). *Deterrence: A conceptual analysis*. Beverly Hills, CA: Sage.

Morrill, C. (1995). *The executive way: Conflict management in corporations*. Chicago: University of Chicago Press.

Morris, M., & Keltner, D. (2000). How emotions work: The social functions of emotional expression in negotiations. In: B. Staw & R. Sutton (Eds), *Research in Organizational Behavior* (Vol. 22, pp. 1–50).

Morrison, E., & Milliken, F. (2000). Organizational silence: A barrier to change and development in a pluralistic world. *Academy of Management Review, 25*(4), 706–725.

Murnighan, J. K., & Conlon, D. E. (1991). The dynamics of intense work groups: A study of British string quartets. *Administrative Science Quarterly, 36*, 165–186.

Neary, H. (1997). A comparison on rent-seeking models and economic models of conflict. *Public Choice, 93*, 373–388.

Nemeth, C. J. (1987). Influence processes, problem solving and creativity. In: M. P. Zanna, J. M. Olson & C. P. Herman (Eds), *Social Influence: The Ontario Symposium* (Vol. 5, pp. 237–246). Hillsdale, NJ: Lawrence Erlbaum.

Nemeth, C. J. (1995). Dissent as driving cognition, attitudes, and judgments. *Social Cognition, 13*(3), 273–291.

Nemeth, C. J. (2001). The art of mentoring: It's personal. In: F. Buschini & E. Lage (Eds), *Penser la Vie, le Social, la Nature: Mélanges en l'honneur de Serge Moscovici*. Paris: Editions de la Maison des Sciences de l'Homme, in press.

Nohria, N. (1991). Garcia-point, Carlos global strategic linkages and industry structure. *Strategic Management Journal, 12*, 105–124.

Park, O. S., Sims, H. P., & Motowidlo, S. J. (1986). Affect in organizations. In: H. P. Sims & D. A. Gioia & Associates (Eds), *The Thinking Organization* (pp. 215–237). San Francisco, CA: Jossey-Bass.

Pelled, L. H. (1996). Demographic diversity, conflict, and work group outcomes: An intervening process theory. *Organization Science, 6*, 615–631.

Pelled, L., Eisenhardt, K., & Xin, K. (1999). Exploring the black box: An analysis of work group diversity, conflict, and performance. *Administrative Science Quarterly, 44*, 1–28.

Pelz, D. C., & Andrews, W. P. (1966). *Scientists in organizations: Productive climates for research and development.* New York: Wiley.

Peterson, R., Owens, P., Tetlock, P., Fan, E., & Martorana, P. (1998). Group dynamics in top management teams: Groupthink, vigilance, and alternative models of organizational failure and success. *Organizational Behavior and Human Decision Processes, 73*, 272–305.

Pillutla, M. M., & Murnighan, J. K. (1996). Unfairness, anger, and spite: Emotional rejections of ultimatum offers. *Organizational Behavior and Human Decision Processes, 68*, 208–224.

Pinkley, R. (1990). Dimensions of the conflict frame: Disputant interpretations of conflict. *Journal of Applied Psychology, 75*, 117–128.

Plutchik, R. (2001). The nature of emotions. *American Scientist, 89*, 344.

Pondy, L. (1967). Organizational conflict: Concepts and models. *Administrative Science Quarterly, 12*, 296–320.

Pondy, L. (1992). Reflections on organizational conflict. *Journal of Organization Behavior, 25*, 261–284.

Priem, R., & Price, K. (1991). Process and outcome expectations for the dialectical inquiry, devil's advocacy, and consensus techniques of strategic decision making. *Group and Organization Studies, 16*, 206–225.

Pruitt, D. (1981). *Negotiation behavior.* New York: Academic Press.

Putnam, L. L. (1994). Productive conflict: Negotiation as implicit coordination. *International Journal of Conflict Management, 9*, 285–299.

Putnam, L. L., & Wilson, C. E. (1982). Communicative strategies in organizational conflicts: Reliability and validity of a measurement scale. In: M. Burgoon (Ed.), *Communication Yearbook* (Vol. 6, pp. 629–652). Beverly Hills, CA: Sage.

Radford, K., Hipel, K., & Fang, L. (1994). Decision making under conditions of conflict. *Group Decision and Negotiation, 3*, 169–185.

Rahim, M., & Magner, N. (1995). Confirmatory factor-analysis of the styles of handling interpersonal conflict – first-order factor model and its invariance across groups. *Journal of Applied Psychology, 80*(1), 122–132.

Raiffa, H. (1982). *The art and science of negotiation.* Cambridge: Belknap Press of Harvard University Press.

Rapoport, A. (1960). *Fights, games, and debates.* Ann Arbor: University of Michigan Press.

Rokeach, M. (1973). *The nature of human values.* New York: Free Press.

Rollin, S., & Dowd, T. (1979). Conflict resolution: A model for effective marital and family relations. *American Journal of Family Therapy, 7*, 61–67.

Roloff, M. (1987). Communication and conflict. In: C. R. Berger & S. H. Chaffee (Eds), *Handbook of Communication Science* (pp. 484–534). Newbury Park, CA: Sage.

Roseman, I., Wiest, C., & Swartz, T. (1994). Phenomenology, behaviors, and goals differentiate discrete emotions. *Journal of Personality and Social Psychology, 67*, 206–221.

Rosenberg, L., & Stern, L. (1970). Towards the analysis of conflict in distribution channels: A descriptive model. *Journal of Marketing, 34*, 40–46.

Rosenbloom, B. (1973). Conflict and channel efficiency: Some conceptual model for the decision maker. *Journal of Marketing, 37*, 26–30.

Ross, L. (1995). Reactive devaluation in negotiation and conflict resolution. In: K. Arrow, R. Mnookin, L. Ross, A. Tversky & R. Wilson (Eds), *Barriers to Conflict Resolution* (pp. 26–42). New York: W. W. Norton & Company.

Ross, M. H. (1997). The relevance of culture for the study of political psychology and ethnic conflict. *Political Psychology, 18*, 299–326.

Ross, R. (1989). Conflict. In: R. Ross & J. Ross (Eds), *Small Groups in Organizational Settings* (pp. 139–178). Englewood Cliffs, NJ: Prentice-Hall.

Rowe, M. (1997). Dispute resolution in the non-union environment: An evolution toward integrated systems for conflict management? In: S. Gleason (Ed.), *Frontiers in Dispute Resolution and Human Resources* (pp. 79–106). East Lansing, MI: Michigan State University Press.

Rubin, J. (1980). Experimental research on third party intervention in conflict: Towards some generalizations. *Psychological Bulletin, 87*, 379–391.

Rudashevskii, V. D. (1974). Risk, conflict and uncertainty in the process of decision-making, and their modelling. *Voprosy Psikhologii, 2*, 84–94.

Russell, J. (1978). Evidence of convergent validity on the dimensions of affect. *Journal of Personality and Social Psychology, 37*, 345–356.

Russell, J., & Fehr, J. (1994). Fuzzy concepts in a fuzzy hierarchy: Varieties of anger. *Journal of Personality and Social Psychology, 67*, 186–205.

Sanna, L., Parks, C., & Chang, E. (2003). Mixed-motive conflict in social dilemmas: Mood as input to competitive and cooperative goals. *Group Dynamics: Theory, Research, and Practice, 7*, 26–40.

Santa-Barbara, J., & Epstein, N. (1974). Conflict behavior in clinical families: Preasymptotic interactions and stable outcomes. *Behavioral Science, 19*, 100–110.

Sathe, V. (1983). Implications of corporate culture: A manager's guide to action. *Organizational Dynamics, 5*, 73–84.

Schein, E. H. (1985). *Organizational culture and leadership.* San Francisco, CA: Jossey-Bass.

Schelling, T. C. (1960). *The strategy of conflict.* Cambridge, MA: Harvard University Press.

Schmidt, S., & Kochan, T. (1972). Conflict: Toward conceptual clarity. *Administrative Science Quarterly, 17*, 359–370.

Schweiger, D., Sandberg, W., & Ragan, J. (1986). Group approaches for improving strategic decision making: A comparative analysis of dialectical inquiry, devil's advocacy, and consensus approaches to strategic decision making. *Academy of Management Journal, 29*, 51–71.

Schweiger, D., Sandberg, W., & Rechner, P. (1989). Experiential effects of dialectical inquiry, devil's advocacy, and consensus approaches to strategic decision making. *Academy of Management Journal, 32*, 745–772.

Schwenk, C. (1990). Conflict in organizational decision making: An exploratory study of its effects in for-profit and not-for-profit organizations. *Decision Sciences, 36*, 436–448.

Schwenk, C., & Cosier, R. (1993). Effects of consensus and devil's advocacy on strategic decision making. *Journal of Applied Social Psychology, 23*, 126–139.

Schwenk, C., & Valacich, J. (1994). Effects of devil's advocacy and dialectical inquiry on individuals versus groups. *Organizational Behavior and Human Decision Processes, 59*, 210–222.

Shah, P. P., & Jehn, K. A. (1993). Do friends perform better than acquaintances? The interaction of friendship, conflict, and task. *Group Decision and Negotiation, 2*, 149–165.

Shapiro, D., & Von Glinow, M. A. (1999). Negotiation in multicultural teams: New world, old theories? In: R. J. Bies, R. J. Lewicki & B. H. Sheppard (Eds), *Research on Negotiation in Organizations* (Vol. 7). Greenwich, CT: JAI Press.

Sheth, J. (1973). A model of industrial buyer behavior. *Journal of Marketing, 37*, 50–56.

Siani, R., & Siciliani, O. (1996). Family, subject, and history from Bateson to psychotic games and family conflicts models: Old limits and new directions in Italian family therapy. *New Trends in Experimental & Clinical Psychiatry, 12*, 81–93.

Simmel, G. (1955). *Conflict*. Glencoe, IL: Free Press.

Simons, T., & Peterson, R. (2000). Task conflict and relationship conflict in top management teams: The pivotal role of intragroup trust. *Journal of Applied Psychology, 85*, 102–111.

Sinclair, R., & Mark, M. (1995). The effect of mood state on judgmental accuracy: Processing strategy as a mechanism. *Cognition and Emotion, 9*, 417–438.

Snyder, G., & Diesing, P. (1977). *Conflict among nations: Bargaining, decision making and system structure in international crises*. Princeton, NJ: Princeton University Press.

Staw, B., Sanderlands, L., & Dutton, J. (1981). Threat-rigidity effects in organizational behavior: A multilevel analysis. *Administrative Science Quarterly, 26*, 501–524.

Strauss, G. (1962). Tactics of lateral relationships: The purchasing agent. *Administrative Science Quarterly, 7*, 161–186.

Stearns, F. (1972). *Anger: Psychology, physiology, and pathology*. Springfield, IL: Charles C. Thomas.

Sternberg, R., & Lubart, T. (1996). Investing in creativity. *American Psychologist, 51*(7), 677–688.

Surra, C., & Longstreth, M. (1990). Similarity of outcomes, interdependence, and conflict in dating relationships. *Journal of Personality and Social Psychology, 59*, 501–516.

Tetlock, P., Armor, D., & Paterson, R. (1994). The slavery debate in antebellum America: Cognitive style, value conflict, and the limits of compromise. *Journal of Personality and Social Psychology, 66*, 115–126.

Thatcher, S. M. B. (1999). The contextual importance of diversity: The impact of relational demography and team diversity on individual performance and satisfaction. *Performance Improvement Quarterly, 12*(1), 97–112.

Thatcher, S., Jehn, K., & Chadwick, C. (1998). *Understanding the impact of differences: Individual demographic differences, group diversity, and conflict*. Annual Meeting of the Academy of Management, San Diego, CA.

Thatcher, S. M. B., Jehn, K. A., & Zanutto, E. (2003). Cracks in diversity research: The effects of faultlines on conflict and performance. *Group Decision and Negotiation, 12*, 217–241.

Thomas, K. W. (1976). Conflict and conflict management. In: M. D. Dunnette (Ed.), *Handbook of Industrial and Organizational Psychology* (pp. 889–935). Palo Alto, CA: Consulting Psychologists Press.

Thomas, K. W. (1992). Conflict and negotiation processes in organizations. In: M. Dunnette & L. Hough (Eds), *Handbook of Industrial and Organizational Psychology* (pp. 651–718). Palo Alto, CA: Consulting Psychologists Press.

Thompson, J. (1967). *Organizations in action*. Chicago: McGraw-Hill.

Tinsley, C. H. Predicting the constellation of strategies used by Germans, Americans, and Japanese to negotiate conflict. *Academy of Management Journal*.

Tjosvold, D. (1990). Power in cooperative and competitive organizational contexts. *The Journal of Social Psychology, 130*(2), 249–258.

Tjosvold, D. (1991). Rights and responsibilities of dissent: Cooperative conflict. *Employee Responsibilities and Rights Journal, 4*, 13–23.

Tjosvold, D. (1998). Making employee involvement work: Cooperative goals and controversy to reduce costs. *Human Relations, 51*(2), 201–214.

Tjosvold, D., Dann, V., & Wong, C. (1992). Managing conflict between departments to serve customers. *Human Relations, 45*, 1035–1054.

Tjosvold, D., Johnson, D., & Johnson, R. (1984). Influence strategy, perspective-taking, and relationships between high- and low-power individuals in cooperative and competitive contexts. *The Journal of Applied Psychology, 116,* 187–202.

Tjosvold, D., Nibler, R., & Wan, P. (2001). Motivation for conflict among Chinese university students: Effects of others' expertise and one's own confidence in engaging in conflict. *The Journal of Social Psychology, 141*(3), 353–363.

Tuckman, B. W. (1965). Developmental sequences in small groups. *Psychological Bulletin, 63,* 384–399.

Turner, M. E., Pratkanais, A. R., Probasco, P., & Leve, C. (1992). Threat, cohesion, and group effectiveness: Testing a social identity maintenance perspective on groupthink. *Journal of Personality and Social Psychology, 63,* 781–796.

Tushman, M., & Nadler, D. (1978). Information processing as an integrating concept in organizational design. In: D. A. Nadler & M. L. Tushman (Eds), *Managerial Behavior* (4th ed., pp. 157–190). New York: Columbia University Press.

Ury, W., Brett, J., & Goldberg, S. (1989). *Getting disputes resolved: Designing systems to cut the costs of conflict.* San Francisco, CA: Jossey-Bass.

Van de Ven, A. (1986). Central problems in the management of innovation. *Management Science, 32,* 590–607.

Van de Ven, A., Delbecq, A., & Koenig, R. (1976). Determinants of coordination modes within organizations. *American Sociological Review, 41,* 322–338.

Van de Ven, A., & Ferry, D. (1980). *Measuring and assessing organizations.* New York: Wiley.

Van de Vliert, E. (1997). *Complex interpersonal conflict behaviour: Theoretical frontiers.* East Sussex, UK: Psychology Press.

Van de Vliert, E., & De Dreu, C. (1994). Optimizing performance by conflict stimulation. *International Journal of Conflict Management, 5,* 211–222.

Van de Vliert, E., Nauta, A., Euwema, M., & Janssen, O. (1997). The effectiveness of mixing problem solving and forcing. In: C. De Dreu, E. Van de Vliert et al. (Eds), *Using Conflict in Organization* (pp. 38–52). London, UK: Sage.

Van Dyne, L., Jehn, K., & Cummings, A. (2001). Pink collar stress: Employee performance, creativity, and satisfaction in hair salons. *Journal of Organization Behavior, 23,* 57–74.

Van Maanan, J. (1992). Drinking our troubles away: Managing conflict in a British policy agency. In: D. Kolb & J. M. Bartunek (Eds), *Hidden Conflict in Organizations: Uncovering Behind-the-Scenes Disputes* (pp. 32–62). Newbury Park, CA: Sage.

Wagner, G., Pfeffer, J., & O'Reilly, C. (1984). Organizational demography and turnover in top-management groups. *Administrative Science Quarterly, 29,* 74–92.

Wall, V., & Nolan, L. (1986). Perceptions of inequality, satisfaction, and conflict in task oriented groups. *Human Relations, 39,* 1033–1052.

Walton, R. E., Cutcher-Gershenfeld, J., & McKersie, R. (1994). *Strategic negotiations: A theory of change in labor-management relations.* Boston: Harvard Business School Press.

Walton, R. E., & McKersie, R. B. (1965). *A behavioral theory of labor negotiations: An analysis of a social interaction system.* New York: McGraw-Hill.

Weldon, E., Jehn, K., Doucet, L., Chen, X., & Wang, Z. (1996). Conflict management in U.S.-Chinese joint ventures. *Academy of Management Electronic Best Paper Proceedings.*

Wert-Gray, S., Center, C., Brashers, D., & Meyers, R. (1991). Research topics and methodological orientations in organizational communication: A decade in review. *Communication Studies, 42,* 141–154.

Whitney, J., & Smith, R. (1983). Effects of group cohesiveness on attitude polarization and the acquisition of knowledge in a strategic planning context. *Journal of Marketing Research, 20*, 167–176.

Williams, K., & O'Reilly, C. (1998). Demography and diversity in organizations. In: B. M. Staw & R. M. Sutton (Eds), *Research in Organizational Behavior* (Vol. 20, pp. 77–140). Greenwich, CT: JAI Press.

Zajonc, R. (1984). On the primacy affect. *American Psychologist, 39*, 117–123.

Zuk (1988). The conflict cycle in families and therapy. *Contemporary Family Therapy, 10*(3), 45–153.

Zuk, C., & Zuk, G. (1989). The conflict cycle in the case of an adolescent in crisis. *Contemporary Family Therapy, 11*, 259–266.

A SOCIAL IDENTITY MODEL OF LEADERSHIP EFFECTIVENESS IN ORGANIZATIONS

Daan van Knippenberg and Michael A. Hogg

ABSTRACT

Research into leadership effectiveness has largely overlooked the implications of the fact that leadership processes are enacted in the context of a shared group membership, where leaders, as group members, ask followers, as group members, to exert themselves on behalf of the collective. In contrast, the social identity model of organizational leadership, proposed here, emphasizes the characteristics of the leader as a group member, and the leader's ability to speak to followers as group members. In salient groups with which group members identify, leadership effectiveness rests on the extent to which the leader is prototypical of the group (i.e. representative of the group's identity) and engages in group-oriented behavior (i.e. behavior perceived to benefit the group). Explicating the added value of our model and going beyond contemporary approaches to leadership effectiveness, we discuss how our model extends, and may be integrated with, three major contemporary approaches to leadership effectiveness (charismatic leadership theories, Leader-Member Exchange theory, and leadership categorization theories). In addition, we outline how our model provides a viable framework to integrate future developments in research on leadership such as a growing attention to leader fairness and the role of emotions in leadership effectiveness.

Research in Organizational Behavior
Research in Organizational Behavior, Volume 25, 243–295
ISSN: 0191-3085/doi:10.1016/S0191-3085(03)25006-1

A SOCIAL IDENTITY MODEL OF LEADERSHIP EFFECTIVENESS IN ORGANIZATIONS

What makes leadership in organizations effective? This is a fundamental theoretical and practical question that continues to tax organizational leadership researchers. To be effective, leaders must be able to motivate and direct followers towards group or organizational goals, mission, or vision, and be able to maintain stability and group harmony even when acting as agents of change (e.g. Chemers, 2001; Yukl, 2001). What, then, makes leaders effective in achieving this? For an answer, leadership researchers have looked to leader traits, behavioral style, situational contingencies, social exchange processes, and charismatic and transformational leadership. Commentators believe, however, that the quest has only been moderately successful (Bass, 1990; Yukl, 1999; Yukl & Van Fleet, 1994).

We propose that an important reason for this lack of success is that researchers have tended to overlook or underemphasize the important fact that leaders not only lead groups of people, *but are also themselves members of these groups*. Organizational leaders are members of the organization, and of various groups and teams within the organization, and they therefore share one or more group memberships with the people they lead. Leadership processes are enacted in the context of a shared group membership, where leaders, as group members, ask followers, as group members, to exert themselves on behalf of the collective. Characteristics of the leader *as a group member*, and the leader's ability to speak to followers *as group members*, therefore play a key role in leadership effectiveness. In this study, we substantiate this claim by outlining a theoretical framework that places psychological group membership center-stage in the explanation of leadership in organizations.

Building on the social identity analyses of leadership by Hogg (2001a, b) and Hogg and van Knippenberg (2003), we propose a framework to analyze leadership effectiveness in organizations, the *Social Identity Model of Organizational Leadership* (SIMOL). In this article, we describe SIMOL, and assess its performance relative to other theories of leadership, and its potential to integrate with three major contemporary perspectives on leadership effectiveness in organizations: (1) Theories of charismatic and transformational leadership (Bass, 1985; Conger & Kanungo, 1987; Shamir, House & Arthur, 1993); (2) Leader-Member Exchange (LMX) theory, which provides a social exchange analysis that emphasizes the quality, and development of interpersonal leader-follower relationships (Graen & Scandura, 1987; Graen & Uhl-Bien, 1995; Schriesheim, Castro & Cogliser, 1999); and (3) leadership categorization theories that focus on follower perceptions of leadership (cf. Meindl, Ehrlich & Dukerich, 1985) and highlight the role of the perceived match between leader characteristics and schemas of effective leaders (Eagly & Karau, 2002; Lord & Maher, 1991; Ridgeway, 2001). The integration of SIMOL with these three approaches provides the building blocks for a broader conceptual framework that integrates different perspectives into a wide-ranging unified theory of leadership effectiveness. First, however, we briefly introduce the social identity approach, which provides the theoretical foundations of SIMOL.

The Social Identity Approach

The social identity approach is a theoretical framework that integrates a number of compatible social-cognitive, motivational, social-interactive, and societal level theories in order to explicate the relationship between self-conception and group and intergroup phenomena (Abrams & Hogg, 2001; Haslam, 2001; Hogg, 2001c, d, 2003). These theories include the original social identity theory (e.g. Hogg & Abrams, 1988; Tajfel & Turner, 1979), the newer self-categorization theory (J. C. Turner, 1985; J. C. Turner, Hogg, Oakes, Reicher & Wetherell, 1987) and other related theories of social identity processes (e.g. Brewer, 1991; Sedikides & Brewer, 2001). At the core of the social identity approach is the assumption that group membership contributes to self-definition. People define themselves not only in terms of idiosyncratic individualizing attributes and interpersonal relationships ("I"), but also in terms of collective attributes of a group to which they belong ("we"). The former delineates one's personal identity and personal self, whereas the latter delineates one's social identity and collective self (Hogg & Williams, 2000; Sedikides & Brewer, 2001; but cf. Brewer, 2001; Brewer & Gardner, 1996).

The value of the social identity concept is that it offers insights into how group memberships shape attitudes, feelings, and behavior. Self-conception in terms of group membership involves a psychological "merging" of self and group, or more precisely all aspects of self are governed by the *ingroup prototype*. From a social identity perspective people cognitively represent groups as prototypes (Rosch, 1978), fuzzy sets of attributes (perceptions, attitudes, feelings, behaviors) that in a particular context capture the essence of the ingroup and clearly differentiate the ingroup from relevant outgroups. The ingroup prototype is an abstract cognitive representation of "us" that draws on immediate situational information that maximizes intergroup differences and ingroup similarity, but also draws on ingroup and intergroup memory and on past group history. The ingroup prototype describes and prescribes group membership appropriate attributes in a specific context. As such the prototype is closer to a representation of the ideal than typical group member (i.e. the prototypical group member is not the average group member).

Through the process of self-categorization, group prototypical characteristics are internalized as characteristics of the self, and whatever concerns the group is experienced as concerning the self. The more fully someone defines self in terms of a specific group membership, the more that his or her perceptions, attitudes, feelings, and behavior conform to the group prototype. In this way, social identification (i.e. self-conception in terms of the group membership) produces a host of group-based attitudes and behaviors, including two phenomena that are central to our social identity model of leadership: susceptibility to group influence, and a group-oriented motivation to further the group's interests.

Influence and Persuasion in Groups
Groups are a critical source of social influence. To make sense of novel or ambiguous situations or events, or where no "objective" reference point exists (as for instance for norms and values), people typically have to rely on others for information about (social) reality (Festinger, 1954). But whom should one be influenced by, and what information should be accepted as valid?

The social identity approach to social influence (Abrams & Hogg, 1990; J. C. Turner, 1991; J. C. Turner et al., 1987) proposes that people turn to anyone who provides information about ingroup-defining norms – the ingroup prototype. Typically, ingroup members are the primary source of information, but outgroup members can also provide information to help one define the ingroup and thus know how to behave. Information about the ingroup prototype plays a very important function in reducing self-conceptual uncertainty by prescribing one's attitudes, feelings, and behaviors in a particular context, and grounding these prescriptions in group consensus (e.g. Hogg, 2000). As a result, group members are open to, and willing to elaborate communications that are perceived to reflect group prototypical attitudes and opinions.

In support of this proposition, research on persuasive communication has shown that messages from membership groups (i.e. ingroups) are more effective at changing attitudes than are messages from non-membership groups (i.e. outgroups), provided they are perceived as group prototypical (D. van Knippenberg & Wilke, 1992). More specifically, this research suggests that ingroup messages are more persuasive for three reasons. First, they are more likely to receive attention and to be processed fully (Mackie, Worth & Asuncion, 1990). Second, ambiguous aspects of prototypical ingroup messages (e.g. unclear argumentation) are more likely to receive the benefit of the doubt and to be responded to favorably than similar aspects in outgroup or non-prototypical ingroup messages (D. van Knippenberg, 1999). Third, when the motivation to systematically process the message is low, for instance because the source's position is known beforehand, prototypical ingroup advocacies are more likely to be accepted without elaborate processing than non-prototypical messages (D. van Knippenberg, Lossie & Wilke, 1994).

The notion that it is the prototype that influences people in groups may also explain differences between group members in how influential they are. As a function of the match between personal characteristics and group prototypical characteristics, some group members are more prototypical than others, just like some traits, attitudes, or behavioral dispositions are more prototypical of the group than others. Being a prototypical group member means being "one of us," embodying the group's identity, and representing what group members have in common and what differentiates the group from other groups. In the same way, then, that ingroup sources are usually more persuasive than outgroup sources, prototypical ingroup members are more persuasive than less prototypical ingroup members (D. van Knippenberg, 2000b; D. van Knippenberg et al., 1994; also see B. van Knippenberg & van Knippenberg, in press).

Group prototypes, and therefore the relative prototypicality of members, are not fixed. They are context-dependent. Prototypes are configured to maximize the ratio of intergroup differences to intragroup differences in a particular comparative context. In this way they accentuate what "we" share and what makes "us" different from "them," in order to maximize the extent to which the group is a clear and distinct entity (e.g. Hamilton & Sherman, 1996). As the comparative context changes, for example by making comparisons with a different outgroup, the prototype changes and thus the relative prototypicality of specific ingroup members changes. The effect on members is straightforward. Assuming they do not dis-identify with the group or form subgroups and factions, their behavior changes to conform to the new prototype, and those people who are most prototypically influential in the group may change.

As a straightforward example of this context-dependency of prototypes and their influence, take the experiment conducted by Hogg, Turner and Davidson (1990). Hogg et al. led participants to anticipate a group discussion involving risky decisions. Participants received bogus feedback about the positions on a number of risky decision problems of the members of their group as well as about the position of an other group enlisted for the same task. Contingent on experimental condition, the other group favored either a more cautious or a more risky decision than participants' own group (position of own group was constant over conditions). As predicted, participants' perception of the prototypical ingroup position, and own decision preferences were contingent on the position of the other group, such that perceived group prototype and individual preferences were more risky when the other group was relatively cautious than when the other group was more risky than the own group.

Group-Oriented Motivation

Self-definition in terms of group membership elicits group-oriented motivation to exert oneself on behalf of the group (e.g. Dutton, Dukerich & Harquail, 1994; Haslam, 2001; Lord & Brown, 2001; Shamir, 1990; Tyler & Blader, 2000; D. van Knippenberg, 2000a). Through the merging of self and group, group interest is experienced as self-interest (i.e. collective self-interest), and events affecting the group are experienced as affecting the self. The more strongly one identifies with the group the more personally motivated one feels to respond in a group-oriented manner to challenges and threats faced by the group, in order to protect the group or promote the group's best interest. The extent to which this motivation translates into action is influenced by a range of factors that hinge on the degree of perceived normative support for the behavioral intention and/or the action (e.g. Terry & Hogg, 1996), and self-efficacy and collective efficacy in translating motivation into effective action (D. van Knippenberg & Ellemers, 2003; cf. Bandura, 1986).

Social Identification and Social Identity Salience

The social identity approach describes how group memberships are self-definitional, and how group membership-based self-definition produces group-based influence and group-oriented motivation. This is however not to say that all group memberships are equally self-definitional or that group membership in all circumstances elicits attitudes and behavior consistent with the self-definition implied by the group membership. The extent to which a group membership is a salient part of the self-concept may vary between individuals, groups, and situations. Social identity phenomena such as group-based influence and group-oriented motivation will only come into play to the extent that individuals identify with the group and social identity is salient.

Social identification is contingent on a number of factors. Identification reflects psychological oneness (e.g. Ashforth & Mael, 1989), and accordingly the perceived context-dependent similarity between individual and group affects identification, such that higher similarity elicits higher identification (e.g. Haslam, 2001; J. C. Turner et al., 1987; but see van Knippenberg & Haslam, 2003). Through the psychological merging of self and group the prestige and status of the group reflects on the self-image. People strive for a positive self-image, and accordingly, they strive for membership of, and are more likely to identify with high status groups (e.g. Ellemers, 1993; also see van Prooijen & van Knippenberg, 2000). People also aim to strike a balance between their need for belongingness and their desire for distinctiveness (i.e. not being part of the "gray masses"). Membership in relatively small and distinct groups is more likely to achieve the desired balance between these opposing desires, and is therefore more likely to elicit identification (Brewer, 1991). Group identification may reduce self conceptual and other uncertainty through the internalization of, and conformity to group normative characteristics (i.e. the prototype). Accordingly, in situations of uncertainty individuals are more likely to seek group affiliations and identify with groups (Hogg, 2000).

Social identification and the salience of the social identity (i.e. the extent to which it is cognitively activated – e.g. Haslam, 2001) mutually affect each other (i.e. people are more likely to identify with salient groups, and high identification is more likely to render group membership salient). Other factors affect social identity salience too, however. As specified by self-categorization theory (e.g. Oakes, Haslam & Turner, 1994; J. C. Turner et al., 1987), a self-inclusive social category, and associated social identity, becomes the psychologically salient basis of self-conception in a specific situation if four conditions are met: (a) The social category is accessible in memory because one identifies strongly with it and one employs it frequently, due to its importance, value, and centrality to self-conception; (b) The social category is perceptually accessible in the immediate social context – situational cues call the category forth; (c) The categorization into ingroup and outgroup fits similarities and differences among people in the immediate context (called structural fit); (d) Stereotypical properties of the categorization account for why people behave as they do (called normative fit). Categorization in terms of gender, for instance, is more likely to become salient for somebody who believes that there are important differences between men and women than for somebody who holds such beliefs about gender differences to a lesser extent.

Social Identity in Organizational Contexts

The social identity approach was originally developed as a social psychological theory of intergroup relations (Tajfel & Turner, 1979), and it has mainly been applied outside organizations. Over the last decade, however, an increasing number of studies have applied social identity analyses to group and organizational processes (for overviews, see Haslam, 2001; Haslam, van Knippenberg, Platow & Ellemers, 2003; Hogg & Terry, 2000, 2001). These studies have addressed a wide range of issues. Some of these concern more individual-level aspects of organizational behavior, such as organizational identification (Ashforth & Mael, 1989; Elsbach, 1999; Pratt, 1998), turnover (Abrams, Ando & Hinkle, 1998; Mael & Ashforth, 1995), work motivation and performance (James & Greenberg, 1989; D. van Knippenberg, 2000a; Worchel, Rothgerber, Day & Hart, 1998), and organizational justice (Tyler, 1999; Tyler & Blader, 2000). Others focus more on group level aspects of organizational behavior, such as group cohesiveness (Hogg, 1993; Hogg, Cooper-Shaw & Holzworth, 1993), organizational diversity (Ely, 1994; Tsui, Egan & O'Reilly, 1992; D. van Knippenberg & Haslam, 2003), and group decision making (J. C. Turner, Wetherell & Hogg, 1989; M. E. Turner, Pratkanis & Samuels, 2003). And there are also analyses relating to the intergroup aspects of organizational behavior, such as intergroup relations within the organization (Hennessy & West, 1999; Kramer, 1991; D. van Knippenberg, 2003), and mergers and acquisitions (Terry, Carey & Callan, 2001; D. van Knippenberg, van Knippenberg, Monden & de Lima, 2002).

The shift in social identity research from an almost exclusive emphasis on intergroup relations to a growing emphasis on group processes has also led to the development of social identity analyses of leadership. The social identity analysis of social influence has been central to the development of self-categorization theory (e.g. Turner et al., 1987), and the analysis of leadership naturally flowed from this analysis of social influence. Whereas the focus of these analyses originally was not on leadership in organizations, the social identity analysis of leadership now has developed to a state where it can provide a social identity model of leadership in organizations. Central to this social identity model of leadership we outline in the following are the notions of group prototypicality, social identity-based influence, and group-oriented motivation we introduced in the previous.

A SOCIAL IDENTITY ANALYSIS OF
LEADERSHIP EFFECTIVENESS

As noted above, theories of leadership effectiveness in organizations tend to underemphasize the fact that leaders are also members of the groups they lead, and that therefore characteristics of the leader as a group member may influence leadership effectiveness. The social identity approach provides a very different perspective from which to understand leadership processes – one that suggests that group membership becomes a strong influence on attitudes and behavior as individuals identify more with the group and group membership becomes more salient. Because leadership effectiveness is critically contingent on the ability to influence followers and on followers' motivation to cooperate with the leader (Chemers, 2001; Yukl, 2001), the social identity analysis suggests that group membership characteristics of the leader are an important determinant of leadership effectiveness. This is the starting point for our Social Identity Model of Organizational Leadership (SIMOL) outlined and developed here.

Based on the social identity analyses of leadership by Hogg (2001a, b) and Hogg and van Knippenberg (2003), SIMOL proposes that as group members identify more strongly with their group and group membership becomes more salient, leadership perceptions, evaluations, and effectiveness become increasingly based on: (a) how group prototypical the leader is perceived to be; and (b) the extent to which the leader is perceived to act with the group's best interest in mind (i.e. is group-oriented).

Leader Prototypicality and Leadership Effectiveness

SIMOL proposes at least four processes that increase the likelihood of more prototypical group members emerging as leaders and being more effective as leaders: influence, consensual social attraction, attribution, and trust.

First, from above, we know that highly prototypical group members are more informative than less prototypical members about the nature of the group prototype, and therefore they serve an important self-conceptual uncertainty reduction function for group members. This is particularly important for leadership, because one of the functions leaders fulfill is that of sense-maker (Cohen & March, 1974) – people turn to leaders to make sense of ambiguous situations. Being representative of the group's identity positions leaders particularly well for this role. This gives prototypical members a form of group-based referent power (cf. French & Raven, 1959), or referent informational influence (J. C. Turner et al., 1987), that renders them more influential than less prototypical members (D. van Knippenberg, 2000b). It imbues prototypical members with status that positions them for a leadership role, both because member expectations favor leadership by a prototypical member and because prototypicality-based status may feed into feelings of entitlement and self-efficacy as a leader (D. van Knippenberg, van Knippenberg & van Dijk, 2000; cf. Ridgeway, 2001; Ridgeway, Johnson & Diekema, 1994).

Members of high salience groups also tend to like prototypical members more than less prototypical members. Social identification transforms the basis of liking for others from idiosyncratic preference and the quality of the interpersonal relationship (personal attraction) to group membership (depersonalized social attraction – liking for the other *as group member*; Hogg, 1992, 1993). Ingroup members are liked more than outgroup members, and, because they are more representative of the shared ingroup identity, prototypical ingroup members are liked more than less prototypical ingroup members. In salient groups social attraction is consensual – members unilaterally like the same highly prototypical member, who appears to be popular and thus have increased status and standing in the group. Because people are more likely to agree with people they like, and to comply with requests and suggestions from people they like (e.g. Berscheid & Reis, 1998), social attraction is an additional basis for prototypical members to be more influential than less prototypical members, and for this influence to be over the group as a whole.

Because prototypicality is a critical feature of group membership, highly prototypical members stand out against the background of less prototypical members, creating circumstances in which people internally attribute the prototypical members' behavior to invariant properties of the person rather than to situational or contextual factors (Gilbert & Malone, 1995; Ross, 1977). Some of the attributes that are internally attributed are those mentioned above; for example, being the focus of attention for the group, being influential, having status, and being consensually liked. These attributes tend to be attributed to intrinsic leadership abilities (e.g. Erber & Fiske, 1984; also see Meindl et al., 1985).

Last, trust in the leader plays an important role. When people identify with a group or organization, and group or organizational membership is salient, they take the group's or organization's interests to heart and care about its well-being. This not only increases motivation to exert oneself on behalf of the collective, but also places a premium on being able to trust others to have the group's best interest at heart. Being able to trust fellow members in this way is especially important in the case of being able to trust one's leaders. After all, leaders typically have more power over the group and group resources than other group members, and have the important job of representing the group and making decisions on behalf of the group. As a result, leaders who are trusted to have the group's best interest at heart will be liked more and endorsed more strongly than others who are perceived to be less group-oriented. People trust ingroup members more than outgroup members (Brewer, 1979; Kramer, 1999). In similar vein, people may place greater trust in prototypical leaders to represent the group well and to have the group's best interest at heart than in less prototypical leaders (Giessner, Sleebos & van Knippenberg, 2003), thus further contributing to prototypical leaders' greater effectiveness (cf. Dirks & Ferrin, 2002).

SIMOL proposes that the importance of leader prototypicality is contingent on group identification and social identity salience. When personal rather than social identity is salient, self and others, including leaders, are viewed through an individuating and interpersonal lens rather than through the lens of (shared) group membership. Accordingly, relationships are governed by personal rather than social attraction (Hogg, 1992, 1993), and prototypicality will have little influence on leadership effectiveness in comparison with the influence of personal characteristics of the leader and interpersonal leader-follower relationships. The more individuals identify with the group and the more social identity is salient, however, the more influential leader prototypicality is in determining leadership effectiveness, and the less important, relative to leader prototypicality, individuating characteristics of the leader and interpersonal leader-follower relationships are in determining leadership effectiveness.

The proposition that leader prototypicality is a determinant of emergent leadership and leadership effectiveness is supported by studies using different paradigms, different operationalizations of prototypicality, and different measures of leadership effectiveness. Moreover, support is found both in experimental studies that established causality (Giessner et al., 2003; Hains, Hogg & Duck, 1997; Hogg, Hains & Mason, 1998; Platow & van Knippenberg, 2001; Platow, van Knippenberg, Haslam, Spears & van Knippenberg, 2002; B. van Knippenberg & van Knippenberg, 2003; D. van Knippenberg et al., 2000) and in studies in field settings (Outward Bound groups, Fielding & Hogg, 1997; leaders of higher-level management teams, B. van Knippenberg & van Knippenberg, in press; leaders from a variety of different organizations, B. van Knippenberg & van Knippenberg, 2003) that established that the hypothesized relationships may also be observed in more naturalistic settings.

In experimental research, leader prototypicality has been manipulated by bogus feedback about the leader's characteristics vis-à-vis the characteristics of the group (and sometimes an outgroup). This feedback took either the form of information about the distribution of ingroup (and outgroup) positions on a group-defining dimension (e.g. attitudes, traits), and about the position of the leader within this distribution, or the form of information about the leader's characteristics as either matching or not matching the perceived characteristics of the group. As an example of the former, Platow and van Knippenberg (2001) assigned participants in their experiment a (simulated) leader, and gave participants bogus feedback about the score of the leader on a personality test that allegedly assessed aspects of personality that were highly representative of the student population from which participants and the leader originated. This feedback was presented graphically within a distribution of ingroup and outgroup (a neighboring student population) scores, and placed the leader either in a highly prototypical position (in the center of the ingroup distribution) or in a non-prototypical position (near one of the tails of the distribution). As an example of the latter, Platow et al. (2002) based their manipulation on a pilot study of traits that were perceived to be prototypical and non-prototypical of the student group from which participants and the (simulated) leader originated, describing the leader either in terms of group prototypical or non-prototypical traits. In the field, leader prototypicality has been assessed in questionnaires requesting group member responses to such items as "This leader is a good example of the kind of people that are member of my team" and "This leader represents what is characteristic about the team" (B. van Knippenberg & van Knippenberg, 2003), and by asking respondents to describe the group prototype and then rate their similarity to this prototype (i.e. where the leader is among the respondents; Fielding & Hogg, 1997).

The majority of these studies have operationalized leader effectiveness in terms of follower perceptions. Perceptions of effective leadership may of course provide an important basis for leadership endorsement and openness to the leader's influence, but should not be equated with evidence that the leader performed well in terms of more objective standards of leadership effectiveness such as follower performance (Lord & Maher, 1991). However, there is also evidence for the effects of prototypicality on follower intentions (Platow & van Knippenberg, 2001), emergent leadership behavior (D. van Knippenberg et al., 2000), and follower performance (B. van Knippenberg & van Knippenberg, 2003) that corroborates the findings from studies focusing on leadership perceptions only.

Several of the studies of leader prototypicality also provide support for the proposition that follower identification and social identity salience moderates the effects of leader prototypicality (Fielding & Hogg, 1997; Hains et al., 1997; Hogg et al., 1998; Platow & van Knippenberg, 2001; B. van Knippenberg & van Knippenberg, in press; also see Giessner et al., 2003). These demonstrations of the moderating role of identification/salience are not only important because they confirm one of the core propositions of the social identity analysis of leadership, but also because they show that the effect of leader prototypicality is tied to social identity rather than to for instance interpersonal similarity (cf. Hogg, 1993).

This latter set of studies also provide support for the proposition that more individualized, personal characteristics of the leader are less important predictors of leadership effectiveness relative to leader prototypicality as identification and social identity salience increases. For example, Hains et al. (1997) conducted a laboratory study of perceptions of leadership effectiveness in relatively minimal groups (ad hoc, short-lived, groups with very few defining features) as a function of three manipulated variables: leader prototypicality, group membership salience, and personalized leader characteristics. To operationalize personal characteristics of the leader that would influence perceptions of leadership effectiveness under conditions of low identity salience, Hains et al. focused participants on the extent to which the leader had characteristics that matched general schemas of effective leaders (taken from Lord, Foti & DeVader, 1984). The match between leader characteristics and leadership schemas has been shown to be predictive of perceptions of leadership effectiveness (e.g. Lord & Maher, 1991; also see the discussion of leadership categorization theories below).

Under conditions of high or low group salience, participants anticipated joining a discussion group ostensibly formed on the basis of attitude similarity among members. Salience was manipulated by referring in instructions to groups or to loose aggregates of individuals, by having participants consider commonalties within the group or differences among members, and by referring to themselves in group terms or in individual terms. Participants were told that a leader had been

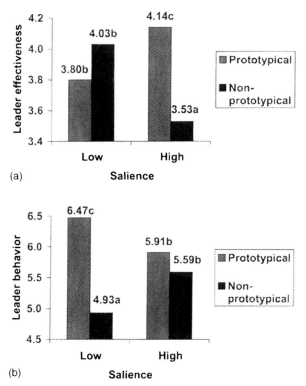

Fig. 1. (a) Leader Effectiveness as a Function of Group Salience, and Group Prototypicality of the Leader. (b) Leadership Behavior as a Function of Group Salience, and Leader Schema Congruence of the Leader, Hains et al. (1997). Means with the Same Subscript do not Differ Significantly.

randomly appointed from among the group members. Bogus feedback described the leader as group prototypical or non-prototypical in terms of the attitude dimension (i.e. a group-defining dimension), and as having a behavioral style that was congruent or incongruent with general schemas of effective leadership. Dependent measures were taken ostensibly in anticipation of the forthcoming discussion.

Results showed that when group membership was salient and people identified more strongly with the group, they perceived the prototypical leader as likely to be more effective than the non-prototypical leader. In contrast, low salience participants did not differentiate between prototypical and non-prototypical leaders (Fig. 1a). Leaders whose characteristics matched the general leader schema were perceived to be more effective overall than leaders whose characteristics did not match the schema. However, this effect disappeared for high salience participants on a leadership effectiveness measure reflecting the extent to which the leader was anticipated to exhibit leadership behavior (Fig. 1b).

Circumstantial evidence for the role of leader prototypicality comes from research on various proxies for prototypicality: Endorsement of ingroup vs. outgroup leaders, and of elected vs. appointed leaders. Leaders may be appointed from within or from outside the group or organization. Because leaders whose origins lie within the group tend to be more prototypical that those whose origins are in an outgroup, it follows that when social identity is salient and members identify with their group, leaders with ingroup origins are more strongly endorsed than leaders with outgroup origins. Studies by Duck and Fielding (1999) and Van Vugt and De Cremer (1999) have confirmed this. Similarly, leaders who are elected by the group would be expected to be perceived to be more prototypical than leaders who are appointed by entities outside the group (for example, management). In psychologically salient groups, ingroup elected leaders should therefore be more strongly endorsed and be more effective. This has been confirmed by Van Vugt and De Cremer (1999) and De Cremer and Van Vugt (2002).

Leader Group-Oriented Behavior and Leadership Effectiveness

Social identification with a group produces group-oriented motivation, and endorsement of leaders who are trusted to share this motivation. Leader prototypicality may be an important source of such trust in the leader, but it is not the only source. Irrespective of their prototypicality, leaders may display their group-oriented motivation through group-oriented attitudes and behavior. As Haslam and Platow (2001a) phrase it, social identity-based leadership endorsement may not only derive from being "one of us" (i.e. being prototypical), but also from "doing it for us" (i.e. displaying group-oriented behavior). Leaders who demonstrate that they have the group's best interest at heart by displaying group-oriented attitudes (e.g. commitment to the group) and group-oriented behaviors (e.g. going the extra mile for the group, making personal sacrifices or taking personal risks on behalf of the group), should therefore be more effective than leaders who do not behave in this way.

As described above, concern with group goals and group interests increases as a positive function of strength of identification with a group. Thus, the more members identify with a group, the more leader group-oriented behavior affects leadership effectiveness, and the less important, relative to group-oriented behavior, individuating characteristics of the leader and interpersonal leader-follower relationships are in determining leadership effectiveness.

A number of studies focusing on different displays of group-oriented attitudes and behavior provide support for this idea. These studies show that leadership effectiveness is contingent on the extent to which the leader has a committed attitude towards the group (De Cremer & Van Vugt, 2002); is ingroup-favoring in distributive decisions (Haslam & Platow, 2001b; Platow, Hoar, Reid, Harley & Morrison, 1997; Platow, Mills & Morrison, 2000; Platow & van Knippenberg, 2001) and procedural decisions (i.e. whether or not to give individuals voice in a decision – Platow, Reid & Andrew, 1998); and sacrifices personal interests on behalf of the group (Choi & Mai-Dalton, 1999; De Cremer, 2002; De Cremer & van Knippenberg, 2002; B. van Knippenberg & van Knippenberg, 2003; Yorges, Weiss & Strickland, 1999). Although some of these studies have relied on leadership perceptions and/or behavioral intentions alone, a number have yielded evidence for the actual behavioral effects of leader group-oriented behavior. De Cremer and Van Vugt (2002) for instance show that leaders that are high (vs. low) in commitment to the group elicit more cooperative behavior from group members, and B. van Knippenberg and van Knippenberg (2003) show that leaders sacrificing personal interests engender higher follower performance.

There is also evidence from these studies that these effects on leadership effectiveness are contingent on follower identification with the group (e.g. De Cremer & Van Vugt, 2002; Platow et al., 1997; Platow & van Knippenberg, 2001), and that personal leader characteristics become less influential on leadership endorsement as followers identify more strongly with the group. De Cremer and Van Vugt (2002) measured high and low identifying group members' cooperative behavior in response to a leader who was either highly committed to the group or who ostensibly scored high on leadership skills (cf. Hains et al.'s, 1997, group prototypicality vs. leader schema consistency manipulations, described above). When member identification was high, the committed leader elicited more cooperative behavior, whereas the leader high in leader skills elicited more cooperation when identification was low (also see Platow & van Knippenberg, 2001).

Leader Prototypicality and Leader Group-Oriented Behavior

Prototypical group members are more likely to identify with the group, and therefore take the group's interest to heart. As a result, leader prototypicality and leader group-oriented behavior may often go together in practice. However, the two do not go together by necessity. Prototypicality is not restricted to behavior that furthers the collective's interest, and, conversely, group-oriented behavior need not be group prototypical. An obvious question therefore is how leader prototypicality and leader group-oriented behavior in combination influence leadership effectiveness.

The key issue here probably is trust in the leader's group-orientedness. SIMOL proposes that both leader prototypicality and leader group-oriented behavior engender trust in the leader – and that this affects leadership effectiveness. Non-prototypical leaders may not be trusted to have the group's best interest at heart without concrete demonstrations to that end. They will be expected to actually behave in group-oriented ways to 'prove' their credentials and engender trust. In contrast, prototypical leaders will have more leeway in their behavior because their prototypicality is taken as read and they are intrinsically trusted to "do it for us." This analysis builds on classic research that shows that legitimate and respected leaders are allowed a great deal of normative leeway in groups (e.g. Sherif & Sherif, 1964), and that leaders who have climbed through the ranks and are highly normative are allowed to behave idiosyncratically and non-normatively (e.g. Hollander, 1958). From the SIMOL perspective the clear prediction is that the expression of group-oriented behavior will impact leadership effectiveness more strongly for low than high prototypical leaders.

A number of studies support this prediction. In a laboratory experiment, Platow and van Knippenberg (2001) showed that individuals who identified with the group endorsed a non-prototypical leader only when the leader was ingroup-favoring in an allocation decision. Prototypical leaders were endorsed irrespective of their allocative behavior, even when it was outgroup-favoring. Leadership endorsement among low identifiers was not affected by leader prototypicality, and was highest for a leader who made even-handed allocations. Similar findings where obtained for the interaction between leader prototypicality and leader self-sacrifice (B. van Knippenberg & van Knippenberg, 2003), the interaction between leader prototypicality and leader's appeal to collective interest versus follower self-interest (Platow et al., 2002), and leader prototypicality and the leader's use of "hard" (coercive) versus "soft" (non-coercive) influence tactics (B. van Knippenberg & van Knippenberg, in press).

Giessner et al. (2003) report an experiment taking this analysis one step further. They focused on the desired outcome of leader group-oriented behavior, namely that the leader benefits the group. Giessner et al. presented German Green Party voters and German voters that did not associate themselves with the Green Party with a scenario describing a hypothetical local Green Party leader. This leader was described as either prototypical or non-prototypical based on the Green Party program. The prototypical leader represented characteristics that were central to the program, the non-prototypical leader represented characteristics that were more peripheral to the program. Crossed with this prototypicality manipulation, the leader was described as either successful or unsuccessful in achieving important Green Party ends in negotiations with local industry. In addition to these experimental manipulations, Giessner et al. distinguished between participants

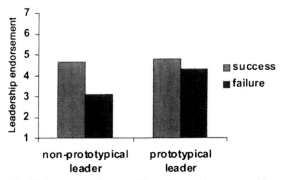

Fig. 2. Leadership Endorsement Among Green Party Voters as a Function of Leader Prototypicality and Leader Success, Giessner et al. (2003).

that identified with the Green Party and participants that did not identify with the Green Party. As predicted, Green Party identifiers endorsed the prototypical leader irrespective of his success or failure in achieving important group goals, whereas the non-prototypical leader was only endorsed when he was successful (see Fig. 2). Giessner et al. also assessed trust in the leader, and found that the effect of prototypicality was mediated by trust, suggesting that endorsement of the prototypical leader was less contingent on his success on behalf of the group, because he was trusted more a priori. For participants that did not identify with the Green Party, leadership endorsement was low irrespective of leader prototypicality or success.

The interaction between leader prototypicality and leader group-oriented behavior points to a key issue in understanding the social identity analysis of leadership: The notion that group prototypicality is a basis for leadership effectiveness does by no means imply that prototypical leaders can only behave like "the average group member." Unusual and unconventional behavior is seen as a basis for leadership effectiveness (Conger & Kanungo, 1987), and if prototypical leaders could only engage in such behavior at costs to their prototypicality-based effectiveness, that would put serious limits on their effectiveness. The contrary is true, however. Prototypicality provides leaders with more leeway in their behavior and thus positions them to effectively engage in behavior that may lead the group or organization in new directions (also see the discussion of charismatic leadership below). Being representative of the group's identity as a basis of leadership effectiveness is not at odds with engaging in special, unusual, or distinctive behavior; indeed, it sets the stage for effectively engaging in such behavior.

The Dynamic Relationship Between Leaders and Social Identity
Processes in Leadership Effectiveness

Our analysis so far has focused on the effects on leadership of leader prototypicality, leader group-oriented behavior, and identification/social identity
salience. These variables are not merely a "given." Leaders may consciously
display and manipulate their own prototypicality, deliberately decide to engage in
group-oriented acts to enhance their leadership effectiveness, and affect follower
identification and social identity salience.

Analyses of political leadership by Reicher and Hopkins (2001, in press; also see
Reid & Ng, in press) suggest that political leaders often engage in strategic displays
of their prototypicality. Political leaders like Ghandi, Sukharno, and Thatcher all
projected an image of themselves as the embodiment of national identity (i.e. as
highly prototypical of the group). By thus portraying themselves, and their advocated course of action, as prototypical of the group, leaders convey that an attack
on them or their policy is an attack on the group and what it stands for. Gandhi,
for example, adopted a sober lifestyle closer to the lives of many of the people
he represented, thus communicating a close match to the contextually salient
prototype of the Indian nation in contrast to the imperial power, Great Britain.

Anecdotal evidence suggests that organizational leaders too engage in prototypicality management strategies. B. van Knippenberg (2003) for instance described
how regional managers in a service organization "dressed down" – changed from
their regular business dress to a jeans-and-sweater outfit – when visiting the
organization's cleaning teams. The explicit aim was to "be more like the team
members" in order to bridge the gap between management and work floor. The one
regional manager who did not dress down when visiting these teams was generally
perceived to be less strongly endorsed than other managers. Similarly, Choi and
Mai-Dalton (1998) describe the example of a strongly endorsed military general
eating with his men rather than using the separate officers' facilities. Although
Choi and Mai-Dalton interpret this as an example of leader self-sacrifice (i.e.
leader group-oriented behavior), we would argue that the more important message
here is the general's communication of prototypicality – "I am one of you."

In their attempts to use the group prototype to mobilize followers for their cause
leaders need not accept the group prototype as fixed. The context-dependence of
prototypes ensures that what is prototypical of the group may change over time,
for instance because the intergroup comparative context has changed (e.g. Elsbach
& Kramer, 1996) or because an organization's core business has changed (e.g.
M. E. Turner et al., 2003). As a consequence of such changes, the basis for a
leader's effectiveness may change. However, leaders may use these processes to
their advantage. For instance, Reicher and Hopkins (in press) discuss how in the
context of elections in Scotland, political leaders from across the entire political

spectrum tried to appeal to the electorate by voicing their deep sense of Scottishness (i.e. their prototypicality of the national category). However, these leaders differed in what they portrayed Scottish identity to be. For the Left, Scottishness was characterized by egalitarianism and communalism, whereas for the Right, it was exemplified by entrepreneurship. Both Left and Right legitimated their claims with reference to Scottish history (cf. Shamir et al., 1993), thus strategically using aspects of national identity and national history to project a particular image of national identity that would portray them, and their advocated course of action, as prototypically Scottish.

Aside from engaging in such prototype-management strategies, leaders may also strategically engage in group-oriented behavior to build their basis of leadership effectiveness. Analyses of charismatic leadership in organizations suggest for example that highly effective leaders often engage in dramatic public displays of group-oriented behavior to build support among followers. For instance, as CEO of Chrysler Lee Iaccoca publicly decided to set his annual salary at US$ 1 to prove his commitment to Chrysler's plight, and to elicit similar commitment from Chrysler's employees (e.g. Conger & Kanungo, 1998).

Similarly, leaders whose position is insecure often seek an outgroup "enemy" to enhance their basis of support (Rabbie & Bekkers, 1978). An enemy provides the leader with an opportunity to be seen to stand up for the group and to represent the group against outside forces, and thus strengthen his or her position. In addition, it may help make group identity and group prototypical attributes salient (Hogg & Reid, 2001). This analysis can also be extended to include ingroup "enemies" or deviants (e.g. Hogg, Fielding & Darley, in press; Hogg & Hornsey, in press; Marques, Abrams, Páez & Hogg, 2001). Leaders can identify specific ingroup members or subgroups to derogate and marginalize as threats to the group's integrity and survival or merely as threats to the nature of what the group stands for, its prototype. Leaders throughout history have used this technique very effectively – for example Stalin's targeting of "dissident intellectuals," and Thatcher's derogation of "communist sympathizers."

Reicher and Hopkins' (in press) analysis suggests that by being *entrepreneurs of identity*, managing what is seen as prototypical of the group, leaders may enhance identification with the collective and render the collective's identity salient, thus mobilizing followers and giving direction to collective action. Similarly, De Cremer and van Knippenberg (2002) have proposed that group-oriented behavior like leader self-sacrifice on behalf of the group may enhance identification and render the collective salient, which in turn increases follower contributions to the collective (also see Lord, Brown & Freiberg, 1999; Shamir et al., 1993). In other words, identification/salience is not only a *moderator* of leadership effectiveness (i.e. leader prototypicality and group-oriented behavior being more influential under conditions of high identification/salience), but also a *mediator* of leadership effectiveness (i.e. leaders ability to mobilize followers for the collective deriving from their influence on identification/salience). This suggests a dynamic model in which leaders may create, through their (displays of) prototypicality and group-oriented actions, the conditions conducive to the effectiveness of their leadership (i.e. high identification and social identity salience).

Leader effectiveness may have a basis in group prototypicality, but group prototypicality may also shape the leader's thoughts and actions. To the extent that leaders identify with their group and social identity is salient, group prototypicality will be an important influence on their attitudes and behavior, and they will be motivated to further the group's best interest. The more that leaders engage in group-oriented behavior, the more powerful the basis of their leadership effectiveness. However, in a provocative analysis of Lyndon Johnson's presidential leadership, Kramer (in press) suggests that in extreme cases the influence of leader self-definition may turn the leader into a "captive' of the prototype, to the detriment of leadership effectiveness.

Kramer (in press) argues that Johnson's self-definition was tied particularly strongly to the United States presidency, and that this self-definition came to decisively shape his decisions in the Vietnam War. Johnson was initially judged to be a very capable politician and statesman and a highly competent and accomplished president. However, his aspirations to be a truly great president in conjunction with his prototypical representation of the presidency, lead him to make increasingly questionable decisions. As Kramer argues, "running away" from the challenge presented by Vietnam was anathema to Johnson's prototypical representation of a great American president. Thus he made a series of decisions that he may have known were wrong.

There is an interesting parallel between Kramer's analysis and M. E. Turner et al. (2003) analysis of decisions made by Intel's leadership to move from the manufacturing of computer memory to microprocessors. Kramer argues that Johnson made the wrong decisions because he was a captive of his prototypical representation of the United States presidency, whereas Turner et al. argue that Intel's leadership made the right decisions because they were able to avoid this "identity trap." If Intel's leadership had been guided more by Intel's identity as "The Memory Company," and had been less able to break free of this identity, the company would probably have fared far worse than it did.

Summary

To summarize the analysis so far, the core propositions of the Social Identity Model of Organizational Leadership (SIMOL) are that in salient social groups with which people identify more prototypical leaders and leaders that engage in group-oriented behavior are more likely to be endorsed and to be effective as leaders. In contrast, more personalized or interpersonal aspects of leadership become less important relative to leader prototypicality and leader group-oriented behavior. Moreover, leader prototypicality and leader group-oriented behavior interact, such that the effects of leader group-orientedness are more pronounced when leaders are non-prototypical. Leaders may use these processes, and actively manage the group prototype and strategically engage in group-oriented behavior to build and maintain their basis of effectiveness. Leaders may also affect follower identification and social identity salience, which both feed directly into leadership effectiveness (the mediator role of identification/salience) and work to construe the conditions for social identity-based leadership endorsement (the moderator role of identification/salience).

SIMOL AND OTHER THEORIES OF LEADERSHIP EFFECTIVENESS IN ORGANIZATIONS

The basic propositions of SIMOL are well-supported by experimental and survey research. Even so, to be a significant perspective on leadership effectiveness in organizations, SIMOL must have added value – it needs to go beyond existing theories of leadership effectiveness in research in organizational behavior. This added value lies in: (a) a focus on group membership characteristics of the leader; and (b) a focus on group identification and identity salience as moderators of leadership effectiveness processes.

We explore this added value by discussing SIMOL in relationship to what arguably are the three main contemporary perspectives on leadership effectiveness in organizational behavior (Chemers, 2001; D. van Knippenberg & Hogg, in press; Yukl, 2001): (1) Leadership categorization theories (Eagly & Karau, 2002; Lord & Maher, 1991), which share with SIMOL a theoretical basis in social-cognitive theories of social categorization processes; (2) Leader-Member Exchange (LMX) theory (Graen & Scandura, 1987; Graen & Uhl-Bien, 1995; Schriesheim et al., 1999), which adopts an interpersonal orientation that is at first sight in opposition to SIMOL's group membership perspective; and (3) Theories of charismatic and transformational leadership (Bass, 1985; Conger & Kanungo, 1987; Shamir et al., 1993), arguably the main contemporary perspective in leadership research and the one most attuned to social identity dynamics.

SIMOL and Leadership Categorization Theories

Since the 1980s, a line of leadership research has developed that focuses on factors leading people to perceive others as effective leaders (Lord, 1977; Lord et al., 1984).

This line of inquiry highlights the role of leadership perceptions, perceptions of the extent to which a target individual has both the qualities of a leader and the potential to exhibit effective leadership in a particular situation (Lord & Hall, in press). It is assumed that leadership perceptions play a key role in leader selection decisions (i.e. organizations assign individuals who are expected to be effective as leaders to leadership positions) and in a leader's power base (i.e. the perception that one is a capable leader provides one with a basis of power to influence others), and thus ultimately in the extent to which people can exercise leadership and influence others (Lord & Hall, in press; Lord & Maher, 1991).

The most extensive research program focusing on leadership perceptions is Lord and colleagues' leadership categorization theory (e.g. Lord, Brown, Harvey & Hall, 2001; Lord et al., 1984; Lord & Maher, 1991). The theory rests on the notion that perceivers have implicit leadership theories that shape perceptions of (potential) leaders. In making leadership judgments, leadership schemas or stereotypes (called prototypes by Lord and colleagues) based on these implicit leadership theories are activated, and characteristics of the target/leader are matched against these schemas of effective leadership.

Earlier conceptions of leadership categorization theory (e.g. Lord et al., 1984) viewed leader stereotypes as relatively general and fixed in nature. The contemporary version (e.g. Lord et al., 2001; Lord & Hall, in press) views leadership representations as being relatively flexible and contextually constrained and constructed. The basic prediction, however, of leadership categorization theory remains the same. The better the match between target characteristics and the perceiver's leadership schema, the more favorable leadership perceptions are. For example, a perceiver whose leadership schema favors "intelligent," "organized," and "dedicated" as core leadership attributes (Lord et al., 1984), is more likely to endorse a leader the more the leader is perceived to be intelligent, organized, and dedicated.

Similar predictions may be found in Eagly's Role Congruity Theory (Eagly, in press; Eagly & Karau, 2002) and in theories of status such as expectation states theory and status characteristics theory (Berger, Wagner & Zelditch, 1985; Ridgeway, 2001, in press). Although these theories do not focus as extensively as Leadership Categorization Theory on the social-cognitive processes underlying leadership perceptions, they too may be called leadership categorization theories. This is because they also suggest that the match between an individual's characteristics and abstracted conceptions of status and leadership affect leadership perceptions. Role Congruity Theory focuses on gender and leadership (Eagly, in press; Eagly & Karau, 2002). It argues that because there is greater overlap between general leader schemas and male stereotypes than between leader schemas and female stereotypes, people tend to have more favorable perceptions of male leaders than of female leaders. Status characteristics theory (e.g. Berger et al., 1985; Ridgeway, 2001, in press) attributes influence (and by implication leadership) within groups to possession of specific status characteristics (qualities that match what the group actually does) and diffuse status characteristics (stereotypical properties of high status groups in society).

Leadership categorization theories link leadership perceptions, and leadership effectiveness contingent on these perceptions, to the match between a leader's characteristics and leadership schemas. In contrast, SIMOL links leadership perceptions and effectiveness to the match between a leader's characteristics and the group prototype. Leadership categorization theories and SIMOL thus share an emphasis on the role of social categorization processes in leadership perceptions, but they differ quite fundamentally over the role of psychological group membership. Group membership, not leadership schemas, is critical for SIMOL, but the opposite is the case for leadership categorization theories (e.g. Lord et al., 1984; Offerman, Kennedy & Wirtz, 1994). Although leadership categorization theories and SIMOL thus converge in the proposition that leadership perceptions are contingent on the cognitive activation of a standard to which a (potential) leader's characteristics are compared, they diverge in the proposed contents of this standard (also see Lord & Hall, in press).

Studies by Hains et al. (1997) and Fielding and Hogg (1997) described above show how these different perspectives can be reconciled. Recall that Hains et al.'s (1997) experiment contrasted group prototypicality and leadership schema congruence (conceptualized as in Leadership Categorization Theory) as determinants of effective leadership, and argued that group identification and social identity salience determine the relative importance of group prototypes versus leadership schemas in leadership perceptions. In line with their social identity analysis they found that the impact of leadership schemas on leadership evaluations weakened under high salience conditions, and that group prototypicality had a greatly increased impact on leadership evaluations under high salience. Similar findings were obtained in a correlational field study by Fielding and Hogg (1997) and in a correlational analysis conducted as part of a laboratory study by Platow and van Knippenberg (2001). The available evidence thus supports the conclusion that social identification and social identity salience affect the standard of comparison (i.e. leadership schema vs. group prototype) against which a (potential) leader's leadership qualities are judged.

Lord and Hall (in press) reach a similar conclusion in their analysis of the construal of leadership stereotypes, arguing that leadership stereotypes that are construed under conditions of high identification/salience may be heavily influenced by group prototypes. In summary, then, the moderating role of identification/identity salience that is core to SIMOL forms the basis of the integration of leadership categorization theories and SIMOL. Leadership schemas that are not bound to a specific group membership are relatively more important for leadership perceptions under conditions of low identification/social identity salience, whereas group prototypicality is relatively more important under conditions of high identification/salience.

Recently, Hogg, Fielding, Johnston, Masser, Russell and Svensson (2003) conducted an experiment on gender and leadership in small interactive groups, which is directly relevant to role congruity theory, status characteristics theory, and general leadership categorization perspectives. They argued, from a social identity perspective, that whether demographic category attributes enhance leadership effectiveness in a small group is an interactive function of psychological membership salience and the extent of congruence between stereotypic attributes of the demographic category and the local group norm or prototype. Using gender as their demographic category, Hogg and associates created, in a computer mediated communication environment, small non interactive groups with male stereotypic or female stereotypic behavioral norms (i.e. instrumental vs. expressive), and ostensibly appointed a male or female member to lead the group. In this way leader-prototype congruence was manipulated. Congruence was high for male leaders of instrumental groups and female leaders of expressive groups, and low in the other cases (Hall, Workman & Marchiore, 1998). Salience was also manipulated using standard social identity procedures to prime self-conception in group or in individual terms.

The prediction was that salience should improve leadership evaluations of congruent leaders, but worsen evaluations of non-congruent leaders. However, there was a third measured variable to qualify this prediction. Participants were divided into higher and lower scorers on the hostile sexism sub-scale of Glick and Fiske's (1996) Ambivalent Sexism Inventory, to identify those who had more or less traditional sex-role attitudes. Based on Swim, Aikin, Hall and Hunter's (1995) suggestion that "progressives" are more aware that occupational segregation may be a result of prejudice, and the argument that progressives might exhibit "reverse discrimination" in favor of women in order to combat gender stereotypes (also see Brief, Dietz, Cohen, Pugh & Vaslow, 2000), Hogg and associates felt that more progressive participants would show entirely the opposite effect to that predicted above.

The results of the experiment largely supported these predictions (see Fig. 3). For people who subscribed to traditional gender stereotypes, salience improved evaluation of leaders whose gender was congruent with the local group norm. For people who had more progressive gender attitudes salience improved evaluation of leaders whose gender was *not* congruent with the local group norm, and worsened evaluations of leaders whose gender was congruent with the local group norm.

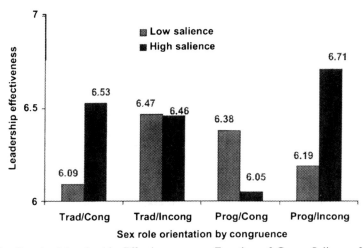

Fig. 3. Perceived Leadership Effectiveness as a Function of Group Salience, Leader-Prototype Congruence, and Sex-Role Orientation, Hogg, Fielding et al. (2003).

This study shows again the role played by prototypicality in leadership evaluations under high salience. It also has implications for an understanding of the glass ceiling effect in which women find it difficult to attain top leadership positions in organizations (Eagly, Karau & Makhijani, 1995) and the glass elevator effect in which males do not suffer in the same way (Eagly, in press; Williams, 1992). The study suggests that gender per se may not be the only impediment to effective leadership. Incongruence between female-stereotypical attributes and the generally masculine environment of many organizations (Cejka & Eagly, 1999) may hold women back under conditions of high organizational salience. The study also suggests that the glass elevator may not exist for men in high salience female stereotypical professions such as nursing and flight attendants (e.g. Young & James, 2001). The analysis can also be extended to other demographic groups, for example those based on ethnicity, race (dis)ability, or age. For these categories too organizational prototypes may typically favor characteristics of majority and higher status groups – indeed, underrepresented group are more or less by definition less prototypical of the collective (Mummendey & Wenzel, 1999; van Leeuwen & van Knippenberg, 2003).

SIMOL and Leader-Member Exchange (LMX) Theory

Another major perspective in contemporary leadership research is the social exchange analysis of leader-follower relations. Originating in work by Hollander

(1958; also see Hollander & Offerman, 1990) it is now primarily represented by Leader-Member Exchange (LMX) theory of leadership (Gerstner & Day, 1997; Graen & Scandura, 1987; Graen & Uhl-Bien, 1995). Testifying to its impact, a recent review of the LMX literature lists 147 studies since the concept was originally introduced in the 1970s (Schriesheim et al., 1999).

LMX theory identifies interpersonal exchange relationships as the key to effective leadership. Effective leadership rests on the development of high quality dyadic exchange relationships between the leader and specific subordinates. High quality LMX relationships are ones where subordinates are favored by the leader and thus receive many valued resources. In return, subordinates are expected to contribute substantially to the relationship. Leader-subordinate exchanges go beyond the formal employment contract, with managers showing influence and support, and giving the subordinate greater autonomy and responsibility. In contrast, low quality LMX relationships are ones where subordinates are less favored by the leader and thus receive fewer valued resources. Leader-subordinate exchanges simply adhere to the terms of the employment contract, with little attempt by the leader to develop or motivate the subordinate. LMX theory predicts that effective leaders should develop high quality LMX relationships with their subordinates, which should enhance subordinates' well-being and work performance.

Research confirms that organizational leaders do differentiate among subordinates and develop different quality dyadic relations with them, and that high quality LMX relations are associated with job satisfaction, well-being, organizational commitment, and organizational citizenship (Schriesheim et al., 1999). LMX theory has, however, some problems; for example the measurement of LMX is problematic (e.g. Keller & Dansereau, 2000), and there is only limited evidence for LMX to predict actual performance (e.g. Vecchio, 1998). There is a more fundamental problem with LMX theory (Hogg & Martin, 2003; Hogg, Martin & Weeden, in press). LMX theory is a perspective that focuses on leader-follower dyadic relations that occur in isolation of group membership dynamics. The extent to which leader and follower identify with the wider group is not considered, nor is the perceived or actual relationship between the specific leader-follower relationship and other such relationships or groupings within the group.

From a social identity leadership perspective Hogg and associates have proposed the novel analysis that although personalized, dyadic, leader-member relations may be effective in many groups, they may be less effective in groups that are highly salient and that people identify strongly with (Hogg & Martin, 2003; Hogg et al., in press). The logic of this analysis is that personalized relations in a high-salience group may run counter to the collective spirit of such groups because they are seen to identify favorites, separate members who feel joined through common identity. Members may actually prefer to be treated alike by the leader. Depersonalized leader-member relations may appear more in the spirit of enhanced collective self-conception, and may promote enhanced feelings of trust and legitimacy for an apparently group-focused egalitarian leader (e.g. Tyler & Lind, 1992).

Hogg, Martin, Epitropaki, Mankad, Svensson and Weeden (2003) report two questionnaire studies of people in organizations to test the very simple prediction that as group membership becomes more salient, depersonalized leader-member relations are perceived to be an increasingly more effective basis for leadership. Associated with this, depersonalized leadership may be perceived to be less effective than more personalized leadership under conditions of low salience, whereas under high salience depersonalized leadership may be seen to be more effective than personalized leadership.

Study 1 was a survey of 439 employees of a range of companies in the U.K. Using multi-item scales, our key measures were of leader effectiveness, organizational salience in self-conceptualization, and the extent to which the leader's style involved personalized or depersonalized relations with subordinates. Figure 4a illustrates the results in a 2 (salience) × 2 (leadership style) ANOVA format. As predicted salience increased the perceived effectiveness of depersonalized leadership, and under high salience the perceived advantage of a personalized style was greatly decreased.

Study 2 was a replication of Study 1 that used similar but better developed, better-focused and more extensive measures, and very importantly measured the extent to which respondents identified with their group rather than how salient they reported it to be. Identification is a more direct measure of social identity processes of leadership than is salience. Study 2 was conducted with 128 employees of organizations in Mumbai, India. Figure 4b illustrates the results in a 2 (identification) × 2 (leadership style) ANOVA format. As predicted, increased identification was associated with increased perceived effectiveness of depersonalized leadership, and under high identification the leadership advantage of a depersonalized over personalized style was much stronger than under low identification.

Together this pair of studies calls into question the LMX view that personalized leader-member relations are always best. On the contrary, and consistent with the social identity analysis of leadership, in salient groups personalized relations do not have an advantage – members may prefer depersonalized leader-member relations. Put differently, with increasing salience and identification depersonalized leader-member relations are more favorably evaluated and leaders who adopt these relations are better received and more effective.

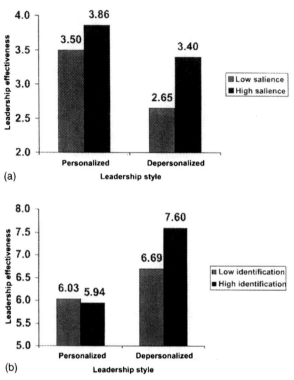

Fig. 4. (a) Perceived Leadership Effectiveness as a Function of Group Salience and Leadership Style, Hogg, Martin et al. (2003, Study 1). (b) Perceived Leadership Effectiveness as a Function of Identification and Leadership Style, Hogg, Martin et al. (2003, Study 2).

SIMOL and Theories of Charismatic and Transformational Leadership

From the late 1970s (Burns, 1978; House, 1977), and gathering momentum in the 1980s (Bass, 1985; Conger & Kanungo, 1987), charismatic and transformational leadership probably has become the main focus of research on leadership effectiveness (e.g. Bass, 1998; Conger & Kanungo, 1998; House & Shamir, 1993; Lowe, Kroeck & Sivasubramaniam, 1996). Although theories of charismatic and transformational leadership vary in the aspects of leadership they highlight (e.g. Bass, 1985; Conger & Kanungo, 1987; Shamir et al., 1993), there is substantial overlap, with differences reflecting differences in emphasis more than disagreement. Therefore, we treat them together under the general heading of charismatic leadership (House, 1995), and discuss SIMOL in relation to this broadly conceptualized perspective.

Charismatic leadership persuades followers to go beyond self-interest to serve collective goals and interests, and motivates followers to exceptional performance (Bass, 1985; Bass & Avolio, 1993; Boal & Bryson, 1988; Conger & Kanungo, 1987; House, 1977; Shamir et al., 1993; Tichy & Devanna, 1986). For this reason, charismatic leadership is an especially effective form of leadership (e.g. Bass, 1998; Conger & Kanungo, 1998; Lowe et al., 1996). The key question is what makes a leader charismatic? In answer to this question, charismatic leaders are proposed to engage in such behaviors as emphasizing collective identity, communicating a collective vision or mission, referring to collective history, making personal sacrifices and taking personal risks in pursuit of collective goals and interests, displaying self-confidence, expressing confidence in followers, role-modeling desired behavior, and coaching and developing followers to pursue the collective vision (e.g. Bass, 1985; Bass & Avolio, 1993; Conger & Kanungo, 1987, 1998; Shamir et al., 1993).

A question that has received relatively less (empirical) attention (Hunt, 1999; Yukl, 1999) is what psychological processes underlie the effects of charismatic leadership on followers. In what is probably the most elaborate discussion of these processes, Shamir et al. (1993) highlight the role of the self-concept and collective identity. Shamir et al. propose that charismatic leadership is effective because it induces identification with the collective and renders the collective identity salient, and engenders follower self-efficacy and collective efficacy in pursuit of collective goals and interests (cf. Bass, 1998; Conger & Kanungo, 1998). In addition, Bennis and Nanus (1985) and Boal and Bryson (1988) highlight trust in the leader as an important factor. Although process-oriented research is scarce in the field of charismatic leadership, there is empirical support for the proposed roles of collective identification (De Cremer & van Knippenberg, 2002), self-efficacy (Shea & Howell, 1999), and trust in the leader (Pillai, Schriesheim & Williams, 1999; Podsakoff, MacKenzie, Moorman & Fetter, 1990).

There are a number of commonalities between theories of charismatic leadership and SIMOL, most notably the emphasis on identification and collective identity. In contrast to SIMOL, however, theories of charismatic leadership do not address the role of group membership characteristics of the leader. The obvious question, then, is how leader prototypicality should be seen in relationship to charismatic leadership, and related to this, how leader group-oriented behavior should be seen in relationship to charismatic leadership. We first address these questions related to the components of charismatic leadership. Then we discuss similarities and differences between SIMOL and theories of charismatic leadership in relation to the psychological processes underlying leadership effectiveness.

SIMOL and the Components of Charisma

Based on SIMOL, we propose that in salient groups with which members identify, leader prototypicality affects perceptions of charisma. As discussed above, leader prototypicality results in status and referent informational influence, social attraction to the leader, and trust in the group-orientedness of the leader. All of this adds to attributions of charisma and to the leader's ability to engender the very processes that are assumed to underlie the effectiveness of charismatic leadership. Indeed, the very fact that prototypical leaders are representative of the group's identity renders them more able to elicit identification and render the collective salient.

For example, Reicher and Hopkins's (2001, in press) analyses of political leadership suggest that many charismatic leaders in the political arena derived much of their ability to mobilize the masses from their emphasis on their own prototypicality and on the collective identity they claimed to represent. In support of this analysis, experiments by Platow et al. (2002) and B. van Knippenberg and van Knippenberg (2003) show that leader prototypicality has a positive effect on perceptions of charismatic leadership (also see Platow, Haslam, Foddy & Grace, in press). In sum, SIMOL suggests that the leader's characteristics as a group member are an important but largely neglected part of charismatic leadership.

In contrast, the role of group-oriented behavior in charismatic leadership has been recognized. Leader self-sacrifice on behalf of the group, in particular, is proposed to be a component of charismatic leadership (Choi & Mai-Dalton, 1998, 1999; Conger & Kanungo, 1987; De Cremer, 2002; De Cremer & van Knippenberg, 2002; B. van Knippenberg & van Knippenberg, 2003; Yorges et al., 1999). Thus, SIMOL and theories of charismatic leadership converge on the proposition that group-oriented behavior is an important determinant of perceptions of charisma and leadership effectiveness.

SIMOL thus suggests that leader prototypicality and leader group-oriented behavior influence perceptions of charisma and perceptions of leadership effectiveness. The same reasoning, then, that leads to the proposition that prototypicality and group-oriented behavior interact in affecting leadership perceptions and effectiveness leads to the prediction that prototypicality and the group-oriented aspects of charismatic leadership interact in affecting perceptions of charisma and leadership effectiveness. Group-oriented behavior is less important to perceptions of charisma and effectiveness the more prototypical the leader is. Support for this proposition is found in studies by Platow et al. (2002) and B. van Knippenberg and van Knippenberg (2003).

In line with theories of charismatic leadership (Bass, 1985; Shamir et al., 1993), Platow et al. argued that appealing to the collective interest rather than to follower self-interest would be perceived as a sign of leader group-orientedness and render the collective identity salient, and would therefore contribute to perceptions of charisma. In addition, they argued that this would hold more for non-prototypical than for prototypical leaders, because prototypical leaders' group-orientedness is more taken for granted (cf. Giessner et al., 2003) and social identity is more likely to be salient when confronted with a leader that is representative of the collective identity. In support of this hypothesis, Platow et al. found in a laboratory study that leader prototypicality and leader's appeal to the collective interest versus follower's self-interest in communication addressed to followers interacted to affect perceptions of charismatic leadership. Prototypical leaders were considered charismatic regardless of the nature of their appeal, whereas non-prototypical leaders were considered charismatic only when they appealed to the collective interest.

B. van Knippenberg and van Knippenberg (2003) tested the prediction that leader prototypicality and leader self-sacrifice interact in affecting perceptions of charisma and leadership effectiveness. Consistent with theories of charismatic leadership (Choi & Mai-Dalton, 1998; Conger & Kanungo, 1987), they argued that leader self-sacrifice would feed into perceptions of charisma and leadership effectiveness, and would make followers more willing to exert themselves on behalf of the collective (De Cremer & van Knippenberg, 2002). Van Knippenberg and van Knippenberg proposed that leader prototypicality moderates these effects, because prototypicality heightens the trust in leader group-orientedness, and therefore renders perceptions of charisma and leadership effectiveness, and the willingness to exert oneself on behalf of the group less contingent on leader self-sacrificial behavior. To test these predictions, they conducted two surveys of employees from a variety of organizations. They found that leader prototypicality and leader self-sacrifice both related positively to perceived leader effectiveness, and more importantly that prototypicality and self-sacrifice interacted in affecting perceptions of leadership effectiveness. As predicted, the relationship between self-sacrifice and leadership effectiveness was stronger for less prototypical leaders. This interaction effect was replicated in a scenario experiment in which leader prototypicality and leader self-sacrifice were manipulated.

Complementing and extending these results, van Knippenberg and van Knippenberg obtained this leader prototypicality by leader self-sacrifice interaction in a laboratory experiment and showed that it generalized to perceptions of charisma and follower performance. Participants in the experiment were assigned an idea generation task by a (simulated) leader. This leader was presented as either prototypical or non-prototypical via bogus feedback about the position of the leader and the other group members on a dimension that defined the group in the experimental context (brain hemisphere dominance), and as self-sacrificing or non-sacrificing based on whether or not the leader would invest time and energy

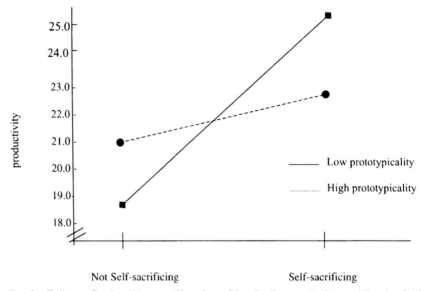

Fig. 5. Follower Productivity as a Function of Leader Prototypicality and Leader Self-Sacrifice, B. van Knippenberg and van Knippenberg (2003).

in the group task at the expense of other, personal, commitments. Figure 5 shows the results for the performance measure. Leader prototypicality and self-sacrifice interacted to affect productivity on the task (number of ideas generated), such that prototypicality attenuated the positive effect of leader self-sacrifice on follower performance.

The role of leader prototypicality proposed by SIMOL is an important extension of theories of charisma. SIMOL has another important implication for the components of charisma proposed in theories of charismatic leadership. Theories of charisma propose that charismatic leadership consists of different components, which are all assumed to contribute to perceptions of charisma and leadership effectiveness (Bass, 1985; Conger & Kanungo, 1987; Shamir et al., 1993). The possibility that the effectiveness of different components is contingent on different circumstances or different processes seems to have been neglected.

Considering the components of charisma proposed in theories of charismatic leadership from the perspective of SIMOL, we note that some components are clearly group-oriented, whereas others are more individualized or interpersonal. On the one hand charismatic leaders are proposed to emphasize collective identity, champion the collective's mission, make self-sacrifices and take great personal risk in pursuit of the collective vision, and foster collective efficacy (Conger & Kanungo, 1987; Shamir et al., 1993; cf. Bass, 1985). On the other hand, charismatic leaders are proposed to show individualized consideration, and coach and develop individual subordinates (Bass, 1985; Bass & Avolio, 1993; Shamir et al., 1993). Accordingly, based on SIMOL we propose that follower identification and social identity salience moderate the effectiveness of the group-oriented versus the interpersonal aspects of charismatic leadership. Group-oriented components of charismatic leadership are more effective under conditions of high identification and social identity salience, whereas interpersonal aspects of charismatic leadership are more effective under conditions of low identification and social identity salience.

A related argument has been proposed by Lord et al. (1999) concerning the effectiveness of transformational versus transactional leadership (i.e. leadership focusing on contingent rewarding and monitoring; Bass, 1985). Lord et al. argue that transactional leadership is more focused on the personal self, whereas transformational leadership is more focused on the collective self, and that, following the same logic as SIMOL, follower self-concept should therefore moderate the effectiveness of these two forms of leadership (also see Platow et al., 2002). This argument aligns well with the current analysis, but in deviation, or extension, of Lord et al.'s (1999) proposition we argue that we should also differentiate between interpersonal aspect and group-oriented aspects of charismatic leadership.

An implication of our argument is that by not recognizing the moderating role of identification/salience, we may underestimate the potential impact of different charismatic leadership behaviors. The context-specific impact of different components of charisma may be greater than the relationships between leader behavior and criteria of leadership effectiveness typically reported in the literature (e.g. Lowe et al., 1996).

SIMOL and Processes Underlying the Effectiveness of Charismatic Leadership
SIMOL and theories of charismatic leadership converge on the processes proposed to underlie leadership effectiveness. Both perspectives allocate a key role to identification/salience, agreeing that leaders may mobilize collective identity to motivate followers (Conger & Kanungo, 1987; Conger, Kanungo & Menon, 2000; De Cremer & van Knippenberg, 2002; Reicher & Hopkins, 2001, in press; Shamir et al., 1993; Shamir, Zakay, Breinin & Popper, 1998). In addition, trust in the leader (Giessner et al., 2003; Pillai et al., 1999; Podsakoff et al., 1990), and follower self-efficacy and collective efficacy (Shamir et al., 1993; Shea & Howell, 1999; van Knippenberg & Ellemers, 2003) have been allocated a role in motivating followers both in the charismatic and the social identity perspective. The operation of one process does not preclude the operation

of the other, and several processes may operate simultaneously to translate leader behavior into follower action. It should be noted, however, that although there is evidence for these different processes mediating leadership effectiveness, no study to date has to our knowledge demonstrated the operation of more than one process simultaneously – which would seem an important challenge for future research.

Even though SIMOL and theories of charismatic leadership seem to agree on the psychological processes underlying charismatic leaders' influence on followers, from SIMOL follows an important qualification. As argued above, some aspects of charismatic leadership have a clear group-oriented focus, whereas others have a more interpersonal focus. The same may be said for the processes underlying the effectiveness of charismatic leadership. Identification, social identity salience, trust in the leader's group-orientedness, and collective efficacy clearly have a group focus. Follower self-efficacy (and self-esteem/self-worth, which Shamir et al., 1993, also propose mediates the effects of charismatic leadership) and interpersonal trust between leader and follower (Podsakoff et al., 1990) are more related to the personal self-concept than to the collective self. In the same way that identification and social identity salience moderate the impact of the group-oriented and interpersonal aspects of charismatic leader behavior, they may moderate the impact of the group-oriented and interpersonal processes translating leader behavior into follower attitudes and actions.

Uncertainty, Crisis, and the Effectiveness of Charismatic Leadership
Crisis is probably the factor that is most cited as conducive to the emergence and effectiveness of charismatic leadership – indeed, even as a precondition for it to occur (e.g. Boal & Bryson, 1988; Conger & Kanungo, 1987; Hunt, Boal & Dodge, 1999; Pillai & Meindl, 1998). Crises, and other ambiguous situations associated with uncertainty (Shamir & Howell, 1999), are proposed to elicit a desire for guidance and leadership that provides potentially charismatic leaders with the opportunity to take charge and realize their charismatic potential. Once the crisis is resolved, followers are supposedly less receptive to charismatic leadership.

This moderating role of crisis is highly consistent with work on uncertainty, social identity, and leadership. A program of research by Hogg and colleagues (for an overview, see Hogg, 2000) has shown that uncertain or stressful situations moti-vate individuals to turn to their group memberships, because group identifications reduce self-conceptual uncertainty. The uncertainty associated with crises may thus lead individuals to identify more with their group and look to the group for guidance and leadership (cf. the sense-maker role proposed by Cohen & March, 1974). This provides the opportunity for prototypical, charismatic leaders to emerge. This analysis is supported in a study by D. van Knippenberg et al. (2000),

Van Knippenberg et al. argued that task groups would be more in need of leadership when their task was ambiguous rather than clear-cut, and that therefore prototypical group members would be more likely to emerge as leaders under uncertainty. Results of two experiments on emergent leadership behavior of prototypical and non-prototypical group members (manipulated by bogus feedback about participants' own and fellow group members' score on a group defining trait) corroborated this proposition.

SIMOL also suggests a second factor that is likely to contribute to crisis' moderating influence: Crisis raises the need, and thus provides the opportunity, for group-oriented behavior, which positions leaders to build their basis of leadership effectiveness. As a case in point, take the example of Lee Iaccoca's self-sacrifice mentioned earlier. The crisis at Chrysler set the stage for the (presumed) effectiveness of this act of leadership – indeed, it would have made little sense if there would not have been a crisis.

Leading Change: Charismatic Leaders as Agents of Change
Analyses of charismatic leadership emphasize the change-orientedness of charismatic leaders. A change-oriented vision for the group or organization is often seen as a key component of charismatic leadership, and charismatic leaders are considered to be more effective change agents than non-charismatic leaders (e.g. Bass, 1998; Conger & Kanungo, 1998; Howell & Higgins, 1990). The social identity analysis too suggests that prototypical, charismatic leaders are particularly effective as agents of change.

The organizational change literature cites resistance to change as one of the principle obstacles to effective change (e.g. Conner, 1995). An analysis of the social identity implications of organizational change processes (Rousseau, 1998) identifies social identity concerns as a significant source of resistance to change. Social identity analyses of mergers and acquisitions have similarly identified social identity processes as a major obstacle to successful merging (e.g. Blake & Mouton, 1985; Terry, Carey & Callan, 2001; van Leeuwen & van Knippenberg, 2003). Major organizational changes, such as mergers and acquisitions, may have a substantial impact on organizational identity and thus on employees' self-definitions as members of the organization. People may strongly resist such changes. Building on work by Rousseau (1998), van Knippenberg and associates (D. van Knippenberg et al., 2002; D. van Knippenberg & van Leeuwen, 2001; van Leeuwen, van Knippenberg & Ellemers, 2003) propose that resistance to change is contingent on a *sense of continuity of identity* – a sense that defining features of the group's identity are preserved. As long as group members feel that, despite the changes, it is still "their group," they may be quite accepting of changes, even substantial ones.

A key task, then, for leadership of change would seem to address these identity concerns, and to ensure such a sense of continuity. Put differently, to be effective agents of change, leaders also need to be *agents of continuity*. Prototypical, charismatic leaders may be particularly good at combining the role of agent of change and agent of continuity. Because prototypical leaders represent the collective identity, changes promoted by prototypical leaders are more likely to be viewed as identity-consistent than the same changes promoted by less prototypical leaders. Accordingly, prototypical, charismatic leaders should be more able to overcome resistance to change and to mobilize followers in pursuit of a change-oriented vision than less prototypical, charismatic leaders. (Note that this proposition aligns well with Shamir et al.'s (1993) suggestion that individuals are motivated by a desire for a consistent self-image, and that charismatic leadership may address this desire.)

First evidence that leader prototypicality may be conducive to overcoming resistance to change is provided in one of the surveys conducted by B. van Knippenberg and van Knippenberg (2003). This survey was conducted in the context of organizational change and also assessed the relationship of leader prototypicality and leader self-sacrifice with willingness to change. As predicted, leader prototypicality and leader self-sacrifice both had a positive relationship with willingness to change. (Moreover prototypicality and self-sacrifice interacted, such that the relationship between self-sacrifice and willingness to change was weaker for more prototypical leaders.)

The suggestion that prototypicality positions a leader to be an effective agent of change by also being an agent of continuity also points to the problems faced by "outgroup leaders" trying to engender change. To lead changes in organizations (boards of) organizations sometimes bring in outside management. Similarly, acquiring organizations may replace the management of the acquired organization by people from the acquiring organization. Changes introduced by such outgroup leaders may be particularly vulnerable to the perception that they introduce discontinuity of identity, and as a result may be particular likely to elicit resistance and lowered identification.

Reicher and Hopkins' (2001, in press) analysis of political leaders as "entrepreneurs of identity" suggests that effective change agents do not just rely on their image of prototypicality and/or group-orientedness to engender change. They may also suggest that the change they envision is highly consistent with the collective identity. Indeed, leaders may in fact suggest that the change they envision is more consistent with the group's identity than the current situation. Steve Jobs' return to Apple seems a good example of the latter. As co-founder of Apple, Jobs had worked on creating an identity for the company that flagged its unconventional and creative nature. After Jobs left, this distinct identity gradually faded. When

Jobs was brought back to reinvigorate Apple after being away from the company for several years, his (highly effective) strategy was to advocate a return to Apple's roots, to return to being the unconventional and creative company it used to be.

Perhaps counter-intuitively, this then would suggest that an important aspect of a charismatic vision of change is a sense of continuity of, or even a return to core aspects of the collective identity, especially when advocating radical change. Indeed, the larger the change envisioned, the more important it would seem to complement the vision of change with a vision of continuity of identity: "we will change, but we will still be us."

Summary

At the core of the Social Identity Approach lies the proposition that social identification and social identity salience underlie the influence of group membership on perceptions, beliefs, attitudes, and behavior. Identification/salience plays a key role in SIMOL too. Not surprisingly, then, one of the core building blocks for the integration of SIMOL with leadership categorization theories, LMX theory, and theories of charismatic leadership is the moderating role of identification/salience. Identification/salience affects the importance of leader stereotypes versus group prototypes as determinants of leadership perceptions, affects the impact of group-oriented versus interpersonal leadership as described in LMX theory, and affects the effectiveness of the group-oriented versus interpersonal aspects of charismatic leadership. In addition, SIMOL allows us to refine the analysis of charismatic leadership by introducing: (a) leader prototypicality as a component of charisma; (b) identification/salience as a moderator of not only the effectiveness of different aspects of charismatic leadership but also of different underlying processes; and (c) the ability to ensure a sense of continuity of identity as a key aspect of leadership effectiveness in dealing with resistance to change.

TOWARDS AN INTEGRATIVE THEORY OF LEADERSHIP EFFECTIVENESS

We have seen how SIMOL can extend three influential and at first sight quite different perspectives on leadership effectiveness in organizations (leadership categorization theories, LMX theory, and theories of charismatic leadership). The social identity model of organizational leadership is not only important in integrating and extending these perspectives on leadership effectiveness, it also provides a viable framework to integrate developments in leadership research.

Indeed, one of the important contributions SIMOL makes to the study of organizational leadership is that it provides a vehicle for the integration of different
perspectives on leadership effectiveness into a unified theoretical framework.

SIMOL advances self-conception and social identity processes as core moderators and mediators of leadership effectiveness, and suggests that other perspectives on leadership effectiveness may be understood, and integrated with SIMOL in
terms of the implied relationships with follower self-concept. This basic notion lies
at the core of the integration presented in the previous section, and we propose that
it may also lie at the core of the integration of other approaches to leadership into
a more unified framework for understanding leadership effectiveness. To illustrate
this point, in the following we focus on two developments that are as yet not
center-stage in leadership research, but which we expect to become increasingly
important in years to come: The study of leader fairness, and the study of leadership
and emotions. The ultimate aim of this discussion is not just to outline how SIMOL
may be developed to encompass leader fairness and emotions, but more generally
to demonstrate the integrative potential and wide applicability of the model.

Leader Fairness

Although there is a rich tradition in organizational justice research (e.g. Greenberg,
1990; Konovsky, 2000), fairness has only received modest attention as an aspect
of leadership. And yet, a core function of leaders is to carry the responsibility
for decisions about outcomes that are important to followers (e.g. promotions,
performance appraisals, allocation of duties, etc.). Not surprisingly, followers
may be concerned about how fair the leader is in making these decisions. These
concerns may relate to the perceived fairness of the outcomes of leaders' decisions
(distributive fairness) as well as the perceived fairness of the procedures used
by the leader to arrive at these decisions (procedural fairness; Thibaut & Walker,
1975). Both distributive and procedural fairness affect reactions to decisions, and
to the authorities making these decisions (Brockner & Wiesenfeld, 1996; Lind &
Tyler, 1988; Tyler & Lind, 1992). It thus seems very likely that leaders' distributive
and procedural fairness affect responses to leadership, and therefore leadership
effectiveness.

Although the relationship with leadership has always been implicitly present
in justice research (cf. Tyler, 1997; Tyler & Lind, 1992), leadership research has
only relatively recently started to explicate the role of leader fairness (e.g. De
Cremer, in press; Tyler, in press). De Cremer and van Knippenberg (2003), for
instance, show that group member cooperation in a mixed-motive situation is
affected by the procedural fairness of the leader (whether or not the leader gave

group members voice in decisions about personal outcomes), especially when the outcomes group members receive are relatively unfavorable.

Of particular relevance to our social identity analysis, justice research suggest that social identity processes play an important role in the effects of leader fairness on followers. Tyler (1999) argues that procedural justice fulfills a social identity function, because fair procedures convey a favorable social evaluation of followers as group members (Koper, van Knippenberg, Bouhuijs, Vermunt & Wilke, 1993). Accordingly, the respect for group members conveyed by procedural fairness may build member identification and thus feed into cooperative behavior (De Cremer & van Knippenberg, 2002; Tyler & Blader, 2000).

Justice research also suggests that social identity processes may moderate responses to procedural and distributive fairness. People who identify strongly with the group care more about the esteem they are held in by the group than people who identify less strongly with the group, and therefore they are more concerned about procedural fairness (Tyler & Degoey, 1995; also see Brockner, Chen, Mannix, Leung & Skarlicki, 2000). People that identify strongly with the group may be expected to value distributive fairness relatively less, because instrumental, outcome-oriented considerations become less important relative to relational considerations as people identify more with the group (Tyler, 1997; cf. Vermunt, van Knippenberg, van Knippenberg & Blaauw, 2001). People also value more highly the esteem in which they are held by ingroup than outgroup leaders. Therefore they respond more strongly to the procedural fairness of ingroup than outgroup leaders (Tyler, Lind, Ohbuchi, Sugawara & Huo, 1997).

In perfect alignment with SIMOL, then, research in social and organizational justice suggests that leader procedural fairness as compared with leader distributive fairness becomes more important as a determinant of leadership effectiveness as group members define the self more in collective terms. Moreover, leader procedural fairness may affect follower identification and thus help mobilize followers for collective endeavors. The role of leader fairness in leadership effectiveness may thus fruitfully be integrated with, and extend, the social identity analysis of leadership effectiveness.

Emotions and Leadership Effectiveness

Until recently, research in organizational behavior paid little attention to the role of affect and emotions (Brief & Weiss, 2002; Weiss & Cropanzano, 1996). Yet, emotions are a powerful force driving human behavior, and there is good evidence that affective reactions and emotions may influence all social interactions (e.g. Forgas, Bower & Krans, 1984; George, 1991), including those between leaders and followers (Brief & Weiss, 2002; George, 2000). Some analyses suggest that leadership effectiveness may in part actually derive from leaders' ability to elicit emotional responses from their subordinates (Conger & Kanungo, 1998; House, Spangler & Woycke, 1991). Until recently, however, there have been few empirical studies of the role of emotions in leadership effectiveness. This has started to change (e.g. Humphrey, 2002), but leadership research is still struggling to make sense of the role of emotions. We propose that SIMOL may provide a useful framework to integrate the role of emotions with other approaches to leadership.

Emotions fulfill an important self-regulatory function, and may serve as internal signals for "motive-readiness" to engender action (e.g. Lang, 1995). Accordingly, leadership effectiveness may be influenced by the leader's ability to elicit follower emotions that motivate pro-organizational attitudes and behavior. A first proposition that follows from SIMOL is that it is important from the perspective of eliciting pro-organizational behavior that emotions are group-oriented emotions, that is, emotions that are associated with, and favoring, the group (e.g. happiness for group success, anger at threats to the group). Emotions may engender motive-readiness, but for this motive-readiness to translate into group-oriented behavior it is important that the emotions are group-oriented. From the perspective of an analysis of leadership effectiveness, then, the key question is how leaders elicit group-oriented emotions.

The most direct way probably is through *emotional contagion* (Hatfield, Cacioppo & Rapson, 1994). Leaders may publicly display group-oriented emotions that are subsequently adopted by their subordinates. Corroborating this proposition, analyses of charismatic leadership suggest that charismatic leaders may use their own emotions to arouse similar feelings in their followers (Conger & Kanungo, 1998; House et al., 1991). The social identity analysis would suggest that for a leader's emotions to translate into follower emotions it is important that leader and followers share a group membership with which followers identify. Identification allows individuals to experience others' internal states, such as feelings, as their own (e.g. Mackie, Devos & Smith, 2000; Norton, Monin, Cooper & Hogg, in press), and for followers to experience leader emotions as self-relevant it would seem important that the leader is linked to followers' self-definition. Leaders may also find it easier to affect followers' emotion through their own emotional displays in emotionally ambiguous situations. As argued above, ambiguous or stressful situations may raise the need for leadership, and cause group members to turn to the group, and to group prototypical members for guidance (D. van Knippenberg et al., 2000; see Hogg, 2000). This may include "emotional guidance," modeling the appropriate emotional response to the situation (Pescosolido, 2002).

Leaders' ability to elicit emotions is of course not limited to display of own emotions. Analyses of charismatic leadership for instance suggest that leaders may also elicit follower emotions through dramatic actions like making personal sacrifices or running personal risk (e.g. Conger & Kanungo, 1998). In these instances too SIMOL would suggest that such factors as follower identification and uncertainty are conducive to translating leader behavior into follower emotion.

CONCLUSION

The starting point of our analysis of leadership effectiveness was the observation that leadership research has largely ignored the implications of the fact that leaders do not only lead groups of people, but also are members of these groups, and that leadership processes are therefore enacted in the context of a shared group membership. To address this issue, we propose a theoretical framework to analyze leadership effectiveness in organizations from this leaders-as-group-members perspective, the Social Identity Model of Organizational Leadership (SIMOL). SIMOL not only explicates the effects of leaders' characteristics as a group member on leadership effectiveness, but it may also be fruitfully integrated with other perspectives on leadership effectiveness, and provides important qualifications and extensions of these perspectives.

The main propositions of the model are summarized in Fig. 6. Follower identification and social identity salience moderate the effects on leadership effectiveness of on the one hand leader prototypicality and group-oriented aspects of leadership, and on the other hand more personalized and interpersonal aspects of leadership. Collective identity processes mediate the effects of leader prototypicality and group-oriented aspects of leadership – and set the stage for future responses to leadership – while processes related to the personal self-concept and interpersonal relations mediate the effects of personalized and interpersonal aspects of leadership.

SIMOL also provides the building blocks for a broader conceptual framework that integrates different perspectives into a more unified theory of leadership effectiveness. One of the main challenges for the future of leadership research in organizational behavior, as we see it, is thus to not only develop SIMOL as a theory of leadership effectiveness in organizations, but also to develop the integration of SIMOL and other perspectives on leadership effectiveness, with the ultimate aim to develop a broad-ranging and integrative theoretical framework for understanding leadership effectiveness. Core to this integrative framework as we see it is an understanding of leadership effectiveness in terms of the moderating and mediating role of follower self-conceptions.

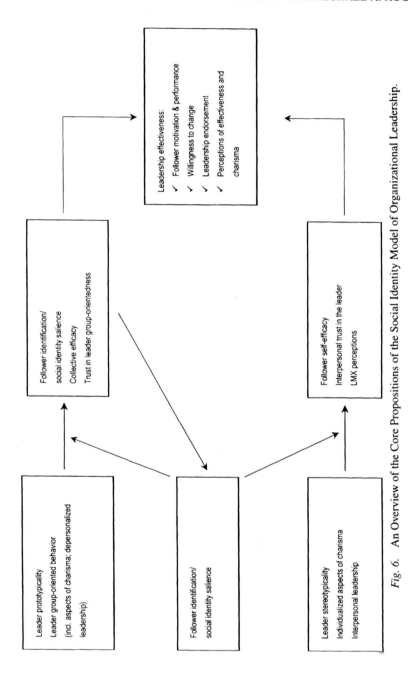

Fig. 6. An Overview of the Core Propositions of the Social Identity Model of Organizational Leadership.

ACKNOWLEDGMENT

We thank Barbara van Knippenberg for her valuable comments on earlier drafts of this manuscript.

REFERENCES

Abrams, D., Ando, K., & Hinkle, S. (1998). Psychological attachment to the group: Cross-cultural differences in organizational identification and subjective norms as predictors of workers' turnover intentions. *Personality and Social Psychology Bulletin, 24*, 1027–1039.

Abrams, D., & Hogg, M. A. (1990). Social identification, self-categorization and social influence. *European Review of Social Psychology, 1*, 195–228.

Abrams, D., & Hogg, M. A. (2001). Collective identity: Group membership and self-conception. In: M. A. Hogg & R. S. Tindale (Eds), *Blackwell Handbook of Social Psychology: Group Processes* (pp. 425–460). Oxford, UK: Blackwell.

Ashforth, B. E., & Mael, F. (1989). Social identity theory and the organization. *Academy of Management Review, 14*, 20–39.

Bandura, A. (1986). *Social foundations of thought and action: A social cognitive theory.* Englewood Cliffs, NJ: Prentice-Hall.

Bass, B. M. (1985). *Leadership and performance beyond expectations.* New York: Free Press.

Bass, B. M. (1990). *Bass and Stogdill's handbook of leadership: Theory, research and managerial applications.* New York: Free Press.

Bass, B. M. (1998). *Transformational leadership: Industrial, military, and educational impact.* Mahwah, NJ: Erlbaum.

Bass, B. M., & Avolio, B. J. (1993). Transformational leadership: A response to critiques. In: M. M. Chemers & R. A. Ayman (Eds), *Leadership Theory and Research: Perspectives and Directions* (pp. 49–80). London: Academic Press.

Bennis, W., & Nanus, B. (1985). *Leaders: The strategies for taking charge.* New York: Harper & Row.

Berger, J., Wagner, D., & Zelditch, M. (1985). Expectation states theory: Review and assessment. In: J. Berger & M. Zelditch (Eds), *Status, Rewards, and Influence* (pp. 1–72). San Francisco: Jossey-Bass.

Berscheid, E., & Reis, H. T. (1998). Attraction and close relationships. In: D. T. Gilbert, S. T. Fiske & G. Lindzey (Eds), *The Handbook of Social Psychology* (4th ed., Vol. 2, pp. 193–281). New York: McGraw-Hill.

Blake, R. R., & Mouton, J. S. (1985). How to achieve integration on the human side of the merger. *Organizational Dynamics, 13*, 41–56.

Boal, K. B., & Bryson, J. M. (1988). Charismatic leadership: A phenomenological and structural approach. In: J. G. Hunt, B. R. Baliga, H. P. Dachler & C. A. Schriesheim (Eds), *Emerging Leadership Vistas* (pp. 5–28). Lexington, MA: Lexington Books.

Brewer, M. B. (1979). Ingroup bias in the minimal intergroup situations: A cognitive-motivational analysis. *Psychological Bulletin, 86*, 307–324.

Brewer, M. B. (1991). The social self: On being the same and different at the same time. *Personality and Social Psychology Bulletin, 17*, 475–482.

Brewer, M. B. (2001). The many faces of social identity: Implications for political psychology. *Political Psychology, 22*, 115–125.

Brewer, M. B., & Gardner, W. (1996). Who is this "we"? Levels of collective identity and self repre-
    sentations. *Journal of Personality and Social Psychology*, *71*, 83–93.

Brief, A. P., Dietz, J., Cohen, R. R., Pugh, S. D., & Vaslow, J. B. (2000). Just doing business: Modern
    racism and obedience to authority as explanations for employment discrimination. *Organiza-
    tional Behavior and Human Decision Processes*, *81*, 72–97.

Brief, A. P., & Weiss, H. M. (2002). Organizational behavior: Affect in the workplace. *Annual Review
    of Psychology*, *53*, 279–307.

Brockner, J., Chen, Y.-R., Mannix, E. A., Leung, K., & Skarlicki, D. P. (2000). Culture and procedural
    fairness: When the effects of what you do depend on how you do it. *Administrative Science
    Quarterly*, *45*, 1238–1259.

Brockner, J., & Wiesenfeld, B. M. (1996). An integrative framework for explaning reactions to deci-
    sions: The interactive effects of outcomes and procedures. *Psycholgical Bulletin*, *120*, 189–208.

Burns, J. M. (1978). *Leadership*. New York: Harper & Row.

Cejka, M. A., & Eagly, A. H. (1999). Gender-stereotypic images of occupations correspond to the sex
    segregation of employment. *Personality and Social Psychology Bulletin*, *25*, 413–423.

Chemers, M. M. (2001). Leadership effectiveness: An integrative review. In: M. A. Hogg & R. S.
    Tindale (Eds), *Blackwell Handbook of Social Psychology: Group Processes* (pp. 376–399).
    Oxford, UK: Blackwell.

Choi, Y., & Mai-Dalton, R. R. (1998). On the leadership function of self-sacrifice. *Leadership Quarterly*,
    9, 475–501.

Choi, Y., & Mai-Dalton, R. R. (1999). The model of followers' responses to self-sacrificial leadership:
    An empirical test. *Leadership Quarterly*, *10*, 397–421.

Cohen, M. D., & March, J. G. (1974). *Leadership and ambiguity*. New York: McGraw-Hill.

Conger, J. A., & Kanungo, R. N. (1987). Towards a behavioral theory of charismatic leadership in
    organizational settings. *Academy of Management Review*, *12*, 637–647.

Conger, J. A., & Kanungo, R. N. (1998). *Charismatic leadership in organizations*. Thousand Oaks,
    CA: Sage.

Conger, J. A., Kanungo, R. N., & Menon, S. T. (2000). Charismatic leadership and follower effects.
    Journal of Organizational Behavior, *21*, 747–767.

Conner, D. R. (1995). *Managing at the speed of change: How resilient managers succeed and prosper
    where others fail*. New York: Villard Books.

De Cremer, D. (2002). Charismatic leadership and cooperation in social dilemmas: A matter of trans-
    forming motives? *Journal of Applied Social Psychology*, *32*, 997–1016.

De Cremer, D. (in press). A relational perspective on leadership and cooperation: Why it matters to
    care and be fair. In: D. van Knippenberg & M. A. Hogg (Eds), *Leadership and Power: Identity
    Processes in Groups and Organizations*. London: Sage.

De Cremer, D., & van Knippenberg, D. (2002). How do leaders promote cooperation? The effects of
    charisma and procedural fairness. *Journal of Applied Psychology*, *87*, 858–866.

De Cremer, D., & van Knippenberg, D. (2003). Cooperation with leaders in social dilemmas: On the
    effects of procedural fairness and outcome favorability in structural cooperation. *Organizational
    Behavior and Human Decision Processes*, *91*, 1–11.

De Cremer, D., & Van Vugt, M. (2002). Intergroup and intragroup aspects of leadership in social
    dilemmas: A relational model of cooperation. *Journal of Experimental Social Psychology*, *38*,
    126–136.

Dirks, K. T., & Ferrin, D. L. (2002). Trust in leadership: Meta-analytic findings and implications for
    research and practice. *Journal of Applied Psychology*, *87*, 611–628.

Duck, J. M., & Fielding, K. S. (1999). Leaders and sub-groups: One of us or one of them? *Group
    Processes and Intergroup Relations*, *2*, 203–230.

Dutton, J. E., Dukerich, J. M., & Harquail, C. V. (1994). Organizational images and member identification. *Administrative Science Quarterly, 39*, 239–263.

Eagly, A. H. (in press). Few women at the top: How role incongruity produces prejudice and the glass ceiling. In: D. van Knippenberg & M. A. Hogg (Eds), *Leadership and Power: Identity Processes in Groups and Organizations*. London: Sage.

Eagly, A. H., & Karau, S. J. (2002). Role congruity theory of prejudice toward female leaders. *Psychological Review, 109*, 573–598.

Eagly, A. H., Karau, S. J., & Makhijani, M. G. (1995). Gender and the effectiveness of leaders: A meta-analysis. *Psychological Bulletin, 117*, 125–145.

Ellemers, N. (1993). The influence of socio-structural variables on identity enhancement strategies. *European Review of Social Psychology, 4*, 27–57.

Elsbach, K. D. (1999). An expanded model of organizational identification. In: R. I. Sutton & B. M. Staw (Eds), *Research in Organizational Behavior* (Vol. 21, pp. 163–200). Greenwich, CN: JAI Press.

Elsbach, K. D., & Kramer, R. M. (1996). Members' responses to organizational identity threats: Encountering and countering the business week rankings. *Administrative Science Quarterly, 41*, 442–476.

Ely, R. J. (1994). The effects of organizational demographics and social identity on relationships among professional women. *Administrative Science Quarterly, 39*, 203–238.

Erber, R., & Fiske, S. T. (1984). Outcome dependency and attention to inconsistent information. *Journal of Personality and Social Psychology, 47*, 709–726.

Festinger, L. (1954). A theory of social comparison processes. *Human Relations, 7*, 117–140.

Fielding, K. S., & Hogg, M. A. (1997). Social identity, self-categorization, and leadership: A field study of small interactive groups. *Group Dynamics: Theory, Research and Practice, 1*, 39–51.

Forgas, J. P., Bower, G. H., & Krantz, S. E. (1984). The influence of mood on perceptions of social interactions. *Journal of Experimental Social Psychology, 20*, 497–513.

French, J. R. P., & Raven, B. H. (1959). The bases of social power. In: D. Cartwright (Ed.), *Studies in Social Power* (pp. 150–167). Ann Arbor, MI: Institute of Social Research.

George, J. M. (1991). Personality, affect, and behavior in groups. *Journal of Applied Psychology, 75*, 107–116.

George, J. M. (2000). Emotions and leadership: The role of emotional intelligence. *Human Relations, 53*, 1027–1055.

Gerstner, C. R., & Day, D. V. (1997). Meta-analytic review of leader-member exchange theory: Correlates and construct issues. *Journal of Applied Psychology, 82*, 827–844.

Giessner, S., Sleebos, E., & van Knippenberg, D. (2003, June). *License to fail?: Leader prototypicality, leader performance, and leadership endorsement.* Paper presented at the EAESP Small Group Meeting on New Directions in Leadership Research, Amsterdam, The Netherlands.

Gilbert, D. T., & Malone, P. S. (1995). The correspondence bias. *Psychological Bulletin, 117*, 21–38.

Glick, P., & Fiske, S. T. (1996). The Ambivalent Sexism Inventory: Differentiating hostile and benevolent sexism. *Journal of Personality and Social Psychology, 70*, 491–512.

Graen, G. B., & Scandura, T. (1987). Toward a psychology of dyadic organizing. In: B. M. Staw & L. L. Cummings (Eds), *Research in Organizational Behavior* (Vol. 9, pp. 175–208). Greenwich, CT: JAI press.

Graen, G. B., & Uhl-Bien, M. (1995). Relationship-based approach to leadership: Development of leader-member exchange (LMX) theory of leadership over 25 years: Applying a multi-level multi-domain approach. *Leadership Quarterly, 6*, 219–247.

Greenberg, J. (1990). Organizational justice: Yesterday, today, and tomorrow. *Journal of Management, 16*, 399–432.

Hains, S. C., Hogg, M. A., & Duck, J. M. (1997). Self-categorization and leadership: Effects of group prototypicality and leader stereotypicality. *Personality and Social Psychology Bulletin, 23*, 1087–1100.

Hall, R. J., Workman, W. J., & Marchiori, C. A. (1998). Sex, task, and behavioral flexibility effects on leadership perceptions. *Organizational Behavior and Human Decision Processes, 74*, 1–32.

Hamilton, D. L., & Sherman, S. J. (1996). Perceiving persons and groups. *Psychological Review, 103*, 336–355.

Haslam, S. A. (2001). *Psychology in organisations: The social identity approach.* London: Sage.

Haslam, S. A., & Platow, M. J. (2001a). Your wish is our command: The role of shared social identity in translating a leader's vision into followers' action. In: M. A. Hogg & D. J. Terry (Eds), *Social Identity Processes in Organizational Contexts* (pp. 213–228). Philadelphia, PA: Psychology Press.

Haslam, S. A., & Platow, M. J. (2001b). The link between leadership and followership: How affirming social identity translates vision into action. *Personality and Social Psychology Bulletin, 27*, 1469–1479.

Haslam, S. A., van Knippenberg, D., Platow, M., & Ellemers, N. (Eds) (2003). *Social identity at work: Developing theory for organizational practice.* Philadelphia, PA: Psychology Press.

Hatfield, E., Cacioppo, J. T., & Rapson, R. L. (1994). *Emotional contagion.* New York, NY: Cambridge University Press.

Hennessy, J., & West, M. A. (1999). Intergroup behavior in organizations: A field study of social identity theory. *Small Group Research, 30*, 361–382.

Hogg, M. A. (1992). *The social psychology of group cohesiveness: From attraction to social identity.* New York: New York University Press.

Hogg, M. A. (1993). Group cohesiveness: A critical review and some new directions. *European Review of Social Psychology, 4*, 85–111.

Hogg, M. A. (2000). Subjective uncertainty reduction through self-categorization: A motivational theory of social identity processes. *European Review of Social Psychology, 11*, 223–255.

Hogg, M. A. (2001a). A social identity theory of leadership. *Personality and Social Psychology Review, 5*, 184–200.

Hogg, M. A. (2001b). From prototypicality to power: A social identity analysis of leadership. In: S. R. Thye, E. J. Lawler, M. W. Macy & H. A. Walker (Eds), *Advances in Group Processes* (Vol. 18, pp. 1–30). Oxford, UK: Elsevier.

Hogg, M. A. (2001c). Social categorization, depersonalization, and group behavior. In: M. A. Hogg & R. S. Tindale (Eds), *Blackwell Handbook of Social Psychology: Group Processes* (pp. 56–85). Oxford, UK: Blackwell.

Hogg, M. A. (2001d). Self-categorization and subjective uncertainty resolution: Cognitive and motivational facets of social identity and group membership. In: J. P. Forgas, K. D. Williams & L. Wheeler (Eds), *The Social Mind: Cognitive and Motivational Aspects of Interpersonal Behavior* (pp. 323–349). New York: Cambridge University Press.

Hogg, M. A. (2003). Social identity. In: M. R. Leary & J. P. Tangney (Eds), *Handbook of Self and Identity* (pp. 462–479). New York: Guilford.

Hogg, M. A., & Abrams, D. (1988). *Social identifications: A social psychology of intergroup relations and group processes.* London: Routledge.

Hogg, M. A., Cooper-Shaw, L., & Holzworth, D. W. (1993). Group prototypicality and depersonalized attraction in small interactive groups. *Personality and Social Psychology Bulletin, 19*, 452–465.

Hogg, M. A., Fielding, K. S., & Darley, J. (in press). Deviance and marginalization. In: D. Abrams, J. Marqués & M. A. Hogg (Eds), *The Social Psychology of Inclusion and Exclusion.* Philadelphia, PA: Psychology Press.

Hogg, M. A., Fielding, K. S., Johnson, D., Masser, B., Russell, E., & Svensson, A. (2003). *Demographic category membership and leadership in small groups: A social identity analysis.* University of Queensland, Manuscript submitted for publication.

Hogg, M. A., Hains, S. C., & Mason, I. (1998). Identification and leadership in small groups: Salience, frame of reference, and leader stereotypicality effects on leader evaluations. *Journal of Personality and Social Psychology, 75,* 1248–1263.

Hogg, M. A., & Hornsey, M. J. (in press). Self-concept threat and differentiation within groups. In: R. J. Crisp & M. Hewstone (Eds), *Multiple Social Categorization: Processes, Models, and Applications.* Philadelphia, PA: Psychology Press.

Hogg, M. A., & Martin, R. (2003). Social identity analysis of leader-member relations: Reconciling self-categorization and leader-member exchange theories of leadership. In: S. A. Haslam, D. van Knippenberg, M. Platow & N. Ellemers (Eds), *Social Identity at Work: Developing Theory for Organizational Practice* (pp. 139–154). New York and Hove: Psychology Press.

Hogg, M. A., Martin, R., Epitropaki, O., Mankad, A., Svensson, A., & Weeden, K. (2003). *Effective leadership in salient groups: Revisiting leader-member exchange theory from the perspective of the social identity theory of leadership.* Manuscript submitted for publication: University of Queensland.

Hogg, M. A., Martin, R., & Weeden, K. (in press). Leader-member relations and social identity. In: D. van Knippenberg & M. A. Hogg (Eds), *Leadership and Power: Identity Processes in Groups and Organizations.* London: Sage.

Hogg, M. A., & Reid, S. A. (2001). Social identity, leadership, and power. In: A. Y. Lee-Chai & J. A. Bargh (Eds), *The Use and Abuse of Power: Multiple Perspectives on the Causes of Corruption* (pp. 159–180). Philadelphia, PA: Psychology Press.

Hogg, M. A., & Terry, D. J. (2000). Social identity and self-categorization processes in organizational contexts. *Academy of Management Review, 25,* 121–140.

Hogg, M. A., & Terry, D. J. (Eds) (2001). *Social identity processes in organizational contexts.* Philadelphia, PA: Psychology Press.

Hogg, M. A., Turner, J. C., & Davidson, B. (1990). Polarized norms and social frames of reference: A test of the self-categorization theory of group polarization. *Basic and Applied Social Psychology, 11,* 77–100.

Hogg, M. A., & van Knippenberg, D. (2003). Social identity and leadership processes in groups. In: M. P. Zanna (Ed.), *Advances in Experimental Social Psychology* (Vol. 35, pp. 1–52). San Diego, CA: Academic Press.

Hogg, M. A., & Williams, K. D. (2000). From I to we: Social identity and the collective self. *Group Dynamics: Theory, Research, and Practice, 4,* 81–97.

Hollander, E. P. (1958). Conformity, status, and idiosyncrasy credit. *Psychological Review, 65,* 117–127.

Hollander, E. P., & Offerman, L. R. (1990). Power and leadership in organizations. *American Psychologist, 45,* 179–189.

House, R. J. (1977). A 1976 theory of charismatic leadership. In: J. G. Hunt & L. L. Larson (Eds), *Leadership: The Cutting Edge* (pp. 189–207). Carbondale, IL: Southern Illinois University Press.

House, R. J. (1995). Leadership in the twenty-first century: a speculative inquiry. In: A. Howard (Ed.), *The Changing Nature of Work* (pp. 411–450). San Fransisco, CA: Jossey-Bass.

House, R. J., & Shamir, B. (1993). Towards the integration of transformational, charismatic, and visionary theories. In: M. M. Chemers & R. Ayman (Eds), *Leadership Theory and Research: Perspectives and Directions.* San Diego, CA: Academic Press.

House, R. J., Spangler, W. D., & Woycke, J. (1991). Personality and charisma in the U.S. presidency: A psychological theory of leadership effectiveness. *Administrative Science Quarterly, 36,* 364–396.

Howell, J. M., & Higgins, C. A. (1990). Champions of technological innovation. *Administrative Science Quarterly, 35,* 317–341.

Humphrey, R. H. (2002). The many faces of emotional leadership. *Leadership Quarterly, 13,* 493–504.

Hunt, J. G. (1999). Transformational/charismatic leadership's transformation of the field: An historical essay. *Leadership Quarterly, 10,* 129–144.

Hunt, J. G., Boal, K. B., & Dodge, G. E. (1999). The effects of visionary and crisis-responsive charisma on followers: An experimental examination of two kinds of charismatic leadership. *Leadership Quarterly, 10,* 423–448.

James, K., & Greenberg, J. (1989). In-group salience, intergroup comparison, and individual performance and self-esteem. *Personality and Social Psychology Bulletin, 15,* 604–616.

Keller, T., & Dansereau, F. (2000). The effects of adding items to scales: An illustrative case of LMX. *Organizational Research Methods, 4,* 131–143.

Konovsky, M. A. (2000). Understanding procedural justice and its impact on business organizations. *Journal of Management, 26,* 489–511.

Koper, G., van Knippenberg, D., Bouhuijs, F., Vermunt, R., & Wilke, H. (1993). Procedural fairness and self-esteem. *European Journal of Social Psychology, 23,* 313–325.

Kramer, R. M. (1991). Intergroup relations and organizational dilemmas: The role of categorization processes. In: B. M. Staw & L. L. Cummings (Eds), *Research in Organizational Behavior* (Vol. 13, pp. 191–228). Greenwich, CN: JAI Press.

Kramer, R. M. (1999). Trust and distrust in organizations: Emerging perspectives, enduring questions. *Annual Review of Psychology, 50,* 569–598.

Kramer, R. M. (in press). The imperative of identity: The role of identity in leader judgment and decision making. In: D. van Knippenberg & M. A. Hogg (Eds), *Leadership and Power: Identity Processes in Groups and Organizations.* London: Sage.

Lang, P. J. (1995). The emotion probe: Studies of motivation and attention. *American Psychologist, 50,* 372–385.

Lind, E. A., & Tyler, T. R. (1988). *The social psychology of procedral justice.* New York: Plenum.

Lord, R. G. (1977). Functional leadership behavior: Measurement and relation to social power and leadership perceptions. *Administrative Science Quarterly, 22,* 114–133.

Lord, R. G., & Brown, D. J. (2001). Leadership, values, and subordinate self-concepts. *Leadership Quarterly, 12,* 133–152.

Lord, R. G., Brown, D. J., & Freiberg, S. J. (1999). Understanding the dynamics of leadership: The role of follower self-concepts in the leader/follower relationship. *Organizational Behavior and Human Decision Processes, 78,* 1–37.

Lord, R. G., Brown, D. J., Harvey, J. L., & Hall, R. J. (2001). Contextual constraints on prototype generation and their multilevel consequences for leadership perceptions. *Leadership Quarterly, 12,* 311–338.

Lord, R. G., Foti, R. J., & DeVader, C. L. (1984). A test of leadership categorization theory: Internal structure, information processing, and leadership perceptions. *Organizational Behavior and Human Performance, 34,* 343–378.

Lord, R., & Hall, R. (in press). Identity, leadership categorization, and leadership schema. In: D. van Knippenberg & M. A. Hogg (Eds), *Leadership and Power: Identity Processes in Groups and Organizations.* London: Sage.

Lord, R. G., & Maher, K. J. (1991). *Leadership and information processing: Linking perceptions and performance*. Boston, MA: Unwin Hyman.

Lowe, K. B., Kroeck, K. G., & Sivasubramaniam, N. (1996). Effectiveness correlates of transformational and transactional leadership: A meta-analytic review of the MLQ literature. *Leadership Quarterly, 7*, 385–425.

Mackie, D. M., Devos, T., & Smith, E. R. (2000). Intergroup emotions: Explaining offensive action tendencies in an intergroup context. *Journal of Personality and Social Psychology, 79*, 602–616.

Mackie, D. M., Worth, L. T., & Asuncion, A. G. (1990). Processing of persuasive in-group messages. *Journal of Personality and Social Psychology, 58*, 812–822.

Mael, F., & Ashforth, B. E. (1995). Loyal from day one: Biodata, organizational identification, and turnover among newcomers. *Personnel Psychology, 48*, 309–333.

Marques, J. M., Abrams, D., Páez, D., & Hogg, M. A. (2001). Social categorization, social identification, and rejection of deviant group members. In: M. A. Hogg & R. S. Tindale (Eds), *Blackwell Handbook of Social Psychology: Group Processes* (pp. 400–424). Oxford, UK: Blackwell.

Meindl, J. R., Ehrlich, S. B., & Dukerich, J. M. (1985). The romance of leadership. *Administrative Science Quarterly, 30*, 78–102.

Mummendey, A., & Wenzel, M. (1999). Social discrimination and tolerance in intergroup relations: Reactions to intergroup difference. *Personality and Social Psychology Review, 3*, 158–174.

Norton, M. I., Monin, B., Cooper, J., & Hogg, M. A. (in press). Vicarious dissonance: Attitude change from the inconsistency of others. *Journal of Personality and Social Psychology*.

Oakes, P. J., Haslam, S. A., & Turner, J. C. (1994). *Stereotyping and social reality*. Oxford, UK: Blackwell.

Offermann, L. R., Kennedy, J. K., Jr., & Wirtz, P. W. (1994). Implicit leadership theories: Content, structure, and generalizability. *Leadership Quarterly, 5*, 43–58.

Pescosolido, A. T. (2002). Emergent leaders as managers of group emotion. *Leadership Quarterly, 13*, 583–599.

Pillai, R., & Meindl, J. R. (1998). Context and charisma: A meso level examination of the relationship of organic structure, collectivism, and crisis to charismatic leadership. *Journal of Management, 24*, 643–671.

Pillai, R., Schriesheim, C. A., & Williams, E. S. (1999). Fairness perceptions and trust as mediators for transformational and transactional leadership: A two-sample study. *Journal of Management, 25*, 897–933.

Platow, M. J., Haslam, S. A., Foddy, M., & Grace, D. M. (in press). Leadership as the outcome of self-categorization processes. In: D. van Knippenberg & M. A. Hogg (Eds), *Leadership and Power: Identity Processes in Groups and Organizations*. London: Sage.

Platow, M. J., Hoar, S., Reid, S. A., Harley, K., & Morrison, D. (1997). Endorsement of distributively fair and unfair leaders in interpersonal and intergroup situations. *European Journal of Social Psychology, 27*, 465–494.

Platow, M. J., Mills, D., & Morrison, D. (2000). The effects of social context, source fairness, and perceived self-source similarity on social influence: A self-categorisation analysis. *European Journal of Social Psychology, 30*, 69–81.

Platow, M. J., Reid, S. A., & Andrew, S. (1998). Leadership endorsement: The role of distributive and procedural behavior in interpersonal and intergroup contexts. *Group Processes and Intergroup Relations, 1*, 35–47.

Platow, M. J., & van Knippenberg, D. (2001). A social identity analysis of leadership endorsement: The effects of leader ingroup prototypicality and distributive intergroup fairness. *Personality and Social Psychology Bulletin, 27*, 1508–1519.

Platow, M. J., van Knippenberg, D., Haslam, S. A., van Knippenberg, B., & Spears, R. (2002, June). *A special gift we bestow on you for being representative of us: Considering leader charisma from a self-categorization perspective.* Paper presented at the General Meeting of the EAESP, San Sebastián, Spain.

Podsakoff, P. M., MacKenzie, S. B., Moorman, R. H., & Fetter, R. (1990). Transformational leader behaviors and their effects on followers' trust in leader, satisfaction, and organizational citizenship behaviors. *Leadership Quarterly, 1*, 107–142.

Pratt, M. G. (1998). To be or not to be? Central questions in organizational identification. In: D. A. Whetten & P. C. Godfrey (Eds), *Identity in Organizations: Building Theory Through Conversations.* Thousand Oakes, CA: Sage.

Rabbie, J. M., & Bekkers, F. (1978). Threatened leadership and intergroup competition. *European Journal of Social Psychology, 8*, 9–20.

Reicher, S. D., & Hopkins, N. (2001). *Self and nation.* London: Sage.

Reicher, S., & Hopkins, N. (in press). On the science and art of leadership. In: D. van Knippenberg & M. A. Hogg (Eds), *Leadership and Power: Identity Processes in Groups and Organizations.* London: Sage.

Reid, S. A., & Ng, S. H. (in press). Identity, power, and strategic social categorizations: Theorizing the language of leadership. In: D. van Knippenberg & M. A. Hogg (Eds), *Leadership and Power: Identity Processes in Groups and Organizations.* London: Sage.

Ridgeway, C. L. (2001). Social status and group structure. In: M. A. Hogg & R. S. Tindale (Eds), *Blackwell Handbook of Social Psychology: Group Processes* (pp. 352–375). Oxford, UK: Blackwell.

Ridgeway, C. L. (in press). Status characteristics and leadership. In: D. van Knippenberg & M. A. Hogg (Eds), *Leadership and Power: Identity Processes in Groups and Organizations.* London: Sage.

Ridgeway, C. L., Johnson, C., & Diekema, D. (1994). External status, legitimacy, and compliance in male and female groups. *Social Forces, 72*, 1051–1077.

Ross, L. (1977). The intuitive psychologist and his shortcomings. In: L. Berkowitz (Ed.), *Advances in Experimental Social Psychology* (Vol. 10, pp. 174–220). New York: Academic Press.

Rosch, E. (1978). Principles of categorization. In: E. Rosch & B. B. Lloyd (Eds), *Cognition and Categorization* (pp. 27–48). Hillsdale, NJ: Erlbaum.

Rousseau, D. M. (1998). Why workers still identify with organizations. *Journal of Organizational Behavior, 19*, 217–233.

Schriesheim, C. A., Castro, S. L., & Cogliser, C. C. (1999). Leader-member exchange (LMX) research: A comprehensive review of theory, measurement, and data-analytic practices. *Leadership Quarterly, 10*, 63–113.

Sedikides, C., & Brewer, M. B. (Eds) (2001). *Individual self, relational self, collective self.* Philadelphia, PA: Psychology Press.

Shamir, B. (1990). Calculations, values, and identities: The source of collectivistic work motivation. *Human Relations, 43*, 313–332.

Shamir, B., House, R., & Arthur, M. B. (1993). The motivational effects of charismatic leadership: A self-concept based theory. *Organization Science, 4*, 577–594.

Shamir, B., & Howell, J. M. (1999). Organizational and contextual influences on the emergence and effectiveness of charismatic leadership. *Leadership Quarterly, 10*, 257–283.

Shamir, B., Zakay, E., Breinin, E., & Popper, M. (1998). Correlates of charismatic leader behavior in military units: Subordinates' attitudes, unit characteristics, and superiors' appraisals of leader performance. *Academy of Management Journal, 41*, 387–409.

Shea, C. M., & Howell, J. M. (1999). Charismatic leadership and task feedback: A laboratory study of their effects on self-efficacy and task performance. *Leadership Quarterly, 10*, 375–396.

Sherif, M., & Sherif, C. W. (1964). *Reference groups*. New York: Harper & Row.

Swim, J. K., Aikin, K. J., Hall, W. S., & Hunter, B. A. (1995). Sexism and racism: Old fashioned and modern prejudices. *Journal of Personality and Social Psychology, 68*, 199–214.

Tajfel, H., & Turner, J. C. (1979). An integrative theory of intergroup conflict. In: W. G. Austin & S. Worchel (Eds), *The Social Psychology of Intergroup Relations* (pp. 33–47). Monterey, CA: Brooks/Cole.

Terry, D. J., Carey, C. J., & Callan, V. J. (2001). Employee adjustment to an organizational merger: An intergroup perspective. *Personality and Social Psychology Bulletin, 27*, 267–280.

Terry, D. J., & Hogg, M. A. (1996). Group norms and the attitude-behavior relationship: A role for group identification. *Personality and Social Psychology Bulletin, 22*, 776–793.

Thibaut, J., & Walker, L. (1975). *Procedural justice: A psychological analysis*. Hillsdale, NJ: Erlbaum.

Tichy, N., & Devanna, M. (1986). *The transformational leader*. New York: Wiley.

Tsui, A., Egan, T., & O'Reilly, C. (1992). Being different: Relational demography and organizational attachment. *Administrative Science Quarterly, 37*, 549–579.

Turner, J. C. (1985). Social categorization and the self-concept: A social cognitive theory of group behaviour. In: E. J. Lawler (Ed.), *Advances in Group Processes* (Vol. 2, pp. 77–122). Greenwich, CT: JAI Press.

Turner, J. C. (1991). *Social influence*. Buckingham, UK: Open University Press.

Turner, J. C., Hogg, M. A., Oakes, P. J., Reicher, S. D., & Wetherell, M. S. (1987). *Rediscovering the social group: A self-categorization theory*. Oxford, UK: Blackwell.

Turner, M. E., Pratkanis, A. R., & Samuels, T. (2003). Identity metamorphosis and groupthink prevention: Examining Intel's departure from the DRAM industry. In: S. A. Haslam, D. van Knippenberg, M. J. Platow & N. Ellemers (Eds), *Social Identity at Work: Developing Theory for Organizational Practice* (pp. 117–136). New York and Hove, UK: Psychology Press.

Turner, J. C., Wetherell, M. S., & Hogg, M. A. (1989). Referent informational influence and group polarization. *British Journal of Social Psychology, 28*, 135–147.

Tyler, T. R. (1997). The psychology of legitimacy: A relational perspective on voluntary deference to authorities. *Personality and Social Psychology Review, 1*, 323–345.

Tyler, T. R. (1999). Why people cooperate with organizations: An identity-based perspective. In: R. I. Sutton & B. M. Staw (Eds), *Research in Organizational Behavior* (Vol. 21, pp. 201–246). Greenwich, CN: JAI Press.

Tyler, T. R. (in press). Justice, identity, and leadership. In: D. van Knippenberg & M. A. Hogg (Eds), *Leadership and Power: Identity Processes in Groups and Organizations*. London: Sage.

Tyler, T. R., & Blader, S. L. (2000). *Cooperation in groups. Procedural justice, social identity, and behavioral engagement*. Philadelphia, PA: Psychology Press.

Tyler, T. R., & Degoey, P. (1995). Collective restraint in social dilemmas: Procedural justice and social identification effects on support for authorities. *Journal of Personality and Social Psychology, 69*, 482–497.

Tyler, T. R., & Lind, E. A. (1992). A relational model of authority in groups. In: M. P. Zanna (Ed.), *Advances in Experimental Social Psychology* (Vol. 25, pp. 115–191). New York: Academic Press.

Tyler, T. R., Lind, E. A., Ohbuchi, K., Sugawara, I., & Huo, Y. J. (1997). Conflict with outsiders: Disputing within and across cultural boundaries. *Personality and Social Psychology Bulletin, 24*, 137–146.

van Knippenberg, B. (2003, February 5th). *Personal communication.*

van Knippenberg, B., & van Knippenberg, D. (2003, June). *Leader self-sacrifice, leader prototypicality, and leadership effectiveness.* Paper presented at the EAESP Small Group Meeting on New Directions in Leadership Research, Amsterdam, The Netherlands.

van Knippenberg, B., & van Knippenberg, D. (in press). Leadership, identity, and influence: Relational concerns in the use of influence tactics. In: D. van Knippenberg & M. A. Hogg (Eds), *Leadership and Power: Identity Processes in Groups and Organizations.* London: Sage.

van Knippenberg, D. (1999). Social identity and persuasion: Reconsidering the role of group membership. In: D. Abrams & M. A. Hogg (Eds), *Social Identity and Social Cognition* (pp. 315–331). Oxford, UK: Blackwell.

van Knippenberg, D. (2000a). Work motivation and performance: A social identity perspective. *Applied Psychology: An International Review, 49*, 357–371.

van Knippenberg, D. (2000b). Group norms, prototypicality, and persuasion. In: D. J. Terry & M. A. Hogg (Eds), *Attitudes, behavior, and social context: The role of norms and group membership* (pp. 157–170). Mahwah, NJ: Erlbaum.

van Knippenberg, D. (2003). Intergroup relations in organizations. In: M. West, D. Tjosvold & K. G. Smith (Eds), *International Handbook of Organizational Teamwork and Cooperative Working* (pp. 381–399). Chichester, UK: Wiley.

van Knippenberg, D., & Ellemers, N. (2003). Social identity and group performance: Identification as the key to group-oriented efforts. In: S. A. Haslam, D. van Knippenberg, M. J. Platow & N. Ellemers (Eds), *Social Identity at Work: Developing Theory for Organizational Practice* (pp. 29–42). New York and Hove, UK: Psychology Press.

van Knippenberg, D., & Haslam, S. A. (2003). Realizing the diversity dividend: Exploring the subtle interplay between identity, ideology, and reality. In: S. A. Haslam, D. van Knippenberg, M. J. Platow & N. Ellemers (Eds), *Social Identity at Work: Developing Theory for Organizational Practice* (pp. 61–77). New York and Hove, UK: Psychology Press.

van Knippenberg, D., & Hogg, M. A. (in press). *Leadership and power: Identity processes in groups and organizations.* London: Sage.

van Knippenberg, D., Lossie, N., & Wilke, H. (1994). In-group prototypicality and persuasion: Determinants of heuristic and systematic message processing. *British Journal of Social Psychology, 33*, 289–300.

van Knippenberg, D., van Knippenberg, B., Monden, L., & de Lima, F. (2002). Organizational identification after a merger: A social identity perspective. *British Journal of Social Psychology, 41*, 233–252.

van Knippenberg, D., van Knippenberg, B., & van Dijk, E. (2000). Who takes the lead in risky decision making? Effects of group members' individual riskiness and prototypicality. *Organizational Behavior and Human Decision Processes, 83*, 213–234.

van Knippenberg, D., & van Leeuwen, E. (2001). Organizational identity after a merger: Sense of continuity as the key to post-merger identification. In: M. A. Hogg & D. J. Terry (Eds), *Social Identity Processes in Organizational Contexts* (pp. 249–264). Philadelphia, PA: Psychology Press.

van Knippenberg, D., & Wilke, H. (1992). Prototypicality of arguments and conformity to ingroup norms. *European Journal of Social Psychology, 22*, 141–155.

van Leeuwen, E., & van Knippenberg, D. (2003). Organizational identification following a merger: The importance of agreeing to differ. In: S. A. Haslam, D. van Knippenberg, M. J. Platow &

N. Ellemers (Eds), *Social Identity at Work: Developing Theory for Organizational Practice* (pp. 205–221). New York and Hove, UK: Psychology Press.

van Leeuwen, E., van Knippenberg, D., & Ellemers, N. (2003). Continuing and changing group identities: The effects of merging on social identification and ingroup bias. *Personality and Social Psychology Bulletin, 29,* 679–690.

van Prooijen, J.-W., & van Knippenberg, D. (2000). Individuation or depersonalization: The influence of personal status position. *Group Processes & Intergroup Relations, 3,* 63–77.

Van Vugt, M., & de Cremer, D. (1999). Leadership in social dilemmas: The effects of group identification on collective actions to provide public goods. *Journal of Personality and Social Psychology, 76,* 587–599.

Vecchio, R. P. (1998). Leader-member exchange, objective performance, employment duration, and supervisor ratings: Testing for moderation and mediation. *Journal of Business and Psychology, 12,* 327–341.

Vermunt, R., van Knippenberg, D., van Knippenberg, B., & Blaauw, E. (2001). Self-esteem and outcome fairness: Differential importance of procedural and outcome considerations. *Journal of Applied Psychology, 86,* 621–628.

Weiss, H. M., & Cropanzano, R. (1996). Affective events theory: A theoretical discussion of the structure, causes and consequences of affective experiences at work. In: L. L. Cummings & B. M. Staw (Eds), *Research in Organizational Behavior* (Vol. 18, pp. 1–74). Greenwich, CT: JAI Press.

Williams, C. (1992). The glass escalator: Hidden advantages for men in the "female" professions. *Social Problems, 39,* 41–57.

Worchel, S., Rothgerber, H., Day, E. A., Hart, D., & Butemeyer, J. (1998). Social identity and individual productivity within groups. *British Journal of Social Psychology, 37,* 389–413.

Yorges, S. L., Weiss, H. M., & Strickland, O. J. (1999). The effect of leader outcomes on influence, attributions, and perceptions of charisma. *Journal of Applied Psychology, 84,* 428–436.

Young, J. L., & James, E. H. (2001). Token majority: The work attitudes of male flight attendants. *Sex Roles, 45,* 299–319.

Yukl, G. (1999). An evaluation of conceptual weaknesses in transformational and charismatic leadership theories. *Leadership Quarterly, 10,* 285–305.

Yukl, G. (2001). *Leadership in organizations* (5th ed.). New York: Prentice-Hall.

Yukl, G., & Van Fleet, D. D. (1994). Theory and research on leadership in organizations. In: H. C. Triandis, M. P. Dunnette & L. M. Hough (Eds), *Handbook of Industrial and Organizational Psychology* (2nd ed., Vol. 4, pp. 769–827). Palo Alto, CA: Consulting Psychologists Press.

ORGANIZATIONAL PERCEPTION MANAGEMENT

Kimberly D. Elsbach

ABSTRACT

The phenomena of organizational perception management is hardly new. The efforts of organizational spokespersons to protect and manage positive images, identities, or reputations of their organizations can be found in historical accounts of the Roman Catholic Church, and the universities of ancient Greece. The same perception management problems that plagued these early organizations (e.g. threats of illegitimacy due to changes in social norms; face-saving following scandals or accidents), continue to confront organizations today. During the past thirty years, these types of issues have been studied by organizational scholars in attempts to understand how perception management tactics affect the views and support critical audiences' (i.e. those audiences on which the organization depends for support). This paper provides an overview of this research and a framework defining the primary components of organizational perception management. This framework distinguishes organizational perception management from individual perception management in terms of its practical implementation and strategic nature.

INTRODUCTION

In the waning months of 1996 the National Rifle Association (NRA) found itself at a low-point in terms of public perceptions and support. Over the previous two years,

Research in Organizational Behavior
Research in Organizational Behavior, Volume 25, 297–332
© 2003 Published by Elsevier Ltd.
ISSN: 0191-3085/doi:10.1016/S0191-3085(03)25007-3

the non-profit organization – incorporated in 1871 to provide firearms training and promote shooting sports – had been forced to end its high-profile assignment as the governing body for U.S. Olympic shooting (Longman, 1994), lost almost 1 million dues-paying members (Broder, 1996), and run up a debt of more than forty million dollars in its attempts to promote pro-gun legislation (Zremski, 1996). These events reflected growing criticism of the organization's focus by mainstream gun owners.

Beginning in the early 1980s the NRA began to shift its focus from supporting sportsmen and hunters, to political battles over gun control (Zremski, 1996). The organization's extreme political stance on gun control was embodied by NRA president, Wayne LaPierre. In late 1996, LaPierre claimed that that the U.S. government agents who stormed the, now famous, Waco compound of the Branch Davidian cult (whose members were protecting themselves with an arsenal of personally-owned firearms) were no more than, "jack-booted thugs" (Zremski, 1996, p. 1A). This remark led former president George Bush to publicly tear up his NRA membership card, and eventually led LaPierre to step down from his position in the organization (Zremski, 1996).

In light of these events, the activist group, Handgun Control Inc., through its legislative director, suggested, in late 1996, that the NRA was in "very severe difficulty," adding that "it's political clout is diminished, and its very future is in doubt" (Broder, 1996, p. A14). In short, it appeared that perceptions of the NRA, among both members and potential members, were increasingly negative. The organization was clearly in need of perception management.

DEFINING ORGANIZATIONAL PERCEPTION MANAGEMENT

Organizational perception management involves *actions that are designed and carried out by organizational spokespersons to influence audiences' perceptions of the organization.* This definition is grounded in psychological research on individual impression management and identity management (Leary, 1996; Schlenker, 1980; Tedeschi, 1981), as well as in empirical studies of impression management and identity management strategies by organizations and their spokespersons (Elsbach, 1999, 2001a; Marcus & Goodman, 1991; Staw et al., 1983).

I use the term perception management, instead of the more commonly-heard term of impression management, as a means of providing a more inclusive, overarching nomenclature for tactics used to affect audiences' perceptions. The term "impression management" has been typically used to refer to the management of externally-focused perceptions of individuals, groups, or organizations (i.e.

images and reputations). In one of the most oft-quoted primers on impression management, Schlenker (1980, p. 6) defines impression management as "*the conscious or unconscious attempt to control images that are projected in real or imagined social interactions.*" This definition implies that impression management is used to influence "projected" images only, and that self-perceptions – such as individual and organizational identities – are not included under the umbrella of this term. I use the expression "perception management" to signal the use of both internally-focused, identity-management management strategies, as well as externally-focused, image and reputation-management strategies.

My definition of organizational perception management contains four key components (summarized in Fig. 1) that are important to understanding the unique

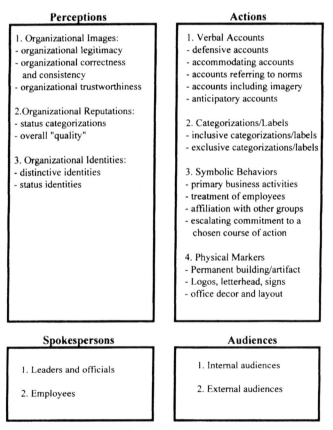

Fig. 1. Components of Organizational Perception Management.

nature of this phenomena. These components include: (1) perceptions of the organization; (2) actions or "tactics"; (3) organizational spokespersons; and (4) organizational audiences. The purposes of this paper are to explicate and illustrate these four components, to demonstrate how they interact following events that trigger organizational perception management, and to distinguish them from the components used in individual-level perception management.

PERCEPTIONS OF THE ORGANIZATION

A first component of organizational perception management is the form of perception that is being managed. Organizational perception management is designed to influence perceptions of the organization as an *entity*. Such perceptions include organizational: (1) images (e.g. current perceptions of legitimacy or trustworthiness); (2) reputations (e.g. being consistently viewed as a tough competitor); and (3) identities (e.g. being categorized as "top-tier"). In many cases, perceptions of *specific organizational actions* (e.g. perceptions of an organization's fairness in implementing a downsizing, or the quality of organizational decision-making that affected economic performance) may motivate organizational spokespersons to engage in perception management of the organization as a whole.

While prior research on organizational perception management has tended to focus on one of these three perceptions (i.e. images, reputations, or identities), it is important to note that, for any given organization, all three kinds of perceptions likely exist, simultaneously. Recently, organizational scholars have made attempts to clearly distinguish these three types of organizational perceptions from one another (Fombrun, 1996; Schultz et al., 2000). This research suggests that organizational images, reputations, and identities may be compared and contrasted along four dimensions: (1) their primary perceivers; (2) their defining categorizations; (3) their typical endurance; and (4) their specificity. In the following sections, and in Table 1, I describe how organizational images, reputations, and identities are defined by these four dimensions. I also illustrate the most common forms of these three types of organizational perceptions.

Organizational Images

Research on organizational perception management suggests that organizational images are *relatively current, and temporary perceptions of an organization, held by internal or external audiences, regarding an organization's fit with particular distinctiveness categories* (e.g. organizational legitimacy, organizational

Table 1.   Comparing Organizational Images, Reputations, and Identities.

	Organizational Image	Organizational Reputation	Organizational Identity
Primary perceivers	Insiders and outsiders	Outsiders	Insiders
Defining categorizations	Distinctiveness	Status	Distinctiveness and status
Typical endurance	Short-lived	Long-lived	Long-lived
Specificity	Specific	General	General and specific
Common impression management context	Organizational crises: • Industrial accidents • Product recall	Organizational competition: • Performance reports • Quality ranking	Organizational change: • Leadership change • Membership change

correctness and consistency, organizational trustworthiness) (Elsbach & Sutton, 1992; Hatch & Schultz, 2000; Mayer et al., 1995; Staw & Ross, 1993). This definition suggests that organizational images are relatively short-lived, specific perceptions of an organization, and that organizations may possess several distinct images at the same time. These attributes distinguish organizational images from organizational identities and reputations (defined below), which tend to be more enduring, and are more likely to be defined by status-oriented categorizations of the organization. This definition also suggests that, in contrast to identities and reputations – which are perceived solely by internal or external audiences, respectively – organizational images may be perceived by *both* internal and external audiences. For example, organizational perception management researchers commonly refer to organizational images as external audiences specific attributions of an organization (Fombrun, 1996; Sutton & Callahan, 1987). In addition, researchers have defined what insiders think outsiders think of the organization as construed external image (i.e. they suggest that insiders can have an image of the organization) (Dutton et al., 1994; Gioia & Thomas, 1996). I describe some of the more common organizational images (that are the focus of organizational perception management) below.

Organizational Legitimacy
The most commonly studied organizational image is organizational legitimacy (Elsbach, 2001b). Organizational legitimacy may be defined as "a generalized perception or assumption that the actions of an entity are desirable, proper, or appropriate within some socially constructed system of norms, values, beliefs, and definitions" (Suchman, 1995, p. 574). Legitimate organizations and their leaders are perceived as "more worthy, . . . more meaningful, more predictable, and more trustworthy" than illegitimate organizations (Suchman, 1995, p. 575). As a result, organizations perceived as legitimate are likely to receive unquestioned support and resources from constituents (Ashforth & Gibbs, 1990; Tyler, 1990). Legitimate organizations are also more likely to gain the commitment, attachment, and identification of members (Lind & Tyler, 1988; Mueller et al., 1994).

Organizational researchers studying legitimacy have typically been concerned with how firms use their legitimacy as a resource to attract and maintain valued stakeholders (i.e. employees, customers, favorable media representatives, industry analysts, concerned public citizens) (Suchman, 1995). The opinions of these stakeholders can influence an organization's performance and survival. For example, organizational strategy researchers have shown that corporate legitimacy allows firms to command premium prices from loyal customers, and gain support from industry experts and analysts, without excessive advertising or promotional expenditures (Weigelt & Camerer, 1988). This focus in organizational research on legitimacy as a resource for improving firm performance differs from the approach of much psychological research, which tends to view individual legitimacy as an attribute that is valued in and of itself (Zelditch, 2001).

The value of legitimacy for organizations and their spokespersons appears to be most evident in times of crisis or controversy when legitimacy is challenged or threatened (Chen & Meindl, 1991; Elsbach & Sutton, 1992). When organizational legitimacy is called into question, public support and the media's positive portrayal of the organization may diminish (Marcus & Goodman, 1991). For example, following the consumer fraud investigation of its auto repair shops in 1992, retail giant Sears, Roebuck & Co. suffered its first quarterly loss in profits since the Great Depression. Sears attributed much of this loss to a 10 to 15% decline in automotive repair sales and the $27 million settlement in its consumer fraud case.

Organizational Correctness and Consistency
A second form of organizational image, that has been an increasing focus of perception management research, is organizational correctness and consistency (Staw & Ross, 1987). Although, much of the work on organizational images of correctness and consistency has focused on how the behaviors of top managers, such as decision-making regarding on-going organizational projects (i.e. a negotiation, a merger, a new product launch), affect images of the organization as a whole. This research suggests that consistency in top-managers' decisions over time may lead audiences to view the organization, as a whole, as more stable, as well as more correct in it's past actions (see Brockner, 1992 for a review).

Similarly, a few studies have examined escalation behaviors by top management *teams* (McNamara et al., 2002; Ross & Staw, 1986, 1993). Research on escalation in such group situations suggests that the need to manage images of correctness and consistency are increased in group situations because groups tend to polarize the initial attitudes of groups members (Brockner, 1992). In this vein, Ross and Staw (1993) describe organizational escalation that occurred during building of the Shoreham Nuclear Power Plant. They describe how Long Island Lighting Company's (LILCO) decisions to continue to support the Nuclear Power Plant project – despite growing evidence that the costs were severely underestimated –

were influenced, in part, by the top-management teams' desire to manage organizational images of correctness and consistency (Ross & Staw, 1993). The top management of LILCO perceived a threat to the organization's images of correctness and consistency when stockholders and the public utilities commission challenged the managers to defend their investment decisions. In response to these image threats, the upper management of the company attempted to justify it's past decisions and maintain its images of correctness and consistency by continuing to back its original plan to build and run the Nuclear Plant. This example suggests that pressures for organizational correctness and consistency may lead to more dysfunctional image management in group or organizational settings than in individual settings.

Organizational Trustworthiness

A third type of organizational image involves perceptions of organizational trustworthiness. Recent work has defined the image of organizational trustworthiness as the perception that an organization displays competence, benevolence, and integrity in its behaviors and beliefs (Mayer et al., 1995). In this definition, competence refers to the abilities and skills that allow an organization to achieve desired goals, benevolence refers to an organization's apparent willingness to do good, and integrity refers to an organization's adherence to principles or ideals that conform to social norms (Mayer & Davis, 1999).

Research on employees perceptions of organizational trustworthiness has shown that equity in compensation practices may be a focal point for determining the integrity and trustworthiness of an organization's actions (Pearce, 1993; Pearce et al., 1994). By contrast, when external audiences (e.g. stockholders, potential business partners) gauge the trustworthiness of organizations, strategy theorists suggest that they will look to the culture and control systems of the organization (Barney & Hansen, 1994). According to these theorists, if an organization is viewed as having a culture and set of control systems that limit its actions through values, standards, and principles of behavior, then it will be perceived as having an image of trustworthiness. In both cases of insider and outsider perceptions, organizational trustworthiness appears to be dependent on the presence of industry or organizational structures and procedures that delimit organizational action. By contrast, research suggests that compliance with broad societal norms are more likely to influence images of individual trustworthiness (Elsbach, 2003a).

Organizational Reputations

Organizational reputations differ from organizational images in several ways. First, reputations are more general than are images. As Cowden and Sellnow (2002, p. 199) note, "image reflects a set of specific associations, whereas reputation denotes an overall judgment regarding the extent to which a firm is held in high esteem or regard." Similarly, Fombrun (1996, p. 37) defines organizational reputation as "the overall estimation in which a company is held by its constituents." Second, organizational reputations have been defined as external audiences' enduring perceptions of how a "firm's products, jobs, strategies, and prospects compare to those of competing firms" (Fombrun & Shanley, 1990). That is, while images are defined primarily by distinctiveness categorizations, reputations are defined by status categorizations (although they may include status based upon a distinct trait – such as "best small school" or "most admired large company"). Finally, organizational reputation and identity researchers have commonly agreed that reputation is both perceived and legitimated by external audiences (vs. internal audiences) (Dukerich & Carter, 2000; Dutton et al., 1994; Fombrun & Rindova, 2000). Together, these findings suggest that organizational reputations involve *enduring status categorizations of an organization (relative to other organizations) as perceived by external audiences and stakeholders.*

Theory and research on organizational reputations has primarily come from the domain of strategy. In particular, strategy researchers have identified two perspectives on the use and management of organization reputations: resource-based views (Wernerfelt, 1984) and market-based views (Milgrom & Roberts, 1982). Resource-based views of organizations focus on the capabilities, attributes, and resources of a firm that are distinctive, rare, durable, and generally inimitable. One key resource is the firm's reputation: "Intangible resources such as reputation significantly contribute to performance differences among organizations because they are rare, socially complex, and difficult to trade and imitate" (Rao, 1994, p. 29). In contrast, market-based views of organizations focus on reputations as strategic attributes that firms use to gain a competitive advantage in incomplete information settings (Milgrom & Roberts, 1982, 1986). In these cases, outsiders are forced, by their lack of information, to predict a firm's future decisions based solely on its past behavior (Camerer & Vepsalainen, 1988). A significant amount of research in both paradigms has shown that attractive or distinctive reputations favorably influence organizational customers and competitors. Researchers have also shown that positive corporate reputations improve inter-organizational bargaining outcomes, allow firms to command premium prices, or help firms to gain support and resources from primary constituents (D'Aveni & O'Neill, 1992; Tsui, 1990; Weigelt & Camerer, 1988).

In recent years, organizations scholars have built on this strategy work and have focused on the cognitive and social antecedents of organizational reputation (Fombrun, 1996; Mohamed et al., 2001). These studies suggest that the stability and positive distinctiveness (a form of status) of an organization's performance will help its audiences form enduring perceptions of the firm. In particular, these studies suggest that stability or consistency in behavior and performance is important in reputation-building because it helps increase audiences' confidence that they can predict future performance based on the past (Weigelt & Camerer, 1988). For example, Rao (1994) showed how many firms in the auto industry built reputations for performance, in part, by repeatedly publicizing their early successes in automobile contests. In addition, researchers have shown that positive distinctiveness is important to reputation-building because it helps audiences to categorize individual organizations on status-relevant traits (Shrum & Withnow, 1988). In this vein, Staw and Epstein (2000) found when a company became associated with new management techniques (e.g. total quality management programs) it gained a reputation of being more innovative than peer organizations that did not adopt these techniques. Ultimately, the techniques were shown to have no effect on organizational performance, and the researchers suggested that they were adopted because they provided a salient signal about the organization's reputation.

Organizational Identities

Organizational identities are the answers organizational members' question: "who are we?" (Dutton et al., 1994; Elsbach, 1999). As a result, organizational identities may be relatively complex and include both status (we're "top tier") and distinctiveness (we're creative) categorizations, as well as specific (we're the most family-friendly company in Sacramento, California) and general (we're one of the most admired companies in America) foci which define the organization (Hatch & Schultz, 2000). By contrast, organizational images or organizational reputations typically answer questions about an organization's fit with one type of distinctiveness or status categorization at a time. Similar to organizational reputations, organizational identities are commonly perceived as being enduring (Dutton et al., 1994). Yet, researchers have suggested that they are not immutable (Gioia & Thomas, 1996), and that identity management can successfully change and organization's identity (Elsbach & Bhattacharya, 2001). Based on these findings, organizational identities may be conceptualized as *insiders' relatively enduring perceptions of their organization's fit with distinctiveness categorizations and status categorizations along both general and specific dimensions* (Dutton, Dukerich & Harquail, 1994; Dutton & Penner, 1993; Hatch & Schultz, 2000; Kramer, 1993).

Individual members who identify with their organization (i.e. who define their own self-concept, in part, by their membership in the organization, and who perceive their own identity to overlap with the organization's identity), are likely to perceive that their own identities are threatened by events that threaten the organization's identity (Dutton et al., 1994). As a result, organizational identity management may be motivated as much by members' desires to maintain positive perceptions of their own individual identities, as by desires to maintain positive perceptions of their organization's identity (Elsbach & Kramer, 1996). This link between individual and organizational identities also makes the management of organizational identities more complex because individual members often vary in terms of their level and focus of identification with the organization. Individuals who strongly identify with an organization's identity as a top-tier organization may engage in symbolic actions to affirm that status-categorization, while other individuals who weakly identify with the status categorization of top-tier may opt-out of such identity affirmation, or even disidentify with that aspect of the organization's identity by distancing themselves from the organization (Elsbach & Bhattacharya, 2001).

Further complicating the management of organizational identities is the fact that organizations may be defined by more than one identity (e.g. a business school may have a teaching identity and a research identity). In some cases, these multiple identities may appear to be in conflict with one another. That is organizations may have *hybrid identities* that are "composed of two or more (identities) that would not normally be expected to go together." (Albert & Whetten, 1985, p. 270). For example, Elsbach (2001a) described the California State Legislature as being defined by an often-derided "political" identity and a more noble "policy-making" identity, which were often in conflict. In other cases, these multiple identities may define distinct, yet compatible aspects of the organization (e.g. a University that prides itself on both excellent teaching and research). In these cases, the dual identities may support each other (e.g. research informs teaching, and teaching provides a context for research). Also, because they are not vulnerable to the same types of threats, they may provide a good offense against overall identity damage (e.g. a University that loses a top researcher to a rival institution, can still tout its excellent teaching faculty) (Elsbach & Kramer, 1996).

SYMBOLIC ACTIONS

Symbolic actions are a second component of organizational perception management. Symbolic actions include *any activities by organizational spokespersons that are used, at least in part, to affect audience perceptions of the organization.* Such actions may be primarily symbolic (e.g. changing the name *Kentucky Fried Chicken*, to *KFC* – to minimize unhealthy images associated with the word "fried" – without changing the menu), or may be primarily practical (e.g. adopting, without fanfare or publicity, a Total Quality Management program based on a desire to improve product quality), or somewhere in between. In most cases, researchers have not been able to completely separate the symbolic from the practical aspects of such actions, and they suggest that most cases of organizational perception management involve both (Russ, 1991).

Research in this area has identified four specific types of symbolic actions used to manage organizational perceptions: (1) verbal accounts (e.g. justifications for a corporate downsizing included in an annual report); (2) distinctiveness and status-oriented categorizations and comparisons of organizations (e.g. defining a business school as "top-tier" in promotional materials); (3) symbolic behaviors (e.g. contribution to charitable foundations and causes); and (4) the display of physical markers (e.g. American flags hung in retail stores following the September 11th, 2001 terrorist acts).

Verbal Accounts

Psychological frameworks of individual and organizational perception management suggest that verbal accounts may be defined as explanations that are designed to influence perceptions of an organization's responsibility for an event, or for the valence of an event (whether it is positive or negative) (Schlenker, 1980; Tedeschi, 1981). Verbal accounts – which have been studied more than any other type of organizational perception management tactic – are used primarily to manage external organizational images and reputations (vs. internal identities). This body of research has defined three primary features of accounts,: (1) form; (2) content; and (3) communication medium.

Account Forms
A number of account forms commonly follow negatively perceived events. *Excuses* are accounts that are designed to minimize perceptions of responsibility for a negative event ("it wasn't our fault"), while *justifications* are accounts that are designed to minimize the perceived negativity of an event, when responsibility is not in question ("it wasn't as bad as you think" or "we had a good reason for doing it"). Similarly, *denials* are accounts that attempt to refute any responsibility for an event ("we didn't do it") or that claim that an event was not at all negative ("it didn't happen"), while *apologies* are accounts that accept full responsibility for a negative event, but claim regret ("we did it, but we're sorry).

Other accounts, are designed to follow positively perceived events. *Entitlings* are accounts that are designed to increase perceptions of responsibility for a positive event ("we did it" or "we were more responsible than you think"), while *enhancements* are accounts designed to increase the perceived positiveness of an event, when responsibility is admitted (i.e. "it was positive" or "it was better than you think").

Organizational studies have routinely characterized the accounts that organizational spokespersons use following negative events as either *accommodative or defensive* (Elsbach, 1994; Marcus & Goodman, 1991), and those that follow positive events as *acclaims* (Benoit, 1999). These more general terms have been used to describe the form of organizational accounts because such explanations tend to include more than one form of accounts (e.g. excuses and denials may be combined in defensive accounts, while justifications and enhancements may be combined in accommodative accounts), and because organizational accounts tend to be designed to meet general the goals of aggressively defending organizational perceptions, accommodatively meeting audience needs, or proactively managing perceptions (Conlon & Murray, 1996).

Sutton and Callahan (1987) provide an example of the use of defensive accounts to manage perceptions of organizational legitimacy. They found that, following corporate Chapter 11 bankruptcy filings, organizational spokespersons commonly combined the excuse that the bankruptcy was due to a national recession, with the denial that a Chapter 11 filing was, in fact a failure (i.e. they claimed that it was a normal and rational business procedure for an organization in certain circumstances). These defensive accounts suggested that the organization was attempting to pursue reasonable and logical goals, but was thwarted by extenuating circumstances or was mistakenly attributed with responsibility for a negative outcome. In another example, Allen and Caillouet (1994, pp. 59–61) found that spokespersons for a recycling facility routinely responded to challenges to the organization's legitimacy (e.g. challenges to its licensing status and disposal methods for hazardous waste from environmental groups like Greenpeace), by offering verbal accounts that combined denials of wrong-doing (we're not an "incinerator" – "we never put one drop of anything in the river") with denouncements of the challengers (e.g."the Department of Environmental Quality is acting unlawfully, illegally, and totally outside their constitutional authority in making the latest hearing and other information requests of the organization").

By way of contrast, Allen and Caillouet (1994, p. 60) found that the recycling facility also used a combination of enhancements (e.g. " The ...U.S. Patent office recognized (our) technology as the first and only process in the country with the ability to substitute large quantities of contaminated soils and other materials for feedstocks and still economically manufacture products that exhibit no hazardous characteristics"), and flattery (e.g. "I want to applaud the efforts of the EPA ...for putting together a very find and excellent draft permit") in acclaims that suggested that the evaluation of the facility was, in fact, a positive event. In a similar example, Elsbach's (1994) study of perception management in the California cattle industry revealed that spokespersons often combined justifications and enhancements in accommodative accounts they gave in response to public concerns about the potentially harmful effects of treating beef cattle with hormones. Company spokespersons justified the use of hormones, arguing that the drugs helped to keep cattle healthy (a common concern of consumers), and added that the reduction in costs achieved by producing larger beef cattle was passed on to consumers as reduced prices (an enhancement).

Account Content
The content of accounts includes the arguments, evidence, and illustrations that back up the basic account form. Research on organizational accounts has shown that, in general, "accounts are seen as more adequate to the extent that they are detailed (e.g. Shapiro et al., 1994), based on sound reasoning (e.g. Bies et al., 1988), (and) sensitive (e.g. Greenberg, 1994)," (Folger & Cropanzano, 1998, p. 155).

More specifically, a small number of studies suggest that adequate accounts often contain of *references to social or industry norms* as a means of indicating sound reasoning and sensitivity to audience needs (Elsbach, 1994). Elsbach and Sutton (1992), for example, found that spokespersons from radical social movement organizations often used references to normative and widely endorsed procedures (i.e. conducting press conferences or non violence workshops) in their accounts of illegitimate protest actions. Similarly, Taylor and Bogdan (1980) described how accounts used by spokespersons for mental health institutions to manage organizational perceptions of legitimacy often referred to new, widely endorsed organizational goals (e.g. habilitation vs. custodial care) and organizational structures (e.g. team approaches, formal policies, and unitization). Finally, Dutton and Dukerich (1991) found that police officers in the New York City Port Authority Bus Terminal backed up their justifications for removing homeless persons from the terminal by noting that they were enforcing an anti-loitering law (i.e. a normative procedure). Later, Port Authority spokespersons backed up their enhancements of their organization's image by highlighting their use of new, socially endorsed structures, including a paid consultant and a human resource administration to provide sensitivity training for police.

In many cases, references to social norms are contained in a "legitimating label" of the organization. For example, when Chrysler was charged with committing fraud by selling used vehicles as new (i.e. the vehicles had been driven by Chrysler executives with the odometers disconnected prior to sale), CEO Lee Iacocca attempted to manage Chrysler's reputation for trustworthiness by denying that the company had done anything wrong, and labeling the actions in question as a "test program" rather than a fraudulent executive perk (Hearit, 1994). In a similar case, the automaker, Volvo, came under attack after it was demonstrated that its car showcased in an advertisement as withstanding repeated overruns by a "Monster Truck" while other vehicles were crushed, had been reinforced with steel and wood. In response, Volvo spokespersons engaged in image repair by claiming that the advertisement was not a hoax or sham as it had been described in the media, but a "re-enactment" of an actual event that had been witnessed by hundreds of people at a Vermont truck rally (Hearit, 1994).

A second, specific type of content used to bolster accounts is *ideological imagery or illustration*, which adds to detail and sensitivity (Benoit, 1995). In a case study of the Apollo 13 space mission, for example, Kaufman (2001) describes how NASA spokespersons used a "frontier" narrative and imagery to portray the space agency in a positive light in enhancements following the mission's failure. At post-mission press conferences, NASA administrators characterized the mission an " 'epic struggle' in which the astronauts were 'pitted' against the 'hostile environment of space.' " (Kaufman, 2001, p. 442). NASA spokespersons also described the astronauts who "dare to brave the perils of space" as possessing "bravery, skill, discipline, courage, ingenuity, resourcefulness, teamwork, and character." (Kaufman, 2001, p. 442). At the same time, then president Richard Nixon claimed that the astronauts' actions reminded Americans of their "proud heritage as a nation." (Kaufman, 2001, p. 442). This type of imagery provided substance to NASA's claims that the Apollo 13 mission was "A Successful Failure" (Kaufman, 2001, p. 443).

Account Medium
Finally, it's important to keep in mind that there are many mediums through which verbal accounts may be communicated. Organizations can seek to communicate directly with audiences through paid advertisements, company newsletters, annual reports, websites, or e-mails. These routes employ media gatekeepers and allow organizational perception managers to craft their accounts to portray specific images (Hearit, 1994). In, perhaps, the only study of account effectiveness based on account medium, Shapiro et al. (1994) found that face-to-face oral communication of an unpopular decision led to more positive reactions from audiences than written communication. This finding suggests that, to the extent that organizational spokespersons can communicate negative news directly to audiences, the more likely they are to effectively manage those audiences' perceptions of the organization.

In other cases, organizations communicate through the news media, where the form and content of their accounts may be altered by the reporter (e.g. an industry-friendly newspaper may report an account of corporate downsizing in a more positive light than would a labor-friendly publication). In fact, it is not uncommon for the media's treatment of the story to create a peripheral controversy, drawing attention away from the facts of the case. For example, the *New York Times* was embroiled in an perception management controversy after they refused to print two sports columns that sided against an organization (the National Council of Women's Organizations, NWCO) that was attempting to get women admitted as members of the Augusta National Golf Club (Johnson, 2002 December 5). This "spiking" of the news stories led critics to claim that the *New York Times* was taking on NWCO's crusade as their own. In this manner, the newspaper, itself, became a player in organizational perception management related to the controversy.

Organizational Categorizations Comparisons

A second verbal strategy for managing perceptions of organizations is to offer organizational categorizations and comparisons. In particular, organizations wishing to affirm desired identities, use categorizations and comparisons to define who they are and who they are not.

Inclusion in Social Categories

Social psychologists have shown that, on dimensions that are self-relevant (e.g. one's stand on ideological issues such as gun control), individuals prefer to see themselves as relatively unique compared to others because "similarity (to many others) on self-defining dimensions may imply that one is undistinguished or mediocre"(Wood, 1989, p. 241). As a result, individuals may affirm their distinctive identities by categorizing themselves in ways that display these unique attributes (Brewer, 1991). Researchers have also shown that individuals often prefer social categorizations that emphasize comparisons to inferior social groups as a means of affirming or enhancing their self-concept (Crocker & Gallo, 1985; Wood, 1989). This form of self-categorization tends to be used in response to threats to self-concept or identity (i.e. mistaken inclusion into an undesirable social group such as "right-wing gun enthusiasts") (Hogg & Abrams, 1988).

Recently, organizational researchers have found that members and spokespersons for an organization may perceive these same types of identity threats when the organization to which they belong is categorized in ways that run counter to their perceptions of its identity. In this manner, Terry et al. (2001) showed that members of higher-status organizations that merged with a lower-status organization perceived the merger as an organizational identity threat because it diluted their organization's relative status. Similarly, in their study of business school members' reactions to the *Business Week* rankings, Elsbach and Kramer (1996) found that members experienced cognitive distress or perceived that dissonance when, as a result of the school's ranking in the survey, they perceived that their organization's identity was threatened by inaccurate categorizations or misleading (and, by implication, unfair) comparisons to other organizations.

Elsbach and Kramer (1996) showed that, in response to this cognitive distress, members attempted to restore and affirm positive self-perceptions, as well as positive perceptions of their organization's identity, by describing their organization in terms of alternate social categories (not included in the *Business Week* rankings) that confirmed its established identity (e.g. being an entrepreneurial school, being a top public institution). These organizational categorizations and comparisons were most commonly claimed for attributes that were widely-known within the organization (e.g. being a research institution). In contrast to individual self-categorizations and comparisons (which need only be verified by their claimant), organizational categorizations and comparisons must be verified by many members to be perceived as legitimate.

In other cases, researchers have suggested that organizational leaders may wish to clarify their categorization along a number of different identity dimensions, as the organization's identity becomes more complex (Pratt & Foreman, 2000). Pratt and Foreman (2000) suggest that organizations may choose to manage multiple organizational identities by compartmentalization (e.g. keeping the identities separate by maintaining multiple identity categorizations), integration (e.g. fusing the identities through a single new categorization), deletion (e.g. removing some identity categorizations), or aggregation (e.g. creating a hierarchy of identity categorizations). Organization's may perceive the need to manage multiple identities as new identities are taken on (e.g. through a change in business practices, or a merger or divestiture), or as the value of existing identities change (e.g. a once important line of the business becomes obsolete).

Exclusion from Social Categories
In addition to denoting the categorizations to which an organization belongs, identity managers identify categorizations to which the organization does not belong. That is, organizational identity management may underscore an organization's disidentification from specific, negatively-viewed categories (Elsbach, 1999; Elsbach & Bhattacharya, 2001). For example, organizations that are proactively changing their identity due to a merger, acquisition, or management directive may want members to give up old identifications so that they can more readily embrace new ones (Pfeffer & Sutton, 1999). Yet, if new organizational identities are too disparate from existing ones, members may have difficulty understanding and embracing them (Reger et al., 1994). Understanding the dynamics of disidentification may allow organizations to help their members make this identity-transition.

Along these lines, the Saturn division of General Motors used identity categorizations (e.g. the slogan "A different kind of car company. A different kind of car") to separate themselves from their parent company, General Motors (Pfeffer & Sutton, 1999). Their commercials and print advertising worked to separate the company from people's stereotype of a car company as big, impersonal, and adversarial. In one advertisement, an African-American sales representative talks about how his father was treated unfairly by a big-company car salesman in the 1950s, and how his approach at Saturn is designed to be in distinct contrast to this approach. All of these tactics by the company appeared designed to help members to disidentify with out-dated and undesirable identities associated with a "traditional car company." Such disidentification helps people to then identify with the "different kind of car company" Saturn professes to be.

Symbolic Behaviors

Symbolic behaviors involve both routine and special actions that are used to indicate something about an organizations image or identity. Symbolic organizational behaviors are most commonly used as perception management when they are perceived to be visible and salient (e.g. the use of patriotic displays in retail stores has been perceived as much more salient since the events of 9/11), and when they affect a salient aspect of the organization's image or identity (e.g. introducing a new product or service related to an organization's central mission, such as on-line education by a renown university). Such behaviors are effective perception management tactics because they literally show the organization "living" its image, identity, or reputation (Arnold et al., 1996). As a case in point, Rao (1994) describes how early auto manufacturers (i.e. at the turn of the 20th century), used speed or endurance contests to display specific features of their cars, such as performance in hill-climbing, or reliability on a rugged, cross-country course to legitimate automobiles as viable alternative to horses, and as noted earlier, to build their reputations for performance in these areas.

Yet, to maximize their impact, symbolic behaviors are often coupled with verbal accounts or communications that explain them. In the study described above, Rao (1994) found that auto manufacturer's used newspaper advertisements to publicize their contest wins and increase public awareness about the automobiles' capabilities. In another case, Arndt and Bigelow (2000), found that hospitals that adopted a diversified corporate structure during the 1990s (in place of their previous not-for-profit structure) used verbal accounts in their annual reports that justified the change as a response to the institutional environment (e.g. pressures on hospitals from HMO's to carry out such restructuring) and desires to maintain high status in their relevant comparison group (e.g. "other hospitals of our caliber are making these changes, so we must also change to keep up").

Organizational research points to four primary forms of symbolic behaviors used to manage perceptions of organizations: (1) behaviors related to primary business activities; (2) treatment of employees or prospective employees; (3) visible affiliation with groups or organizations; and (4) escalation behaviors.

Behaviors Related to Primary Business Activities

The most common forms of symbolic behavior used as organizational perception management involve visible actions (e.g. attacking competitors, re-calling products) related to primary business activities (e.g. serving customers, manufacturing products, or complying with government regulations). Typically, this means signaling organizational reputations or images through activities related to putting out products or services (Weigelt & Camerer, 1988).

Extensive research from the domain of management strategy suggests that organizations may attempt to signal a reputation of "toughness," for example, by enduring performances losses (e.g. by pricing below cost, or by proliferating their product line to fill every market niche – even unprofitable ones) to deter other firms from entering their market (Kreps & Wilson, 1982; Milgrom & Roberts, 1986; Schmalensee, 1978). In other cases, firms may attempt to signal a reputation for "high quality" by lavish expenditures on advertising (Nelson, 1974), social causes, or costly office furniture, none of which provide direct information about products, improve costs, or increase demand (Milgrom & Roberts, 1986). Finally, organizations may attempt to build reputations for distinctive competencies (e.g. a business school's academic orientation) by offering specific products and services (e.g. large number of faculty on editorial boards, high use of doctoral students as teachers) that meet the particular needs of a primary constituency, such as faculty (D'Aveni & O'Neill, 1992). As noted earlier, Staw and Epstein (2000) describe how several corporations adopted popular management techniques, such as total quality management programs, to enhance their reputation for innovation.

Treatment of Employees

Symbolic behavior related to the treatment of employees (or prospective employees) can also be used to enhance or affirm an organization's identity (Turban & Greening, 1997). Murrell (2001) found that firms that engaged in employment practices that promoted family life (e.g. good advancement opportunities for women, available on-site childcare, leave for childbirth, job sharing, flextime, and work-at-home options), signaled an identity categorization of "family friendly" and were recognized by *Working Mother Magazine*.

Similarly, researchers of organizational justice have suggested that fair and equitable treatment of employees in decisions regarding hiring, firing, promotion, performance evaluation, and compensation are important to maintaining distinctive identity categorizations of fairness and trustworthiness (Folger & Cropanzano, 1998; Greenberg, 1990). For example, research on hiring decisions has shown that applicants view cognitive ability tests, personality tests, drug screens, and biographical inventories as unfair means of employment selection (Folger & Cropanzano, 1998). Further, applicants subjected to these types of procedures are more likely than those who are not tested to view the organization negatively (e.g. perceive the organization as having an image of "unfairness") (Smither et al., 1993; Stoffey et al., 1991).

Finally, recent empirical studies have described how managers or organizational leaders can enhance organizational identities of trustworthiness among employees through daily interactions. A recent review of this work (Whitener et al., 1998) suggests five behavioral characteristics that are important to achieving organizational identities of trustworthiness among employees. First, they suggest that *behavioral consistency* (i.e. reliability or predictability) by leaders increases employees' confidence in the organization's competence, and willingness to take risks on their behalf (Butler, 1991; Robinson & Rousseau, 1994). Second, *behavioral integrity* (i.e. telling the truth and keeping promises) by leaders, reduces the risk employees associate with working in an organization (Mayer et al., 1995). Third, a leader's willingness to *share control* enhances employees' abilities to protect their own interests, and affirms their self-worth as valued part of their organization – thereby increasing their perception of the organization's benevolence (Tyler & Lind, 1992). Fourth, *accurate, open, and thorough communication* by leaders about decisions and organizational issues helps employees to feel that there is a sharing and exchanging of ideas, and increases their perceptions of the organization's integrity (Butler, 1991; Hart et al., 1986). Finally, *demonstrating concern* for employees' well-being (e.g. showing consideration and sensitivity for employees' needs and interests, acting in a way that protects employees' interests, and refraining from exploiting employees) by leaders helps employees to perceive the organization as loyal and benevolent. In support of these recommendations, a fourteen month field study of management performance appraisal systems by Mayer and Davis (1999) showed that enhancing perceived benevolence, integrity, and competence by implementing a new performance appraisal system, increased employees "willingness to let top management have control over" employee and organizational well-being.

Affiliation with Other Groups or Organizations

A third, common, symbolic behavior that has been used as an organizational perception management tool involves formal or informal affiliation with other groups or organizations. In some cases, affiliation behaviors and their advertisement can be used to manage an organization's identity. For example, visible affiliation with a high-status or distinctive organization (e.g. advertising one's recent inclusion in *Fortune Magazine's* "most admired" list) can enhance an organization's identity by creating the perception that the organization is in the same league as other, perennially admired companies (Elsbach & Kramer, 1996). At the same time, visible disidentification from a low-status or distinctive organization (e.g. touting one's title as the corporation "most hated" by the National Rifle Association) underscores that a company is not in the same league (Elsbach & Bhattacharya, 2001).

Affiliation with well-respected groups can also be used to manage organizational images of legitimacy. For example, research on the uses of philanthropy by organizations (Himmelstein, 1997) shows that many organizations that are facing legitimacy threats donate money to prestigious causes and organizations as a means demonstrating that their underlying values and ideals are aligned with those of the recipients (e.g. the oft-attacked tobacco giant, Phillip Morris, has sponsored the Arts for over 40 years, including donating money to Lincoln Center, The Whitney Museum, The Dance Theater of Harlem, and the Alvin Ailey Dance Theater (Sisario, 2002 November 18)).

Escalation Behaviors

Finally, as suggested earlier, a fourth symbolic behavior that has been used to manage organizational images of correctness and consistency is escalation of commitment to a previously chosen (often failing) course of action (Brockner, 1992). Such escalation behaviors commonly occur in the following situations:

> ... decision makers allocate some resources ... in the hope of attaining some goal or goals. After having made an investment, however, ... they receive negative feedback suggesting that, at the very least, they have not yet attained their goals; moreover, they are not certain that additional investments will be sufficient to bring about goal attainment (Brockner, 1992, p. 40).

As noted earlier, organizational theorists suggest that, in these situations, the decision makers continue to invest resources toward their originally stated goals as a symbolic means of "self-justification" (i.e. to justify that their past actions were correct). Further, such actions demonstrate consistency in behavior over time, which has been shown to be a valued trait (at least in Western societies) (Staw & Ross, 1987).

Research has suggested that these symbolic goals motivate organizations and their leaders to go on devoting resources to a failing course of action (Ross & Staw, 1986, 1993). Ross and Staw (1993, p. 717) described this phenomena in their discussion of escalation behaviors during the construction of the Shoreham Nuclear Power Plant:

> ... external justification effects are particularly strong among those who are politically vulnerable or whose initial policy choice has met with resistance. In constructing Shoreham,

LILCO's management continually faced LILCO's management continually faced the need to assure external constituencies, such as shareholders and the public utilities commission, that it's investment was a wise one ... It seemed that as the management of LILCO's commitment was challenged, each challenge was met with renewed justification (and investment), only serving to further increase commitment to Shoreham.

Physical Markers

Physical markers include the display of temporary or permanent physical artifacts, at least in part, to signal an organization's images, identities, and reputations. In connection with organizational perception management, such physical markers commonly include size, style, and location of office buildings (e.g. investment banks located on or off Wall Street), type of furnishings (e.g. traditional vs. contemporary office furnishings), and decor (e.g. the presence or absence of artwork and live plants), as well as company logos, signs, and letterheads.

Research from the area of environmental psychology (Sundstrom & Altman, 1989; Sundstrom & Sundstrom, 1986), suggests that physical markers are most often used to manage perceptions of an organization's long-term and enduring identities and reputations (Olins, 1995). Proponents of the "visual school" of corporate identity, for example, suggest that the visible and tangible decor, design, and structures of an organization may be viewed as manifestations of the organization's identity (Balmer, 1995). Perhaps because physical markers, such as buildings and furnishings, are relatively permanent and highly visible, they are viewed as a natural means of symbolizing and managing perceptions of the enduring and central character of an organization (Elsbach, 2003b). Along those lines, Ornstein (1986, 1992) found that the design of public reception areas in corporate office buildings conveyed organizational identity categorizations of authoritarianism (signaled by displays of flags, pictures of organizational leaders, and chairs facing each other) or non-authoritarianism/ comfort (signaled by displays of artwork, live plants, and couches and chairs at 45 degree angles). Similarly, Arnold et al. (1996) found that patriotic displays in retail stores (e.g. Wal Mart) were effectively used to communicate and build the organization's long-standing reputation for community involvement and concern to customers. Finally, Ridoutt et al. (2002) found that organizations that displayed wood in their interior design were most preferred by observers, and were most likely to be described by the identity categorizations: innovative, energetic, and comfortable (vs. rigid, unpleasant, and impersonal, which were assigned to organizations without wood in their interiors).

In addition, physical markers can be used effectively to manage temporary organizational images in anticipation of future controversies (e.g. the use of "green" imagery by an automaker in anticipation of public concern over their launch of a new, gas-guzzling sport-utility vehicle). In such cases, physical markers work well for preemptive perception management because they are continually visible to customers, employees, or the public, and may send a consistent signal well-before the anticipated controversy occurs. Elsbach et al. (1998), for example, found that hospitals strategically changed the structure of their invoices (e.g. making sure common items like aspirin were priced close to drugstore prices) to present an image of organizational legitimacy, which they hoped would deter patients from challenging their charges.

ORGANIZATIONAL SPOKESPERSONS

A third component of organizational perception management is the organizational spokesperson. Organizational spokespersons convey or explain symbolic actions (verbal accounts, symbolic behaviors, display of physical markers) to organizational audiences. *Spokespersons include anyone who is perceived by audience members as representing the organization.* They do not have to be members of the organization or hold formal or official titles or roles that designate them to speak on its behalf.

Speaking on behalf of a large and diverse organization presents unique challenges for organizational perception managers. Most notably, they must often manage multiple organizational perceptions, to multiple audiences. This situation is difficult not just because there are many distinct perceptions to track, but also because these perceptions are, at times, incongruent. Elsbach and Kramer (1996) found, for example, that a school may find it challenging to maintain its reputation for top quality teaching while also trying to maintain an identity as a preeminent research institute. The role of the spokesperson in such situations becomes crucial to success.

Empirical organizational research reveals that the most common types of organizational spokespersons are: (1) organizational leaders, public relations professionals; and (2) employees.

Leaders and Official Spokespersons

For several reasons, visible organizational leaders or official public relations professionals are the most common types of spokespersons who carry out organizational perception management. First, they are typically the ones who offer initial accounts following both positive and negative events (Pearson & Clair, 1998). For example, in annual reports, the letter to shareholders explaining past performance is always signed by the company leader (Staw et al., 1983). Researchers have found that audiences react most positively if leaders take responsibility, in these letters, for both successes and failures (Salancik & Meindl, 1984). Audiences expect leaders to take both credit and blame for the performance of their organizations (Meindl & Ehrlich, 1987).

Second, several studies show that organizational leaders are most likely to engage in symbolic behaviors on behalf of the organization, such as presenting restitution to harmed parties following an industrial accidents (Marcus & Goodman, 1991). Conlon and Murray (1996) found that responses to letters of complaints about poor product quality typically came from an official organizational spokesperson in charge of customer satisfaction and product quality. When the harm done is more serious (e.g. physical harm or death caused by an organization), the company president or CEO is likely to respond. For example, Ford Motor Company CEO, Jacques Nasser announced Ford's program to replace faulty Firestone tires on its Ford Explorers, following publicity about numerous deaths that resulted from Explorer accidents (*60 Minutes*, October 8th, 2000).

Finally, organizational leaders are often involved in the choice or design of company buildings and work spaces – an organization's most prominent physical markers. The sprawling, campus-like environment of the Microsoft Headquarters in Redmond, Washington is often attributed to the mindset of the company's founder, Bill Gates (Meyer, 1994). Similarly, John Chambers, CEO of Cisco Systems portrays his company's collaborative spirit in his choice to put top managers in cubicles alongside fellow workers (Donlon, 2000).

Employees

For events on a smaller and less controversial scale, symbolic actions, intended to manage day-to-day perceptions or to provide anticipatory perception management, are often conducted by rank and file employees. These employees routinely interact with the customers and/or the public, and thus, are often in a position to provide symbolic information about an organization. In one example, Elsbach et al. (1998), showed how customer service staff in hospital billing departments used symbolic behaviors in their interactions with customers (e.g. threatening to send a patient's bill to an outside collection agency, warnings that an audited bill can lead to additional charges). These behaviors were intended to portray the hospital as an intimidating and threatening organization that would not easily given in to patients' requests to reduce the amount of their bills.

In certain situations, however, the employees as a group are symbolically defined as the spokesperson in organizational perception management. Most commonly, this occurs when the organization is dominated by an employee union or unions that speak on behalf of the rank and file. In this manner, Cowden and Sellnow (2002) described how the employees of Northwest Airlines were represented as the "organization" in a contentious battle with the National Airline Pilots Association. In a series of full-page newspaper advertisements, rank and file Northwest Airlines employees spoke as a group committed to meeting the needs of customers, but hand-cuffed by a small band of rogue pilots.

ORGANIZATIONAL AUDIENCES

The fourth component of organizational perception management is organizational audiences. *Organizational audiences include all the parties who are targets of organizational perception management.* These audiences may be made up of persons external to the organization, such as members of other organizations (e.g. regulatory agencies, competing organizations, suppliers), public interest groups (e.g. consumers, environmental activists, voters), and the general public. Alternatively, audiences may be made up of persons internal to the organization, such as employees, stockholders, volunteers, dues-paying members, and students.

External Audiences

The general public is the most common external audience studied by researchers of organizational perception management. It is often the largest group affected by organizational events that threaten short-term organizational images, and includes consumers or potential consumers who hear about faulty products or services, citizens of communities harmed by environmental pollution from a corporate plant, and citizens in communities affected by corporate layoffs (Marcus & Goodman, 1991). Because these groups include so many people, and may be associated with influential political parties, their complaints receive substantial attention from the public media (Lamertz & Baum, 1998). In addition, because of the diversity of members within a group, multiple and complex perception management messages are required to adequately address all of the audiences' concerns following a negative organizational event (Sutton & Callahan, 1987).

In the absence of an immediate or impending crisis, members of special interest groups (including customers, competitors, and activists) may be the only external audiences still scrutinizing the actions of an organization. These audiences pay special attention to routine symbolic behaviors and the permanent display of physical markers that are indicative of the enduring reputations of an organization (vs. temporary or short-term images). For example, Fombrun and Shanley (1990) found that, in rating corporations reputations in the *Fortune* magazine survey of most admired companies, corporate executives, were strongly influenced by an organization's routine behaviors, including their advertising intensity, their contribution to charity, and their choice of risky strategies.

Internal Audiences

Organizational perception management aimed at internal audiences has received much less attention than that aimed at external audiences. Recent research has begun, however, to examine how managing the perceptions of internal audiences may require additional or distinct tactics (Pratt & Foreman, 2000). Specifically, organizational identities are important to internal audiences, and identity management becomes necessary when internal audiences perceive that organization's status or distinctiveness is threatened, or that its identity is internally conflicted. For example, Elsbach (2001a) found that long-time staffers working for the California State Legislature connected with the "policy making" identity of that organization, while newer and short-term staffers often identified with the "political campaigning" identity of that organization. Maintaining these two identities was a difficult act for many members, who often used physical markers to denote their decision to affiliate themselves with one of these identities rather than work to reconcile the two.

SUMMARY: A FRAMEWORK OF ORGANIZATIONAL PERCEPTION MANAGEMENT

I have defined organizational perception management as symbolic actions by organizational spokespersons to influence audiences' perceptions of the organization. Further, I have used empirical studies of organizational perception management to explicate the specific types of: (1) organizational perceptions; (2) symbolic actions; (3) organizational spokespersons; and (4) organizational audiences that are involved in managing organizational perceptions. These findings contribute to our understanding of organizational perception management by demonstrating several factors that make organizational perception management a distinct field of study from individual perception management.

First, the research presented here defines the primary forms of perceptions of organizations that may be managed through perception management (i.e.

images, reputations, and identities). While individuals may manage the same kinds of perceptions of themselves, it appears that particular perceptions are more relevant to organizations. For example, an organization's preoccupation with images of legitimacy may result from our society's more stringent regulation and requirement for standardization of organizational practices than of individual practices. Because organizations are increasingly confronted with both formal and informal certification requirements(from meeting accounting standards to fulfilling social norms about donations to charity), it seems natural that managing perceptions of legitimacy should be a priority for organizational perception managers. Similarly, organizations' emphasis on the status (vs. distinctiveness) components of identity and reputation may result, at least in part, because organizations are increasingly ranked in public surveys. By contrast, individuals are not as commonly subjected to such public rankings, and thus, they may focus more on the distinctiveness dimensions of their identity.

Second, the empirical findings reviewed in this paper suggest that an organization's symbolic actions include many of the same categories of tactics used by individual perception managers, including verbal accounts, verbal categorizations and comparisons, symbolic behaviors, and the display of physical markers. Yet these findings also reveal how such tactics are uniquely deployed within the domain of organizational perception management. In particular, organizational tactics appear to build on institutional and legitimate benchmarks for their content. Organizational accounts, for example, commonly refer to industry norms or trends to validate their excuses, justifications, or denials. Elsbach (1994) found that cattle industry spokespersons used denials of food safety violations that they backed-up with references to their use of industry norms and guidelines. Similarly, in accounts of corporate performance included in annual reports, Bettman and Weitz (1983) found that excuses for poor performance were bolstered by references to industry trends, such as higher prices for materials or a slowdown in the industry. By contrast, individual-level accounts of failures at work are more likely to refer to broad social norms, rather than industry norms, to back up their excuses or justifications (i.e. I was late for work because I had to care for a sick child) (Riordan et al., 1989). Because the actions of organizations (vs. individuals) are more likely to be evaluated in the context of industry norms (vs. social norms), it is more appropriate and effective for organizational accounts to refer to such norms.

In addition to differences associated with verbal accounts, organizational actions and physical markers appear to be operationalized differently by organizations vs. individuals. Organizations can devise, publicize, and enact corporate *strategies* that incorporate a number of activities designed to signal a single perception. For example, a corporate strategy of "environmental awareness" can be enacted through a recycling program that involves actions by marketing, manufacturing, and research and development groups, as well as the display of physical markers such as the construction of energy-efficient buildings and plants (Gotsi & Wilson, 2001). In this manner, organizations can enact a single reputation through multiple, simultaneous activities and displays of physical markers that reach diverse audiences. It would be difficult for an individual to manage his or her identities or reputations on so many fronts through so many simultaneous actions. Instead, individuals are likely to focus on one type of perception management at a time, and perhaps vary their focus over time. For example, Chen and Meindl (1991) described how the image of People's Express Airline founder, Donald Burr, evolved over time through a series of different perception management tactics, including press releases, symbolic behaviors, and verbal accounts.

Third, the research reviewed in this paper documents how organizational perception management may be carried out by a variety of organizational spokespersons – many of whom have no link to the specific organizational event or controversy that prompted the perception management. That is, unlike the individual perception manager who is primarily responsible for his or her own images, identities, and reputations, organizational perception managers are responsible for the images, identities, and reputations of a collective. Further, more than one spokesperson may manage the perceptions of this collective. Speaking or acting on behalf of an organization (versus only on behalf of an individual) presents additional dilemmas, such as dealing with the often inevitable inconsistencies between various images, identities, and reputations that define an organization, as well as inconsistencies in the expectations held by various internal and external organizational audiences. On the upside, researchers have found that maintaining more than one spokesperson means that organizations may project different (even conflicting) images to specific audiences to meet the particular needs of those audiences (Sutton & Callahan, 1987; Zbaracki, 1998).

Finally, this paper identifies both internal and external audiences of organizational perception management, and demonstrates how these are distinct from the audiences that individuals may face. In the same way that organizational spokespersons are a diverse group, audiences of organizational perception vary in their size and characteristics. Demands for identity management from employees, an internal audience, may focus on maintaining a distinct culture (e.g. of "smallness" or "collegiality"). Yet, multiple internal audiences may disagree about what identity is appropriate for the organization, leading to hybrid organizational identities that are difficult to maintain (Elsbach, 2001a). These identity conflicts would not manifest themselves in the same way for individuals as for organizations.

In other cases, there may be conflicts between the demands of an organization's internal and external audiences. Organizational consumers may demand cost cutting behaviors as symbols of their commitment to lowering prices, while employees may chafe against such actions. While such internal/external conflicts may occur for individuals (i.e. individuals may hold internal beliefs that conflict with what their friends would like them to be), such conflicts are not typically thrust into the public eye unless the individual chooses to make the conflict public.

Finally, organizations may face disagreements between the demands from various external audiences. External audiences that routinely interact with the organization (e.g. consumers) may pay most attention to routine symbolic behaviors and communications from leaders, while external audiences that only casually observe the organization may pay most attention to crisis communications or communications in anticipation of controversial events.

Taken together, these findings suggest that organizational (vs. individual) perception management involves a consideration of unique strategic issues. In particular, the above discussion suggests that organizational perception management involves matching spokesperson actions to audiences' interpretations of salient perception forms (i.e. images, reputations, or identities), as well as to organizational norms and strategies. As shown in Fig. 2, the key to successful organizational perception management starts with recognizing how different types of triggering events focus audiences' attention on: (1) specific forms of organizational perceptions; and (2) specific strategic issues (i.e. coping with audience conflicts, coordinating multiple spokespersons). Interestingly, this framework suggests that the major mistakes that spokespersons can make in carrying out organizational perception management are *not*, for example, the use of the wrong types of accounts or symbolic behaviors to manage a threatened organizational image. Rather, the major mistakes such spokespersons can make are to incorrectly identify the *form* of organizational perception that needs managing (e.g. using identity management responses, when reputation management is called for), and the *strategic issues* that need consideration (e.g. disregarding how perception management tactics fit with the organization's overall performance strategy).

In sum, there is ample evidence that organizational perception management involves a set of components that are distinct from those used in individual perception management. There is also evidence that putting these components together to effectively manage perceptions of an organization is not a simple or easy task. Still, there are many cases that illustrate how such organizational perception management may be effectively carried out. As a case in point, let us return to the trials of the National Rifle Association, originally discussed at the beginning of this paper.

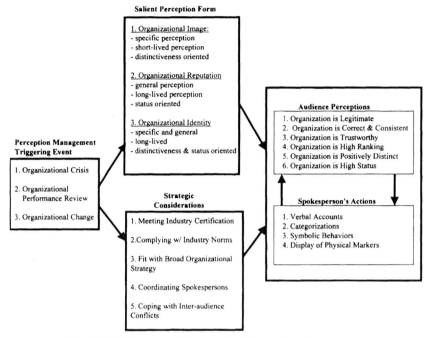

Fig. 2.   The Process of Organizational Perception Management.

The NRA: Follow-Up

In the months and years following Handgun Control Inc.'s prediction of the NRA's demise, the NRA and its leadership undertook a series of campaigns to manage these perceptions. First, it attempted to improve its current *images of legitimacy and morality* with external and internal audiences by electing a new leader. In the Spring of 1997 the NRA elected screen icon, Charleton Heston to be vice-president. Members elected him as president of the organization one year later. Heston was seen a legitimate, mainstream gun owner, and a morally and ethically sound spokesperson for the organization (most American's remember him in his film roles as Moses and Ben Hur) (Getlin, 1998, p. A1).

Second, the NRA re-affirmed its central, distinctive, and enduring *identity* as a mainstream organization by producing a series of magazine and newspaper advertisements that described the NRA's role in mainstream life. These advertisements featured famous, and widely respected members of the NRA (e.g. Heston, former NFL quarterback and Congressman, Steve Largent, and television star Tom Selleck) who claimed, "I am the NRA" in full-page advertisements

(Janofsky, 1998). Their statements equated the NRA with their personalities (e.g. mainstream, upstanding, legitimate role models).

Finally, the NRA attempted to influence its widely-perceived *reputation* by publicizing its links to other well-established and well-respected organizations and by engaging in symbolic actions that highlighted its status. For instance, it publicized its affiliation with the Boy Scouts of America in promoting shooting safety, and the NRA cartoon mascot, Eddie the Eagle, was used in gun safety programs designed by the Boy Scouts and used by other community organizations (Moscoso, 2000). It also designed and taught a college curriculum on gun safety that was offered for credit at Colorado's Trinidad State Junior College (Curtin, 1999).

Together, these tactics were credited with major improvements in audience perceptions of the NRA. By the summer of 2001, LaPierre (now the organizations CEO) reported that membership of the "New NRA" was at an all time high of 4.3 million members, that approval ratings for the organization based on national polls were running at a 20 year high of 60–65%, and that state-supported right-to-carry firearms laws were now in place in 32 states (up from only 6 states a decade earlier) (Staff, 2001). While it is likely that other events also helped to produce this turnaround (e.g. the replacement of a Democratic President, with a Republican), it seems probable that LaPierre was correct in crediting the makeover of the organization's images, identities, and reputations for its improved pubic support.

In the end, the NRA appears to have successfully implemented organizational perception management by considering the components and strategic issues outlined in this paper. This case illustrates how an understanding of the unique nature of organizational perception management can help even the most controversial organizations to repair and maintain positive and desired perceptions among its valued audiences.

REFERENCES

Albert, S., & Whetten, D. A. (1985). Organizational identity. In: B. M. Staw & L. L. Cummings (Eds), *Research in Organizational Behavior* (Vol. 7, pp. 263–295). Greenwich, CT: JAI Press.

Allen, M. W., & Caillouet, R. H. (1994). Legitimation endeavors: Impression management strategies used by an organization in crisis. *Communication Monographs, 61*, 44–62.

Arndt, M., & Bigelow, B. (2000). Presenting structural innovation in an institutional environment: Hospitals' use of impression management. *Administrative Science Quarterly, 45*, 494–522.

Arnold, S. J., Handelman, J., & Tigert, D. J. (1996). Organizational legitimacy and retail store patronage. *Journal of Business Research, 35*, 229–239.

Ashforth, B. E., & Gibbs, B. W. (1990). The double-edge of organizational legitimation. *Organization Science, 1*, 177–194.

Balmer, J. (1995). Corporate branding and connoisseurship. *Journal of General Management, 21*, 22–46.

Barney, J. B., & Hansen, M. H. (1994). Trustworthiness as a source of competitive advantage. *Strategic Management Journal, 15,* 175–190.

Benoit, W. L. (1995). *Accounts, excuses, and apologies: A theory of image restoration strategies.* Albany, NY: State University of New York Press.

Benoit, W. L. (1999). Acclaiming, attacking, and defending in presidential nominating acceptance addresses, 1960–1996. *Quarterly Journal of Speech, 85,* 247–267.

Bettman, J. R., & Weitz, B. A. (1983). Attributions in the board room: Causal reasoning in corporate annual reports. *Administrative Science Quarterly, 28,* 165–183.

Bies, R. J., Shapiro, D. L., & Cummings, L. L. (1988). Causal accounts and managing organizational conflict: Is it enough to say it's not my fault? *Communications Research, 15,* 381–399.

Brewer, M. B. (1991). The social self: On being the same and different at the same time. *Personality and Social Psychology Bulletin, 15,* 475–482.

Brockner, J. (1992). The escalation of commitment to a failing course of action: Toward theoretical progress. *Academy of Management Review, 17,* 39–61.

Broder, J. M. (1996). NRA's still flexing its muscle as some question its influence. *The Los Angeles Times,* October 31st, A14.

Butler, J. K., Jr. (1991). Towards understanding and measuring conditions of trust: Evolution of a conditions of trust inventory. *Journal of Management, 17,* 643–663.

Camerer, C., & Vepsalainen, A. (1988). The economic efficiency of corporate culture. *Strategic Management Journal, 9,* 115–126.

Chen, C. C., & Meindl, J. R. (1991). The construction of leadership images in the popular press: The case of Donald Burr and People Express. *Administrative Science Quarterly, 36,* 521–551.

Curtin, D. (1999). Critics take aim at NRA courses. College will offer group's curriculum. *The Denver Post,* April 10th, A1.

Conlon, D. E., & Murray, N. M. (1996). Customer perceptions of corporate responses to product complaints: The role of explanations. *Academy of Management Review, 39,* 1040–1056.

Cowden, K., & Sellnow, T. L. (2002). Issues advertising as crisis communication: Northwest Airlines' use of image restoration strategies during the1998 pilots' strik. *Journal of Business Communication, 39,* 193–219.

Crocker, J., & Gallo, L. (1985). Prejudice against outgroups: The self-enhancing effects of downward social comparisons. Paper presented at the Annual Convention of the American Psychological Association, Los Angeles, CA, August.

D'Aveni, R. A., & O'Neill, R. (1992). *Toward a multiple-constituency model of organizational scope and distinctive competence: A study of strategic positioning and groups among business schools.* Unpublished Manuscript, Amos Tuck School of Business Administration, Dartmouth University.

Donlon, J. P. (2000). Why John Chambers is the CEO of the future? *Chief Executive, 157,* 26–36.

Dukerich, J. M., & Carter, S. M. (2000). Distorted images and reputation repair. In: M. Schultz, M. J. Hatch & M. H. Larsen (Eds), *The Expressive Organization. Linking Identity, Reputation, and the Corporate Brand* (pp. 97–114). New York: Oxford University Press.

Dutton, J. E., & Dukerich, J. M. (1991). Keeping an eye on the mirror: Image and identity in organizational adaptation. *Academy of Management Journal, 34,* 517–554.

Dutton, J. E., Dukerich, J. M., & Harquail, C. V. (1994). Organizational images and member identification. *Administrative Science Quarterly, 39,* 239–263.

Dutton, J. E., & Penner, W. J. (1993). The importance of organizational identity for strategic agenda building. In: J. Hendry & G. Johnson (Eds), *Strategic Thinking: Leadership and the Management of Change* (pp. 89–113). New York: Wiley, Strategic Management Society.

328   KIMBERLY D. ELSBACH

Elsbach, K. D. (1994). Managing organizational legitimacy in the California cattle industry: The construction and effectiveness of verbal accounts. *Administrative Science Quarterly, 39*(1), 57–88.
Elsbach, K. D. (1999). An expanded model of organizational identification. In: B. M. Staw & R. I. Sutton (Eds), *Research in Organizational Behavior* (Vol. 21, pp. 163–200).
Elsbach, K. D. (2001a). Coping with hybrid organizational identities: Evidence from California legislative staff. In: J. Wagner (Ed.), *Advances in Qualitative Organizational Research* (Vol. 3, pp. 59–90). Oxford, UK: Elsevier.
Elsbach, K. D. (2001b). The architecture of legitimacy: Constructing accounts of organizational controversies. In: J. T. Jost & B. Major (Eds), *The Psychology of Legitimacy: Emerging Perspectives on Ideology, Justice, and Intergroup Relations* (pp. 391–415). Cambridge, UK: Cambridge University Press.
Elsbach, K. D. (2003a, in press). Managing images of trustworthiness in organizations. In: R. M. Kramer & K. Cook (Eds), *Trust and Distrust in Organizations: Enduring Questions, Emerging Perspectives*. Thousand Oaks, CA: Sage.
Elsbach, K. D. (2003b). Interpreting workplace identities: The role of office decor. *Journal of Organizational Behavior*, forthcoming.
Elsbach, K. D., & Bhattacharya, C. B. (2001). Defining who you are by what you're not: Organizational disidentification and the National Rifle Association. *Organization Science, 12*, 393–413.
Elsbach, K. D., & Kramer, R. M. (1996). Members' responses to organizational identity threats: Encountering and countering the Business Week rankings. *Administrative Science Quarterly, 41*, 442–476.
Elsbach, K. D., & Sutton, R. I. (1992). Acquiring organizational legitimacy through illegitimate actions: A marriage of institutional and impression management theories. *Academy of Management Journal, 35*, 699–738.
Elsbach, K. D., Sutton, R. I., & Principe, K. E. (1998). Averting expected controversies through anticipatory impression management: A study of hospital billing. *Organization Science, 9*, 68–86.
Folger, R., & Cropanzano, R. (1998). *Organizational justice and human resource management*. Thousand Oaks, CA: Sage.
Fombrun, C. (1996). *Reputation*. Boston, MA: Harvard Business School Press.
Fombrun, C., & Rindova, V. P. (2000). The road to transparency: Reputation management at Royal Dutch/Shell. In: M. Schultz, M. J. Hatch & M. H. Larsen (Eds), *The Expressive Organization. Linking Identity, Reputation, and the Corporate Brand* (pp. 77–96). New York: Oxford University Press.
Fombrun, C., & Shanley, M. (1990). What's in a name? Reputation building and corporate strategy. *Academy of Management Journal, 33*, 233–258.
Getlin, J. (1998). Heston chosen to lead NRA back to mainstream. *The Los Angeles Times*, June 9th, A1.
Gioia, D. A., & Thomas, J. B. (1996). Institutional identity, image, and issue interpretation: Sensemaking during strategic change in academia. *Administrative Science Quarterly, 41*, 370–403.
Gotsi, M., & Wilson, A. (2001). Corporate reputation management: "Living the brand". *Management Decision, 39*, 99.
Greenberg, J. (1990). Looking fair vs. being fair: Managing impressions of organizational justice. In: B. M. Staw & L. L. Cummings (Eds), *Research in Organizational Behavior* (Vol. 12, pp. 111–157). Greenwich, CT: JAI Press.
Greenberg, J. (1994). Using socially fair treatment to promote acceptance of a work site smoking ban. *Journal of Applied Psychology, 79*, 288–297.
Hart, K. M., Capps, H. R., Cangemi, J. P., & Caillouet, L. M. (1986). Exploring organizational trust and its multiple dimensions: A case study of General Motors. *Organizational Development Journal, 4*, 31–39.

Hatch, M. J., & Schultz, M. (2000). Scaling the Tower of Babel: Relational differences between identity, image, and culture in organizations. In: M. Schultz, M. J. Hatch & M. H. Larsen (Eds), *The Expressive organization. Linking identity, reputation, and the corporate brand* (pp. 11–35). New York: Oxford University Press.

Hearit, K. M. (1994). Apologies and public relations crisis at Chrysler, Toshiba, and Volvo. *Public Relations Review, 20*, 113–125.

Hogg, M. A., & Abrams, D. (1988). *Social identification: A social psychology of intergroup relations and group processes.* London: Routledge.

Janofsky, M. (1998). N.R.A. tries to improve image, with Charlton Heston in lead. *New York Times,* June 8th, A1.

Johnson, P. (2002). Spiked golf columns drive "Times" debate. *USA Today,* December 5th, 3D.

Kaufman, J. (2001). A successful failure: NASA's crisis communications regarding Apollo 13. *Public Relations Review, 27,* 437–448.

Kramer, R. M. (1993). Cooperation and organizational identification. In: J. Keith Murnighan (Ed.), *Social Psychology in Organizations* (pp. 244–268). Englewood Cliffs, NJ: Prentice-Hall.

Kreps, D. M., & Wilson, R. (1982). Reputation and imperfect information. *Journal of Economic Theory, 27,* 253–279.

Lamertz, K., & Baum, J. A. C. (1998). The legitimacy of organizational downsizing in Canada: An analysis of explanatory media accounts. *Canadian Journal of Administrative Sciences, 15,* 93–107.

Leary, M. R. (1996). *Self-presentation: Impression management and interpersonal behavior.* Oxford, UK: Westview Press.

Lind, E. A., & Tyler, T. R. (1988). *The social psychology of procedural justice.* New York: Plenum.

Longman, J. (1994). NRA heeds Olympic call to end team affiliation. *The New York Times,* March 15th, B14.

Marcus, A. A., & Goodman, R. S. (1991). Victims and shareholders: The dilemmas of presenting corporate policy during a crisis. *Academy of Management Journal, 34,* 281–305.

Mayer, R. C., & Davis, J. H. (1999). The effect of the performance appraisal system on trust for management: A field quasi-experiment. *Journal of Applied Psychology, 84,* 123–136.

Mayer, R. C., Davis, J. H., & Schoorman, F. D. (1995). An integrative model of organizational trust. *Academy of Management Review, 20,* 709–734.

McNamara, G., Moon, H., & Bromiley, P. (2002). Banking on commitment: Intended and unintended consequences of an organization's attempt to attenuate escalation of commitment. *Academy of Management Journal, 45,* 443–452.

Meindl, J. R., & Ehrlich, S. B. (1987). The romance of leadership and the evaluation of organizational performance. *Academy of Management Journal, 30,* 91–109.

Meyer, M. (1994). Culture club. *Business Week Magazine,* July 11th, 38–42. New York: McGraw-Hill.

Milgrom, P., & Roberts, J. (1982). Predation, reputation, and entry deterrence. *Journal of Economic Theory, 27,* 280–312.

Milgrom, P., & Roberts, J. (1986). Price and advertising signals of product quality. *Journal of Political Economy, 94,* 796–821.

Mohamed, A. A., Orife, J. N., & Slack, F. J. (2001). Organizational reputation: A literature review and a model. *International Journal of Management, 18,* 261–269.

Moscoso, E. (2000). NRA flap: Eagle ruffles feathers. *The Atlanta Journal Constitution,* June 11th, 7F.

Mueller, C. W., Boyer, E. M., Price, J. L., & Iverson, R. D. (1994). Employee attachment and noncoercive conditions of work. The case of dental hygienists. *Work and Occupations, 21,* 179–212.

Murrell, A. (2001). Signaling positive corporate social performance. *Business & Society, 40,* 59–78.

Nelson, P. (1974). Advertising as information. *Journal of Political Economy, 81,* 729–754.

Olins, W. (1995). *Corporate identity: Making business strategy visible through design*. Boston, MA: Harvard Business School Press.

Ornstein, S. (1986). Organizational symbols: A study of their meanings and influences on perceived psychological climate. *Organizational Behavior and Human Decision Processes, 38*, 207–229.

Ornstein, S. (1992). First impressions of the symbolic meanings connoted by reception area design. *Environment and Behavior, 24*, 85–110.

Pearce, J. L. (1993). Toward an organizational behavior of contract laborers: Their psychological involvement and effects on employee co-workers. *Academy of Management Journal, 36*, 1082–1096.

Pearce, J. L., Branyiczki, I., & Bakacsi, G. (1994). Person-based reward systems: A theory of organizational reward practices in reform-communist organizations. *Journal of Organizational Behavior, 15*, 261–282.

Pearson, C. M., & Clair, J. A. (1998). Reframing crisis management. *Academy of Management Review, 23*, 59–76.

Pfeffer, J., & Sutton, R. I. (1999). *The knowing-doing gap: How smart companies turn knowledge into action*. Harvard, MA: Harvard Business School Press.

Pratt, M. G., & Foreman, P. O. (2000). Classifying managerial responses to multiple organizational identities. *Academy of Management Review, 25*, 18–42.

Rao, H. (1994). The social construction of reputation: Certification contests, legitimation, and the survival of organizations in the American automobile industry: 1895–1912. *Strategic Management Journal, 15*, 29–44.

Reger, R. K., Gustafson, L. T., DeMarie, S. M., & Mullane, J. V. (1994). Reframing the organization: Why implementing total quality is easier said than done. *Academy of Management Review, 19*, 565–584.

Ridoutt, B. G., Ball, R. D., & Killerby, S. K. (2002). First impressions of organizations and the qualities connoted by wood in interior design. *Forest Products Journal, 52*, 30–36.

Riordan, C. A., James, M. K., & Runzi, M. J. (1989). Explaining failures at work: An accounter's dilemma. *Journal of General Psychology, 116*, 197–205.

Robinson, S. L., & Rousseau, D. M. (1994). Violating the psychological contract: Not the exception but the norm. *Journal of Organizational Behavior, 15*, 245–259.

Ross, J., & Staw, B. M. (1986). Expo 86: An escalation prototype. *Administrative Science Quarterly, 31*, 274–297.

Ross, J., & Staw, B. M. (1993). Organizational escalation and exit: Lessons from the Shoreham Nuclear Power Plant. *Academy of Management Journal, 36*, 701–732.

Russ, G. S. (1991). Symbolic communication and image management in organizations. In: R. A. Giacalone & P. Rosenfeld (Eds), *Applied Impression Management* (pp. 219–240). Newbury Park, CA: Sage.

Salancik, G. R., & Meindl, J. R. (1984). Corporate attributions as strategic illusions of management control. *Administrative Science Quarterly, 29*, 238–254.

Schlenker, B. R. (1980). *Impression management: The self-concept, social identity, and interpersonal relations*. Monterey, CA: Brooks/Cole.

Schmalensee, R. (1978). A model of advertising and product quality. *Journal of Political Economy, 86*, 485–503.

Schultz, M., Hatch, M. J., & Larsen, M. H. (Eds) (2000). *The expressive organization. Linking identity, reputation, and the corporate brand*. New York: Oxford University Press.

Shapiro, D. L., Buttner, E. H., & Barry, B. (1994). Explanations for rejection decisions: What factors enhance their perceived adequacy and moderate their enhancement of justice perceptions? *Organizational Behavior and Human Decision Processes, 58*, 346–368.

Shrum, W., & Withnow, R. (1988). Reputational status of organizations in technical systems. *American Journal of Sociology, 93*, 882–912.

Sisario, B. (2002). The arts: The corporations behind the curtain: Six supporters of the arts. *The New York Times*, November 18th, F13.

Smither, J. W., Reilly, R. R., Millsap, R. E., Pearlman, K., & Stoffey, R. W. (1993). Applicant reactions to selection procedures. *Personnel Psychology, 46*, 49–76.

Staff (2001). NRA chief ties membership drive to renewal. *The Buffalo News*, June 24th, C9.

Staw, B. M., & Epstein, L. D. (2000). What bandwagons bring: Effects of popular management techniques on corporate performance, reputation, and CEO pay. *Administrative Science Quarterly, 45*, 523–556.

Staw, B. M., McKechnie, P. I., & Puffer, S. M. (1983). The justification of organizational performance. *Administrative Science Quarterly, 28*, 582–600.

Staw, B. M., & Ross, J. (1987). Behavior in escalation situations: Antecedents, prototypes, and solutions. In: B. M. Staw & L. L. Cummings (Eds), *Research in Organizational Behavior* (Vol. 9, pp. 39–78). Greenwich, CT: JAI Press.

Stoffey, R. W., Millsap, R. E., Smither, J. W., & Reilly, R. R. (1991). The influence of selection procedures on attitudes about organization and job pursuit intentions. Paper presented at the Annual Conference of the Society for Industrial and Organizational Psychology, Saint Louis, MO.

Suchman, M. C. (1995). Managing legitimacy: Strategic and institutional approaches. *Academy of Management Review, 20*, 571–610.

Sundstrom, E., & Altman, I. (1989). Physical environments and work-group effectiveness. In: L. L. Cummings & B. M. Staw (Eds), *Research in Organizational Behavior* (Vol. 11, pp. 175–209). Greenwich, CT: JAI Press.

Sundstrom, E., & Sundstrom, M. G. (1986). *Work places: The psychology of the physical environment in offices and factories*. Cambridge, UK: Cambridge University Press.

Sutton, R. I., & Callahan, A. L. (1987). The stigma of bankruptcy: Spoiled organizational image and its management. *Academy of Management Journal, 30*, 405–436.

Taylor, S. J., & Bogdan, R. (1980). Defending illusions: The institution's struggle for survival. *Human Organization, 39*, 209–218.

Tedeschi, J. T. (Ed.) (1981). *Impression management theory and social psychological research*. New York: Academic Press.

Turban, D. B., & Greening, D. W. (1997). Corporate social performance and organizational attractiveness to prospective employees. *Academy of Management Journal, 40*, 658–672.

Terry, D. J., Carey, C. J., & Callan, V. J. (2001). Employee adjustment to an organizational merger: An intergroup perspective. *Personality and Social Psychology Bulletin, 27*, 267–280.

Tsui, A. S. (1990). A multiple-constituency model of effectiveness: An empirical examination at the human resource subunit level. *Administrative Science Quarterly, 35*, 458–483.

Tyler, T. R., & Lind, E. A. (1992). A relational model of authority in groups. In: M. Zanna (Ed.), *Advances in Experimental Social Psychology* (Vol. 25, pp. 115–191). San Francisco: Jossey-Bass.

Weigelt, K., & Camerer, C. (1988). Reputation and corporate strategy: A review of recent theory and applications. *Strategic Management Journal, 9*, 443–454.

Wernerfelt, B. (1984). A resource-based view of the firm. *Strategic Management Journal, 5*, 171–180.

Whitener, E. M., Brodt, S. E., Korsgaard, M. A., & Werner, J. M. (1998). Managers as initiators of trust: An exchange relationship framework for understanding managerial trustworthy behavior. *Academy of Management Review, 23*, 513–530.

Wood, J. V. (1989). Theory and research concerning social comparisons of personal attributes. *Psychological Bulletin, 106,* 231–248.

Zbaracki, M. J. (1998). The rhetoric and reality of total quality management. *Administrative Science Quarterly, 43,* 602–636.

Zelditch, M. (2001). Theories of legitimacy. In: J. T. Jost & B. Major (Eds), *The Psychology of Legitimacy: Emerging Perspectives on Ideology, Justice, and Intergroup Relations* (pp. 33–53). Cambridge, UK: Cambridge University Press.

Zremski, J. (1996). Debt, falling membership threaten NRA's firepower. *The Buffalo News,* June 5th, 1A.

UNPACKING COUNTRY EFFECTS: ON THE NEED TO OPERATIONALIZE THE PSYCHOLOGICAL DETERMINANTS OF CROSS-NATIONAL DIFFERENCES

Joel Brockner

ABSTRACT

Most cross-national research examines employees from two or more countries, who are assumed to differ on psychological dimensions in ways that influence their work attitudes or behaviors. However, the psychological dimensions assumed to influence employees' attitudes or behaviors sometimes have not been operationalized (i.e. measured or manipulated) in previous research. Moreover, even when the relevant psychological dimensions have been operationalized, their role in mediating the relationships between people's country and their work attitudes and behaviors have not been fully examined. By operationalizing (and appropriately examining the mediating role of) these psychological dimensions, cross-national researchers may make a variety of conceptual contributions, including: (a) accounting for both between- and within-country differences in work attitudes and behaviors; (b) providing greater clarity in accounting for unexpected null effects of country; and (c) providing insight into the basic theoretical processes underlying the relationships between people's country and their work attitudes and behaviors. Future research opportunities based on operationalizing the

Research in Organizational Behavior
Research in Organizational Behavior, Volume 25, 333–367
ISSN: 0191-3085/doi:10.1016/S0191-3085(03)25008-5

psychological dimensions hypothesized to account for country effects also are discussed.

INTRODUCTION

As business has globalized, organizational scholars have focused a great deal of attention on how employees' national culture influences their work attitudes and behaviors (e.g. Adler, 2002; Triandis, 1995). The guiding assumption underlying these efforts is that being brought up in a particular country fundamentally influences people's standings on a variety of psychological dimensions (e.g. values, beliefs, attributions, and decision-making tendencies), which, in turn, influence their attitudes and behaviors at work (Erez & Earley, 1993; Hofstede, 1980; Markus & Kitayama, 1991).

Cross-national research has made several important contributions to our understanding of attitudes and behaviors in the workplace. For one thing, it has enabled researchers to evaluate the cross-cultural generality of their findings. Many organizational/social phenomena have been demonstrated in Western countries (e.g. the United States), which raises the important question, as Hofstede (1980) put it, of whether "American theories apply abroad." Indeed, recent research has shown that some of the most important and robust phenomena in Western-based organizational/social psychology do not emerge to the same degree, if at all, in other countries.

Three examples of these country-dependent findings are presented next: the fundamental attribution bias, social loafing, and employees' reactions to participation in decision-making. These exemplars were selected because they refer to a variety of important organizational phenomena (e.g. manifesting themselves on different workplace dependent variables), and because they illustrate the importance of several psychological dimensions in accounting for cross-national differences. Moreover, the fact that country differences have emerged in these and other important phenomena in organizational behavior further illustrates the contributions of cross-national research. That is, in addition to speaking to matters of generalizability or external validity, cross-national research has heightened our understanding of the phenomena themselves (i.e. the factors and processes that account for them).

Cross-National Differences in Work Attitudes/Behaviors: Some Noteworthy Examples

The Fundamental Attribution Bias

The fundamental attribution bias (Ross, 1977) refers to the tendency for people to attribute the behavior of others to internal factors (e.g. others' personality, attitude, or ability), rather than external factors (e.g. organizational and environmental conditions). Originally a central finding in social psychology, the fundamental attribution bias also has important implications for behavior in organizations. For example, the remedies enacted by managers in attempting to address others' problem behaviors are likely to be based upon the perceived causes of the problems. If managers have misperceived the root causes of certain problem behaviors, then their interventions are likely to be similarly misguided.

Studies conducted in non-Western countries suggest, however, that the fundamental attribution bias may not be so "fundamental" after all (e.g. Markus & Kitayama, 1991; Morris & Peng, 1994). Rather, the tendency to make internal attributions for behavior is a product of an individualistic culture, in which people develop more independent forms of self-construal. In individualistic countries, Markus and Kitayama (1991) suggested that "achieving the cultural goal of independence requires construing oneself as an individual whose behavior is organized and made meaningful primarily by reference to one's own internal repertoire of thoughts, feelings, and actions, rather than by reference to the thoughts, feelings and actions of others" (p. 226). In contrast, the tendency to make internal attributions for behavior is less pronounced in collectivistic countries, in which people have more interdependent forms of self-construal. In collectivistic countries, achieving the cultural goal of interdependence "entails seeing oneself as part of an encompassing social relationship and recognizing that one's behavior is determined, contingent on, and . . . organized by what the actor perceives to be the thoughts, feelings, and actions of *others* in the relationship" (Markus & Kitayama, 1991, p. 227).

For those with independent self-construals, individual actors are figural whereas the context is much less salient. For those with interdependent self-construals, however, the context is figural (in particular, people's relationships with one another) whereas individual actors are much less salient. Given the perceptual/cognitive differences emanating from self-construal, it becomes easier to understand why people from collectivistic countries are less likely to exhibit the fundamental attribution bias, relative to their counterparts from more individualistic countries (Miller, 1984; Morris & Peng, 1994; Shweder & Bourne, 1984).

Social Loafing
Social loafing (also known as "free-riding") refers to the tendency for people to withhold effort in certain group settings relative to when they are acting alone. In many group contexts, members prefer to share in the collective's benefits without having to share in the costs. Consequently, group members may diffuse their personal responsibility to perform effortful activities to fellow group members. Diffusion of personal responsibility, in turn, leads to a reduction in individuals' own level of effort (social loafing). If fellow group members successfully pick up the slack, individuals may be able to reap the collective's benefit without having to

share in the costs. Of course, the performance level of the group as a whole may be adversely affected if a substantial number of group members engage in diffusion of responsibility. Put differently, one important determinant of sub-optimal group performance is social loafing.

Whereas social loafing effects have been found in many studies (e.g. Latane, Williams & Harkins, 1979), research also shows that they are less likely to emerge in a collectivistic rather than in an individualistic country (Earley, 1989). Social loafing essentially amounts to gaining individual benefit at the expense of the collective. One of the distinguishing features of an individualistic versus collectivistic belief system is the relative importance people attach to their personal interests versus those of their ingroup. Individualists attach more importance to their personal interests, whereas collectivists are more willing to subordinate their personal interests to those of the collective, particularly when the collective consists of an ingroup. It therefore stands to reason that people from countries emphasizing collectivistic beliefs would be less apt to engage in social loafing, relative to their counterparts in countries that foster more individualistic beliefs. This is precisely what Earley (1989) found in a study comparing managers from the People's Republic of China (more collectivistic) to managers from the United States (more individualistic).

Participation in Decision-Making
A basic tenet of management, at least among Western countries, is that employees' work attitudes and behaviors may be enhanced when they have input into decisions that affect them. For example, people are more likely to be supportive of decisions, decision makers, and organizations when they have participated in a decision process, relative to when the same decisions were autocratically imposed on them. Related findings have appeared in the organizational justice literature (e.g. Folger, 1986; Greenberg, 1996). Whereas many factors have been shown to influence people's judgments of procedural fairness, probably the most widely studied factor is voice, that is, whether people were given the opportunity to provide input into a decision or whether they were given any say in the actual making of the decision (Lind & Tyler, 1988; Thibaut & Walker, 1975).

Theory and research suggest that the tendency for people to respond more favorably when voice is high rather than low depends upon their country. Hofstede (1980) suggested that countries differ not only in individualism-collectivism, but also in power distance. Power distance refers to the extent to which inequality among persons in different positions of formal power is viewed as a natural (and even desirable) aspect of the social order. The norms of high power distance countries legitimize differences in decision-making power between those who are in high power positions versus those who are in low power positions.

In contrast, the norms of low power distance countries reduce power differences among people in positions of varying levels of formal decision-making power. In low power distance countries, people in positions with legitimate decision-making power are more likely to share their power with those in lower power positions.

Given the difference in cultural norms based on power distance, it stands to reason that people in high power distance countries are less likely to expect or want to have input into a decision making process, relative to their counterparts in low power distance countries. And if this is the case, then the work attitudes/behaviors of people from high power distance countries should be less influenced by the extent to which they actually had voice in a decision making process. Put differently, the tendency for people to respond more favorably when voice is high rather than low should be less pronounced in a high power distance country than in a low power distance country. The results of a recent series of studies support this reasoning (Brockner et al., 2001).

In summary, some of the most important and well-replicated phenomena in Western-based organizational behavior do not manifest themselves to equal degrees in other countries. Such cross-national differences are both theoretically and practically noteworthy. At the theoretical level, the findings provide clear limits to the external validity of certain findings, even those previously thought to be "fundamental." Moreover, the findings shed light on the basic psychological processes that account for a given result. For example, the positive effects of voice depend upon the extent to which people expect/want to have voice; the more that people expect/want voice, the more likely is their actual level of voice to influence their work attitudes and behaviors. Country-based differences in power distance beliefs, in turn, are one determinant of how much people expect/want to have voice. Thus, studies of cross-national differences help to inform the conceptual foundations on which the studies are predicated. At the practical level, the findings suggest that strategies designed to improve employees' work attitudes and behaviors must take their country into consideration. For example, Earley (1989) found that making people individually accountable reduced social loafing in the U.S., but had no effect on participants from the PRC.

In spite of these and other advances offered by previous cross-national investigations, much more needs to be learned. Indeed, the point of departure for the remainder of this chapter is that the information yield of much prior cross-national research has been compromised by the design of the study (and, to a lesser extent, by how researchers have analyzed their findings). More specifically, in most workplace studies aimed at identifying culture's consequences employees from two or more countries are examined. Whereas it is assumed that participants from the different countries differ on psychological dimensions in ways that influence their work attitudes and behaviors, the psychological dimensions often have not been operationalized (that is, measured or manipulated). The failure to operationalize the key psychological dimension(s), in turn, reduces that which may be learned from the study. For example, not operationalizing the key psychological dimension(s) makes it difficult to determine: (1) whether participants from the countries actually differed from one another in the expected directions; and (2) whether the psychological dimensions actually accounted for or mediated the relationship between employees' country and their attitudes and behaviors. Oyserman, Coon and Kemmelmeier (2002) recently commented on this design flaw in their exhaustive review of the most widely studied culturally-based values, namely individualism (IND) and collectivism (COL):

Comparisons (between participants from different countries) focus on either showing that variables of interest vary in ways that might be expected if cross-cultural differences in IND or COL exist *without directly showing the connection to IND or COL or assessing IND or COL* to show that differences in IND or COL predict differences in the variables of interest (p. 6, my parentheses and emphasis added).

To be sure, many studies have included operationalizations (e.g. measures) of the psychological dimensions that were expected to account for country differences in work attitudes and behaviors. In many of these studies, however, researchers have not fully conducted (or at least reported) the analyses that would inform readers of whether the psychological dimensions played the mediating role that they were posited to play. The current chapter calls attention to these shortcomings of much of the prior research on cross-national differences in work attitudes and behaviors. Said differently (and more optimistically), my goal is to show how the information yield of future cross-national research may be enhanced in no fewer than four important ways if investigators were to operationalize the psychological dimensions that they believe to be accounting for country differences in employees' work attitudes and behaviors (and if they were to conduct the appropriate data analytic tests of their reasoning).

First, research on cross-national differences in work attitudes or behaviors needs to do more than document the fact that country differences exist. For both theoretical and practical reasons, it is important to know *why* such differences emerge. A common cycle in science is first to demonstrate an effect, and subsequently to try to better understand when and why it occurs. There is by now ample evidence that employees from different countries often think and act differently from one another. Sorely needed at this point are theory and research that help to explain why such differences emerge. Operationalizing the psychological dimensions posited to account for country differences in work attitudes or behaviors may help researchers to account for their findings. Second, cross-national researchers often find unexpectedly null effects of country. In general, null results are more difficult to interpret than are statistically significant results. I will describe how the unexpected null effects of country in cross-national research may be more informative if researchers were to operationalize the psychological dimensions that they expected to elicit country differences. In short, whenever cross-national studies are conducted two likely outcomes are for the expected country differences to emerge or for null results to (unexpectedly) emerge. In either instance, the findings are likely to be less revealing if researchers fail to operationalize the psychological dimensions that were expected to account for significant country effects.

Third, cross-national research has the potential to contribute to our understanding of basic theoretical processes. Note the reciprocal relationship between the study of country differences in work attitudes and behaviors, and the conceptual foundation on which such studies are based. On the one hand, the conceptual foundation provides a basis for predicting and testing for country differences. On the other hand, the results that emerge may inform the conceptual foundation. Studies that test for cross-national differences in employees' attitudes or behaviors are less likely to inform basic theory, however, if researchers fail to operationalize the psychological dimensions that they expected to produce significant country effects. Let us return to the example of country differences in the effects of participation in decision-making. It seems reasonable that the effects of participation in decision-making on employees' attitudes/behaviors will be positively related to the extent to which employees expect or want to participate in decision-making. One way to evaluate this reasoning is by including as independent variables in the research design factors reflective of how much employees expect or want to participate in decision-making. One such factor, in turn, consists of (country-based differences in) power distance. It is not enough simply to treat participants' country as a proxy for the psychological dimension. Rather, a far better design strategy is to operationalize the psychological dimension itself. Fourth, cross-national studies that simply classify people on the basis of their country ignore potentially meaningful within-country variation on the psychological dimensions that may account for country differences in employees' attitudes or behaviors (Vandello & Cohen, 1999). Indeed, within-country variation on the psychological dimensions is treated as error variance whenever people are classified simply on the basis of their country. By operationalizing the psychological dimensions expected to elicit *between*-country differences in work attitudes or behaviors, researchers also may be better able to understand the basis of *within*-country variation on those same attitudes or behaviors. Relatedly, participants' country is a categorical variable whereas the psychological dimensions expected to account for country effects often may be treated as continuous variables. Regardless of whether researchers are trying to account for *between*- or *within*-country differences in work attitudes and behaviors, classifying participants on the basis of continuous (rather than categorical) variables allows for more powerful and nuanced hypothesis-testing.

The remainder of the chapter is divided into two main sections. First, I elaborate on each of these four points of how cross-national research may be enhanced if researchers were to devote greater attention to operationalizing the psychological dimensions expected to elicit country differences in work attitudes and behaviors. I also will provide examples of the relatively few studies that have operationalized (and appropriately tested for the mediating influence of) the relevant psychological dimensions, and how such studies have enhanced the information yield of cross-national research. The second section of the paper describes how future cross-national research may benefit from studies in which researchers attend to the psychological mediators of country effects on employees' attitudes and behaviors.

Benefits of Operationalizing the Psychological Mediators:
Some Recent Evidence

It is ironic that researchers sometimes do not operationalize the psychological dimensions that they are assuming to account for country differences in work attitudes and behaviors. In most cross-national studies, investigators not only expect to find country differences in employees' attitudes or behaviors, but also they have hypotheses about why such country differences may be found. Implicit in their theorizing is that certain psychological dimensions differ by country, which in turn, will lead to differences in employees' work attitudes and behaviors. Given that researchers have already developed a conceptual basis for predicting country differences in employees' attitudes and behaviors, it often is not too difficult to evaluate their reasoning by operationalizing the psychological dimensions that they are assuming to be influential. In some instances all that may be needed is to measure the psychological dimensions (e.g. via self-report). In short, the costs of operationalizing the psychological dimensions may be relatively low, and the benefits (to be described next) may be substantial.

BENEFIT NO. 1: ACCOUNTING FOR (NOT MERELY DEMONSTRATING) BETWEEN-COUNTRY DIFFERENCES

The mere demonstration of between-country differences in phenomena such as the fundamental attribution bias or social loafing does not necessarily mean that they are due to the reasons hypothesized to account for them (e.g. Earley & Mosakowski, 1996; Leung & Bond, 1989; Van de Vijver & Leung, 2000). Consider, for example, the well-replicated "truth" in various management literatures that giving employees voice (or having them participate) in organizational decision-making procedures makes them more likely to support the decisions that are reached, the authorities responsible for planning the decisions, and the institutions in which the decisions are rendered (Folger, 1986; Greenberg, 1996; Lawler, 1992; Lind & Tyler, 1988). The positive effects of participation in decision-making are not universal; they are considerably less pronounced among people from high power distance countries than they are among people from low power distance countries (Brockner et al., 2001).

Whereas country-based differences in power distance beliefs are one explanation of these findings, they are by no means the only one. At a conceptual level, perhaps it was some other psychological dimension, in addition to or instead of power distance beliefs that accounted for country differences in reaction to voice. At a methodological level, perhaps people from different countries used the rating scales (accompanying the dependent variables) differently. For example, research has found country differences in people's willingness to use the endpoints of rating scales (e.g. Hui & Triandis, 1989). Moreover, there is some evidence that people from certain high power distance countries (e.g. those in parts of Asia) are less willing to make ratings on the endpoints of scales, relative to their counterparts in low power distance countries (Stening & Everett, 1984). If the tendency to avoid using scale endpoints were related to people's power distance beliefs, then such a relationship may pose a potential methodological artifact to the finding that employees' actual level of participation in decision-making has more of an influence on their attitudes and behaviors in low power distance countries than in high power distance countries.

As a first step towards evaluating the conceptual and methodological alternative explanations raised above, researchers need to examine whether the hypothesized country difference in participants' power distance beliefs actually emerged. *The expected between-country difference in power distance beliefs cannot simply be assumed to be present.* Psychological factors that differ between countries also vary to a considerable extent on a within-country basis (e.g. Vandello & Cohen, 1999). Given the within-country variation, researchers need to evaluate whether the expected between-country difference was present *in their particular samples.*

Moreover, and of greater theoretical significance, it is not sufficient merely to verify the presence of the expected between-country difference. It also is necessary to conduct mediational analyses to evaluate whether the expected between-country difference accounted for the predicted findings. Previous studies often have failed to test for mediation completely, even when the investigators have gathered the information necessary to do so. For example, in some studies researchers have assessed the psychological dimensions assumed to differentiate people from various countries, and have even observed the expected country difference (akin to a "manipulation check" in experimental research). However, in testing their main hypotheses they continue to classify participants only on the basis of country rather than the psychological dimension hypothesized to be influential (e.g. Tower, Kelly & Richards, 1997). In other instances researchers examine participants from multiple countries and assess the relevant psychological dimensions, but only present the results of analyses in which participants are classified on the basis of their standing on the psychological dimensions. That is, country effects (that the psychological dimensions may be able to account for) often are not reported (e.g. Tyler, Lind & Huo, in press).

Based on the general principles set forth by Baron and Kenny (1986), a more complete demonstration of psychological mediation of country effects consists of showing that: (1) people's country is related to their work attitudes or behaviors; (2) people's country is related to the psychological dimension; (3) the psychological dimension is related to people's work attitudes or behaviors; and (4) the relationship between people's country and their work attitudes or behaviors is significantly reduced when the psychological dimension is statistically controlled. Even more persuasive evidence of mediation is shown if the relationship between the psychological dimension and people's work attitudes or behaviors remains significant when their country is controlled.

Several recent studies have tested for mediation in these ways, and have shown compelling evidence. For example, in the research examining the effect of country-based differences in power distance and participation in decision-making on employees' organizational commitment, participants completed a measure of their power distance beliefs (Brockner et al., 2001). In three separate studies, participants drawn from countries expected to foster relatively high power distance beliefs (Hong Kong, Mexico, and the PRC) were shown in fact to be higher in power distance, relative to their counterparts from countries assumed to foster lower power distance beliefs (Germany and the U.S.). As expected, level of participation was more positively related to the work attitudes and behaviors of participants from the lower than the higher power distance countries. Moreover, in all three studies the results of mediational analyses showed that it was participants' power distance beliefs (and not simply their country) that influenced the magnitude of the positive effects of participation on their work attitudes and behaviors.

Other researchers recently used the same investigative strategy (that is, operationalizing the key psychological dimensions via measurement) to better account for observed country differences in people's attitudes and behaviors. One such study dealt with ingroup favoritism, the pervasive tendency for people to believe that the groups to which they belong (hereafter referred to as their ingroups) are inherently better or more desirable than groups to which they do not belong (hereafter referred to as their outgroups; Brewer, 1979; Tajfel & Turner, 1986).

At first blush, it may be expected that people from countries that emphasize collectivism would show greater ingroup favoritism, relative to their counterparts from countries that emphasize individualism. A recent study by Chen, Brockner and Katz (1998) sought to refine this assertion by delineating some of the conditions under which ingroup favoritism would be more pronounced among people in collectivistic versus individualistic countries. In particular, Chen et al. (1998) theorized that the relationship between collectivism and ingroup favoritism would be more pronounced under conditions that were more threatening to the ingroup.

To test this hypothesis, participants from the PRC (expected to be more collectivistic) and the U.S. (expected to be more individualistic) were assigned to a group (the ingroup) and led to believe that another group (the outgroup) was working on the same task. Individual performance feedback and ingroup performance feedback were manipulated orthogonally. Half of the participants were told that they performed well on an individual basis whereas the remaining half were told that they performed poorly on an individual basis. Moreover, independent of their own level of performance, half were told that their ingroup performed well whereas half were told that their ingroup performed poorly. All participants were then asked to evaluate both their ingroup and the outgroup on a variety of dimensions (e.g. motivated, ambitious, creative, friendly, sincere, trustworthy, considerate, and intelligent). Ingroup favoritism was defined as the tendency to evaluate the ingroup more positively than the outgroup. Presumably, the condition that was most evaluatively threatening to the ingroup was the one in which the ingroup performed poorly while the individual performed well (in that the ingroup's performance was negative on both an absolute basis and on a relative basis). As predicted, the tendency for participants from the PRC to show greater ingroup favoritism than those from the U.S. was much more pronounced when the individuals performed well and the ingroup performed poorly, relative to all other conditions.

To operationalize the psychological dimension presumed to account for the country difference in ingroup favoritism, Chen et al. (1998) also had participants complete a measure of individual-collective primacy, which refers to "the extent to which people will be willing to sacrifice personal benefits to achieve the benefits of their ingroup when the interests of the individual and the ingroup are in conflict with one another" (p. 1491). As expected, participants from the PRC exhibited much greater collective primacy than did those from the U.S. Moreover, when participants were classified on the basis of their individual-collective primacy beliefs rather than on the basis of their country, it was found that the relationship between participants' collective primacy and their ingroup favoritism was most pronounced when they performed well individually and their ingroup performed poorly, relative to all other conditions. Of greater importance, mediational analyses showed that it was participants' individual-collective primacy beliefs (and not their country) that interacted with individual and ingroup performance feedback to influence their ingroup favoritism. In other words, the effect of participants' country on their ingroup favoritism was attributable to their individual-collective primacy beliefs.

Evidence of this sort also goes a long way towards addressing the challenge of achieving cross-cultural equivalence. As Leung and Su (in press) pointed out, the internal validity of cross-cultural research is threatened by the possibility that participants from different countries may differ on many other dimensions (both methodological and conceptual) besides the focal psychological factors hypothesized to account for country differences in employees' attitudes or behaviors. The mediational evidence cited above showed that the relationship between the psychological dimension (e.g. individual-collective primacy) and the dependent variable (e.g. ingroup favoritism) took the same form in both countries, thereby making it less likely that the various sources of non-equivalence between cultures provided a rival explanation of the findings.

Of course, this is hardly the first time that cross-national researchers have been encouraged to operationalize the psychological dimensions posited to account for country differences in employees' attitudes and behaviors (e.g. Earley & Mosakowski, 1996; Leung & Su, in press; Whiting, 1976). In fact, a few studies have heeded this recommendation (across different substantive areas in organizational behavior). Morris et al. (1998) showed that the tendency for Chinese managers to be more conflict-avoidant than their U.S. counterparts was attributable to the Schwartz (1992) value dimension of societal conservatism. Earley (1994) found that country-based differences in people's individualistic or collectivistic beliefs interacted with the type of training they received (self- or group-focused) to influence their self-efficacy and task performance. Managers with individualistic beliefs did better with self-focused training, whereas those with collectivistic beliefs did better with group-focused training. In these studies (see also Brockner, Chen, Mannix, Leung & Skarlicki, 2000), the authors demonstrated a significant relationship between employees' country and their attitudes or behaviors, and then conducted further (mediational) analyses to explain why the country differences emerged. The results of the mediational analyses showed that it was employees' standing on the relevant psychological dimensions that accounted for the country difference in their attitudes or behaviors. In sharp contrast, in the vast majority of cross-national studies researchers have not done both of the following: (1) test for country differences in work attitudes and behaviors; *and* (2) conduct complete mediational analyses to evaluate whether participants' standing on the relevant psychological dimensions accounted for the relationship between their country and their work attitudes and behaviors.

The relatively few studies in which complete mediational analyses were conducted used a similar procedure to operationalize the psychological dimensions hypothesized to play the mediating role. Psychological dimensions such as power distance beliefs, self-construal, individual-collective primacy, and societal conservatism were operationalized on the basis of self-report, individual difference measures. Whereas self-report, individual difference measures are one way to operationalize the psychological dimensions hypothesized to account for the effects of country, they are by no means the only way. Additional ways to operationalize the key psychological dimensions are discussed in a subsequent section of the chapter, in which future research opportunities are considered.

Prior to that discussion, I should mention that it is both methodologically and conceptually important to use methods other than self-report, individual difference measures to operationalize the psychological dimensions presumed to be influential. At the methodological level, the use of alternative modes of operationalization may help to show that the findings presented above are not an artifact of the method used to operationalize the influential psychological dimensions. That is, it is important to demonstrate that it is the dimensions themselves (and not how they are operationalized) that are influential. At the conceptual level, all of the findings presented above show that the effects of country disappeared once researchers controlled for individual differences in the psychological dimensions. This pattern of findings could lead to the misleading impression that people's country is merely a proxy for individual difference variables. I do *not* mean to suggest that once it is known where people stand on the individual difference dimensions, it is not necessary to know their country in order to account for their work attitudes or behaviors. I elaborate on this point in the final section of the chapter.

BENEFIT NO. 2: ACCOUNTING FOR
UNEXPECTED NULL RESULTS

Researchers sometimes conduct studies in multiple countries in a quest to discover universal laws of behavior. In these so-called generalizability studies (Van de Vijver & Leung, 1997) the relationships between the main variables are not expected to differ by country. More typically, however, cross-cultural researchers do not conduct studies in multiple countries in a quest for universalism. On the contrary, one of the main drivers of cross-national research is that the findings are expected to vary by country. Nevertheless, it is not uncommon for research motivated by the expectation of country differences in work attitudes and behaviors to yield null effects. In this section I suggest that even when null effects of country unexpectedly emerge, researchers may be able to increase the informativeness of their findings by operationalizing the psychological dimensions that they expected (but did not find) to elicit between-country differences.

A basic tenet of research is that it is often more difficult to interpret the meaning of null results relative to those that are statistically significant. Null results may come about for numerous reasons. Perhaps the conceptualization guiding the study was flawed or incorrect. In addition, null results could occur for operational reasons. Operational reasons, in turn, subsume a variety of ways in which the independent or dependent variables lacked reliability or validity. For example, the independent variable may have been operationalized "weakly," thereby increasing the chances of a Type II error (which could manifest itself as a null result).

The ambiguity of null results applies to those instances in which cross-national investigators fail to obtain predicted country differences in employees' attitudes or behaviors. Perhaps the null results were due to the possibility that the conceptual basis or rationale for predicting the between-country difference was incorrect. Alternatively, the conceptual basis may have been appropriate, but participants from the different countries may not have differed enough (or at all) on the underlying psychological dimensions; that is, people's country may not have been an adequate or accurate proxy for the psychological dimension that was expected to account for the between-country difference. For instance, as cultures change, so might the psychological dimensions that they affect. Younger participants may not identify with traditional cultural beliefs and values, and therefore may not exhibit the psychological tendencies shown by older participants.

One way to evaluate these different explanations of unexpected null country effects, of course, is by examining whether participants from the different countries actually differed from one another on the psychological dimension that was expected to elicit a country effect in the first place. The results of a recent study by Chen, Brockner and Chen (2002) help to illustrate this point. Building on the results of an earlier study (Chen et al., 1998), Chen et al. (2002) hypothesized that greater collective primacy may predispose people to show more ingroup favoritism under conditions that are evaluatively threatening to the ingroup. As in the earlier study, all participants were assigned to a group (the ingroup) to work on a task, and were told that another group (the outgroup) was working on the same task. Moreover, participants were drawn from two countries: the PRC (in which participants were expected to have greater collective primacy) and the U.S. (in which participants were expected to be higher in individual primacy).

Threat to the ingroup was operationalized on the basis of feedback about the performance of the ingroup and the outgroup. Half of the participants were told that their ingroup performed well whereas the remaining half were informed that their ingroup performed poorly. Orthogonally manipulated was information about the performance of the outgroup; half of the participants were led to believe that the outgroup performed well whereas the remaining half were told that the outgroup performed poorly. Chen et al. (2002) predicted that the tendency for participants from the PRC to show greater ingroup favoritism than those from the U.S. would be especially pronounced when the ingroup performed poorly and the outgroup performed well. In other words, greater collective primacy was expected to lead to more ingroup protection. Note that this prediction, if confirmed, would provide a conceptual replication of the findings of Chen et al. (1998), who found that collective primacy was especially positively related to ingroup favoritism in the face of other information that was evaluatively threatening to the ingroup (i.e. when the ingroup performed poorly while the individual performed well).

As an extension of the earlier findings, Chen et al. (2002) also predicted that being higher in collective primacy would lead people to show greater ingroup favoritism when their ingroup performed well and the outgroup performed poorly. In other words, not only were high collective-primacy individuals expected to protect their ingroup (by showing greater ingroup favoritism when the ingroup performed poorly and the outgroup performed well), but also high collective primacy persons were expected to enhance their ingroup (by showing greater ingroup favoritism when the ingroup performed well and the outgroup performed poorly). In contrast, the relationship between individual-collective primacy and ingroup favoritism was expected to be weaker when the ingroup and outgroup both performed poorly or when they both performed well.

When participants were classified on the basis of their country (PRC or U.S.), the results were in the direction of these predictions but they were not significant. Participants also completed the identical survey used by Chen et al. (1998) to measure their individual-collective primacy beliefs. Whereas participants from the PRC showed more of a collective primacy orientation than those from the U.S., this country difference in collective primacy was not nearly as pronounced as it was in the Chen et al. (1998) study. In particular, the U.S. participants in the Chen et al. (2002) study exhibited much more of a collective primacy orientation than did the U.S. participants in the Chen et al. (1998) study. In fact, this *between*-study differ- ence in individual-collective primacy *among* the U.S. participants was significantly greater than the difference in individual-collective primacy between the U.S. and PRC participants *within* the Chen et al. (2002) study. The fact that participants' country was not a strong proxy for their individual-collective primacy beliefs in the Chen et al. (2002) study may help to explain why the authors found a null (country) effect.

Of course, an alternative possibility is that the conceptual rationale used by Chen et al. (2002) to predict country differences in ingroup favoritism may have been inaccurate. Perhaps the authors simply were wrong to predict that people with more of a collective primacy orientation would be especially likely to show greater ingroup favoritism when the ingroup performed worse or better than (rather than the same as) the outgroup. To evaluate this possibility, Chen et al. (2002) conducted an additional analysis in which participants were classified not on the basis of their country, but rather on the basis of their individual-collective primacy beliefs. As predicted, the results showed that collective primacy and ingroup favoritism were positively related when: (1) the ingroup performed poorly and the outgroup performed well, reflecting greater ingroup protection among those with more of a collective primacy orientation; and (2) the ingroup performed well and the outgroup performed poorly, reflecting greater ingroup enhancement among those with more of a collective primacy orientation. Furthermore, individual-collective primacy and ingroup favoritism were unrelated when the ingroup and outgroup both performed well or when they both performed poorly (in which the motivation to protect or enhance the ingroup should have been less pronounced).

In short, by evaluating whether people from different countries differ on the key underlying psychological dimensions, researchers may be better able to account for unexpected null effects of country. Put differently, had Chen et al. (2002) *not* measured individual-collective primacy, they would have been left with a very unenlightening set of findings. Not only would they have found null results in examining when country differences in ingroup favoritism would emerge, but also (and perhaps even more troubling) they would have had no way of knowing *why* the null results emerged. For example, they may have inappropriately concluded that their conceptual rationale was incorrect. In fact, the problem appeared not to be with the conceptual rationale, but rather with the fact that participants' country was not as much of a proxy for their individual-collective primacy beliefs as had been expected.

Dealing With Null Mediation Effects

Another type of null effect may be present even when significant country effects emerge. More specifically, it is entirely possible for predicted country effects to be found on both the psychological dimensions and on the ultimate dependent variables. Such findings do not necessarily suggest that the psychological dimensions account for country differences on the ultimate dependent variables. Put differently, even if Variable A (country) is related to each of Variable B (the psychological dimension) and Variable C (the ultimate dependent variable) in the expected directions, it does not necessarily follow that Variable B accounts for or mediates the relationship between Variables A and C.

How might one deal with null mediation effects? One possibility is that the mediating variable needs to be refined. For example, suppose that the psychological construct hypothesized to be the mediator actually consisted of multiple sub-factors. In the extensive literature on individualism and collectivism, Oyserman et al. (2002) suggested that no fewer than seven factors have been considered to be aspects of the former, and that eight different factors have been considered to be aspects of the latter. Given the multi-dimensional nature of IND and COL, it is entirely plausible for certain sub-factors to be more germane than others in accounting for country differences in work attitudes and behaviors. For example, Chen et al. (1998) expected participants from the PRC to show greater ingroup favoritism than their counterparts from the U.S. when their ingroup performed poorly while they performed well individually. Furthermore, this effect was expected to be accounted for by IND and/or COL. Chen et al. included several "off the shelf" measures of individualism and collectivism, including Triandis' (1995) constructs of horizontal and vertical individualism and collectivism, interdependent self-construal (Singelis, 1994), and an independent self-construal scale that the authors had employed in a previous study (Brockner & Chen, 1996). In fact, significant country differences emerged on many of these measures, and in the expected directions. For instance, the U.S. sample was significantly higher in horizontal individualism and independent self-construal than were those from the PRC, whereas the PRC sample was significantly higher in vertical collectivism and interdependent self-construal than were those from the U.S.

Whereas the predicted country difference in ingroup favoritism emerged, and whereas participants from the two countries differed from one another in the expected directions on the various measures of IND and COL, mediational analyses showed that none of the "off the shelf" measures of IND and COL accounted for the relationships between participants' country and their tendencies towards ingroup favoritism. Upon further reflection, Chen et al. (1998) hypothesized that it may have been a particular aspect of IND and COL that was most likely to play a mediating role. This factor, known as individual-collective primacy, refers to whether people are more likely to pursue their individual interests versus those of their ingroup when forced to choose between the two. The authors then went back to select those items from the various scales that appeared to be the most face valid measures of individual-collective primacy. Not only did participants from the PRC show greater collective primacy than their U.S. counterparts, but also mediational analyses showed that the individual-collective primacy dimension accounted for the relationship between participants' country and their tendency to show ingroup favoritism.

The Chen et al. (1998) findings suggest that in attempting to identify mediators of between-country differences in employees' attitudes and behaviors, researchers may be more successful when they do not simply use pre-existing scales (at least in their entirety). Instead, careful theoretical reasoning should guide the choice and design of the measure to ensure that it reflects the specific psychological dimension hypothesized to be influential. With this intention, Chen et al. designed a measure that drew upon a subset of items from existing scales, which directly tapped the hypothesized mediator. As Chen et al. found, the most appropriate measure of the mediating variable may consist of a subset of items from multiple scales that are already in use. Or, it may be necessary to generate new items if those from extant scales are not deemed to represent the intended construct adequately.

In summary, it is entirely possible for cross-national researchers to find null effects in their attempts to: (1) demonstrate; or (2) account for, country differences in employees' attitudes and behaviors. The preceding discussion suggests, however, that the information yield of (even) null results may be heightened if researchers were to operationalize the psychological dimensions that they expected to mediate the relationships between employees' countries and their attitudes/behaviors.

BENEFIT NO. 3: CONTRIBUTING TO OUR UNDERSTANDING OF BASIC THEORETICAL PROCESSES

Operationalizing the psychological dimensions expected to account for country differences in work attitudes and behaviors may enable researchers to test the adequacy of their conceptual rationales, not only as a means towards better understanding unexpected null results, but also as a conceptually important activity in its own right. Earlier, I noted the reciprocal relationship between the study of country differences in work attitudes and behaviors, and the conceptual foundation on which such studies are based. Just as the conceptual foundation provides a basis for predicting country differences, the results that emerge may inform the conceptual foundation. Consider, for example, the conceptual basis for studying the moderating effect of power distance on people's reactions to participation in decision-making. Brockner et al. (2001) posited that people are more influenced by their level of actual participation in decision-making to the extent that they expect or want to participate. That is, the more that people expect or want to participate in decision-making, the more likely is their level of actual participation to influence their attitudes and behaviors.

Note that the proposition in the preceding sentence is worth testing in its own right, regardless of whether it is done in a cross-national context. That is, country-based power distance beliefs are one factor that may influence the extent to which people expect or want to participate in decision-making. However, other factors that influence how much people expect or want to participate in a decision-making process also should have a moderating influence on their reactions to their level of actual participation. For example, in a study conducted among U.S. participants only, Greenberg, Eskew and Miles (1991) experimentally manipulated whether students expected to have input into a grading process. Students' actual level of input into the grading process also was varied. Greenberg et al. found that the typical relationship between participation and perceived fairness (e.g. Lind & Tyler, 1988; Thibaut & Walker, 1975) depended upon participants' prior expectations. The more that they expected to participate in the decision process, the more likely they were to rate the process as fair when their actual level of input was high rather than low.

Thus, another reason to operationalize the psychological dimensions expected to account for country effects on work attitudes and behaviors is that doing so facilitates the study of conceptually important questions. Regardless of whether participants from different countries exhibit the expected differences from one another on the psychological dimensions, researchers should take advantage of the opportunity provided by cross-national research to test propositions of more basic theoretical importance.

For example, let's return to the study by Chen et al. (2002) that was originally designed to identify the conditions under which country-based differences in individual-collective primacy would elicit greater ingroup favoritism. Whether participants came from the U.S. or the PRC had no effect on their ingroup favoritism, probably because participants' country was not as much of a proxy for their individual-collective primacy beliefs as had been expected. In addition to the null effects of country, however, Chen et al. found results of theoretical importance. That is, collective primacy and ingroup favoritism were positively related to one another when: (1) people's needs to protect their ingroup had been elicited (i.e. when the ingroup performed worse than the outgroup); and (2) people had an opportunity to enhance their ingroup (i.e. when the ingroup performed better than the outgroup). When the ingroup and outgroup performed equally (well or poorly), collective primacy and ingroup favoritism were not related.

One interpretation of these findings is that ingroup favoritism does not merely depend upon evaluative information about the ingroup and outgroup (e.g. their relative levels of performance). What may also be influential is the degree of psychological importance that people attach to their ingroup. The greater the importance people assign to their ingroup, the greater the ingroup favoritism (particularly under conditions that elicit people's need to protect their ingroup or provide them with an opportunity to enhance their ingroup).

Of course, this reasoning may be evaluated in further research (cross-national or otherwise). Presumably, other factors that influence the degree of importance that people assign to their ingroup may interact with evaluative information about the ingroup and outgroup to influence ingroup favoritism. For example, the amount of importance people assign to their ingroups may depend not only on individual difference factors (such as individual-collective primacy), but also on contextual variables. Thus, whenever group members are united in their belief that a group's goals are important or worthwhile, they are likely to assign significance to the ingroup (Mackie & Goethals, 1987). The role of these and other contextual determinants of the importance people assign to their ingroups may be investigated in future research on the antecedents of ingroup favoritism.

In summary, operationalizing the psychological dimensions expected to account for country differences in work attitudes and behaviors provides researchers with an opportunity to examine conceptually important questions, regardless of whether the expected differences between countries emerge on the psychological dimensions themselves.

BENEFIT NO. 4: ACCOUNTING FOR VARIATION WITHIN COUNTRIES

Psychological dimensions that may account for between-country differences in work attitudes/behaviors also vary considerably within countries. Indeed, a recent study by Vandello and Cohen (1999) found significant regional differences in people's individualistic-collectivistic beliefs *within* the United States. The presence of within-country variation on the psychological dimensions that account for between-country differences presents yet another conceptual and empirical opportunity. Just as variations on these dimensions may help to explain between-country differences in work attitudes and behaviors, so may variations on these dimensions help to account for within-country differences in work attitudes and behaviors.[1]

For example, Brockner and Chen (1996) took as their point of departure a well-established finding in the self-esteem literature (based primarily on theory and research in Western countries): that high self-esteem persons will engage in greater self-protection in the face of negative self-evaluative feedback, relative to their low self-esteem counterparts (Crocker, Thompson, McGraw & Ingerman, 1987; Taylor & Brown, 1988). The authors tested this hypothesis on a group of participants from both the U.S. and the PRC. After completing a measure of their self-esteem, participants worked on a task and were given feedback that they had performed poorly or not. The results within the U.S. replicated those found previously: when participants were given negative feedback, high self-esteem persons were more self-protective than were those low in self-esteem.

Within the PRC, however, there was no overall tendency for high self-esteem persons to show greater self-protection in response to negative feedback. This may have been because the authors' conception of self-esteem was derived from theory and research conducted in Western (individualistic) countries, in which people tend to have more independent forms of self-construal (Diener & Diener, 1995; Markus & Kitayama, 1991; Schaubroeck, Lam & Xie, 2000). Such a conception may have been less applicable to people from the PRC, a collectivistic country in which people's self-construals generally are more interdependent. This is not to say, however, that *all* people in the PRC have interdependent rather than independent forms of self-construal.

Participants in the Brockner and Chen (1996) study completed a self-report measure of independent self-construal. It was predicted that those from the PRC with more independent forms of self-construal should behave similarly to those from the U.S., who tend to have independent self-construals. (Moreover, those from the U.S. with less independent forms of self-construal should behave similarly to those from the PRC, who tend to have less independent self-construals.) This is precisely what was found. For example, among those in the PRC with more independent forms of self-construal, the greater their self-esteem the more they engaged in self-protection in response to negative individual feedback. No such tendency emerged, however, among those from the PRC with less independent forms of self-construal.

Other research previously considered (in the context of accounting for between-country differences in work attitudes and behaviors) also included studies that had been conducted within a single country. For example, Brockner et al. (2001, Study 4) examined a group of employees only from the PRC in testing for the moderating impact of people's power distance beliefs on their reactions to participation in organizational decision-making. Among employees with higher power distance beliefs, participation in decision-making was less strongly related to their organizational commitment and job performance, relative to those lower in power distance. Such findings, of course, are conceptually analogous to those found in the between-country studies. In another within-country study conducted in the PRC, Farh, Earley and Lin (1997) measured the extent to which participants adhered to traditional cultural values. Those with less traditional or more modern values were more likely to exhibit a positive relationship between their perceptions of organizational justice and their willingness to engage in organizational citizenship behavior.

In sum, people vary on pivotal psychological dimensions (e.g. power distance beliefs, traditionality) both on a between-country basis and on a within-country basis. As students of cultural influence, we care about both between-country effects as well as within-country effects. By operationalizing the psychological dimensions that are presumed to influence people's work attitudes and behaviors, we are better able to account for both between-country and within-country sources of variance.

Future Research Opportunities

The preceding section considered the different types of conceptual benefits that already have been gained when researchers operationalized (and appropriately examined the impact of) the psychological dimensions hypothesized to account for between-country differences in work attitudes and behaviors. In this final section I consider some other types of benefits that may be achieved in the future, emanating from researchers having operationalized the psychological dimensions posited to account for country differences in work attitudes and behaviors.

FUTURE OPPORTUNITY NO. 1: FURTHER PINPOINTING THE ROLE OF THE PSYCHOLOGICAL DIMENSIONS

The operationalization of psychological dimensions such as individual-collective primacy (e.g. Chen et al., 1998), power distance beliefs (e.g. Brockner et al., 2001), and societal conservatism (Morris et al., 1998) has enabled researchers to identify factors that may account for between-country differences in employees' work attitudes and behaviors. Nevertheless, further research is needed to clarify the role played by these and other psychological dimensions, and may do so in at least three different ways. First, it is important to differentiate the effect of the focal psychological dimension from that of other (empirically related but conceptually distinct) dimensions. Second, it is necessary to identify more precisely the factor(s) and process(es) through which the focal psychological dimensions account for the relationships between employees' country and their work attitudes and behaviors. Third, it is important to broaden the terrain of psychological dimensions that may account for cross-national differences in employees' attitudes or behaviors. Much if not most previous research has emphasized the role of (country differences) in values, drawing on the frameworks set forth by Hofstede (1980) and Schwartz (1992), among others. Whereas values: (1) differ between countries; and (2) influence employees' attitudes and behaviors, they are not alone in those two regards. Moreover, in the quest to identify influential psychological dimensions (values or otherwise), it is natural and worthwhile to draw upon frameworks whose primary purpose is to explain cross-national differences in people's attitudes and behaviors. However, it will be suggested that literatures not originally designed to account for cross-national differences may provide some useful leads in this regard.

Differentiating Between Psychological Dimensions

Given the nature of the research designs in many previous studies (in which the focal psychological dimensions were operationalized via measurement), it may have been other factors correlated with the focal psychological dimensions that were truly influential, instead of or in addition to the focal psychological dimensions themselves. Several procedures may be used in future research to differentiate between empirically related but conceptually distinct psychological dimensions. One method is to measure not only the focal psychological dimension, but also the other related factors. Researchers could then statistically evaluate the relative influence of the focal psychological dimension and these other factors in accounting for between-country differences. For example, whereas power distance beliefs already have been shown to have a moderating influence on participation in decision-making (Brockner et al., 2001), recent research has shown that individualistic beliefs moderated the relationship between participation in decision-making and job performance (such that participation had more of an influence on those with more individualistic beliefs; Lam, Chen & Schaubroeck, in press). Given that power distance and individualism tend to be modestly (inversely) related to each other, future research is needed to delineate the relative influence of these two factors in moderating the relationship between participation and job performance. Yet another possibility that could be examined if multiple psychological dimensions were to be operationalized is whether the psychological dimensions jointly influence the effect of interest. For example, perhaps the effect of participation on job performance will be particularly acute among people who are both high in individualism and low in power distance.

Second, the role of the focal psychological dimension and related factors may be investigated in the context of an experimental design (Leung & Su, in press). If certain psychological dimensions account for the effects of country, then experimental manipulations of those dimensions should produce similar effects. To return to the previous example, within each of the multiple countries being studied it should be possible to manipulate orthogonally people's individualism and power distance beliefs. Not only will orthogonal manipulations help to disentangle the effects of the two variables, but also the experimental design offers high internal validity.

Identifying the Process
Causes have causes. That is, the psychological dimensions that account for (or statistically mediate) the relationships between employees' country and their attitudes and behaviors may themselves be accounted for by other factors and processes. Further research is needed to identify the factors and processes through which the psychological dimensions exert influence. For example, Van Dyne et al. (2000) found that the previously established positive relationship between collectivism and organizational citizenship behavior (Moorman & Blakely, 1995) was mediated by organization-based self-esteem. More specifically, Van Dyne et al. found that high collectivism per se does not elicit organizational citizenship behavior. Rather, it is high organization-based self-esteem (that is,

feeling valued as an organizational member) that may be associated with high levels of collectivism that leads employees to engage in organizational citizenship behavior.

Within the extensive individualism-collectivism literature, Oyserman et al. (2002) similarly called for further research designed to specify the mechanisms through which IND and COL influence (or at least relate to) people's self-concepts. For instance, whereas many studies have shown that greater IND predisposes people to use personal traits rather than social identities to describe themselves (and vice versa for COL), Oyserman et al. suggest that "an open question is whether cultural differences in IND and COL have the most influence by affecting what is chronically salient about one's self-concept or by affecting how the self-concept is structured" (p. 32).

Moving Beyond Values

There is a growing debate among cross-cultural scholars about the relative influence of motivational variables (e.g. values) and cognitive factors in accounting for country-based differences in employees' attitudes and behaviors. Earley and Mosakowski (1996) and Morris and Young (2002) suggested that specific cognitions (e.g. expectancies about the consequences of behaving in a certain way) that proximally precede what people feel or do may do a better job than culturally-based values (i.e. constructs that generally define what is right or wrong, such as power distance) in accounting for the effects of country on their work attitudes and behaviors. At the very least, future research should consider the role of cognitive factors, if not instead of, then certainly in addition to values in accounting for cross-national differences in work attitudes and behaviors.

One ambitious exemplar of a cognition-based approach is the recent work of Leung and Bond (in press), who surveyed university students and adults from over 40 national/cultural groups. They identified five universal sets of beliefs about what people hold to be true or how the world works, which they dubbed "social axioms." Examples of social axioms include cynicism (which includes the extent to which people maintain "a negative view of human nature, especially as it is easily corrupted by power"; p. 24), social complexity (the extent to which people believe "that there are no rigid rules, but rather multiple ways of achieving a given outcome"; p. 24), and reward for application ("a general belief that effort, knowledge, careful planning and the investment of other resources ... will lead to positive results and help avoid negative outcomes"; p. 24). At the aggregate level, Leung and Bond have provided evidence that social axiom scores are significantly related to country-level indexes. For example, relatively low levels of cynicism and reward for application, and relatively high levels of social complexity are associated with greater country affluence. Of course, cause and effect relationships can not be discerned from the existing studies. Moreover, whereas the social axioms lend themselves to the kinds of cross-national studies featured in the present chapter (in which researchers evaluate whether people's standing on a given dimension accounts for country differences in work attitudes or behaviors), Leung and Bond report that only one such study has been done to date. Thus, future research should examine the joint influence of country-based differences in values (e.g. derived from the Hofstede (1980) or Schwartz (1992) frameworks) and country-based differences in beliefs (e.g. derived from Leung and Bond's (in press) social axioms) on employees' attitudes and behaviors.

Delineating Other Psychological Dimensions
Understandably, most of the psychological dimensions unearthed to date (be they values or cognitions) had their roots in cross-national theory and research. Of these various frameworks (e.g. Kluckhohn & Strodtbeck, 1961; Schwartz, 1992), the one developed by Hofstede (1980) has stimulated the most research, at least among organizational scholars. In fact, Hofstede's conceptualization has generated so much research that a recent review limited itself only to those studies that drew upon his cultural values dimensions (Kirkman, Lowe & Gibson, 2003). Whereas frameworks rooted in cross-cultural theory have identified a number of important psychological dimensions, they may be prone to "errors of omission." That is, other psychological dimensions not rooted in cross-national theory and research also may help to account for country differences in work attitudes and behaviors. Rather than limit themselves to the psychological dimensions that have emerged from cross-national investigations, researchers may take as their point of departure psychological dimensions with proven conceptual and empirical "track records."

One case in point is self-efficacy, originally defined by Bandura (1977) as people's estimates of their capacity to perform a given task. Basic research showed that self-efficacy had significant effects on people's motivation, cognition, and emotion (Bandura, 1986). Organizational scholars then proceeded to consider the implications of self-efficacy for behavior in the workplace (Gist & Mitchell, 1992; Wood & Bandura, 1989). More recently, self-efficacy has been examined cross-nationally, in attempts to evaluate whether there are meaningful country differences in its level (Schwarzer & Born, 1997), antecedents (Earley, Gibson & Chen, 1999), or expression. For example, self-efficacy may be a stronger predictor of work attitudes and behaviors in individualistic countries, whereas collectivistic self-efficacy (people's beliefs about their group's capacity to perform a task) may be a stronger predictor in collectivistic countries. More generally, psychological dimensions that have been shown to have pervasive effects on people's attitudes and behaviors may provide additional insight into country effects on employees' attitudes and behaviors. Furthermore, cross-national investigations of these psychological dimensions should help to determine whether their effects are equally pervasive in countries other than the one in which they were initially examined.

FUTURE RESEARCH OPPORTUNITY NO. 2: TOWARDS ADDITIONAL METHODS OF OPERATIONALIZATION

Most of the research done to date reveals a potentially important slippage between the organizing thesis of this paper (the need to operationalize the psychological dimensions that may account for relationships between employees' country and their attitudes or behaviors) and the methods that have been used to operationalize the psychological dimensions. Psychological dimensions generally are a product of both dispositional and situational factors. Moreover, psychological dimensions generally may be operationalized either through measurement or manipulation. Within each of the two categories of measurement or manipulation, there are multiple ways to operationalize the psychological dimensions. For example, operationalization via measurement may consist of self-reports. In the previously described studies researchers operationalized the psychological dimensions by having participants complete self-report, individual difference measures.

Whereas the self-report/individual difference approach is one method of operationalization, it is not the only way to go. An equally appropriate approach is to measure the psychological dimensions in ways that reflect the contribution of both individual difference and situational factors. For example, if a self-report instrument were to be employed participants may be instructed beforehand to respond to the survey as a "state" measure, i.e. based on their current thoughts and feelings. State measures are better equipped to capture the influence of situational (and hence more temporary) factors, than are conventional individual difference (or "trait") measures, which typically ask people to express their general thoughts and feelings.

Of course, operationalization via measurement may be done in ways other than self-report. The utility of self-reports depends on their accuracy or validity. For a variety of reasons, people may be unwilling or unable to describe themselves (e.g. their values and beliefs) accurately. An alternative method of operationalization may be gleaned from the social cognition literature, which has shown that the impact of cognitive structures such as beliefs depends upon their accessibility (Higgins, 1996). In the social cognition literature, accessibility refers to the ease with which cognitive structures may be activated in relation to the judgment or task at hand. As Morris and Young (2002) have suggested, "In order to measure a mediating process, we want to not only tap whether the cognitive structure is available to the individual but also whether the structure has become activated in relation to the task" (p. 331).

Accessibility, in turn, may not be optimally assessed via self-reports. Instead, response latencies have been shown to be a reliable indication of accessibility. The less time that people need to express their beliefs/attitudes, the more accessible they are; the greater the accessibility of these psychological constructs, the more likely they are to influence people's thoughts, feelings, and behaviors (Higgins, 1998). Future research designed to account for country differences in work attitudes and behaviors needs to operationalize the focal psychological dimensions through methods other than self-report. This is especially the case when the focal psychological dimensions consist of (or exert influence via) implicit knowledge to which people may have little introspective access (Morris & Young, 2002).[2]

Herein lies yet another reason for future research to operationalize the psychological dimensions via experimental manipulation (e.g. Hong, Morris, Chiu & Benet-Martinez, 2000). For example, consider the findings of Earley (1989), who showed that country-based differences in collectivistic beliefs led participants from the PRC to exhibit less social loafing than their counterparts from the U.S. In future research, participants from two or more countries known to vary in collectivism may be randomly assigned to conditions that elicit high or low levels of collectivistic thinking. Earley's findings suggest that in such a study, people from both countries who were assigned to the condition eliciting higher levels of collectivistic thinking will engage in less social loafing than their counterparts who were assigned to the condition eliciting lower levels of collectivistic thinking. Moreover, if the experimental manipulation of collectivistic thinking is strong or constraining (Mischel, 1973), it may reduce or even eliminate the effect of people's country on their tendency to engage in social loafing.

The results produced by strong (Mischel, 1973) experimental manipulations of the psychological dimensions may well be highly similar to those found in previous research, in which the psychological dimensions were operationalized via measurement. That is, not only might the operationalized factor (the manipulated variable) influence work attitudes and behaviors in the expected direction, but also the presence of the operationalization of the psychological dimension may make it less likely for people's country to influence their work attitudes and behaviors. Such findings were observed by Morris, Leung and Iyengar (in press), in a study examining the relationship between people's tendencies to make trait attributions for others' behavior and their preference for different types of conflict resolution procedures. In sum, future research based on operationalizing the psychological dimensions via manipulation provides researchers with yet another way to shed light on why employees from different countries exhibit different attitudes and behaviors. Moreover, operationalizing the psychological dimensions via experimental manipulation lends greater internal validity to the research design than does operationalizing those same dimensions through measurement

(Leung & Su, in press), which has been the preferred tendency in previous research.

FUTURE OPPORTUNITY NO. 3: STUDYING PSYCHOLOGICAL DIMENSIONS IN THEIR BROADER (COUNTRY) CONTEXT

In studies presented to this point, the results of mediational analyses showed that when the joint influence of the psychological dimension and people's country was examined, the former was more important than the latter. Indeed, the effect associated with the psychological dimension continued to be statistically significant whereas the effect associated with country was no longer significant when the two effects were studied simultaneously.

One interpretation of these findings is that when the country variable is analyzed in conjunction with the psychological dimensions, the country factor is not relevant to people's work attitudes and behavior; all that matters is people's standing on the focal psychological dimensions. Whereas this pattern of findings emerged in the particular studies that have been cited to this point, I certainly do not mean to suggest that psychological dimensions *always* "trump" people's country in accounting for their attitudes or behaviors. Rather, the influence of people's country (when examined in conjunction with the psychological dimensions) probably depends upon the conceptual nature of the research question.

Let us assume that people's country is a proxy not only for their own standing on various psychological dimension, but also for the standing of others with whom they are interacting in the same work environment (within that country). For certain research questions, it is vitally important to know *the relationship between* people's standing on the psychological dimensions and the standing of other people on those same dimensions in their work environments. When this is the case, people's country is likely to have a significant influence. Rather than producing a null effect when examined in conjunction with the psychological dimensions, people's country may interact with the psychological dimensions to influence their work attitudes and behaviors.

For example, Chen, Mannix and Okumura (2003) showed that the psychological dimension of egoistic motivation (i.e. negotiators' desire to satisfy their own concerns) moderated the influence of having higher aspirations than their negotiation partner on their individual negotiation outcomes in Japan and China, but not in the U.S. In Japan and China, being high in egoistic motivation elicited more of a positive relationship between having higher aspirations than the partner and individual negotiation outcomes, whereas no such tendency emerged in the

U.S. Further analyses showed that having high egoistic motivation in Japan and China elicited a beneficial effect of having higher aspirations than one's partner because the partner was likely to have a lower level of egoistic motivation. No such benefit associated with high egoistic motivation was present in the U.S., because people's negotiation partners also were likely to have relatively high levels of egoistic motivation themselves. Thus, it was not simply people's own level of egoistic motivation that influenced whether it would have a moderating impact on aspiration differentiation. It *was the relationship between* their own egoistic motivation and that of their negotiation partner that dictated whether their egoistic motivation would moderate the influence of aspiration differentiation on their individual negotiation outcomes. Thus, whereas previously cited studies showed that the psychological dimension eliminated the effect of country when the two factors were examined together (e.g. Morris et al., 1998), Chen et al. (2003) showed that the psychological dimension (egoistic motivation) *interacted with* people's country to influence individual negotiation outcomes.

One way to examine people's standing *in relationship to* others in their work environments is by evaluating whether people are above, below, or equal to others on the relevant psychological dimensions, as in the study by Chen et al. (2003). In other instances, the impact of people's standing on psychological dimensions in relationship to others' standing is not based as much on whether people surpass or are surpassed by others. Rather, the relational influence stems from the extent to which people's standing on the psychological dimensions *fits* with the standing of others in their work environments.

There is a rich tradition in organizational behavior examining the influence of person-environment congruence or fit (Chatman, 1989; Nadler, Tushman & Nadler, 1997) on employees' attitudes/behaviors. The typical finding is that employees respond more favorably under conditions of greater congruence or fit. For example, Newman and Nollen (1996) found that financial indicators of work unit performance (return on assets and sales) were more positive when managers exhibited greater fit between their organizational practices and the prevailing national cultural values (e.g. by encouraging relatively high levels of participation in decision-making in low power distance countries, while allowing for relatively low levels of participation in high power distance countries). In like fashion, studies examining the joint influence of people's country and their standing on certain psychological dimensions on work attitudes and behaviors may also show congruence effects, manifested as interactive relationships between people's standing on the psychological dimensions and their country.

For example, people high in IND in countries emphasizing IND may think and act very differently than people with the same level of IND in countries emphasizing COL. Moreover, people high in COL in countries emphasizing COL may respond differently than people with the same level of COL in countries emphasizing IND. Given the generally positive effects of person-environment fit found in previous research, it may be expected that people whose psychological orientation is more congruent with that emphasized in their country may feel and act less alienated in their interactions with other people in their country, especially when the others have bought into the prevailing psychological orientation in that country.

The results of several studies support this reasoning. Oyserman et al. (2002) reported that the relationship between assessed IND and mental health indices (social anxiety, depression) was moderated by people's country. In America, IND was inversely related to social anxiety and depression, whereas no such relationships emerged in Asian societies. Chatman and Barsade (1995) examined the relationship between MBA students' collectivism beliefs and their level of cooperative behavior. Chatman and Barsade found that participants' collectivistic beliefs were more positively related to cooperation when the simulated organizational culture to which they had been randomly assigned emphasized collectivism rather than individualism.

In short, in conceptualizing the joint influence of: (1) employees' psychological orientation; and (2) their country, on their attitudes and behaviors, we need not limit ourselves to the assertion that the former is more important than the latter. To be sure, past research has shown that the former sometimes *is* more important than the latter; country effects may disappear when people's psychological orientation is controlled (e.g. Morris et al., 1998). Future research, especially that which examines the influence of the relationship between people's psychological orientations and those emphasized in their country, may well find that both factors (in interaction with one another) are important determinants of people's work attitudes and behaviors.

CONCLUSION

Previous cross-national research has tended to demonstrate that people from different countries differ in their work attitudes and behaviors, at least some of the time. Through assessment of the psychological dimensions presumed to account for these differences, recent studies help to explain both why between-country differences emerge and when they will (or will not) emerge. The present analysis also illustrates how important matters other than accounting for between-country differences (e.g. elucidating unexpected null results) may be addressed when researchers operationalize the psychological dimensions expected to account for between-country differences. Finally, the suggestions for future research (based on investigators having operationalized the psychological determinants of country effects) identify several opportunities to expand the considerable conceptual progress that has been made in recent cross-national theory and research.

NOTES

1. This is not to suggest that within-country variation on the psychological dimensions is necessarily greater or lesser than the between-country variation. Both sources of variance are likely to be present, in which case their potential impact on work attitudes and behaviors warrant investigation.

2. Whereas accessible information can be held consciously, it need not be. Thus, it is not necessary for accessible information to be influential with the individual's conscious awareness of the information or its impact.

ACKNOWLEDGMENTS

I am greatly indebted to Art Brief, Yaru Chen, Chris Earley, Sheena Iyengar, Rod Kramer, Kwok Leung, Michael Morris, Barry Staw, and Elke Weber for their constructive comments on earlier drafts of the manuscript.

REFERENCES

Adler, N. (2002). *International dimensions of organizational behavior* (4th ed.). Cincinnati, OH: South-Western Publishing.

Bandura, A. (1977). Self-efficacy: Toward a unifying theory of behavioral change. *Psychological Review, 84,* 191–215.

Bandura, A. (1986). *Social foundations of thought and action: A social cognitive theory.* Englewood Cliffs, NJ: Prentice-Hall.

Baron, R. M., & Kenny, D. A. (1986). The moderator-mediator distinction in social psychological research: Conceptual, strategic, and statistical considerations. *Journal of Personality and Social Psychology, 51,* 1173–1182.

Brewer, M. B. (1979). Ingroup bias in the minimal intergroup situation: A cognitive motivational analysis. *Psychological Bulletin, 86,* 307–324.

Brockner, J., Ackerman, G., Greenberg, J., Gelfand, M., Francesco, A. M., Chen, Z. X., Leung, K., Bierbrauer, G., Gomez, C., Kirkman, B., & Shapiro, D. (2001). Culture and procedural justice: The influence of power distance on reactions to voice. *Journal of Experimental Social Psychology, 37,* 300–315.

Brockner, J., & Chen, Y. (1996). The moderating effects of self-esteem and self-construal in reaction to a threat to the self: Evidence from the People's Republic of China and the United States. *Journal of Personality and Social Psychology, 71,* 603–615.

Brockner, J., Chen, Y., Mannix, E., Leung, K., & Skarlicki, D. (2000). Culture and procedural fairness: When the effects of what you do depend upon how you do it. *Administrative Science Quarterly, 45,* 138–159.

Chatman, J. A. (1989). Improving interactional organizational research: A model of person-organization fit. *Academy of Management Review, 14*, 333–348.

Chatman, J., & Barsade, S. (1995). Personality, organizational culture, and cooperation: Evidence from a business simulation. *Administrative Science Quarterly, 40*, 423–443.

Chen, Y., Brockner, J., & Chen, X. (2002). Individual-collective primacy and ingroup favoritism: Enhancement and protection effects. *Journal of Experimental Social Psychology, 38*, 482–491.

Chen, Y., Brockner, J., & Katz, T. (1998). Towards an explanation of cultural differences in ingroup favoritism: The role of individual vs. collective primacy. *Journal of Personality and Social Psychology, 75*, 1490–1502.

Chen, Y., Mannix, E. A., & Okumura, T. (2003). The importance of who you meet: Effects of self-versus other-concerns among negotiators in the United States, the People's Republic of China, and Japan. *Journal of Experimental Social Psychology, 39*, 1–15.

Crocker, J., Thompson, L., McGraw, K., & Ingerman, C. (1987). Downward comparison, prejudice, and evaluations of others: Effects of self-esteem and threat. *Journal of Personality and Social Psychology, 52*, 907–916.

Diener, E., & Diener, M. (1995). Cross-cultural correlates of life satisfaction and self-esteem. *Journal of Personality and Social Psychology, 68*, 653–663.

Earley, P. (1994). Self or group? Cultural effects of training on self-efficacy and performance. *Administrative Science Quarterly, 39*, 89–117.

Earley, P. C. (1989). Social loafing and collectivism: A comparison of the United States and the People's Republic of China. *Administrative Science Quarterly, 34*, 565–581.

Earley, P. C., Gibson, C. B., & Chen, C. C. (1999). How did I do? versus How did we do?: Cultural contrasts of performance feedback use and self-efficacy. *Journal of Cross-Cultural Psychology, 30*, 594–619.

Earley, P. C., & Mosakowski, E. (1996). Experimental international management research. In: B. J. Punnett & O. Shenkar (Eds), *Handbook of International Management Research* (pp. 83–114). London: Blackwell.

Erez, M., & Earley, P. C. (1993). *Culture, self-identity, and work.* New York: Oxford University Press.

Farh, J. L., Earley, P. C., & Lin, S. C. (1997). Impetus for action: A cultural analysis of justice and organizational citizenship behavior in Chinese society. *Administrative Science Quarterly, 42*, 421–444.

Folger, R. (1986). Rethinking equity theory: A referent cognitions model. In: H. W. Bierhoff, R. L. Cohen & J. Greenberg (Eds), *Justice in Social Relations* (pp. 145–162). New York: Plenum.

Gist, M., & Mitchell, T. R. (1992). Self-efficacy: A theoretical analysis of its determinants and malleability. *Academy of Management Review, 17*, 183–211.

Greenberg, J. (1996). *The quest for justice on the job: Essays and experiments.* Thousand Oaks, CA: Sage.

Greenberg, J., Eskew, D. E., & Miles, J. (1991). Adherence to participatory norms as a moderator of the fair process effect: When voice does not enhance procedural justice. Paper presented at the meeting of the Academy of Management, Miami Beach, Florida.

Higgins, E. T. (1996). Knowledge activation: Accessibility, applicability, and salience. In: E. T. Higgins & A. E. Kruglanski (Eds), *Social Psychology: Handbook of Basic Principles* (pp. 133–168). New York: Guilford.

Higgins, E. T. (1998). Promotion and prevention: Regulatory focus as a motivational principle. In: M. P. Zanna (Ed.), *Advances in Experimental Social Psychology* (Vol. 30, pp. 1–46). New York: Academic Press.

Hofstede, G. (1980). *Culture's consequences: International differences in work-related values.* Beverly Hills, CA: Sage.

Hong, Y. Y., Morris, M. W., Chiu, C. Y., & Benet-Martinez, V. (2000). Multicultural minds: A dynamic constructivist approach to culture and cognition. *American Psychologist, 55,* 709–720.

Hui, C., & Triandis, H. C. (1989). Effects of culture and response format on extreme response style. *Journal of Cross-Cultural Psychology, 20,* 296–309.

Kirkman, B. L., Lowe, K. B., & Gibson, C. B. (2003). *Two decades of culture's consequences: A review of empirical research incorporating Hofstede's cultural values framework.* Manuscript under editorial review.

Kluckhohn, R., & Strodtbeck, F. L. (1961). *Variations in value orientations.* Evanston, IL: Row Peterson.

Lam, S. S. K., Chen, X. P., & Schaubroeck, J. (in press). Participative decision-making and employee performance in different cultures: The moderating effects of allocentrism-idiocentrism and efficacy. *Academy of Management Journal.*

Latane, B., Williams, K., & Harkins, S. (1979). Many hands make light the work: The causes and consequences of social loafing. *Journal of Personality and Social Psychology, 37,* 823–832.

Lawler, E. E. (1992) *Employee involvement and total quality management: Practices and results in Fortune 500 companies.* San Francisco: Jossey-Bass.

Leung, K., & Bond, M. (1989). On the empirical identification of dimensions for cross-cultural comparison. *Journal of Cross-Cultural Psychology, 20,* 133–151.

Leung, K., & Bond, M. H. (in press). Social axioms: A model of social beliefs in multi-cultural perspective. In: M. P. Zanna (Ed.), *Advances in Experimental Social Psychology.* New York: Academic Press.

Leung, K., & Su, S. K. (in press). Experimental methods for research on culture and management. In: B. J. Punnett & O. Shenkar (Eds), *Handbook for International Management Research* (2nd ed.). Cambridge, MA: Blackwell.

Lind, E. A., & Tyler, T. R. (1988). *The social psychology of procedural justice.* New York: Plenum.

Mackie, D. M., & Goethals, G. R. (1987). Individual and group goals. In: C. Hendrick (Ed.), *Review of Personality and Social Psychology* (Vol. 8, pp. 144–166). Thousand Oaks, CA: Sage.

Markus, H. R., & Kitayama, S. (1991). Culture and the self: Implications for cognition, emotion, and motivation. *Psychological Review, 98,* 224–253.

Miller, J. G. (1984). Culture and the development of everyday social explanation. *Journal of Personality and Social Psychology, 46,* 961–978.

Mischel, W. (1973). Toward a cognitive social learning reconceptualization of personality. *Psychological Review, 80,* 252–283.

Moorman, R. H., & Blakely, G. L. (1995). Individualism-collectivism as an individual difference predictor of organizational citizenship behavior. *Journal of Organizational Behavior, 16,* 127–142.

Morris, M. W., Leung, K., & Iyengar, S. S. (in press). Person perception in the heat of conflict: Attributions about the opponent and conflict resolution preferences in two cultures. *Asian Journal of Social Psychology.*

Morris, M. W., & Peng, K. (1994). Culture and cause: American and Chinese attributions for social and physical events. *Journal of Personality and Social Psychology, 67,* 949–971.

Morris, M. W., Williams, K. Y., Leung, K., Larrick, R., Mendoza, M. T., Bhatnagar, D., Li, J., Kondo, M., Luo, J., & Hu, J. (1998). Conflict management style: Accounting for cross-national differences. *Journal of International Business Studies, 29,* 729–748.

Morris, M. W., & Young, M. J. (2002). Linking culture to behavior: Focusing on more proximate cognitive mechanisms. In: F. J. Dansereau & F. Yammarino (Eds), *Research in Multi-Level Issues* (Vol. 1, pp. 327–341). Oxford, UK: Elsevier.

Nadler, D., Tushman, M., & Nadler, M. (1997). *Competing by design: The power of organizational architecture*. New York: Oxford University Press.

Newman, K. L., & Nollen, S. D. (1996). Culture and congruence: The fit between management practices and national culture. *Journal of International Business Studies, 27*, 753–779.

Oyserman, D., Coon, H. M., & Kemmelmeier, M. (2002). Rethinking individualism and collectivism: Evaluation of theoretical assumptions and meta-analyses. *Psychological Bulletin, 128*, 3–72.

Ross, L. (1977). The intuitive psychologist and his shortcomings: Distortions in the attribution process. In: L. Berkowitz (Ed.), *Advances in Experimental Social Psychology* (Vol. 10, pp. 174–221) New York: Academic Press.

Schaubroeck, J., Lam, S. S. K., & Xie, J. L. (2000). Collective efficacy versus self-efficacy in coping responses to stressors and control: A cross-cultural study. *Journal of Applied Psychology, 85*, 512–525.

Schwartz, S. (1992). Universals in the content and structure of values: Theoretical advances and empirical tests in 20 countries. In: M. P. Zanna (Ed.), *Advances in Experimental Social Psychology* (Vol. 25, pp. 1–65). San Diego: Academic Press.

Schwarzer, R., & Born, A. (1997). Optimistic self-beliefs: Assessment of general perceived self-efficacy in thirteen cultures. *World Psychology, 3*(1–2), 177–190.

Shweder, R. A., & Bourne, E. J. (1984). Does the concept of the person vary cross-culturally? In: R. A. Shweder & R. A. LeVine (Eds), *Culture Theory: Essays on Mind, Self, and Emotion* (pp. 158–199). Cambridge, England: Cambridge University Press.

Singelis, T. M. (1994). The measurement of independent and interdependent self-construals. *Personality and Social Psychology Bulletin, 20*, 580–591.

Stening, B. W., & Everett, J. E. (1984). Response styles in a cross-cultural managerial study. *Journal of Social Psychology, 122*, 151–156.

Tajfel, H., & Turner, J. C. (1986). The social identity theory of intergroup behavior. In: S. Worchel & W. G. Austin (Eds), *Psychology of Intergroup Relations* (pp. 7–24). Chicago: Nelson-Hall.

Taylor, S. E., & Brown, J. D. (1988). Illusion and well-being: A social psychological perspective on mental health. *Psychological Bulletin, 103*, 193–210.

Thibaut, J., & Walker, L. (1975). *Procedural justice: A psychological analysis*. Hillsdale, NJ: Lawrence Erlbaum.

Tower, R. K., Kelly, C., & Richard, A. (1997). Individualism, collectivism, and reward allocation: A cross-cultural study in Russia and Britain. *British Journal of Social Psychology, 36*, 331–345.

Triandis, H. C. (1995). *Individualism and collectivism*. Boulder, CO: Westview Press.

Tyler, T. R., Lind, E. A., & Huo, Y. J. (in press). Cultural values and authority relations: The psychology of conflict resolution across cultures. *Psychology, Public Policy, and Law*.

Vandello, J. A., & Cohen, D. (1999). Patterns of individualism and collectivism across the United States. *Journal of Personality and Social Psychology, 77*, 279–292.

Van de Vijver, F. J. R., & Leung, K. (1997). Methods and data analysis of comparative research. In: J. W. Berry, Y. H. Poortinga & J. Pandey (Eds), *Handbook of Cross-Cultural Psychology* (2nd ed., Vol. 1, pp. 257–300). Boston: Allyn & Bacon.

Van de Vijver, F. J. R., & Leung, K. (2000). Methodological issues in psychological research on culture. *Journal of Cross-Cultural Psychology, 31*, 33–51.

Van Dyne, L., Vandewalle, D., Kostova, T., Latham, M. E., & Cummings, L. L. (2000). Collectivism, propensity to trust, and self-esteem as predictors of organizational citizenship in a non-work setting. *Journal of Organizational Behavior, 21*, 3–23.

Whiting, B. (1976). The problem of the packaged variable. In: K. Riegel & J. Meacham (Eds), *The Developing Individual in a Changing World: Historical and Cultural Issues* (Vol. 1, pp. 303–309). Hague, The Netherlands: Mouton.

Wood, R. E., & Bandura, A. (1989). Social cognitive theory of organizational management. *Academy of Management Review, 14*, 361–384.

Printed in the United States
129979LV00004BA/7/A

9 780762 310548